POLITICS AND POWER IN THE MAGHREB

MICHAEL J. WILLIS

Politics and Power in the Maghreb

Algeria, Tunisia and Morocco from Independence to the Arab Spring

HURST & COMPANY, LONDON

First published in the United Kingdom in 2012 by
C. Hurst & Co. (Publishers) Ltd.,
41 Great Russell Street, London, WC1B 3PL
© Michael J. Willis, 2012
This paperback edition published 2014
All rights reserved.
Printed in India

The right of Michael J. Willis to be identified as the author
of this publication is asserted by him in accordance with
the Copyright, Designs and Patents Act, 1988.

A Cataloguing-in-Publication data record for this book
is available from the British Library.

ISBN: 978-1-84904-392-2

This book is printed using paper from registered sustainable
and managed sources.

www.hurstpublishers.com

CONTENTS

Note on Transliteration   vii

Introduction   1
1. The Imprint of History   9
2. Post-Independence State-Building   37
3. The Military   81
4. Political Parties   121
5. Islamist Movements   155
6. The Berber Question   203
7. Politics and Economics   231
8. Regional Relations   265
9. International Relations   293
Conclusion   335

Notes   341
Select Bibliography   387
Index   395

NOTE ON TRANSLITERATION

A standard dilemma faced by works in English about the Maghreb has been whether to adopt recognised forms of transliteration of Arabic words and names into English, or to use ones that rely on French forms of transliteration into Latin characters. Whilst the former has the merit of academic and linguistic rigour, the latter has the benefit of relating much more closely to actual usage within the region itself. The continued pervasiveness of the French language in Algeria, Tunisia and Morocco since the post-colonial period has meant that the governments and people of the region not only continue to make use of the language on an almost daily basis but also have adopted and use fairly standardised French-based transliterations of Arabic names in ways that do not occur with, for example, English, in the Arab Mashreq. On this basis, this book has used French-based transliterations for the majority of Arabic words and especially names, for it makes sense to use the form that most people in the region themselves use on a regular basis, so that, as Richard Pennell has put it, 'people should be able to recognise their own names.'[1] Thus, for example, the Arabic letter ش is transliterated as 'ch' rather than 'sh.' In the cases where there are inconsistencies, in even local forms of transliteration, the most commonly used has been adopted.

INTRODUCTION

The overthrow of the regime of President Zine Al-Abdine Ben Ali in Tunisia on 14 January 2011 took the world by surprise. The popular revolt in a small Arab country which few people knew anything about, beyond the holiday brochures, and the effect that this had on the wider Arab world, prompted questions as to why there had been so little awareness of the country until it surged into the news headlines. Although partly a product of the country's size and enforced absence of internal politics, this lack of knowledge of Tunisia was also indicative of a wider ignorance about the surrounding region in which it lay: the Maghreb. The Maghreb, or western Arab world, had long attracted a tiny fraction of the interest shown by the outside world in the eastern Arab world, or Mashreq. The conflicts in Israel, Palestine, Lebanon, Iraq and the Gulf went a good way to explaining why more outside attention focused on the eastern end of the Arab world; but they did not, however, account for the near complete neglect of events in the Maghreb which, although not matching the impact and magnitude of the Mashreq crises, contained their own sizeable conflicts that were to send significant ripples well beyond the region. The dramatic unfolding of events in Algeria in the 1990s, which saw not only one of the most complete political openings and unfettered sets of elections hitherto seen in the modern Arab world, but which also came close to electing the Arab world's first Islamist majority government, received fleeting coverage in the global media and a tiny proportion of that devoted to Hamas's victory in the Palestinian territories a decade and a half later. The descent into civil conflict that followed the cancellation of these elections and the tens of thousands of Algerians who lost their lives in the resultant bloodletting received even less attention, despite the death toll being far higher than that in more fully covered conflicts further east in Lebanon, the Gulf and in Israel-Palestine during the same period. Drama and violence were not just limited to the Algerian part of the Maghreb; the conflict between Morocco and the Polisario Front over the Western Sahara developed into a full-scale war to which other regional states, such as Algeria and Libya, contributed. The dispute remains unsolved after four decades and now occupies one of the longest serving United Nations peacekeeping operations in the world. Yet few outside the region and the corridors of the UN know anything about the conflict, its causes and its stakes. If Tunisia's lack of domestic turmoil and involvement in territorial conflicts better explained its absence from the headlines than its Maghrebi neighbours, the dramatic events of January 2011 demonstrated that it too was worthy of attention.

More surprising and worrying has been the lack of academic interest in the region, for whilst the media is driven by immediacy and public interest, sustained enquiry is more expected in academia. Here too, attention, whilst present, has been scant, certainly in comparison not only to the Mashreq but also to other regions of the world. For whilst studies of the politics of most geographical areas of the globe are many in number, few such studies exist for the Maghreb region despite all the compelling reasons for having them. Those that do exist are frequently excellent; but they are dwarfed in number by similar studies of the Mashreq. Moreover, much of the academic work on the politics of the Maghreb has focused on individual countries, and even those works that attempt to look at the whole region predominantly consist of discussions of the individual countries in separate sections with only a limited attempt to put forth a general discussion that compares developments and issues across the states. The need for a broad comparative text addressing the politics of the Maghreb therefore lies at the origin of this book. The parallel absence of a broad modern history of the region, especially for the post-colonial period, has led, perhaps ill-advisedly, to an attempt to address both the politics and modern history of the Maghreb in a single book. In this way, most of the chapters in the book address political actors, themes and issues; but within each, a largely chronological and narrative historical approach is adopted to explain the development of the topic. Such an approach runs the clear risk of falling between the two stools of political science and political history, but the intention is to provide a basic framework

INTRODUCTION

for those interested in both the politics and modern history of the region. The book is thus an introductory text for the study of the Maghreb, and therefore existing scholars of the region are unlikely to find much that is novel or unknown to them in it. The original contribution the book hopes to make is in providing a broad and comparative study. It draws heavily on existing secondary literature to construct its narrative and analysis, not least because of the excellence of much that has been written on the region over the past fifty years and the desire to integrate what were often texts on individual countries into a comparative analysis, but also as a way of pointing the reader to this literature in more detail. Use has also been made of media sources, especially those produced in the region itself, and material I have gathered from interviews with both political actors and ordinary people during the times I have visited and lived in the region over the past twenty years.

The opening two chapters of the book cover two defined historical periods that aim to give context to the political developments and actors that are discussed in a more thematic fashion in subsequent chapters. Chapter 1 constitutes a brief survey of the region's history up until the achievement of independence from European colonial rule, with the aim of bringing out some of the broad features and themes of Maghrebi politics that have emerged over time and which help explain developments in the post-colonial period. The period immediately after the achievement of independence is addressed in Chapter 2, which looks at the political regimes that were established in the three states following the departure of the French and Spanish, examining how they were constituted and which groups and individuals assumed and consolidated political power in the first decade and a half after independence. Chapters 3–5 examine the role played by three key actors in the region, the military, political parties and the Islamist movements, that have strongly shaped the way politics has developed within the region, demonstrating how they both challenged and were used by the ruling elites that established themselves in the states after independence. Chapters 6 and 7 look at two issues that have come to have, in very different ways, an increasingly substantial impact on politics in the Maghreb over recent decades: Berber identity and economics. Finally, Chapters 8 and 9 move beyond the domestic politics of Algeria, Tunisia and Morocco to look at, firstly, relations between the three states, which have oscillated wildly between conflict and cooperation in the post-colonial era; and, secondly, interaction with the wider world; particularly Europe, the United States and the Middle East. The adoption of a largely thematic structure is intended to allow potential readers to consult individual chapters as well as the whole text. This has necessitated a slight degree of repetition and also of reference between chapters, but it is hoped that this will not prove too distracting for those reading the book as a single text.

Although it is hoped that a fairly comprehensive picture of political dynamics is given through these chapters, it cannot be pretended that this coverage is exhaustive. Fuller and more specific discussion of the role of society in the politics of the region would have been useful had space permitted. Society has traditionally been dwarfed and dominated by the state in the three countries, and some discussion of this occurs in the chapters on political parties, Islamist movements and Berber identity; but there is, nonetheless, need for a more thorough treatment of this subject, especially in the light of the popular uprisings of 2011 which arguably saw society take on and, in places, defeat the power of the state. A number of important works on this subject have now begun to appear.[1] The role played by women in politics is of similar importance. Despite making often substantial contributions to the anti-colonial struggles in the region, women were effectively excluded from elite politics in the three countries in the decades that followed independence. Individual women exercised considerable political influence in the presidential palace in Tunisia in the closing years of the presidencies of both Habib Bourguiba and Zine al-Abdine Ben Ali, but this was fully due to their being part of the president's family rather than of any formal institution. Bourguiba introduced some of the Arab world's most extensive reforms to the legal status of women in the early years of his rule, but promoted few women to senior positions in the country. Ben Ali continued this pattern, placing heavy emphasis on his predecessor's reforms to persuade supporters in Europe and the United States of the social liberalism of his rule. It was even rumoured that Ben Ali planned to have his venal and popularly reviled wife, Leila Trabelsi, succeed him as president in the hope that the appointment of the Arab world's first female head of state would so dazzle the outside world that the repressive, dictatorial and corrupt system over which she would preside might continue to be overlooked. In Algeria and Morocco, it was not until the first decade of the twenty-first century that governments introduced legal reforms relating to women that even

INTRODUCTION

approximated to those of Tunisia. Both countries appointed a sprinkling of women to ministerial positions but only a small number of women were ever elected to the national parliaments—Morocco featuring none until 1993. Of more significance were the increasingly vocal women's movements in both countries, who took part of the credit for the reform of the legal status of women. The notable presence of Maghrebi women in the protest movements of 2011 promises to change this situation substantially.

An absence of a more geographic rather than thematic nature is that of discussion of countries that are frequently considered to be a part of the Maghreb, specifically the states of Libya and Mauritania. Both not only have long historical connections with the three states covered in this book, but also in 1989 joined with Algeria, Tunisia and Morocco in creating the Arab Maghreb Union. Their exclusion from the coverage of this book is primarily explained by the substantially different nature of their recent political histories and political systems when compared to those of the other three states in the region. Part of the interest and value in comparing Algeria, Tunisia and Morocco is that they share a core of historic characteristics (see Chapter 1) that makes exploration and explanation of their more modern political differences both easier and more instructive. Whilst a number of these common features are shared by both Libya and Mauritania, several are absent and, more importantly, both states have dimensions which are largely absent from the three states of the central Maghreb. Indeed the more peripheral nature of their geographical position in the Maghreb means that Libya and Mauritania fall, at least partially, within the history, traditions and influences of the regions adjoining the Maghreb: notably the Arab Mashreq, the Sahel and sub-Saharan Africa. In more specific terms, Mauritania shared the experience of French colonialism with Algeria, Tunisia and Morocco, but its complex and pivotal ethnic politics have no immediate parallel in the rest of the Maghreb. Its small and sparse population and tiny economy contrast with the much larger, wealthier and more urban populations concentrated in the big coastal cities of its northern neighbours. Libya's population may also be largely urban and coastal, but its experience of European colonialism was of an Italian rather than French flavour. Much more important was the very unique and particular political path the country took following the seizure of power by Colonel Muammar Qadhafi and his free officers in 1969, which rendered meaningful comparison with the rest of the Maghreb states increasingly difficult. The recent development of a multi-party system and the possible discovery of hydrocarbon resources in Mauritania may mean that its differences with the rest of the Maghreb will narrow as, indeed, does the ending of the rule of Muammar Qadhafi in Libya following the rebellion of 2011. For now, though, the exclusion of both states from a comparative analysis of the politics of the Maghreb makes both the historical narrative and comparisons simpler.

The book consciously makes no real attempt to engage with theoretical literature and to compare the political developments of the Maghreb with those occurring in other regions. These elements were omitted because of a desire to give full space and focus to events within the region itself which, as explained above, have been significantly neglected. This is not to say that theoretical approaches to the study of the Maghreb are not valuable or needed, or that the region's politics cannot be usefully compared to those occurring in other parts of the globe; but the primary purpose of this book is to focus on developments within the region in their own right. It is hoped, nevertheless, that this book might potentially provide a basic source for the elaboration of more theoretical approaches to the region and for attempts to compare developments there with those taking place elsewhere.

Writing a book accrues debts of gratitude to those who have helped in its completion, and this book has run up lists that are more sizeable than most. First and foremost, thanks must go to my two employers during the period it has taken to write this book: Al Akhawayn University in Ifrane, Morocco and St Antony's College, University of Oxford. Both institutions have not only given me generous amounts of academic leave to research and write the book but have also been extremely patient during the long wait to see its completion. I am particularly grateful to Driss Ouaouicha in this regard. Sincere thanks must also go to the Moroccan British Society (MBS) and Her Highness Princess Lalla Joumala for not only establishing my post at Oxford but also for their continued support for my research. Credit for the original idea for this book goes to the students who took the 'North African Government and Politics' class that I taught at Al Akhawayn University from the late 1990s. The absence of a single basic text for the course prompted them to encourage me to write one, and their enthusiasm, ideas and feedback have made a huge contribution to the writing of the book. No less a contribution has been made by the students who took the graduate version of the course when I moved to

INTRODUCTION

Oxford in 2004. Their suggestions and, above all, research, have informed significant parts of this book, as has that of the DPhil students I have been fortunate to have supervised and whose work has frequently led me to change my views on a number of issues. Some of these contributions have been formally acknowledged in the text, but I am grateful to all of them. My gratitude also goes to those people in and from all three countries who agreed to be interviewed in the course of research for this book, particularly those who did so in difficult political environments. I would also like to thank those people who were helpful in putting me in touch with many of these interviewees and in making contacts more generally, particularly Nicholas Pelham, Eileen Byrne and successive staff in the British embassies in Rabat and Tunis. I am also very much indebted to all the members of the NAF, especially Saad Djebar for his generosity, good humour and patience in explaining many of the intricacies of Algerian politics, and George Joffé for his valuable advice and constant encouragement. I want also to thank George along with Eugene Rogan, Michael Brett, Hakim Darbouche and Farid Boussaid for reading and commenting on various parts of the manuscript of this book. The errors and shortcomings of the text nevertheless remain entirely mine. The Middle East Centre at Oxford has provided the most encouraging and stimulating of environments in which to research and write, and whilst the prolific publishing output of most of my colleagues was often intimidating, it also afforded me a valuable pool of advice to draw on and pushed me to complete this book. Final thanks go to my parents, Brian and Ann, for all their belief, support and help; and to Michael Dwyer of Hurst & Co., who originally contracted me to write this book and, whilst he must have often despaired that it would never be finished, was a model of patient encouragement.

1

THE IMPRINT OF HISTORY

No examination of the contemporary politics of the Maghreb is possible without some appreciation of the history of the region. The political systems that emerged after the achievement of independence from colonial rule by the Maghrebi states were clearly the product of past forces, influences and experiences. Reference to history is doubly important in the case of the Maghreb since the precise nature and impact of the historical heritage remains an important part of contemporary political debate in the region and frequently goes a long way to explaining current political alignments, disputes or practices. In short, exactly what history has bequeathed to the region remains until today the subject of intense discussion and controversy.

Part of the reason for this controversy lies in the varied nature of the historical influences of the region. Geography alone has placed the Maghreb in the corner of the African continent that is closest to Europe, thus making it a ready bridge for the exchange of influences in both directions. It is similarly not too far removed from the part of the continent that is linked to the Asian landmass, specifically the Middle East. Appropriately, most historians have focused on these three elements—the African, European and Middle Eastern—to explain the various influences to which the Maghreb has been subject. However, more recently, historians have drawn attention to two facts. Firstly, that whilst these three sources of influence have clearly been crucial to the political and social development of the Maghreb, the importance of trends and actors more indigenous to the region should not be overlooked. Abdallah Laroui has argued that the Maghreb is frequently portrayed as 'a land that is conquered, that is exploited, that is "civilised"' by external forces—in other words a place that is simply the 'object' of history rather than the product of its own experiences.[1] John Ruedy points out that all too often historians have 'periodized the Maghrib's history to coincide with the rise and fall of externally imposed regimes and dynasties'—mainly those emanating from either the Middle East or Europe.[2]

The second fact is the related tendency to overemphasise the importance of one period or one source of influence over all others. Ruedy states that this has particularly been the case with the Arab-Islamic heritage of the Maghreb which, whilst being of undeniably paramount importance, should not totally exclude the significance of either the Berber heritage that predates it or the European influence and periodic presence.[3] Indeed, it is the relative importance attached to these three elements—the Berber, the European and the Arab-Islamic—that has caused much controversy and argument in the states of the contemporary Maghreb, particularly as they have sought to establish defined national identities for themselves. The perceived demands of post-independence nation-building led to the importance attached by regimes to the affirmation of 'the singularity of the nation and commonality of its historical origins, culture and experience.'[4] The inevitable reaction to this assertion by different parts of the population who took issue with this restrictive definition of identity explains these conflicts, which will be explored in more detail in later chapters.

The unavoidable truth of the historical experience and legacy of the Maghreb is that it is highly mixed. No one experience or influence can be seen as eclipsing all others. Similarly, debates over which influences are 'authentic' or 'genuine' and which are simply 'imposed' are also misplaced. Such value judgements cannot be attached to historical processes. Countries and regions, like people, are simply the products of their experiences, no more and no less. As John Ruedy has concluded:

The undebatable historical reality is that Islam and Arabism in North Africa were elaborated within the context of a predominantly Berber cultural framework which has stamped the region linguistically, sociologically, institutionally, and perhaps intellectually. At the same time, the fact that the Maghrib was and is closer geographically to southern Europe and the Sudan than to the Middle Eastern *métropole* has dictated that the elaboration of Islam in Barbary was almost constantly modified and conditioned by influences from these regions.[5]

These points need to be considered when seeking to understand how history has affected political developments in the contemporary

Maghreb. Another issue to be aware of is the potential dangers of seeking to interpret the past solely through the experiences of the present. The main problem with this—teleological—approach is that it risks portraying contemporary developments as inevitable and having deep historical roots that may not necessarily be the case. It is likely that whilst much of the political landscape of the modern Maghreb has been produced by longer-term historical processes, parts of it are the product of much more recent developments.

Early History: Berbers, Arabs and Islam

The earliest forms of political organisation in north-west Africa arguably emerged with the Berber populations. Although not truly indigenous to the region—arriving around 2000 BC—the Berbers were a predominantly tribal people whose political organisations reflected this fact. A number of academics and historians have suggested that the segmentary nature of tribal organisation continues to be reflected in the splintered nature of political competition in modern Algeria and Morocco—with shifting factions and clans struggling with each other for political power and influence.[6] The idea of any form of state was thus largely foreign to early Berber society. However, the penetration of the region by other peoples and civilisations—notably the Phoenicians (who established Carthage) and the Romans—led to some tribes adopting structures more akin to a state and the emergence of three Berber kingdoms that, together with the subjugated city of Carthage, formed the basis of the Roman Empire's four provinces in north-west Africa.[7]

The arrival of the Arabs in the region beginning in the seventh century AD had a mixed effect on political organisation. The decision by the states emerging from colonial rule 1,200 years later that it would be this Arab component of their historical identity that would be the official and defining characteristic of the state has made the issue of the Arab historical influence a politically controversial one. Nevertheless, there is little disagreement that this influence over time was huge: particularly religiously (through the introduction of Islam) and to a lesser extent linguistically (through the introduction of the Arabic language). Evidence of the impact of Islam can be seen through the fact that the Islamic armies which left North Africa for the conquest of Spain at the beginning of the eighth century were predominantly Berber in make-up. However, the specifically Arab political presence in the Maghreb remained limited in the early centuries—as it had with the Phoenicians, Romans and other similar groups before them—to a few important cities. It was not until the arrival of further large numbers of Arab tribesmen through the 'Hilalian' invasions in the eleventh century that a more widespread 'Arabisation' occurred outside the main cities. However, whilst the large-scale arrival of these nomadic Arabic tribesmen from the east did much to spread the use of Arabic as a language and helped further entrench Islam as the dominant religion of the Maghreb, the political effect it had was diverse. Whilst Arab in origin, they were tribal and nomadic in organisation. In this way, they did not fundamentally alter the existing political dichotomy that had emerged in the region between the cities and towns of the plains and coast, with their own political organisation, and the tribal rural hinterland. This dichotomy and the complex relationship between these two *milieux* had already become an important part of the politics of the region, and it was a dichotomy and relationship that has arguably persisted into the modern politics of the region. At the same time, the Hilalian invasions, whilst substantially affecting the steppe and lowland regions, left the mountain and desert areas largely untouched. This meant that these regions, while progressively converting to Islam, remained predominantly Berber rather than Arabic speaking and would stay so right into the modern period.

The Forging of a Maghrebi Identity: The Almoravids and Almohads

Overall, the arrival of the Arabs and Islam did herald the beginning of the forging of a specifically Maghrebi identity. In the view of Abdallah Laroui, this process began with the establishment of cities such as Kairouan, Tlemcen and Fez, which became regional centres in their own right rather than merely satellites of other civilisations.[8] The process was consolidated with the emergence in the eleventh to thirteenth centuries of two successive dynasties—the Almoravids (*al-murabitun*) and Almohads (*al-muwahhidun*)—which came to dominate the region. The significance of the impact of these two dynasties was twofold. Firstly, both emerged largely from within the Maghreb region itself (the Almoravids were originally from a little further south into the Sahara) and more significantly were Berbers—thus giving a more indigenous dimension to political power following a long period of largely Arab political control (at least in the cities). Secondly, the Almoravids (1042–

1147) and Almohads (1147–1276) were the first (and indeed last) groups to establish unified political control over more or less the whole region of the Maghreb. This control led to the development of the Maghreb as a much more defined concept than had previously been the case. Both dynasties introduced more uniform social, cultural and particularly religious forms and practices that were to produce a recognisably Maghrebi identity distinct from those around it. Their influence helps explain the distinction that exists between the Maghreb, as the western part of the Arab world, and the Mashreq, the eastern Arab world. The split identity that the modern state of Libya has developed—sometimes being classified as Maghrebi, sometimes as Mashreqi—is due to the fact that it sits astride a historical fault line that was initially instituted during the Almohad period: the Almohads taking control of the western part of modern-day Libya.[9]

Significantly, both dynasties were forged on an explicitly religious basis. Both emerged from the desert (in the case of the Almoravids) and mountainous (in the case of the Almohads) Berber-populated periphery to impose a more rigorous and arguably puritanical interpretation of Islamic practice on the plains and cities that had—in their view—strayed from the correct religious path.[10] This was significant for three reasons. Firstly, it effectively ended any residual speculation that the conversion of the Berber populations to Islam had been a largely superficial affair. Secondly, in political terms, it established Islam as the basis for 'legitimising any supratribal authority'—both dynasties having been able to unite both Berber and Arab tribes around Islam as a unifying and mobilising force.[11] Lastly, the highly religious dimension and justification both dynasties attached to their rule established a link between religious righteousness and political authority that some would argue persists up until this day. In more specific terms the Almoravids and Almohads entrenched the Maliki school of Islamic law as the 'official' basis of sharia across the Maghreb. Although originating in the Arabian peninsula (in Medina), Maliki law was consolidated in Kairouan (in modern-day Tunisia) and remains today the dominant and official school of law in the region.[12]

The Emergence of Differentiated Identities

If the Almoravid and Almohad empires had established a specific cultural and religious identity for the Maghreb, the period following their dominance was characterised by a growing differentiation within the region. For many historians, the fifteenth to sixteenth centuries mark the beginnings of the emergence of separate political entities that would be the eventual forerunners of the modern states of the Maghreb. This development was most marked in the hinterland that surrounded the city of Tunis. This fertile and accessible region—surrounded by sea on two sides—had already started to develop a distinct identity from the time of the early Arab invasions, when it became known as Ifriquia. As Almohad power gradually fragmented and receded, the direct descendants of the dynasty (known as the Hafsids) found their sphere of control restricted to the Tunis region, which progressively became known as Tunisia.[13] The emergence of other successor dynasties in the central (Zayyanid) and far western (Merenid) parts of the Maghreb also laid the foundation for future territorial distinctions (Algeria and Morocco), but in a much less pronounced way than that which occurred for Tunisia under the Hafsids.

These growing distinctions within the wider Maghreb region were not just the product of the natural processes of imperial disintegration. It has been argued that they were also the result of economic changes that saw greater emphasis put on relationships to the south and the north of the region. Developments in seafaring strengthened trading links with Europe, while expanded use of camel caravans expanded the trans-Saharan trade routes into and from Africa. The rise in importance of these links came at the expense not only of the long dominant link with the Middle East but also of contacts *between* regions of the Maghreb as east-west travel and trade declined. As a result, not only did contact between the two regions decrease, but the common factors that had linked them also weakened as each region began to develop its own individual identity.[14]

The Ottoman Regencies and the Moroccan Exception

The processes of differentiation were accelerated from the sixteenth century. The major reason for this was the entrance of the majority of the Maghreb region into the political orbit of the increasingly powerful Ottoman Empire. All of present-day Libya, Tunisia and Algeria passed under effective Ottoman control during this century. Very significantly, though, the area of modern-day Morocco did not. It is something of a misnomer, however, to speak of Ottoman 'control' of the

Maghreb. Ottoman involvement in the region largely came in response to increasing incursions into North Africa by forces from Christian Europe. The intervention of the Muslim Ottomans was therefore largely welcomed by their co-religionists in the Maghreb. Their involvement once in the region took the form of the establishment of 'regencies' in the key strategic cities of Tripoli, Tunis and Algiers. Once in place, these regencies only had a limited impact on the daily lives of most people in the Maghreb. Apart from tax collecting and the most basic forms of administration, the Ottoman presence was restricted to the regency cities and other coastal towns. Even in the cities, the regencies' reliance on a small bureaucratic elite brought in from Istanbul, supported by a similarly imported military caste, meant that there was limited interaction with the indigenous population. The increasing autonomy from Istanbul enjoyed by the regencies served to increase the impression that they were localised political entities rather than provinces of the Ottoman Empire. Indeed, the supreme Ottoman officials in Algiers (the military *deys*) and particularly in Tunis (the administrative *beys*) progressively took on the attributes of hereditary dynasties—the latter openly becoming known as the Hussaynids.

Whilst lacking the characteristics of a traditional colonising empire, the Ottomans' presence in the Maghreb (which lasted over three centuries) was not without impact. The establishment of the regency of Tunis helped further shape the identity and importance of the city and its surrounds. In spite of the limited contacts with the Ottoman establishment, the urban elite of the coastal cities and Tunis were clearly affected by trends and ideas that emerged in the Ottoman heartland. Chief amongst these was the growing reform movement that developed in Istanbul during the nineteenth century. In conscious evocation of the 'Young Ottomans' movement there, the embryonic reform movement in Tunisia during the same period named itself the 'Young Tunisians.' Although reforms introduced as a result of this movement were limited, the overall effect in a geographically compact and ethnically fairly homogenous territory was noticeable. In the view of Michel Le Gall, it allowed Tunisia to emerge by the end of the nineteenth century as 'an integrated state with a renewed and modernised tradition of centralised administration.'[15]

No similar tradition of reform emerged in the lands administered by the regency of Algiers. This was mainly due to the vast size of the territory it oversaw. Contact between the ruling Ottoman elite and the local population was even more limited than in Tunisia. Nevertheless, the mere existence of the regency in Algiers was significant. The Ottomans were the first rulers to establish a 'separate political entity between Tunisia and Morocco.'[16] Unlike Tunisia and Morocco, which over the centuries had developed fairly distinct identities, the area covered by modern-day Algeria had not. Thus the establishment of the regency of Algiers gave the territory at least an administrative identity (the territory of Algiers—'Algeria') and institutions that would provide a framework for future regimes.

The failure by the Ottomans to establish a regency or even a presence in Morocco during this period meant that the most westerly part of the Maghreb was free of Ottoman influences and began to establish its own unique political forms that would increasingly mark it out from its neighbours to the east. Whereas the Ottoman regencies had the effect of establishing forms of government more influenced by Turkic, Mamluk and Mongol political models, with their 'patrimonial bureaucracies' supported by a military elite, it has been argued that a more classically Arab form of rule was preserved in Morocco. There the model of the righteous caliph not only survived but also was arguably expanded during the Ottoman period. The Saadian dynasty (1510–1659) began this process by laying stress on its *sharifian* descent from the Prophet Mohamed and its commitment to the enforcement of a purer form of Islam.[17] Although both these factors had been present before in the rule of previous dynasties, they had not been combined in this way for several centuries. Its success owed much to the encroachment of the Spanish and Portuguese on Moroccan territory, which allowed the Sultan to use his sharifian status to unite the socially fragmented territory over which he ruled around religion as a bulwark against the Christian enemies from the north.[18] The Alawite dynasty that succeeded the Saadians continued and strengthened this pattern—elements of which arguably have survived with the Alawites even up to the present day. Indeed the persistence of the model led John Waterbury to observe that the political organisation of Alawite Morocco on the eve of the establishment of the European protectorates in 1912 'bore a close resemblance' to that established by the dynasty in the seventeenth century when they came to power.[19] Morocco therefore not only failed to be influenced by Ottoman forms of governance, but also missed out on the modernising and reforming trends that later emerged under their administration and which had a particular effect in Tunisia.

THE IMPRINT OF HISTORY

Although the Ottoman period in the Maghreb did produce an important fault line between those areas that fell under Ottoman administrative control and those that did not, there are also some broader common trends of this period that defy these distinctions. The divide between the urban and rural worlds that had emerged in earlier centuries persisted. The confinement of the Algiers regency to the coastal cities meant that the rural hinterland retained its existing, largely tribal, structures. Moreover, in this vast territory different groups were able to preserve their own identities and practices untroubled by the sort of efforts at centralisation and uniformity that many other lands were experiencing during this period.[20] In Morocco, its varied terrain meant that large areas of rural, mountainous and desert territory regularly operated outside of the political control of the Sultan. As in Algeria, tribal forms of political organisation dominated in these regions. In common with Algeria as well was the important influence wielded by Sufi *sheikhs* (religious leaders) and *tariqa* (brotherhoods). These structures related to the more ecstatic and popular forms of Islamic belief and practice that dominated the rural hinterland of the Maghreb throughout the Ottoman period. They came to play an important intermediary role between local populations and the official power structures when the latter periodically ventured out from their urban and coastal enclaves.[21] In both Morocco and Algeria they showed themselves to be highly effective mobilising agents for popular resistance to central authority: most notably in Algeria during belated attempts by the Ottoman regency to establish more control over the interior in the early years of the nineteenth century. In their own way, they emphasised the broader importance of religion as an important facet of political authority and support. Although this rural-urban dichotomy was more pronounced in Algeria than in Morocco where the Sultan's rule relied on tribal alliances and where his religious authority had discernibly sufi aspects, this common experience increasingly differentiated Morocco and Algeria from Tunisia. Whilst still possessing rural regions where tribal and sufi leaders held sway, the dominance of urban political models and practices became more pronounced in Tunisia.

In sum, the Ottoman period in the Maghreb introduced new elements into the political development of the region, whilst at the same time other existing trends were confirmed and entrenched. The territorial and political distinctions between the future states were strengthened with the further development of the nascent Tunisian state, the absence of Morocco from Ottoman influence and the establishment of the first and faintest contours of the future Algerian state. Parallel with this was the continuing relevance of the urban and rural dichotomy and the overarching importance of Islam as a central and legitimising aspect of political power. In the view of the historian Michel Le Gall, it was during the sixteenth century (which saw the rise of both the Ottomans in Tunisia and Algeria and the Saadians in Morocco) that 'the seeds of the current political organisation of North Africa took root, and is there that we can uncover the political origins of those regions that were to become the modern states of Morocco, Algeria [and] Tunisia.'[22]

European Colonisation

Ottoman influence in the Maghreb gave way by the nineteenth century to influence and eventually control from the different and much more disruptive direction of Europe. The Christian states of the northern shore of the Mediterranean, most notably Portugal, Spain and the Italian city states, had made great efforts during the fifteenth and sixteenth centuries to establish control over the southern Maghrebi shore. However, with the help of the Ottomans, the Europeans were eventually pushed out of all but two of the various footholds they established.[23] The rise of Europe by the nineteenth century and the corresponding progressive weakening of the Ottomans renewed European pressure on the Maghreb. This time, as with most of the rest of Africa and vast tracts of Asia, European efforts at domination could not be resisted. By the time of the outbreak of the First World War in 1914, all of the Maghreb had fallen under the political control of European states.

European colonial control had a profound effect on the region at all levels, arguably rivalling even the arrival of the Arabs and Islam a millennium earlier. The closeness of the period of colonial control to the present day, persisting into the second half of the twentieth century, ensures that its effects still significantly mark not only the contemporary political forms of the region but also most other aspects of Maghrebi society, economy, language and culture at the beginning of the twenty-first century. As with the other historical influences already examined, the period of European colonial control served both to differentiate the emerging distinctions between the separate territories of the Maghreb yet further, as well as to provide them all with some common experiences.

The establishment, nature and duration of the colonial presence differed significantly across the Maghreb and further consolidated the distinct emerging identities of Tunisia, Algeria and Morocco. To look simply at the length of the period of European control in the three areas is to go some way to understanding these differences. In Morocco this period lasted just 44 years (1912–56); in Tunisia it was 75 years (1881–1956); and in Algeria 132 years (1830–1962). The duration of Algeria's time under colonial rule is striking. Indeed, Algeria's experience sets it apart from that of Tunisia and Morocco not only for its length. The nature of the rule was also rather different. Whereas the legal rubric under which France established control over Tunisia and (with Spain) Morocco was that of 'protectorate,' by the time these protectorates were established, Algeria had passed from being a colony to forming three fully integrated *départements* of metropolitan France. This was a distinction of both form and substance. Integration into France itself entailed a forced transformation of Algeria to a degree to which neither Tunisia nor Morocco was subjected. The colonial imprint on Algeria was thus far more marked than it was on either of its two neighbours to the immediate east and west.

The different pattern of French control had effectively been entrenched during the half century that elapsed between the arrival of French troops on the Algerian coast in 1830 and the establishment of the protectorate in Tunisia in the 1880s. Whereas French control over Tunisia, and later Morocco, came as part of the elaborate competition for overseas territory that was played out between the major European powers in the closing decades of the nineteenth century, French intervention in Algeria predated this. Whereas France was able to take effective control of Tunisia and Morocco through creeping influence over those countries' finances and economies (facilitated by their mushrooming debts to France and other European states), with final control being established following quid pro quo territorial agreements with other states,[24] control of Algeria was facilitated by methods more typical of early nineteenth-century diplomacy—namely the use of military force following an alleged diplomatic insult.[25] The rapid capitulation of the Dey of Algiers to French forces in 1830 opened the way for the establishment of firmer French control of territory beyond Algiers. This process which gained pace over the following decades was facilitated by three actions taken by the French military who acted with little initial restraint from the civilian powers in Paris. Firstly, the political structures of the old regency, together with the Ottoman elite itself, were largely swept aside and replaced with direct French political and military control. Secondly, armed resistance to French control that did emerge was soundly militarily defeated and, following the last such instance in 1870–71, significantly repressive measures were taken against the general population to ensure that there would be no similar recurrence for a generation. Thirdly, large-scale European migration to Algeria was encouraged and took place—European settlers coming to number nearly half a million by 1880.[26] The cumulative effect of these three policies was not only to transform Algeria radically but also to ensure that its pre-colonial population had a 'long, brutal and thorough colonial experience.'[27] Native Algerians not only saw their political structures and lands taken away from them by the colonial administration and the incoming European settlers (*colons*), but frequently lost much more: the non-European population actually suffering a net *decline* in numbers over the first forty years of the French presence.[28]

By contrast, Tunisia's and Morocco's experiences of colonial rule were far less traumatic. Although the term 'protectorate' was something of a euphemism which sought to obscure the reality of full French and Spanish political control, the mechanisms through which this control was exercised were rather different and ultimately less destructive to the existing political, social and economic structures. In both cases, the decision was taken to retain existing political structures and rulers, and attempt to rule indirectly through them, rather than simply to sweep them aside as had been done in Algeria. In this way both the Hussaynid *bey* in Tunis and the Alawite sultan in Morocco were allowed to keep their nominal positions. Both the *bey* and the sultan were obliged to do the bidding of the local French *Résident Général* appointed by Paris who became the de facto ruler of the protectorate. Although this appeared to make them little different from Algeria, the preservation of these traditional roles and their supporting structures was to have important consequences once colonial rule had come to an end and the states had to introduce their own political structures. In the case of Morocco and Tunisia, use could be made of the structures that had survived colonial rule; in the case of Algeria, where they had been destroyed, these had to be built from scratch. Furthermore, whilst both Tunisia and Morocco experienced land confiscation, significant European immigration and repression of expressions of resistance to colonial control, these were not on nearly the same scale as in Algeria and did not occur over such a long time period.

The Tunisian and Moroccan colonial experiences had much in common when compared to that of Algeria, but they also had important differences between them, many related to their divergent experiences in the pre-colonial period. The arrival of the French in Algeria had a substantial impact on both neighbouring countries, even before the official establishment of direct colonial control. Both the Hussaynids in Tunisia and the Alawites in Morocco moved to try to strengthen and modernise their economies and armed forces to withstand increasing pressures and penetration from the European powers, and especially the French. In Tunisia, a concerted period of reform under the prime ministership of Khayr al-Din (1873–7), although partial and short-lived, strengthened aspects of the administration, education system and the military, enabling the latter to put down the rural rebellion of 1864 and thus establishing for the first time the near full control of the central administration over the countryside.[29] This contributed to the French finding in Tunisia 'all the elements of a solid and durable administration' when they came to establish the protectorate.[30] In the view of Clement Henry Moore, French rule during the protectorate period in Tunisia served to aid further the development of a significant urban, reform-minded middle class that had already begun to emerge during the Ottoman period.[31] Much of this part of the population actually welcomed the formal establishment of the protectorate in 1883, viewing French rule as facilitating the infusion of new modern ideas and reforms from Europe. Although, as will be shown, this view was modified over time, middle-class Tunisians did their best to benefit from contact with France, particularly in the field of education. Henry Moore points out that, despite having a smaller population than both Morocco and Algeria, three-quarters of the—admittedly small—number of North African students studying at universities in France during the early 1930s were Tunisian.[32] In the view of Ruedy, this further consolidation of the Tunisian middle class came at the expense of the residual and traditional aristocracy in Tunisia whose power and influence weakened as a result.[33] The Moroccan sultans' efforts at reform were, by contrast, much less effective and had a destabilising impact on the pre-colonial state, since many served to undermine the traditional forms of networks of patronage that reinforced the sultan's rule.[34] Gradual European penetration of Morocco in the latter part of the nineteenth century led to continual tribal revolts against the sultan in protest against this from a society that had been far less exposed to the outside world than that in Tunisia: a result of the absence of the Ottoman connection and the more isolationist policy pursued by Sultan Moulay Suliman in the early decades of the nineteenth century.

Morocco was arguably the least affected by colonial rule. This was not solely due to the relatively late imposition of colonial control. The effects of the comparatively short duration of the European protectorates were further alleviated by the policies of the first French *Résident Général*, Marshall Louis-Hubert-Gonzales Lyautey. Lyautey's policy of minimal interference in traditional Muslim life together with his respect for the sultan (perhaps prompted by his own monarchist convictions) during his lengthy stay as *Résident Général* between 1912 and 1925 further preserved and protected Morocco's traditional social and political institutions. Monarchical traditions were permitted and in some cases revived under Lyautey, and the *Résident Général* also ensured that bands played the Moroccan rather than the French national anthem on important occasions and that it was the Moroccan flag that flew over public buildings.[35] Lyautey's policies, whilst generally not maintained by his successors, helped reinforce Morocco's traditional political institutions which, as observed earlier, had been strengthened by the passage of several centuries of hereditary monarchy uninterrupted by the Ottoman influence felt in Algeria and Tunisia. This was not to say that Morocco was politically unaffected by the colonial presence but, as Waterbury has observed, whilst French rule inevitably significantly disrupted the governmental and administrative continuity of Morocco, it left the 'political style' of Moroccans largely intact.[36]

Benjamin Stora has observed that French colonial control of the Maghreb can be divided into two phases. The first phase, beginning in around 1870 and lasting until 1930, is characterised by expansion and consolidation of the French presence and dominance in economic, political, demographic and military terms. Full control in all these spheres had been established, creating a social and political order that placed a French administration over a dominant European community which enjoyed superior status and rights over a more numerous but cowed native population that appeared to have largely—if grudgingly—accepted their inferior status. Indeed 1930 marked the highpoint of colonial rule and was symbolised by the high-profile celebrations held by the French administration and *colons* in Algeria that year to mark the centenary of the arrival of the French. The second phase of colonial rule identified by Stora and commencing from 1930 is conversely characterised by a decline in power, eventually culminating in independence being granted to the region in the 1950s and 1960s. Stora attributes this decline to a number of different factors. They include the onset of economic crisis in France, the rising influence of the United States and its endorsement of the principles of self-determination, the effects of the Second World War, the proportional decline of the European population and the emergence and growth during this period of nationalist movements in the region.[37] Although all clearly interlinked, undoubtedly the most important factor was the last.

Resistance, Nationalism and Independence

Native North African reactions to the imposition of European control had varied across the region. Although there were elements (notably in Tunisia and Morocco) that cautiously welcomed the arrival of the Europeans, the bulk of the population was clearly hostile. This hostility took some violent forms in all three countries in the early period of colonial control, most notably in Algeria. Substantial and coordinated armed resistance had been mounted against the French by the celebrated Amir Abd Al-Qadir in the 1830s and 1840s. From an influential sufi order in rural western Algeria, Abd al-Qadir succeeded in uniting large parts of Algeria under his control against the French. For a brief period this control took on many of the attributes of a state, and since it covered nearly two-thirds of modern day Algeria, many historians have regarded the Amir as laying the first foundations of the Algerian state. However, despite these important precedents, Abd-al Qadir's revolt was eventually comprehensively crushed by the French army in 1847—a fate that befell all other attempted revolts that occurred over the following twenty years. The final and most serious and widespread uprising, occurring in 1870, was not only crushed, but the repression and demands for physical and financial reparations from the French authorities so heavy that they effectively broke the back of the native Algerian population and ended its ability to put up any form of renewed resistance for a generation.

In Morocco, the French colonial authorities methodically 'pacified' the tribes of the rural and mountainous regions in their part of the protectorate. In the northern Spanish controlled zone, the Spanish authorities experienced a far more serious uprising. The revolt led by Abd al-Krim al-Khattabi amounted to much more than tribal dissidence and was more of a concerted and well-organised revolution that effectively drove the Spanish army out of the Rif mountains in the early 1920s. However, despite being on the verge of establishing a separate state in the Rif, al-Khattabi's decision to attack the French administered zone brought the much greater weight of the French military machine on him and led to the defeat of both his army and nascent state in 1926.

The effectively conclusive defeat of attempts at armed resistance to European colonial control gave way by the 1920s and 1930s to more politicised forms of opposition and criticism of colonial control. From this period, all three states saw the emergence of groups and associations that sought a more organised and modernist response to colonialism. In contrast to the earlier largely rural-based armed revolts these new groupings formed in the towns and cities of the Maghreb and used structured organisations, meetings and the written word to spread their ideas and recruit supporters. The emergence of these new associations and their timing owed much to the factors already identified by Stora (European economic and demographic decline, the US discourse on self-determination) but also to other factors. These included the influence of new ideologies such as religious reformism brought from the Arab East and, perhaps even more importantly, ideals of socialism and nationalism encountered by the tens of thousands of Maghrebi soldiers who had served in Europe during the First World War.

Although sharing many common characteristics, these movements developed in their own specific way, assuming their own forms and trajectories in the three future Maghrebi states. Perhaps befitting its more urban and educated make-up, Tunisia was the first of the three countries to develop a recognisably nationalist organisation with the formation of the Destour (Constitution) party in 1920. The party's name accurately reflected the central plank of its platform, which consisted of a call for the introduction of a constitution for the protectorate which would establish an elected parliament, an accountable government and formal legal equality between Tunisians and French citizens living in the protectorate. Centred on the capital Tunis, the Destour was 'essentially the party of the old indigenous elite.'[38] However, despite being the first real organisation to call for greater rights for Tunisians, the Destour was rapidly outflanked by a much more radical current that emerged within it, split from it and eventually vanquished it. Restricted by their reluctance to launch effective appeals to Tunisians beyond their own social circles and beyond Tunis itself, the Destour's leaders fell prey to younger more radical voices who not only sought to break through these social and geographical barriers but who were also much more willing to confront head-on the French colonial authorities—something the Destour's leadership had been unwilling to do. The challenge to the leadership of the Destour came from younger figures who distinguished themselves from the old elite through having their origins beyond the capital (largely the Sahel region) and by possessing higher levels of education, many of them having studied at French universities. In other words, they were the representatives of Tunisia's burgeoning provincial bourgeoisie who had continued to grow under the protectorate. Typical of this group was the figure who rapidly came to dominate it, Habib Bourguiba, who himself came from Monastir in the Sahel and who had earned a law degree in Paris. Breaking with the old Destour to form the self-styled Neo-Destour in 1934, Bourguiba and his contemporaries worked to expand their new party's base by establishing links both with the urban working classes, through co-option of trade unions, and with the tribes of the rural interior. By the late 1930s the new party had come to dominate opposition to French rule and was able to survive arrest of its leadership by the authorities through the construction of a sophisticated cell-type structure, also benefiting from public support generated by the public martyrdom of their imprisonment by the French.

In Morocco, the roots of the main nationalist movement can be found in groups that emerged in various elite circles from the 1920s. These groups were not as geographically or ideologically homogenous as they had been in Tunisia. This was demonstrated by the fact that the two main centres of these groups and the nascent nationalist movement were the very different cities of Rabat and Fez. In keeping with the different identities and orientations of the two places, the groups that consolidated in Fez were religious in reference and more traditional and conservative than the groups from Rabat, who were more European in outlook and ideology, many of the leaders having been educated in France and Europe. However, unlike Tunisia, these two main centres did not find themselves at odds but rather worked increasingly closely together, forming a single organisation which by the early 1930s became known as the *Kutla al-Amal al-Watani* (National Action Bloc); in 1944 it transformed itself into a political party, the Istiqlal (Independence) party, which made plain its objective. Like the Neo-Destour, the Istiqlal worked hard from the 1940s to spread its appeal and support base beyond its intellectual and largely elite origins to bring in much larger cross sections of the ordinary Moroccan populace, particularly the urban workers whose numbers had begun to grow significantly during this period. Nevertheless, it was notable that Istiqlali activism was focused in Morocco's towns and cities rather than in rural areas. Although this reflects, in the view of Waterbury, the growing political marginalisation of the old rural elites, it was to be of significance later on in fostering a divide between the urban and rural worlds which—as has been shown—was a persistent feature of Maghrebi political history.[39] In a similar way, the development of the Istiqlal in the French zone of the protectorate led to a progressive marginalisation of nationalist organisations that emerged in the Spanish zone in the wake of the defeat of Abd al-Krim Al-Khattabi. As with the rural-urban divide, the differences between the two protectorate zones would assume political significance at a later date.

In Algeria, the more fragmented and disrupted nature of Muslim society under the French led to the emergence of a correspondingly more fragmented opposition to colonialism from the 1920s. Three different strands emerged. The first was from the small elite section of the population that had received a French education, and whose leading light became Ferhat Abbas. This group petitioned France to grant the Muslim part of the Algerian population the same rights as those accorded to the European population. The second group to emerge was rather different in nature and took as its reference religious ideas that had emerged with the *salafiyya* movement from the Arab East since the turn of the century and which had influenced the Fez branch of the emerging nationalist movement in Morocco. Originally an intellectual movement, led by figures such as Muhammed Abduh from Egypt, the *salafiyya* had argued for a return to the original values and practices of the first Muslims (*salaf*) as a means of reviving Muslim society and responding to the near total dominance by the European powers under which the Muslim heartlands had fallen from the end of the nineteenth century.[40] A number of young Algerians, led by Abdelhamid Ben Badis from an important family in the city of Constantine, were influenced by these ideas and worked together publishing articles and forming discussion groups, eventually forming their own Association of Algerian Ulema (Scholars) in 1931. Initially the association paid little attention to the issue of French colonial rule, preferring to concentrate on what were considered the more important tasks related to religious education. However, despite adopting a strictly apolitical stance, they soon attracted the ire and hostility of the colonial authorities who saw the association's emphasis on Islamic education and the Arabic language (as the language of the Quran) as undermining official attempts to efface Algeria's Muslim and Arab identity.

Hostility and harassment from the authorities led the association to adopt a more critical and oppositional stance towards the French in return. In this they were joined by the French-educated elites, who had found even their demands for equal status effectively rebuffed by the French government. As a consequence, both groups found themselves drawing increasingly closer to the third organisational strand that emerged amongst Algerian Muslims in the 1920s and 1930s: the radical nationalists. In common with the leaders of the Neo-Destour in Tunisia and the Rabat faction of the Istiqlal in Morocco, Algeria's new nationalist leaders had spent time in metropolitan France where they had similarly picked up a number of new and radical ideas which they brought back to their home countries. However, unlike the Neo-Destour and the Istiqlal, the Algerian nationalists had not been studying in France but had been migrant workers. As a consequence the influences and ideas absorbed by the Algerian nationalists were more proletarian and more socialist in orientation than their Maghrebi counterparts. Indeed, Algerian nationalism owed much to the organisational example of the French labour unions and the Communist party of this period, the latter actually aiding the Algerian organisations.[41] The fact that the nationalist movement in Algeria drew its leadership from more working- and lower-middle-class sections of society has been seen by some as an indication of the absence of any traditional elite grouping or cohesive bourgeoisie which could lead the nationalist movement, as was the case to a large degree in Morocco and Tunisia—these groups having being effectively eliminated by the French. It also potentially explains the greater radicalism of this group and its later greater willingness to resort to violence because of the reluctance of the French to recognise them as suitable leaders of the Algerian community.[42] However, despite this, the nationalists under the charismatic leadership of

Messali Hadj, who as a migrant factory worker and street vendor in France had done much to organise and influence Maghrebi associations there, were able progressively and successfully to unite the very different strands of Algerian opinion and society under one broad umbrella cause: that of the demand for independence.

John Ruedy's characterisation of the essential differences between the three nationalist movements—Tunisia's being reformist, Morocco's conservative and Algeria's radical—goes some way to highlighting the different origins of the three movements.[43] Nevertheless, they had much in common and indeed leaders from the three movements met together on several occasions. All three were also successful in being able to unite all those groups calling for greater rights and eventually independence from European colonial control under one organisational banner.

Another important feature of the activities and discourse of the nationalist movements was the use and reference to religion. In all three countries, Islam became an important rallying cry for the nationalist organisations. As has been noted, Islam had historically always played a central role in Maghrebi politics: most notably in legitimising political authority and activism. In this sense, the importance given to Islam should not be surprising. The fact that nationalism was articulating opposition to rule by European *non*-Muslims further strengthened this tendency. Moreover, the fact that the colonial authorities themselves increasingly used religion (rather than the more complex markers of ethnicity and language) to differentiate and discriminate the settlers from the native population—referring to the latter as 'Muslims'—added further to this. Abun-Nasr has identified three influential campaigns launched by the nationalists in each of the three states that used Islam as a central rallying theme against the colonial authorities. In Morocco it was the notorious Berber *dahir* (edict) introduced by the French in 1930, which was perceived to remove the Berber populations from under religious sharia law and place them under a separate tribal and customary law. This became a rallying cry for the nationalists and did much to consolidate the emerging National Action Bloc and its support base. In Algeria it was the stipulation by the French that any Algerian Muslim wishing to become a French citizen (and thus able to enjoy full and equal rights with Europeans) should renounce their personal legal status as a Muslim. This similarly raised the opposition and campaigning fervour of nationalists who saw this—as with the Berber *dahir* in Morocco—as an attempt to undermine and divide Muslim identity. In Tunisia it was a campaign to remove the remains of those few Tunisians who had opted for French citizenship (and thus renounced Muslim status) from Muslim cemeteries that became a major focus of nationalist activity. Abun-Nasr goes even further in emphasising the mobilising capabilities of Islam. He points out that several of these campaigns were led by figures—such as Habib Bourguiba in Tunisia and Ferhat Abbas in Algeria—who came from highly secular backgrounds and who, before and after, appeared to have little personal attachment to religion.[44] In both Algeria and Morocco religious organisations—specifically the urban *salafiyya ulema*—became an integrated and important part of the nationalist movement. This alliance was one that notably did not develop in Tunisia where the *ulema* were substantially co-opted by the colonial authorities who appeared to have recognised the dangers to them of such an association.[45] In Algeria and Morocco the French had concentrated their efforts into co-option of the *rural* religious leaders—the sufi sheikhs and *marabouts* (saints)—in order to control the historically rebellious hinterland. Salafi doctrine's hostility towards the more popular and traditional forms of practice of the rural religious leaders—believing them to be syncretic and unacceptable deviations from scriptual Islam—pitted the two religious trends against each other. The fact that the rural religious leaders had become clearly associated and allied with the French colonial authorities served to cement further the alliance that the *salafiyya* movement had established with the nationalists. The absence of such an alliance in Tunisia, combined with Bourguiba's own apparently weak personal attachment to Islam, was to have important consequences for Tunisia later on.

From the late 1940s the nationalist movements in all three countries moved into increasingly direct confrontation with the colonial authorities, and by the 1950s this confrontation had begun to take a violent form, evolving into outright armed insurrection. In all three states the path to violence had been similar. Early demands for increased autonomy, political representation and rights for the Muslim population were rejected almost out of hand by the colonial authorities, who were subjected to heavy pressure from the European *colons* to avoid making any concession to the nationalists. This progressively pushed the nationalist parties into increasingly more militant positions and eventually, by the 1950s, into support for armed rebellion. The first serious outbreaks of armed violence came in Tunisia and Morocco, with sporadic guerrilla attacks in the countryside becoming augmented by more coordinated activity in the town and the cities.

In the case of Morocco, violence was finally sparked by the French decision to exile Sultan Mohamed V because of his increasing links and cooperation with the Istiqlal and his reluctance to do the bidding of the French authorities. This effective alliance with the Palace strengthened the Istiqlal, and whilst helping to earn it the epithet of 'conservative' given to it by Ruedy, it presented the French with a united front as the widespread and popular affront at the exile of the popular sultan generated a unifying cause. The alliance was, however, to have significant implications for the shape of post-independence politics in Morocco.

Significantly, a similar alliance did not develop between the Neo-Destour and the *bey* of Tunis. Moncef Bey had been a popular figure who had, like Mohamed V, stood up to the French. However, although he too was exiled by the French, this came a decade earlier (1943) than the expulsion of Mohamed from Morocco, and therefore did not elicit quite the same reaction. His death in 1948 similarly came before nationalist agitation had reached its critical mass. His replacement, Amin Bey, not only suffered from a lack of legitimacy from being imposed by the French, but was also old and weak and was thus sidelined by the Neo-Destour.

Relatively soon after of the beginnings of the campaigns of violence against the protectorate regimes, the colonial authorities negotiated an end to the protectorates and a speedy transition to independence for both Morocco and Tunisia. Both officially achieved independence in 1956. In neither case did the still fairly small-scale, if concerted, attacks genuinely threaten the colonial authorities standing against them. The reason for their early capitulation was the fact that a similar insurrection had been launched in Algeria in November 1954. Faced with the prospect of fighting insurgencies on three fronts, France decided to concentrate its efforts on retaining control of the territory that mattered most to it: Algeria.

The start of the Algerian insurrection on 1 November 1954 heralded the beginning of the most bitter and most protracted of the independence struggles not only in the Maghreb but also globally in the whole of the period of decolonisation of European colonial territories in the 1950s and 1960s. Its violence and length owed much to the fact that— unlike Tunisia and Morocco—Algeria was a formally integrated part of France. Even more important was the presence of nearly one million

European *colons* (over 10 per cent of the total population) who were intent on maintaining *l'Algérie Française* whatever the cost and were set on preventing the government in Paris from making any concessions to the nationalists.

In a further departure from the experience of Morocco and Tunisia, the nationalists who led the insurrection of 1954 were not the established organisations and parties that had been at the forefront of the nationalist struggle since the 1930s. To the surprise of many it was not Messali Hadj's *Mouvement pour la Triomphe des Libertés Démocratiques* (MTLD) that launched the attacks of November 1954. Instead it was a hitherto unknown organisation which called itself the *Front de Libération Nationale* (FLN). Consisting of disillusioned former supporters of Messali Hadj, the FLN had broken with the MTLD and put together its organisation a matter of months before the launch of the insurrection in November. The precipitate launch of the FLN had a number of important implications. Firstly, as a brand new organisation it possessed very little historical and ideological 'baggage,' and was explicit in its assertion that its sole ideological goal was the securing of independence from the French. Such a step was taken to avoid ideological wranglings that would distract from the enormous but central task of national liberation. For the same reasons, the FLN deliberately avoided appointing a single central figure to head its organisation. Many of the leaders of the FLN had in fact quit the MTLD over Messali Hadj's autocratic and individualistic style of leadership, which they believed had come to overshadow the greater goal of national self-determination. As a result, the FLN was careful to maintain a strictly collective leadership throughout the period of struggle against the French. This policy proved highly effective in focusing energies on achieving independence, but, as will be seen, it meant that important questions of ideology and leadership were left to be resolved only after the successful conclusion of the liberation struggle. It also created a precedent for collective over individual leadership that would prove remarkably enduring in post-independence Algeria.

The struggle proved long and bloody and lasted nearly eight years before France finally conceded independence. In the process, several hundred thousand French military personnel, European *colons* and Algerian Muslims lost their lives. Of the latter category there was not an insignificant number of Algerian Muslims killed by other Algerian Muslims for reasons of being either allied with the colonial regime or supporters of Hadj's rival *Mouvement National Algérien* (MNA), which sought unsuccessfully to recover leadership of the nationalist struggle from the FLN. The FLN proved highly effective in developing itself from being a relatively small and unknown force in 1954 to being one that attracted within a few years the support of the vast majority of the ordinary Muslim population and secured the adherence of organisations such as the Association of Ulema and the organisations of Ferhat Abbas. Although suffering repeated military setbacks during the struggle, it was the persistence and widespread support for the FLN that finally secured the recognition from the French government that, although the continuation of *l'Algérie Française* was still militarily possible, it was no longer economically or politically feasible or desirable in the longer term. Brought back to power to resolve the mounting crisis, General de Gaulle rode out the rage of the *colons* and even many senior generals to bring the conflict to an end—an outcome that had the agreement of the majority of metropolitan France, sickened and weary from the war. Thus in July 1962 Algeria was finally granted formal independence from France, bringing to an end 132 years of colonial rule.

The Threshold of Independence

The ending of European colonial rule in Tunisia and Morocco in 1956 and in Algeria in 1962 brought all three countries to the threshold of independence, from which point they could construct their own states and political systems largely free from foreign interference. The purpose of this opening chapter is to show that none of the countries emerged from colonial rule as blank sheets of paper. All of them had been marked by both their common and their individual historical experiences which stretched back beyond the colonial period and would shape their post-independence political paths.

Colonial rule provided perhaps the most important but also the most complex political legacy to the three states of the Maghreb. The experience of European—notably French—rule had both uniting and dividing effects, both across the three countries as well as within them. There is little doubt of the unifying effect that colonial rule had in breaking down the barriers that existed between the often historically very different sections of society within the three countries. Part of this was consciously done, part of it was not. The full and effective subjugation of the rural areas and the tribes that lived there by the colonial powers, and their success in bringing them under the control of central political authority, had never previously been achieved by even the most powerful pre-colonial regimes in the Maghreb. In Morocco and Algeria, this strengthened the position of both the urban areas and central political authority in a substantial way. In smaller, more urban and compact Tunisia, this development sounded the effective death knell of any real residual political influence or autonomy exercised by the rural tribes and sufi brotherhoods. This weakening of the independence of the rural areas in favour of the towns and cities was an obvious aim of the colonial authorities who wished to centralise and thus enhance their political control. However, the removal of barriers between rural and urban and between various other communities in different regions and different cities had another unintended effect that actually served to undermine colonial rule. The centralising of political control by the French also helped the anti-colonial nationalists, who used it to unify and mobilise often diverse populations. The substantial administrative and infrastructural networks, established particularly by the French, increased the contact between different parts of the indigenous population. New roads and railways meant that the inhabitants of Marrakech and Fez or Algiers and Constantine, came into much more frequent contact with each other. Rural communities came into the towns and cities more often to trade and also increasingly to live, providing the nucleus of an urban proletariat with which the nationalist parties could work. This contact was instrumental in helping forge a genuinely national consciousness that supported the aims of the nationalists. It was a development that was further aided by the common experience that Maghrebi Muslims, whatever their origins, had under colonial rule: discrimination and inferior status uniting town and country, Arab and Berber, peasant and French-educated.

In the case of Algeria, this development was crucial to the creation of a national identity in a place where—as has been shown—there was virtually no specific pre-colonial national identity. It would be true to say that a hitherto non-existent Algerian national identity was created during the colonial period, developed through the resistance mounted by Amir Abd al-Qadir (whose banner became the national flag of independent Algeria) and the revolt of 1870, and culminating during the long and harrowing struggle for independence of the period 1954–62. Whilst Morocco and Tunisia had distinct national identities and histories stretching back before the arrival of the Europeans, Algeria did not, and thus its post-independence identity and politics are inextricably bound up with its colonial experience.

The crucial role played by the nationalist movements in both forging a national consciousness and mobilising the populations against the colonial presence ensured that even before the achievement of independence these movements and their leaders would play equally central roles in the post-independence politics of the three countries. As Benjamin Stora has commented:

> The mechanisms of power which prevailed after the achievement of independence in the central Maghreb continued the long and complex histories of the major nationalist orientations established during the time of the French colonial presence.[46]

The comprehensive nature of the central administrative control established by colonial rule and its attendant infrastructure left another hugely important legacy for the post-independence period. It meant that whatever political authority succeeded colonial control at independence would inherit a highly efficient, highly centralised and thus highly powerful state apparatus. Post-independence regimes would therefore enjoy far greater control over territory and populations than had been exercised during the pre-colonial period, when large parts of both habitually operated independently and outside the ambit of the central government. Indeed, the post-colonial regimes would inherit and make use of many of the methods of political control established by the colonial powers, such as the networks of alliances and control established in the rural areas in Morocco.[47] Such political power presented a major political prize for any group or individual after independence, and goes a long way to explaining the often turbulent politics that immediately followed independence, which are explored in detail in Chapter 2.

The effects of colonial rule were not only beneficial to the development of national consciousnesses and central authority and control in the post-independence period. The adverse economic, demographic and social dislocation that the colonial regimes had visited on the Maghreb was both very significant and very obvious, and had resulted in the deprivation, suffering and often death of large numbers of Maghrebis over several generations. However, there were other more profound and less obvious effects of the colonial period that complicated and made more difficult the processes of constructing and building cohesive and coherent states after independence. The comprehensive and pervasive nature of colonial control meant that its effects would not cease with the withdrawal of the last European troops and colonial administrators. The post-independence regimes would necessarily inherit administrative, political, economic and educational systems and structures that frequently had little continuity with the pre-colonial structures that they had replaced. This presented challenges to the post-independence societies and polities at not just the practical and technical levels but also at the psychological and cultural levels. It would also lay the foundations for future debates and divisions about what elements of the European colonial legacy could and should be preserved and to what extent it was possible or even desirable to attempt to recreate structures that had existed prior to the colonial period. It was widely agreed that attempts should be made to throw off the negative aspects of the colonial experience whilst preserving its more positive sides. However, there was only limited agreement as to how this should be done amongst populations that had been differentially affected by the experience. These debates would form a major part of the discourses and controversies of the post-independence period and touch on crucial subjects such as education, religion and language, as well as more tangibly political issues.

All of the above effects of colonial rule are clearly applicable to all three of the Maghreb states. However, it should be restated that the effects were not uniform across the three. As has been shown, the duration, nature and thus total effect of colonialism differed between Morocco, Tunisia and Algeria, with the latter's experience being far and away the most affecting and with Morocco's arguably being the least so. In this way, an appreciation of Algeria's history under colonial rule is more critical to gaining an understanding of its post-independence politics than either Tunisia or—particularly—Morocco. For Morocco, John Waterbury has observed that the two most important political legacies that the country inherited at independence were that of the pre-colonial period as well as that of the protectorate itself.[48]

Looking at the wider perspective of history, Michel Le Gall has observed a number of other trends which reach back before the colonial period but which are also informative in understanding the political legacy that the Maghrebi states inherited at independence. He cites primarily the absence of a tradition of popular participation in politics, with a tradition of popular *mobilisation* being more common. As part of this mobilisation process, Le Gall identifies the periodic co-option of various military and religious elites. Evident before the colonial period—in the Almohad, Almoravid and Ottoman periods—these trends clearly appeared again in the activities of the nationalist movements that used policies of co-option and mobilisation in very similar ways.[49] To these factors one could also add the role played by religion in legitimising political authority and discourse and as a unifying force, and the persistence (albeit reduced during the colonial period) of the rural-urban dichotomy.

The exact impact of these diverse and complex legacies will be made clearer as we move to examine the attempts to establish new political structures in all three states in the wake of independence.

2

POST-INDEPENDENCE STATE-BUILDING

The achievement of independence for Tunisia, Morocco and Algeria was treated by the colonised populations both during the colonial period and in its immediate aftermath as very much an end in itself. But it also clearly marked the beginning of a more profound and important process: the creation of modern states in the context of the latter part of the twentieth century. It was apparent that this process was inevitably going to be quite a complex one, since the impact and exactions of the colonial period had been such as largely to preclude a simple re-creation of the pre-colonial arrangements.

The period immediately following the achievement of independence was therefore characterised by attempts on the part of the states to create and forge political structures and arrangements for themselves. All the states pursued their own individual paths in the pursuit of this end, but there were remarkably consistent similarities in these processes across the three states. Firstly, and in spite of the remarkable national unity created by the respective nationalist movements, this unity—at least at the elite level—broke down almost immediately after (and sometimes before) the formal winning of independence. Consensus on the imperative of independence from colonial control between groups and individuals that had stood shoulder to shoulder in the liberation struggles rapidly gave way to open and even violent competition between these same elements over the shape and particularly the control of the post-colonial state. Secondly, the victors in all three of these post-independence power struggles set about creating highly centralised, fairly authoritarian and increasingly personalised structures of rule and political authority in each state. Thirdly, the retention of power by these forces became dependent upon their ability to successfully manage and balance an array of political groups and forces beneath them, in order to prevent a challenge to their dominance. Lastly, the political space and influence afforded to the ordinary populations in the three countries was minimal and largely restricted to participation in activities that served to reinforce the authority of the existing power-holders and their political structures.

The Struggle for Power

Tunisia: The Battle for the Neo-Destour

The consensus among the nationalist elite in Tunisia broke down even before the full achievement of independence. Since the eclipse of the original Destour party by its more aggressive and robust offspring, the Neo-Destour, during the 1930s, there had been little doubt that they would dominate the post-independence political arena, having comprehensively encompassed and led the anti-colonial movement against the French. However, the very comprehensive nature of the Neo-Destour meant that it was quite heterogeneous in its membership and leadership. A feature of all three of the nationalist movements in the Maghreb, this heterogeneity meant that divisions were likely to emerge sooner or later once the binding consensus on the necessity of ridding the country of foreign rule was weakened by the achievement of independence.

In Tunisia's case, a fault line emerged between the Neo-Destour's two most senior leaders: its secretary general, Salah Ben Youssef, and the party president, Habib Bourguiba. Rivalry between the two figures gathered pace in the early 1950s as each man allied himself with different groups and factions within the Neo-Destour in an effort to secure supremacy. The issue that became the chosen battleground was that of the process of transition from colonial rule to independent rule. Bourguiba made sure that he became the central figure in the Neo-Destour team that began negotiations with the French in 1954. In so doing Bourguiba tied himself to the process, and when in May 1955 France offered the option of autonomy (as opposed to full independence) for Tunisia, Bourguiba accepted this plan as a stepping stone to the achievement of greater independence. The Franco-Tunisian Autonomy Conventions were, however, rejected by Salah Ben

Youssef, who denounced the agreement as an unacceptable compromise that did not give Tunisia the full independence it deserved. Ben Youssef's rejection of the Conventions was supported not only by people from the secretary general's home region of Djerba, but also by more radically nationalist and religiously conservative elements who were suspicious of any compromise with the French. When Ben Youssef openly began to condemn the Conventions, Bourguiba moved to marginalise him in the Neo-Destour, finally engineering his expulsion from the party in October 1955. Bourguiba's ability to use and manipulate the Neo-Destour—an ability he would demonstrate consistently and repeatedly over following years—was shown again at the party's congress, held in Sfax in November 1955. At the Congress Bourguiba succeeded, with some help from young loyal militants and trade unionists who ensured Ben Youssef's supporters did not attend in large numbers, in getting backing for the Franco-Tunisian Conventions and thus his own leadership.

These events led to what amounted to a formal declaration of war by Ben Youssef on Bourguiba and his supporters. Despite his expulsion from the Neo-Destour and marginalisation at the Sfax congress, Ben Youssef had substantial support across Tunisia. However, Bourguiba's superior grip on the party apparatus and his winning over of the initially critical leadership of the powerful *Union Générale des Travailleurs Tunisiens* (UGTT) trade union headed off Ben Youssef's attempts to launch a counter-coup within the party. When this failed, Ben Youssef's supporters resorted to armed insurrection, with the first outbreak of violence occurring in November 1955. To deal with this more serious challenge, Bourguiba and his supporters were forced to call upon the colonial power of France, which, after an initial delay, intervened to crush the rebellion. Ben Youssef was forced into exile in January 1956, and the final surrender of the last of his supporters in southern Tunisia occurred five months later.[1] French willingness to come to Bourguiba's aid was explained by an interest in supporting the moderate Bourguiba, who had negotiated the autonomy conventions as opposed to the perceived radical Ben Youssef, who had rejected them. Ironically, French desire to sustain Bourguiba hastened the according of full independence to Tunisia, which was granted in March 1956, Bourguiba having made it clear that, unlike Ben Youssef, he would retain close relations with the former colonial power even after formal independence, which by early 1956 was appearing increasingly inevitable. Bourguiba's achievement of Ben Youssef's demand for full independence thus undercut support for the latter's rebellion by depriving it of its *raison d'être*. Nevertheless, the challenge had been a serious one, costing over a thousand lives and killing nearly twice as many as those killed in clashes between the French and the armed Tunisian resistance between 1953 and 1955.[2]

The extinguishing of what became known as the 'Youssefist' rebellion confirmed the supremacy of Bourguiba and his supporters within the nationalist movement, but it did not fully settle the issue of supremacy within the post-independence state. In spite of the domination of the national scene by the Neo-Destour, there remained one other domestic actor that could potentially challenge the party: the *bey*. The dynastic inheritors of the old Ottoman regency of Tunis enjoyed nowhere near the same popular level of support as the sultan in Morocco, whose exile and return had ignited nationalist opposition to the protectorate there. Much of this was due to the fact that the *beys*, with one notable exception, had largely resisted throwing in their lot with the nationalists, as Mohamed V had done in Morocco, in order to preserve their French protected privileges. Nevertheless, due to the protectorate policy of preserving at least the form of absolute beylical authority, the *bey* represented a potential legal and constitutional obstacle to the assertion of full Neo-Destour control. Bourguiba and the Neo-Destour therefore moved to marginalise and eventually eliminate the *bey*. In early 1956, the Neo-Destour coerced the ageing and weak Lamine Bey to sign a decree creating a Constituent Assembly, a body which would clearly undermine his authority as it would have full power to decide upon Tunisia's future form of government.[3] Once elected, the Constituent Assembly (consisting almost exclusively of Neo-Destour members) appointed Bourguiba as its president and the *bey* was obliged to appoint him prime minister. As prime minister, Bourguiba worked over the following year to undermine what popular support might remain for the *bey*. In speeches in and outside the Assembly, he made increasing reference to the past misrule of the *beys* and the way in which they had cooperated with the colonial authorities. This criticism became increasingly specific to the person of Lamine Bey, reaching a climax in July 1957 when a whole day of ferociously anti-*bey* speeches in the Assembly, led by Bourguiba, culminated in a formal and unanimous vote to depose the *bey* and create a republic. Within a matter of minutes, a second unanimous vote confirmed Habib Bourguiba as first president of this new republic.[4]

Bourguiba's desire to remove the *bey* from the Tunisian political scene was only partly due to his desire to have no other potential challengers to the leadership of both himself and the Neo-Destour. Even before independence Bourguiba had unabashedly set as a goal the establishment of a truly modern state in Tunisia. It was clear that a traditional monarchy could play no real role in such a state: even its retention in a symbolic form could potentially taint the modernist credentials of the new regime.[5] Most of the leadership of the Neo-Destour was also clearly committed to the idea of a republic, and indeed, the lack of popular reaction that greeted the final deposition of the *bey* was indicative of the wider agreement by Tunisian society in general.[6] To complete a full clear-out of the *ancien régime* the Assembly passed a series of laws aimed at penalising all those deemed to have collaborated with the colonial authorities, which primarily struck at the old elite families whose economic and political power and influence consequently withered away.

Morocco: the Triumph of the Monarchy

In Morocco the post-independence struggle for power took a less violent path, but was no less profound in nature. In contrast to Tunisia, the campaign for national liberation had been led and won by a partnership between the traditional monarch—the sultan—and the dominant nationalist party—the Istiqlal. No blueprint had been established in the run-up to independence regarding the political arrangements to be put in place following the departure of the French and Spanish. Crucially, there had also been little discussion regarding the central question of the relative powers of the sultan and the Istiqlal in any post-independence political system. Both elements foresaw a place for each other in this system, but inevitably each believed that they should hold the dominant position. Even though the senior Istiqlali, Allal al-Fassi, was to declare the nationalist party's subservience to the sultan at the independence negotiations with France in 1955, such subservience was clearly intended to be only symbolic in nature.[7] Most of the Istiqlal leadership was of the view that any political power wielded by the monarchy in the post-independence period would be largely ceremonial in form and certainly inferior to that possessed by the Istiqlal. For his part, Sultan Mohamed V, despite re-titling himself king, believed that a simple return to the pre-colonial political arrangement with a dominant and near absolutist sultan was the way forward, with the Istiqlal playing a purely supportive role.

These differing visions meant that cooperation between the monarch and the Istiqlal gradually gave way to competition in the years that followed. As in the case of Tunisia, this competition for power eventually resulted in decisive victory for one side which was able to successfully impose its own political vision on the other. Whereas in Tunisia it was the traditional monarchy that gave way to the nationalist party, in Morocco the reverse occurred, with the monarchy securing full political primacy over the nationalists in the Istiqlal. The reasons for this different outcome relate both to the events and course of the power struggle that ensued between the monarchy and the Istiqlal, as well as to more profound factors relating to the two competitors. The Moroccan monarchy benefited not only from the historic legitimacy it enjoyed from its religious *sharifian* status, but also from the central and active role it had played in uniting Moroccans behind attempts to bring an end to colonial rule. Neither of these factors was present with the Tunisian *bey*. This therefore effectively precluded—on both popular and tactical grounds—the mounting of rhetorical attacks on the monarchy of the sort so successfully used by Bourguiba and his supporters in Tunisia.[8]

Although the Istiqlal also enjoyed a certain prestige associated with the winning of independence, it suffered from the outset from being a large and unwieldy conglomeration of different interests and personalities. The absence of a single uniting charismatic figure in the mould of Bourguiba meant that these differences and factionalism proved more debilitating to the Istiqlal than to the Neo-Destour. Allal al-Fassi is often pointed to as being the leading figure in the party at this time, but the reality was that his prolonged periods in exile abroad meant that he did not become the undisputed leader of the party until 1959—three years after independence.[9]

The strengths of the monarchy and the parallel weaknesses of the Istiqlal were exacerbated by the effectiveness of the tactics employed by the monarchy in the years following independence. Four main tactical moves stand out. Firstly, there was the establishment of quiet but firm control by the palace over the key institutions of the police, the army, the Ministry of Interior and local administration in the immediate wake of independence. Secondly, there was the initiative the palace took in setting up transitional political institutions at the national level on its own terms. Thirdly, there was the drawing together by the palace of a coalition of forces that were either outside or opposed to the

Istiqlal. Finally, there was the encouragement of formal splits and divisions within the Istiqlal itself.

In May 1956 the king established a police force made up largely of members of the old colonial police force, meaning that it had only limited links with the Istiqlal. In a similar way Morocco's independent armed forces were set up under the supervision of the king. They combined members of the old French colonial army and members of the Army of Liberation that had led the independence struggle in rural Morocco. The new force's loyalty to the palace was secured by its predominantly rural and Berber make-up: the palace assiduously cultivating this section of the population as a counterweight to the predominantly Arab and urban Istiqlal (for more details on this issue see Chapters 3 and 6). The quiet consolidation of the palace's control over the police and the army as well as the Ministry of Interior and local administration gave the monarchy crucial advantages in its struggle with the Istiqlal, which was preoccupied with dominating official political institutions at the national level. When the Istiqlal belatedly realised this mistake and in 1960 moved to bring national security under governmental rather than palace control, the power struggle had already swung decisively in the king's favour.

Even at the national institutional level, the Istiqlal found itself outmanoeuvred by the palace. Despite the party's pre-eminent standing, Istiqlal members represented only minorities in both the first two post-independence cabinets, as well as in the provisional National Consultative Assembly established in August 1956.[10] The composition of both bodies was determined by royal appointment with, significantly, even the Istiqlal members being appointed by the palace. This was certainly a far cry from the discussions at the Istiqlal's extraordinary party congress of December 1955, which had planned for a homogenous Istiqlal government headed by one of the party's leaders. The Istiqlal's acquiescence to the initiative taken by the king in these areas can be explained by both the post-independence honeymoon that operated in the immediate aftermath of independence as well as by the nationalist party's great eagerness to participate in government.[11] There was also undoubtedly the belief that the provisional nature of both the Assembly and the early governments meant that the party could afford to wait for the real prize of the institutions established once a formal constitution was written and introduced. However, the entrenchment of the precedent and principle of royal appointment, together with creeping control of the system by the palace, meant that by the time

Morocco eventually got its first constitution in 1962, the king was fully in control of all of the meaningful levers of power.

The monarchy enjoyed enormous popularity at independence as the symbol of national resistance and independence. However, such support was not institutionalised, in contrast to the Istiqlal which had its own established structure of cells and militants. Aware of this potentially crucial weakness, the monarchy set about creating its own networks of supporters and allies to counter those already possessed by the Istiqlal. The palace naturally turned to those groups in Morocco who felt they had been sidelined by the Istiqlal, or felt some degree of antipathy to the party. It encouraged the activities of the *Parti Démocratique de l'Indépendence* (PDI), a grouping that had split from the Istiqlal in 1946 and which the Istiqlal was committed to excluding from the political scene. Another group alienated from the Istiqlal was the country's rural elites. These overwhelmingly Berber groups had found themselves largely shunned by the Istiqlal during the colonial period, not only because of the predominantly urban and Arab origins of the nationalist party, but also because of the often close collaboration that had operated between many of the Berber *notables* and the French colonial administration. The Istiqlal's dispatching of party activists to Morocco's rural areas to take control of local administration in the immediate aftermath of independence heightened resentment towards the party in many such areas and prompted talk of 'Fassi (Fez) colonisation.'[12] In some areas this discontent at the perceived arrogance of the Istiqlal actually led to unrest. A number of rural leaders in 1957 independently and clandestinely formed themselves into an organisation to coordinate resistance to the Istiqlal's incursions: the *Mouvement Populaire* (MP) or *Al Haraka Shaabia*. Headed by leading figures from the rural-based Army of Liberation, the MP represented a natural and more substantial ally for the monarchy in its battle with the Istiqlal. Consequently, the king successfully blocked attempts by the Istiqlal to crush and dissolve the organisation, and in 1959 the MP gained recognition as a formal political party. Recognition of the MP signalled the final failure of attempts by the Istiqlal to establish itself as a single ruling party—the dream of many of its leading figures. The monarchy successfully frustrated its attempts to subjugate all other forces to its authority—as Bourguiba and the Neo-Destour had successfully done in Tunisia. The *Mouvement Populaire*, together with elements of the PDI and sundry other groupings, became the organisational bulwark used against the Istiqlal in the early years following independence and over time the basis of royalist governments and parliamentary majorities. In Morocco's first constitution, introduced in 1962, the principle of multi-partyism was specifically entrenched. To the outside world this appeared like a liberal and enlightened development in a developing world that was dominated by single-party regimes. The reality, of course, was that its purpose was to defend the monarchy against a powerful and united Istiqlal.

The final tactic employed by the palace to secure its dominance at the expense of the Istiqlal was to encourage splits and divisions within the nationalist party. In many ways this was a relatively easy task given the fractious and heterogeneous nature of the party. The palace had only to apply the lightest of touches to hasten and secure a scission in the party, which formally occurred with the creation of the *Union Nationale des Forces Populaires* (UNFP) in 1959. Although the process of the split in the Istiqlal was a complex affair, the broad characterisation of it as a rupture between the younger radical and more leftist elements with the older, more traditional and conservative ones is fundamentally accurate. The inevitability of a split between these two trends was hastened by the palace, which sought to play one faction off against the other. By appointing a member of the more conservative faction, Ahmed Balafrej, as prime minister in May 1958 and then replacing him seven months later with the more radical Abdullah Ibrahim, Mohamed V exacerbated frictions within the Istiqlal.[13] The creation of the UNFP split the Istiqlal down the middle, dividing and fatally weakening the historic nationalist movement and depriving it of its last hope in its battle for supremacy against the monarchy. In almost symbolic acknowledgement of his victory, Mohamed V dismissed Abdullah Ibrahim (now leader of the UNFP) as prime minister in May 1960 and assumed the role himself. In January 1963 the last nationalist members of the government were similarly removed and ultimately replaced by royalists. As Waterbury observes, 'The split of the Istiqlal prepared the way for a royal offensive, a gradual subordination of all governmental activity, directly and indirectly, to the palace.'[14]

Algeria: From Ben Bella to Boumedienne

On the achievement of independence across the three countries, it was far less clear in Algeria than it had been in Tunisia and Morocco which group or individual would be most likely to assume power. Whereas in Morocco and Tunisia the number of competitors had been limited and the outcome of any power struggle more predictable, this was not the case in Algeria. The long and bitter struggle Algerians had undergone to achieve independence had forced a unity of purpose on the population under the all-encompassing umbrella of the FLN. Memories of the authoritarian leadership of Messali Hadj and awareness of the potentially debilitating and divisive effects of individual and personality-based leadership had persuaded the FLN to assume a fully collegial approach to the conduct of the liberation struggle, an approach that also had roots in the tradition of the tribal *jama'a* of the rural Kabyle region, from which much of the early leadership of the FLN came.[15] However, whilst such an approach had proved its ultimate effectiveness in achieving an end to colonial rule, it presented a problem at independence as to who exactly should take the lead in post-colonial political arrangements. The collegiality that had bound the leadership of the FLN during the war covered a mass of often very different groups and factions.[16]

Organisationally, in 1962 the FLN was split between the *Gouvernement Provisoire de la République Algérienne* (GPRA) that had been formed in exile in 1958, the six regional military commands (*wilayas*) that had operated inside Algeria during the struggle, the *Armé de Libération Nationale* (ALN) that had been formed from Algerians exiled in Morocco and Tunisia, and the *Fédération de France du Front de Libération Nationale* (the FFFLN) arm of the FLN that had been formed by Algerians living in the French metropole. In addition to this were the six surviving 'historic chiefs' or founders of the FLN, the majority of whom had spent most of the war imprisoned by the French, having been captured early on in the struggle.[17]

An attempt to bring together and coordinate this complex and volatile mix of personalities and groups was made in the immediate run-up to independence in May 1962 when, under the umbrella of the National Council for the Algerian Revolution (CNRA), a conference was held in Tripoli in Libya. The Tripoli conference aimed to establish both the goals and programme of the Algerian 'revolution' and the political structures for the newly independent state. The first of these objectives was achieved with the drawing up of an ideologically robust text, documenting and hailing the achievements of the Algerian people in the liberation struggle and the desire to create a state based on popular democracy and opposed to imperialism. Very little progress, however, was made on the second objective of establishing political institutions for the new Algerian state.

Already simmering personal and factional rivalries had become more evident at Tripoli and there was much jockeying for position. In the wake of the conference, the Provisional Government (GPRA), which had been established mainly as a means of negotiating with the French, sought to establish what it saw as its rightful claim to leadership. However, other groups perceived the GPRA as only a part of the FLN and believed it should be subservient to the wider movement under the framework of the CNRA. The GPRA's move to assert its power through the unilaterally taken decision to dismiss the chief of staff of the powerful ALN liberation army—Houari Boumedienne—in June 1962 was the event that signalled the polarisation of the various groups and individuals into two opposing camps. The GPRA rallied the support of a number of the internal *wilaya* commands, who were both fearful and resentful of the ALN. They were fearful because of the ALN's plans simply to integrate the *wilaya* commands into its own structures and resentful because of what they saw as the disproportionate burden of the liberation struggle inside the country that they had borne compared with that of the externally based ALN. For its part, the ALN attracted much of the rest of the FLN that was angered by the perceived arrogance of the GPRA.

With the granting of formal independence on 2 July 1962, the GPRA arrived in Algiers, effectively proclaiming itself the legitimate government. In response to this move, a five-member politbureau was formed for the CNRA by one of the historic chiefs and founders of the FLN, the man who had rapidly assumed the leadership of the anti-GPRA forces: Ahmed Ben Bella. As the ALN moved its own forces into Algeria and towards Algiers, clashes and eventually heavy fighting broke out between the ALN and two of the *wilaya* commands supporting the GPRA. The fighting claimed the lives of over a thousand members of both sides during August and early September 1962 before a ceasefire was agreed on 5 September, which amounted to the victory of the better armed ALN over the *wilaya* commands—the latter finally accepting the authority of the politbureau.

Following its victory, the politbureau moved to establish a National Assembly that would formally assume the powers of the GPRA. Sidelining any electoral procedures, the politbureau effectively appointed members to the new National Assembly, which met for the first time at the end of September. In a move that repeated the pattern established by Bourguiba and the Neo-Destour a few years earlier in Tunisia, one of the first acts of the new Assembly was to name the head of the politbureau—Ahmed Ben Bella—as the first president of independent Algeria.

The defeat of the GPRA and its supporters did not signify the end of the post-independence struggle for power in Algeria, it signalled merely the end of the first round of the contest. Once president, Ben Bella sought to cut himself free from both the coalition of forces that had brought him to power and those that sought to impinge on his own powers as the new president. Other senior figures in the FLN were marginalised, resigned or were removed as he swiftly bypassed the new National Assembly and assumed control of the FLN as its secretary general. In September 1963, Ben Bella oversaw the introduction of Algeria's first constitution, which created a strongly presidential regime with powers concentrated in the hands of Ben Bella, who was elected unopposed as president for a five-year term. Buoyed by these successes, Ben Bella then felt secure enough to move against key allies associated with the ALN (now renamed the *Armée Nationale Populaire*—ANP) and its chief of staff Houari Boumedienne. During 1964–5 Ben Bella progressively replaced Boumedienne's associates in the regime with his own supporters, but it was when he sought to remove as foreign minister the chief of staff's chief lieutenant—Abdelaziz Bouteflika—that Boumedienne and the ANP struck. In a swift and virtually bloodless *coup d'état* on 19 June 1965, Ben Bella was removed as president and replaced by a Council of the Revolution headed by Boumedienne. Having alienated virtually all the constituent parts of the coalition that had brought him to power in 1962, by 1965 Ben Bella retained only a small coterie of personal loyalists and ideological leftists who had supported him and his programme. This meant that there was little resistance to a coup when it came.

Although the coup was primarily motivated by the direct threat Ben Bella had posed to Boumedienne and the army, other considerations also prompted the ANP's chief of staff to act. Ben Bella's increasing drift to the ideological left offended the more conservative and religious sensibilities of Boumedienne and some of his supporters. The increasingly erratic and chaotic management of the country, with the president relying more and more on his own admittedly considerable personal charisma and triumphalist trips abroad than on anything more structured, went against Boumedienne's military-ingrained belief in order and discipline.[18] Similarly, Ben Bella's increasingly personalised and centralised rule stood in contrast to the wartime FLN's commitment to collegiality.

The passing of control from Ben Bella to Boumedienne and the Council of the Revolution effectively marked the end of the post-independence power struggles in Algeria. Boumedienne and his supporters then moved—in the same way as had Bourguiba in Tunisia and the monarchy in Morocco—to put in place the political structures that would characterise the state from that point forward.

Ideology and Personality

It is important to understand what the post-independence power struggles were about. Contradicting what many of the actors in the three states claimed themselves, the struggles for power were not primarily conflicts over ideas and ideology with competing groups aiming to impose their own distinct visions of the new countries' futures. Rather, they were more basic struggles for simple power and dominance between clans, factions and particularly personalities who often all shared very similar ideological positions and objectives. This was particularly true of the power struggles that took place in Tunisia and Algeria.

In Tunisia, the violent conflict that erupted between Salah Ben Youssef and Habib Bourguiba, while officially articulated in ideological terms and attracting different sections of the Tunisian population, was essentially about personal rivalry between the two men. Ben Youssef, for his part, had explicitly proclaimed that he never wanted to be second to Bourguiba;[19] and as Clement Henry Moore observes of the two leaders' clash over the autonomy conventions, 'Personal jealousy of Bourguiba more than Cairo pan-Arabism seems to have been at the root of Ben Youssef's intransigent rejection of the Conventions.'[20] Moreover, it is argued that, before the clash, Ben Youssef's dealings with France had been 'more disposed to concessions sometimes than Bourguiba himself' and that Ben Youssef chose to oppose Bourguiba over the accords in order to win the support of the substantial number of Tunisians who were genuinely opposed to the Conventions on ideological grounds.[21] The adoption of partisan positions vis à vis Bourguiba and Ben Youssef has been described as being 'a clash of constituencies,' but often had little to do with the two leaders and more to do with local divisions and rivalries.[22]

In Algeria, the violent power struggle that occurred in the summer of 1962 had similarly little to do with ideology and much to do with personalities. It is noticeable that the Tripoli conference that brought together the whole leadership of the FLN had relatively few difficulties in drawing up an ideological programme for the new Algerian state, with the vast majority being in favour of a broadly socialist model. The alignment of groups and individuals in the conflict that pitted the GPRA against the ALN could often be explained in terms of personal antipathies or ambitions. Ferhat Abbas, the veteran nationalist figure, backed the ALN supposedly out of resentment of the fact that he had been ousted as a previous president of the GPRA. More crucially, Ben Bella reportedly said of his alliance with the ALN, 'I'm not wedding myself to their ideas, I'm wedding myself to their force.'[23] As in Tunisia, much of the debate and conflict that took place between 1962 and 1965 was couched in ideological terms, but as Ruedy observes, these 'served instead as ideological cover for conflict grounded in personal ambition and the interests of "clans" gathered about ambitious men.'[24]

The phenomenon of the 'clan' was something that was to become and remain a central feature of Algerian political life and is crucial to an understanding of elite politics in Algeria. Although competition for power between rival groups is a common feature of political systems in many countries, the specificity of the Algerian case is important to grasp. As Ruedy explains:

These clans seldom represented ongoing family or regional loyalties, as in the Arab East, because the generations-long detribalization of Algeria had been too thorough. Rather, they represented relationships based on school, wartime, or other networking.[25]

These relationships were to prove remarkably enduring, and even decades after the achievement of independence, otherwise surprising personal alliances between individuals could be explained by reference to a past personal connection in one of the wartime *wilayat* or in a given town in exile in Tunisia or Morocco. Other writers have, however, perceived more profound aspects of the 'clan' phenomenon, believing it to have much deeper historical roots. Ottaway and Ottaway see in it a reflection of the medieval Maghrebi historian Ibn Khaldun's theory of *asabiyya* (group solidarity) where rival clans united through this *asabiyya* to bring successively different sultans and dynasties to power.[26] Such was the case for the coalitions that brought firstly Ben Bella and then Boumedienne to power.

POST-INDEPENDENCE STATE-BUILDING

Personal Power

The personal nature of the power struggles in the wake of independence was a trailer for the very personalised nature of the regimes that developed out of these struggles. In all three states, to a greater or lesser extent, regimes and political systems came to be constructed around the personalities of individual leaders, who drew into their own hands the vast majority of state powers to the virtual exclusion of nearly all other political actors.

Tunisia: Bourguiba as the System

The most complete example of the institutionalisation of personal power occurred in Tunisia. As has been seen, Bourguiba adroitly neutralised the challenge to his authority posed by Ben Youssef and his supporters and then moved successfully to remove and exclude the *bey*. In the aftermath of this, Bourguiba then worked to ensure that all power rested in his own hands. Already voted provisional president by the Constituent Assembly following the deposition of the *bey* in July 1957, Bourguiba saw to it that the constitution produced by the Assembly granted him maximum power as president. The final constitutional draft that emerged and was adopted in 1959 conferred huge powers on the president. Other bodies, such as the Tunisian parliament, were confined to a strictly secondary role with most important laws being enacted by simple presidential decree.

Bourguiba did not simply rely on constitutional provisions to establish his personal power. He sought to impose his own image and personality upon the newly independent state. From an early stage he worked to make the identity of Tunisia closely connected and ultimately indistinguishable from his own. In his regular public speeches to the population he associated his own personal life history with that of Tunisia and its people as a whole. He sought to convey the impression that he embodied Tunisia itself. He famously responded to a journalist who asked about the Tunisian 'system' by exclaiming: 'The system? What system? I am the system!'[27] Bourguiba backed up this rhetoric with very practical measures to reinforce his image. As early as June 1956, Avenue Jules Ferry in central Tunis was renamed Avenue Bourguiba, a practice that was to be repeated for the main avenue in virtually all of Tunisia's towns and cities. Shops and businesses were soon required to have a portrait of the president on display.

It is important to understand Bourguiba's motivations in both this accumulation of power and this personal identification with the Tunisian state and people. It was not primarily a result of Bourguiba's individual vanity and appetite for personal power. It was certainly true that he enjoyed the trappings of power, as was demonstrated by his assumption not only of the former *beys*' palaces, but also of many of the old royal practices, such as being saluted by the former royal guard and distributing charity on religious holidays.[28] However, for Bourguiba political power was a means to an end and not simply an end in itself. Even the quasi-monarchical pomp and burgeoning personality cult that he built around himself served for him the purpose of reinforcing the political power and authority of both himself and the Tunisian state, to enable him to put into practice his programme. Significantly, this programme was not one that sought to enrich or benefit Bourguiba as an individual, but one which Bourguiba believed was essential to build a modern and prosperous Tunisia. In this way the familiar refrain of dictatorial rulers, that their overriding objectives were for their country rather than for themselves, was arguably closer to being true for Bourguiba than most others. He was primarily driven by a vision to develop and modernise Tunisia as a nation. His belief that only he fully understood Tunisia's needs and required future direction led him to concentrate all this power in his own hands and away from other individuals and groups whom he believed did not share his perfect vision.

Evidence that such altruism was genuine rather than a convenient rhetorical cover for the exercise of gratuitous and selfish political power can be found in several quarters. Examination of Bourguiba's work schedule as president reveals a man dedicated to the business of effective government and reform rather than to the simple retention of power and enjoyment of its material benefits. His regular speeches to the Tunisian population were 'factual analyses of current developments, not exercises in ideology and propaganda, which kept the public informed of policies and the reasoning behind them.'[29] Indeed the very solid and genuinely enthusiastic support he received from the Tunisian people was another indication of the reality of Bourguiba's commitment to Tunisia. Whereas other populations may have been easily seduced by empty rhetoric from idle and despotic rulers, Tunisia's relatively well-educated population with a large middleclass would not have been so easily beguiled by someone who was clearly not as committed to national objectives as Bourguiba.

Nevertheless, public acceptance of centralised rule was also, at least in part, facilitated by the context of the late 1950s which was 'rich with national and international developments, the dramatic possibilities of which Bourguiba knew how to exploit to justify the necessity of national unity represented by a strong executive.'[30] Specifically, there were the growing tensions with the former colonial power, France, as it tried to retain control over neighbouring Algeria; and domestically there was the challenge mounted by Ben Youssef and his supporters.[31] Whilst Bourguiba may have exploited the 'Youssefist' rebellion, he was also clearly affected by it himself, and this was a likely factor in convincing him of the importance of concentrating power in his own hands in order to avoid these types of dangerous and debilitating schisms that would stand in the way of Tunisia's all-important modernisation and development. In this way the Youssefist rebellion, and the ruthlessness and violence with which its supporters were repressed even after independence, can possibly be seen as laying some historical foundations for the authoritarianism and intolerance of dissent that would characterise Tunisian politics even more sharply than the politics of either Algeria or Morocco.[32]

It was perhaps inevitable that, whatever the higher motives for the institutionalisation of personal power in Tunisia, such concentration of power would—with time—lead to increasingly erratic and idiosyncratic rule. This was certainly the case with Bourguiba, and the process was not helped by the president's advancing age. He was already well over fifty at the time of independence, and as the 1960s progressed Bourguiba showed no indications of wanting to relinquish leadership of the country, either through the preparation of a successor or through the establishment of a more collegiate leadership. Indeed the reverse occurred: in 1974 Bourguiba proclaimed himself president for life and began to act even more unilaterally than ever. Although always taking the final decision, Bourguiba had previously made a habit of consulting widely with advisers and ministers. However, as the 1970s progressed and moved into the 1980s, he relied less and less on the advice of anyone beyond a small circle, consisting mainly of family members, within the presidential palace itself. He became even more intolerant of criticism and dissent than ever, and became increasingly obsessed with the preservation of his achievements for Tunisia.[33] These developments meant that Bourguiba was ill-prepared to deal with the new political and economic challenges brought by the 1980s, and it was his manifest inability to cope that finally led to his peaceful deposition by his prime minister Zine Al-Abidine Ben Ali in November 1987, by which time Bourguiba was into his mid-eighties.

Morocco: Institutionalising the Monarch

In Morocco, the monarchy, as victor of the post-independence power struggle with the nationalist movement, similarly moved to concentrate virtually all political power in its hands by 1960. The 1960s witnessed the palace further entrenching its dominance and, moreover, increasingly personalising political power in the personage of the king. This process was both made necessary as well as aided by the passing of the throne from Mohamed V to his son Hassan II, following the former's death in February 1961.

The entrenchment and personalisation of the political power of the monarch was made necessary by the fact that, despite having had a high profile and active role before becoming king, Hassan lacked the same huge aura of popularity and thus legitimacy that his father had as the symbol of the Moroccan nation in the liberation struggle against the French. Hassan therefore deemed it necessary to work at both institutionalising his political power as well as creating his own personal aura of legitimacy. The process was aided by the fact that, in terms of personality, Hassan was arguably a much tougher and politically attuned figure than his more reserved father.

Following his accession to the throne, Hassan assumed to himself a formidable array of formal positions. In addition to being king he also served as his own prime minister (a role his father had assumed in 1960) as well as taking simultaneous and personal control of the ministerial portfolios of Interior, Defence and Agriculture. He also further institutionalised the enormous powers of patronage developed by his father, assuming the authority to appoint every meaningful position of power and responsibility in the kingdom, including the government, police and army. Whilst Mohamed V had initially negotiated important appointments with the Istiqlal, Hassan made all appointments unilaterally. To entrench his powers more formally, Hassan, like Bourguiba in Tunisia, worked to ensure that the first post-independence constitution of Morocco would place the monarchy in an unchallenged political position. In essence, it took Hassan two attempts to achieve constitutionally what Bourguiba was able to achieve at his first attempt.

Although defeated, the nationalist movement represented by the Istiqlal and the UNFP ensured that, although most power was accredited in the new constitution of 1962 to the king, parliament and the government had some role, unlike the situation in Tunisia. However, this role remained marginal and the ultimate dominance of the monarchy was demonstrated by Hassan's suspension of both the constitution and the parliament in 1965 before introducing a new constitution in 1970 whose provisions more accurately reflected the political reality of near absolute monarchical power. However, even within the 1962 constitution important provisions had been incorporated that vested power in the monarchy in a very personal way. Not only were the government and ministers made responsible primarily to the king (rather than parliament), but both the person and institution of the monarchy were made constitutionally inviolable and beyond criticism or question in all matters. The very real political power of this provision was made apparent in the months following the introduction of the 1962 constitution when several senior members of the UNFP were arrested and imprisoned for appearing publicly to question the sovereignty of the monarchy through the organs of the party's press.[34] The choice of date to introduce the first constitution—18 November 1962—was also made deliberately to coincide with the anniversary of Mohamed V's return from exile to Morocco exactly seven years earlier in 1955.[35] This further emphasised the desired continuity between the two kings, as well as seeking to attach something of the former king's legitimacy to the new document.

A second more subtle yet equally effective means of establishing a very personal dimension to the power wielded by the monarchy was through the development of and emphasis placed upon the religious aspects of the Moroccan monarchy. The Islamic dimension of the Sultan as *Amir Al-Muminim* (Commander of the Faithful) and a descendant of the Prophet Mohamed had been present long before independence; but it had taken on additional significance during Mohamed V's confrontation with the French protectorate, and Hassan II sought to expand its significance yet further. The monarchy began to employ greater religious symbolism and language in its protocol and ceremonies. The king took the lead in events to mark religious holidays, publicly sacrificing a sheep himself at Id Al-Adha and instituting and leading series of lectures by renowned Islamic scholars during Ramadan, which he significantly named the *Hassanian* lectures. The practice of receiving formal and tradition allegiance (*ba'ya*) from the country's political, military and regional elites every year was retained and also had strongly religious dimensions. In adopting these rituals and this symbolism, Hassan sought to establish a link with pious ordinary Moroccans over the heads of the elites, which further strengthened his hand in dealing with these elites. It also gave theoretical justification to the articles in the constitution making the person of the king inviolable by explicitly stating his religious and 'sacred' status.[36]

In the successful exercise of this religious dimension of political power, Hassan II made use of an aspect of power essentially unavailable to Habib Bourguiba in Tunisia. It also provided for greater long-term stability and endurance by linking it to the institution of the monarchy as well as to the current king. The monarchy in Morocco experienced a successful and smooth transition of power from Mohamed V to Hassan II in a fashion that would have been unthinkable in Tunisia. Nevertheless, the monarchy's grip on political power was perhaps less sure than that exercised by Bourguiba, who had successfully eliminated all other rival sources of power. By contrast, the Moroccan monarchy had merely temporarily contained and tamed them. It could be argued that Tunisia's smaller population and more compact topography made the establishment of political control much easier than in Morocco, with its much larger and more varied geographical and social landscape. Either way, both states had witnessed the establishment of quite effective (in terms of political control) systems of personal rule by the close of the 1960s.

Algeria: The Failure of Ben Bella and the Ultimate Triumph of Boumedienne

In Algeria a clear attempt was made by Ahmed Ben Bella to establish a highly personalised system of rule. As shown, Ben Bella moved to eliminate or marginalise all rival power centres and to concentrate all meaningful political power in his owns hands. Using the politbureau, Ben Bella engineered the appointment of supporters to the National Constituent Assembly. The Assembly then appointed him as provisional national president before producing a constitution in September 1963 that created a strong presidency to which Ben Bella was immediately elected through the formality of a plebiscite in which he was the only candidate. His removal and marginalisation of other senior figures meant that Ben Bella had accumulated an impressive array of functions in a short space of time. By 1965 Ben Bella was not only President of the Republic, but also head of government, secretary general of the FLN and personally in charge of the ministries of Interior, Finance and Information. Despite creating such institutions as the politbureau, the national assembly and the organs of the FLN, the reality was that Ben Bella made policy unilaterally, consulting only his small circle of close personal associates.

Like Bourguiba in Tunisia and Hassan in Morocco, Ben Bella sought both to legitimise and to sustain this great concentration of power through his own considerable personal charisma. He made use of the symbolism of his return from lengthy imprisonment by the French during the liberation struggle and emphasised his rural origins, which played well with the populist nationalism of the time.[37] However, his over-reliance on his charisma at the expense of more careful alliance building and institutionalisation of power contributed to his downfall in the coup of June 1965. It was notable that the primary reason given by Boumedienne and his supporters after the coup for the removal of Ben Bella was the latter's personalisation of power.[38] The focus on the issue of personalised power rather than the other multiple failings of the Ben Bella period is notable and indicative of the established hostility within the FLN leadership to single dominant leaders, dating back to the period of Messali Hadj. Indeed, in the communiqué issued by the new Council of the Revolution, Ben Bella was specifically compared to the historic nationalist leader and accused of trying to establish the same type of autocratic rule that Messali Hadj had attempted in the 1940s and that had led to the breakaway and creation of the FLN. This antipathy in Algeria to single strong leaders was clearly another important factor in explaining Ben Bella's failure to create the same sort of personalised regime produced by Bourguiba and Hassan II.

Further evidence of widespread dislike of personalised leadership in Algeria was provided by Boumedienne's clear attempts in the aftermath of the June coup to portray the regime that replaced Ben Bella as collective in nature rather than one dominated by himself. Communiqués were issued in the name of the Council of the Revolution and all government actions were made in the name of the Council. Boumedienne himself did not take a leading role, and moreover, did not even make a formal public appearance until four months after the coup. This public reticence was only partly tactical in origin, but was also related to

Boumedienne's more reserved and austere character: very different to that of the more expansive Ben Bella.[39] In spite of his leading role in the coup, Boumedienne was apparently reluctant to head the new government which succeeded Ben Bella, a stance that was as much due to his fear of being similarly accused of seeking personal power as to his 'phobia for personal publicity.'[40]

In keeping with these preferences, Boumedienne, as head of the Council of the Revolution, sought to create a much more collegial form of leadership for the country. The Council itself, which assumed full governing powers from June 1965, was comprised of twenty-six members. Boumedienne appointed hitherto sidelined figures to high profile positions in an attempt to broaden the basis of the regime and decentralise some control. However, the administrative drawbacks of a more collegial form of leadership, together with other more immediate problems, contributed to a gradual reconcentration of power. The process was undoubtedly started following an attempted *coup d'état* in December 1967 by the ANP's chief of staff, Tahar Zbiri. Although unsuccessful, the coup attempt prompted Boumedienne to begin to curtail the practices of greater collegiality and inclusiveness that had brought in figures like Zbiri and which might lead to another similar strike against the regime. The late 1960s saw Boumedienne appoint increasing numbers of apolitical technocrats to positions for which he had initially felt bound to appoint figures satisfying different political factions. By the advent of the 1970s, buoyed by an increasing self-confidence brought about by playing a more active international role and through more self-assured public appearances and pronouncements, Boumedienne felt confident enough to begin to start replacing his own long-standing coterie of close political allies. This group had been with Boumedienne since the period of the liberation struggle, when he had been the ALN commander in Oujda in Morocco, and had thus become known as the 'Oujda Clan.' His progressive replacement of nearly all of these figures in the period 1972–5 opened the way for Boumedienne to construct a regime based much more on his own personal vision than on the need to balance or include other individuals or clans.[41] The Council of the Revolution was slimmed down and that same year was itself replaced by new constitutional arrangements that provided for a strong individual president. In the new constitution, which replaced the one of 1963 that had been suspended when Ben Bella was removed, the President of the Republic was given substantial powers which Boumedienne formally assumed following his election to the post (as the only candidate), immediately following the introduction of the new constitution. It also attributed to Boumedienne as president the roles of head of state, head of government, head of national defence and head of the FLN.

Boumedienne's election as president in December 1976 marked the successful culmination of his efforts to focus all political power in his own hands. It was a process that was remarkably similar to that attempted by Ben Bella in 1962–5, to achieve the same end. A vital difference was that, whilst Ben Bella's efforts had aimed to make his dominance reality through the creation of constitutional mechanisms, Boumedienne's represented the introduction of constitutional mechanisms that merely reflected the existing political reality of full political control by him. Boumedienne's success in achieving what Ben Bella had tried and failed to do had much to do with his patience in building the bases of his personal power over a much longer time span than his impulsive predecessor. Boumedienne's 'more somber and low-key style of authority,'[42] together with his more deliberative and thorough approach to the organisational aspects of power, clearly outweighed the drawbacks of personal shyness and lack of overt charisma that were also traits of his personality. He was further aided by the sure grip he maintained over the key institution of the military, which remained the bedrock of his political support over this period (see Chapter 3). Another important facet of his exercise of political power was his adroitness in handling the complex politics of the elite clans, the mishandling of which had led to Ben Bella's downfall.

Indeed the ability to control and manipulate elites became another central feature of politics in the post-independence phase in all three Maghreb states.

Elite Manipulation and Control

The complex and heterogeneous nature of the societies in the three countries had produced similarly complex and heterogeneous groups and elites that competed for power in the newly independent states. United briefly under the banner of the anti-colonial struggle, this unity largely disintegrated following the achievement of independence. Although the post-independence power struggles did produce decisive victors in all three states, these victors were aware that their victories had come with the assistance of a least some of the various elite groups with whom they had struck an alliance. Moreover, they were also conscious of the need not to alienate fatally those groups or individuals who had lost out in the power struggles, for fear of creating a strong and unified opposition. A key factor in the maintenance of political power was the ability to manage and control these different and diverse elites, so that they were never able to mount a challenge to the victors of the post-independence power struggles.

Tunisia: Rotation and Replacement

Habib Bourguiba was an accomplished master in the field of elite manipulation and control, and both his personal political survival as well as his effectiveness as a leader owed as much to this talent as to his popularity and charisma. The main tool Bourguiba used was the simple practice of circulating senior figures (and their supporters) in the regime between positions. This had the obvious aim of never allowing any one powerful individual to stay long enough in a position to allow him to build up a power base from which a political challenge to Bourguiba's position could be made. His conflict with Ben Youssef had persuaded him of the dangers of allowing any other senior figure within the ruling party to develop a significant following.[43] Ministers and senior figures in the Neo-Destour were shuffled on a regular basis. However, whilst circulation and rotation was the major feature of these reshuffles, the longer-term trend was towards replacement of the elite itself. As time progressed Bourguiba sought gradually to replace the original leading figures of the regime with younger more technocratic figures, who were much more dependent on him individually than the figures whom they replaced who had risen alongside Bourguiba during the colonial period. An indication of this process was the fact that none of the members of the first post-independence cabinet of 1956 were still present in the cabinet of 1963.[44]

Despite the trend towards overall replacement, Bourguiba was, however, careful to avoid permanent alienation of potentially dangerous groups and individuals. As a result, individuals who had been removed from power were often reappointed to another position at a later date: 'the president customarily restored those with whom he had fallen out to significant positions in the party or government after a sobering stay in the political wilderness.'[45] As a result, whilst the threat and fear of removal served to keep existing office-holders both loyal and attentive, the possibility of rehabilitation and reintegration back into the system kept those removed from the system from drifting into serious and organised opposition to Bourguiba and his regime.[46] Bourguiba also used his extensive powers of appointment to buy off potentially powerful adversaries. Such was the case with Ahmed Ben Salah, the onetime head of the powerful UGTT, whom Bourguiba had edged out of the union in favour of one of his allies, but whose subsequent criticism of the government he successfully silenced by appointing him as an influential minister in 1961. Eight years later Bourguiba once again engineered Ben Salah's dismissal and public disgrace by blaming Tunisia's growing economic problems on the minister. Whilst Ben Salah was to some degree responsible for failures of policy, his dismissal and particularly public castigation by the president were more connected to the potential threat he posed to Bourguiba. Thus by placing himself as arbiter over a fluid system of appointment and dismissal, which prevented the emergence of potentially threatening clans and factions based on patronage at lower levels, Bourguiba was able to ensure the security of his own position. Bourguiba did not use these tools indiscriminately. His manipulations demonstrated 'shrewd insight into personality and position,' and on the individual level he built support 'through carefully cultivated debts of loyalty.'[47] At an organisational level, Bourguiba instituted changes such as enlarging the politbureau of the Neo-Destour to weaken its power by diluting the influence of leading members.[48] Yet over time Bourguiba's 'obsession with betrayal' led him to discard a growing number of confidants and senior ministers on whom he consistently laid the blame for the failures of the regime, thus progressively weakening and narrowing the bases of his rule.[49]

Morocco: The King as Arbiter and Patron

Very similar tactics to those used by Bourguiba in Tunisia were used by the kings of Morocco. The palace made substantial use of its huge powers of patronage and appointment not only to rotate leading figures but, more importantly and even more so than Bourguiba, to buy off opposition and dissident opinion. In this case, the 'carrot' of patronage was much more widely used than the 'stick' of the threat of dismissal and exclusion. There was also a need to balance various powerful groups and factions against each other through the use of appointment. Such a tactic had been used to great effect in hastening the split in the

Istiqlal party in 1958–9. The importance of doing this was underlined by Waterbury's view that for the monarchy this was a question of 'divide and survive' rather than simply 'divide and rule.'[50] Like Bourguiba, the Moroccan monarchy played the role of arbiter above different and competing groups. Indeed it was a role that Hassan II explicitly referred to when in 1962 he defended the substantial powers the new constitution had given him by using the analogy of the need for a referee in a football match. Waterbury draws a much older analogy through reference to the role played by the *zaïm* or tribal leader in traditional Moroccan and Arab society, whose role was to arbitrate between groups.[51] The Moroccan monarchy's greater emphasis on tradition and religion enabled it to play this role with more effectiveness and legitimacy than the unabashedly modernist Tunisian president.

The much more traditional nature of Moroccan politics and society also affected the way the king was able to control and manipulate the elites. Family, kinship and region were far more important in Morocco than in Tunisia and certainly Algeria, and the palace used this to win over whole families and regions through its patronage. Royal sisters and daughters were married into some of the key big families to cement personal and family loyalties.[52] However, elite politics were complicated by the traditional division that existed between the urban and rural elites. The pervasiveness of the Istiqlal party amongst the urban elites of the country persuaded the monarchy to seek alliances with the rural elites so that together they could fend off encroachment from the nationalist party. Frictions between the rural and urban worlds and elites also enabled the monarchy to pose as an arbiter between the two and thus boost its credentials as a central and unifying influence and presence.[53]

Algeria: Factional Struggle

The role played by elite manipulation in Algeria differed somewhat from that which was seen in Tunisia and Morocco, primarily because of the absence of a single dominant individual who sought to orchestrate, balance and dominate political factions. Instead, in Algeria's case, there was the experience of one coalition of factions defeating another similar coalition, followed by one element from within the victorious alliance seeking subsequently to cut itself free from the other often disparate factions with which it had allied itself. This process was of course repeated twice: in the case of first Ben Bella and then Boumedienne. Whilst Ben Bella was not successful in his attempt to establish independence and full political control, Boumedienne largely was. It has been argued that this process of elimination of former allies was seen as an unavoidable necessity by both Ben Bella and Boumedienne, because of the belief that the alternative was their own elimination by former allies. Moreover, it was clear that what initially bound the coalition of factions behind each leader were not the ties of region, kinship or even patronage, but simple hostility to a common enemy and rival. The coalition that had brought Ben Bella to power in 1962 had been united by antipathy to the GPRA, whereas Boumedienne's backers in 1965 were drawn together by a common wish to oust Ben Bella.[54] Once this common binding factor was removed, it was perhaps inevitable that faction fighting would resume.

The importance of the phenomenon of the 'clan' or faction to Algerian politics and the eternal struggle for pre-eminence between various rival clans marks Algeria out from Tunisia and Morocco, where one group or individual was able to establish effective dominance.[55] It is certainly true that Boumedienne was, by the mid 1970s, able to put in place a system of personal rule similar to that established by Bourguiba in Tunisia and Hassan II in Morocco. However, it is highly significant that, following Boumedienne's unexpected death in December 1978, Algeria's political leadership was once more plunged back into a situation of inter-faction conflict and rivalry with no one element becoming fully dominant—a state of play that was to persist through at least the following three decades.

It was notable also that, during the periods when Ben Bella and then Boumedienne sought to establish their dominance, they did not practice the same tactic of elite circulation favoured by the Moroccan kings and especially Bourguiba in Tunisia. Whilst both leaders began by distributing positions to a wide cross section of the alliance of factions that had brought them to power, they progressively weeded out and excluded former allies rather than simply rotating them. Nor was there any use of the tactic of temporary exclusion followed by reintegration. Once individuals were ejected from the system there was no later attempt to readmit them: their exclusion was permanent and absolute.[56] The similarity between the way in which both Ben Bella and Boumedienne came to power and sought to stay in power led Ahmed Rouadjia to conclude with justification that the *coup d'état* of June 1965 did not represent any meaningful break in Algerian politics, but instead 'marks only the victory of one clan over others.'[57]

POLITICS AND POWER IN THE MAGHREB

Political Structures

Although the political systems established in the wake of independence in the three states were characterised by personal rule and elite manipulation, these elements alone were not capable of running and controlling often large and diverse states with millions of inhabitants. In all three cases there was a need to establish formal political and administrative structures both to run the country as well as to ensure and institutionalise political control by those who had won the post-independence power struggles. None of the states felt the need to construct entirely new political systems from scratch. All three fundamentally maintained the political and administrative structures they inherited from the departed colonial powers, not just out of necessity but in full consciousness of the fact that the colonial structures had been designed with the specific objective of establishing full and exclusive political control of the country.

Tunisia: The 'Party State' and the 'Presidential Monarchy'

The post-colonial Tunisian state was primarily structured by and around the personality of Habib Bourguiba. However, whilst Bourguiba was undeniably the architect and the centrepiece of the system, even he himself was aware of the fact that one man alone could not run and control a whole country, no matter how charismatic and popular he might be. He was even more conscious of the fact that the sort of modern and dynamic vision he had for Tunisia could not be constructed by his hands alone. His rule therefore needed structures and institutions.

Bourguiba's chosen tool for institutionalising his rule was the Neo-Destour party. It was a logical choice. Not only was it the mass movement that had brought both independence to Tunisia and Bourguiba to power, but already by 1956 the Neo-Destour was a significant institutional force. Unlike the often ramshackle coalitions of interests that passed as nationalist parties in other states, the Neo-Destour from its creation in the 1930s had constructed for itself a well organised apparatus based on a strong pyramid structure and local party cells.[58] In the aftermath of independence, Bourguiba used and developed the structures of the nationalist party to institutionalise and establish his rule and control over Tunisia. In this way the party became central to the

Tunisian state in a way that clearly did not occur in Morocco or even—despite the official rhetoric—Algeria. The dominant role created for the Neo-Destour in post-independence Tunisia was fundamentally similar to that established in states in the communist world. In 1958 Bourguiba introduced reforms that created extensive structures for the party, mirroring the structures of local and regional government administration in Tunisia. Moreover, in textbook communist fashion, these party structures increasingly merged with those of the state to create an effective fusion of party and state, with the party having the predominant influence.

Bourguiba's position as both state president and head of the politbureau of the Neo-Destour ensured his full control over both state and party, and in this way the whole country. Such control exercised through the structures of the party was vital for the implementation of the bold programme of reforms which Bourguiba began to introduce from independence, and which sought, in places, to change fundamental aspects of Tunisian society. The mass organisation of the Neo-Destour provided Bourguiba with both popular support and legitimacy during the difficult post-independence years.[59] The extensive structures of the party which stretched all the way down to the local level and which incorporated an estimated 380,000 members (30 per cent of the adult population) by 1965 also provided Bourguiba with a valuable means of communication with the Tunisian populace.[60] The reforms of 1958 also placed the structures of the Neo-Destour much more firmly under the control of the politbureau, which in turn was firmly under the control of Bourguiba. The president consulted but always took the final decision. As the highest organ of the party, the politbureau was formally selected by the Central Committee of the party. However, Bourguiba controlled this process and by the 1970s dispensed with all formal appearance and simply directly appointed the politbureau members himself. The official 'annual' congress of the Neo-Destour in reality met much less frequently, and between 1956 and 1964 not at all. Even the politbureau itself met only at the behest of the president. In the view of some, the Neo-Destour had as early as the mid1960s transformed itself from a mass popular organisation into a simple piece of bureaucratic machinery for the president.[61]

Subservient to the structures of the party, the structures of the state also placed Bourguiba at their controlling pinnacle. Bourguiba's inheritance of the traditional powers of the former *bey* led Henry Moore to observe that 'Bourguiba had displaced the Bey to become Tunisia's new Monarch.' Indeed, Henry Moore dubbed the political system installed by Bourguiba a 'presidential monarchy' to encapsulate Bourguiba's combination of modern political structures with traditional autocratic style.[62] In this way the state and party were fused in the personality of Bourguiba himself.[63]

The new constitution of 1959 did provide for other political institutions, but these were largely toothless and subject to the control and veto of the president. A National Assembly was established but was made up entirely of Neo-Destour members, whom Bourguiba had more or less selected himself. The president paid scant attention to it as a body, using presidential decrees to pass most of his most important pieces of legislation, which constitutionally he was allowed to do during the half of the year that the Assembly was not sitting.

Algeria: Institution Building and the Constitutions of 1963 and 1976

In Algeria, Benjamin Stora has observed that, in terms of their authoritarianism, following independence 'the structures of the new Algerian regime remained those of the old colonial regime.'[64] Ahmed Ben Bella tried to follow the same path taken earlier by Bourguiba in Tunisia. In an almost identical fashion to Bourguiba, Ben Bella manoeuvred himself into a position where he was firstly able to create a politbureau of his own close allies, which then in turn selected a constituent assembly, which then drew up a constitution that placed all meaningful powers in the hands of a president. Ben Bella then ensured his own election to this pre-eminent position. In the same fashion as the Tunisian constitution of 1959, the new Algerian constitution of 1963 created political structures that served as simple adornments to the centralised power of the presidency. A national assembly was established, but its role was similarly 'one of elaboration and ratification' rather than of genuine debate and decision-making.[65] Parallels with Tunisia ended, however, with Ben Bella's *coup d'état* of June 1965. Ben Bella's failure to transform the clear popular enthusiasm he generated into tangible political support was evident in the lack of popular protest against his removal.[66] This failure was attributed in turn to Ben Bella's failure to create solid institutions to marshal this enthusiasm. By contrast, Bourguiba's establishment of strong popular political institutions through the Neo-Destour party protected him from a possibly similar fate.

Houari Boumedienne arguably learnt from Ben Bella's mistakes and took time and trouble to build more solid institutional foundations to his regime following the coup of 1965. Much of the institutional 'ballast' of the post Ben Bella regime was automatically provided by the Algerian military, whose support and loyalty Boumedienne, at its head, was careful to nurture and consolidate. The constitution of 1963 was suspended along with all the institutions—both meaningful and cosmetic—it had created. Formal institutional power passed to the Council of the Revolution, whose membership provided a much broader basis for the exercise of political power. A Council of Ministers which reported to the Council of the Revolution dealt with the day-to-day running of the country. Although Boumedienne followed Ben Bella's path in gradually moving to reduce the core leadership of the country (as represented on both the Council of the Revolution and the Council of Ministers) down to his own close circle of personal allies, he avoided the political isolation that Ben Bella had created for himself by simultaneously creating new political institutions such as local government structures which, although more administrative than political in function, helped shore up more general popular support for the regime.

It was not until 1976 that Boumedienne finally officially institutionalised his rule through the introduction of a new constitution. This formally replaced the interim arrangement of the Council of the Revolution that had operated since 1965 and put in writing the extensive political powers that Boumedienne had been effectively exercising over the preceding few years. A new National Assembly—the *Assemblée Populaire Nationale* (APN)—was established, but like its Tunisian counterpart and Ben Bellist predecessor, it was given a marginal role and was certainly not permitted to impinge on the power and prerogatives of the president. In the first elections to the APN in 1977 all the candidates were members of the FLN, and their selection was overseen by Boumedienne as secretary general of the FLN. As Benjamin Stora observes:

The Constitution of 1976 consecrated the presidentialism of the Algerian political system, the pre-eminence of the State and the government over every other partisan or elected representative organ.[67]

A key difference between the regimes established by Bourguiba in Tunisia and by Boumedienne in Algeria was the lack of a dominant Algerian political party. In spite of the official position the FLN enjoyed under both Ben Bella and Boumedienne as the single 'ruling' political party, its role and importance was not remotely analogous to that of the Neo-Destour in Tunisia. To begin with, the FLN did not have the same long history (having been created on the very eve of the independence struggle) and thus was not a long-established structure, unlike that of its nationalist counterpart in Tunisia. Moreover, as Charles-Robert Ageron points out, the FLN that was recognised in the constitution of 1963 was arguably not the same FLN that had led and won the liberation struggle against France between 1954 and 1962. Instead, he argues, it was a reconstructed entity that simply represented the factions that were victorious in the various post-independence power struggles—the old historic FLN having effectively died in the course of these struggles.[68] Following Ben Bella's assumption of the post of secretary general of the party in April 1963, the FLN lost all institutional meaning as both Ben Bella and then Boumedienne allowed it to 'atrophy' under their own stewardship.[69] Both wanted to benefit from the powerful symbolism and legitimacy the party's name enjoyed, but both feared that any meaningful role given to the party might provide a potential rival with a useful institutional base from which to attack the leader. For his part, Boumedienne clearly relied on the military as an institutional prop and support just as he might have relied on a dominant political party. The first signs that the FLN might once again be given a more active role began to emerge in the mid 1970s with a more politically secure Boumedienne indicating that he might use the party to mobilise mass popular support for his increasingly ambitious economic programmes. (There were also rumours about Boumedienne wishing to free himself from such heavy reliance on the military.) However, the death of Boumedienne in December 1978 brought a premature end to such potential plans, as they did to the rest of the president's developing vision for the country.

Morocco: The Dominant Monarchy

A similar pattern of creating political structures that supported and reflected almost untrammelled executive—in this case monarchical—power was witnessed in Morocco. This occurred in several stages. The kingdom's first post-independence constitution of 1962 reflected some of the realities of the power struggles of the late 1950s between the palace and the nationalist movement. Institutions like the national parliament were given some powers. Nevertheless, the monarch was given the dominant position particularly with regard to the inviolability of the person of the king and the fact that ministers were primarily answerable to the palace rather than parliament. The insertion of the clause in the constitution that explicitly specified and guaranteed the existence of a multi-party political system in Morocco also represented the final defeat of any ambitions the Istiqlal (or indeed any other party) might have still harboured to monopolise the political institutions and thus challenge the dominance of the monarchy.

Deadlock in the first parliament between opposition and royalist parties meant that very little was achieved by the parliament in its opening years. This lack of achievement allowed Hassan to belittle the parliament as an institution and to stress its irrelevance. He described it as an actual impediment to the pressing problems of need and poverty in Morocco and contended that it was actually at odds with true democracy.[70] The state of emergency declared by the king in March 1965 following widespread rioting in Casablanca was used by Hassan as both a backdrop and a pretext to dispense with the parliament. He suspended the 1962 constitution and thus automatically prorogued the parliament. In its place, Hassan simply legislated by personal decree.

The suspension and sidelining of the parliament symbolised the final and full victory of the Moroccan monarchy over the nationalist movement. However, although Hassan was more than happy to continue ruling simply through the use of personal decree, he recognised the largely cosmetic advantages of having formally defined political structures and institutions. As a result, in 1970 he introduced Morocco's second constitution which replaced the first introduced only eight years earlier and simply 'consecrated the practice of the state of emergency' which had existed since 1965 and through which the king had enjoyed almost unchallenged political power by ruling through personal decree.[71] The fact that both the UNFP and the Istiqlal boycotted both the heavily rigged referendum approving the new constitution and the parliamentary elections that followed it was evidence of the complete lack of place afforded to any actor other than the monarch in the new constitutional system. That the king pressed ahead with the introduction of these new arrangements meant that he now felt sufficiently powerful to scarcely care what the nationalist parties thought.

State and Society: Popular Participation

It is noticeable that, in discussing the political evolution of the Maghreb states after independence, little mention has been made of the ordinary populations in the three states. This reflects the reality that the vast majority of Tunisians, Moroccans and Algerians were essentially peripheral to political processes during this period. They played little or no role in either the struggles for power or in the construction of the post-independence state—both processes being almost exclusively the preserve of the elites in the three countries. Few efforts were made to solicit the opinions of ordinary people, and even those institutions and mechanisms supposedly established to represent the population, such as the national parliaments, were largely appointed and controlled by the countries' leaders, with no real representative function or political power.

It was also noticeable that such exclusion from politics seemed to be fully accepted by the bulk of the ordinary population. With the partial exception of Morocco, there were no instances of social unrest or popular discontent during the first decade and a half of the post-independence period. The population appeared content with the passive political role it had been assigned by the states' political leaders. That the political leaders were able to achieve this passivity was due to their having successfully persuaded the mass of the people that their interests were best served by accepting and supporting the leadership of the elites. It was stress on the imperatives of national unity and development that provided the leaders in the three states with the ideological elements through which they could legitimise the absolute political authority which they claimed for themselves.[72] There was little need to stress the importance of national unity since this had been at the core of the nationalist struggle against colonial rule which had united the mass of the ordinary populations in the three states in the run-up to the achievement of independence. The fact that the Moroccan monarchy, Bourguiba and the Neo-Destour in Tunisia, and the FLN in Algeria had led the independence struggles in their respective countries meant that all already enjoyed massive popular legitimacy in the eyes of the masses who were willing to accept their continued political leadership and control in the post-independence period. Moreover, 'the emphasis on unity also promoted an authoritarian approach to politics under which a single leader claimed to embody the real interests of an entire society.' It was the success of figures such as Bourguiba and Boumedienne in having themselves popularly recognised as 'the custodians of the national unity' of their countries that enabled them to establish such secure political regimes.[73]

Tunisia: Authoritarian Paternalism and the Mass Organisations

Tunisia followed the pattern of marginal popular participation in political processes. However, there were two variant features to this pattern that marked Tunisia out from its neighbours to the west.

The first feature related to the reasons for the marginalisation of popular opinion and participation. Whilst political centralisation and control were prompted, as in Morocco and Algeria, by an appetite for personal power and a belief in the importance of unity, in Tunisia these factors were buttressed by local experiences. The experience of the Youssefist revolt had had a profound impact on the way Bourguiba viewed the Tunisian people and any political role they might play in the post-independence state. The ease with which large numbers of Tunisians had flocked to Salah Ben Youssef severely undermined Bourguiba's faith in the rationality and trustworthiness of the Tunisian population.[74] He became convinced that Tunisians 'lacked the political sophistication to evaluate wisely options confronting them' which led him to believe that a strong hand was required to lead Tunisia towards progress and away from harmful and distracting alternatives.[75] He regarded regular elections as 'feverish periods' liable to aid 'the proliferation of germs dangerous to the health of the country.'[76] Thus formal institutions or mechanisms designed to allow ordinary Tunisians to participate in the decision-making process were kept to a minimum in favour of a form of authoritarian paternalism that sought to guide Tunisia along a 'correct path.'

The second factor that marks Tunisia out from Algeria and Morocco on the issue of popular participation was its use of the mechanism of the single party to interact with Tunisian society. The transformation of the Neo-Destour into a mass ruling party with a wide membership allowed the Tunisian regime to penetrate and thus control society through the classic model of the communist state-party structure. Almost in recognition of this fact, the Neo-Destour renamed itself the Parti Socialiste Destourian (PSD) in 1964. The establishment of mass party organisations for youth, women workers, and the parallel exclusion of any organisations outside the ambit of the party further reinforced this penetration and control.

Algeria: Institutionalised Populism

Algeria deviated little from the regional pattern. The one group that was noticeably absent from the power struggles of 1962 was the ordinary Algerian people themselves.[77] Boumedienne made few attempts in the late 1960s to communicate with the ordinary population, preferring to devote his time exclusively to the consolidation and bureaucratic institutionalisation of power which Roberts has characterised as 'essentially elitist in concept and method' and in which the role of the mass of the population was 'reduced to the role of onlooker.'[78] In the view of John Ruedy, by the 1970s Algeria had become 'increasingly depoliticized' with the homogenisation of the government, the bureaucratisation of the FLN and the integration of the mass organisations into the state.[79] Boumedienne's introduction of local government structures in 1967–9 was seen by some as an attempt to involve the ordinary population but, as has been seen, these structures were more administrative than political or representative in function. In a similar way the 'Socialist Revolution' announced by Boumedienne in 1971 clearly marked a fresh effort by the regime to appeal to and involve the ordinary Algerian population in new ways through agricultural reform, Arabisation and industrialisation. However, such involvement was to be fully controlled and orchestrated by the state, meaning that the initiative was simply a form of populism. In the view of Leca and Vatin, this populism—which drew on the traditions of the wartime FLN—came to be the predominant form of official political culture in Algeria by the mid 1970s.[80] Most observers were struck by the 'surprisingly candid' nature of the public debate that preceded the drawing up of the National Charter and resultant constitution in 1976.[81] However, the placing of all meaningful political powers into the hands of Boumedienne as president in the latter document appeared to indicate that the debate had little or no impact on the reality of exercise of power in the country.

Morocco: A Restive but Controlled Population

The case of Morocco was somewhat different from that of Tunisia and Algeria. To begin with, the Moroccan population proved to be far less quiescent than their cousins to the east. Social unrest occurred sporadically throughout the early post-independence period, the most notable examples of which being the tribal disturbances in a number of rural areas (notably the Rif) in the late 1950s and the urban riots in Casablanca in March 1965. All were successfully quelled by the state, often with significant force and violence. The causes of these incidents of unrest were varied but reflected the more fragmented, unsettled and contested nature of the political scene in Morocco.[82]

The struggle for dominance between the king and the nationalist movement in the immediate wake of independence did not involve the wider public and was largely conducted at elite level. This was because of the failure of both the Istiqlal and the UNFP to mobilise and channel popular support behind them and the reluctance of Mohamed V to attempt to whip up similar support for the monarchy out of a fear that, once roused, such support could turn against the palace.[83] Nevertheless, Mohamed clearly benefited from the immense public prestige and legitimacy he enjoyed as the symbol of the liberation struggle against the French. As shown, the lack of such similar historic legitimacy on the part of his son, Hassan, when he came to the throne in 1961, led the new king to look for other ways to bolster his power and legitimacy. It was noticeable that Hassan made use of religious and other rituals to establish a personal bond and link with the ordinary Moroccan people over the heads of the politicians in the nationalist movement. However, like Bourguiba and Boumedienne, he used these links with the population as a means of strengthening his own personal authority rather than as a means of facilitating greater participation in political processes and decision-making.

State Agenda and Policies

The gradual consolidation of political power in certain hands in the three states raises the question as to what exactly those who had secured power wanted to do with it. The simple securing of power was not necessarily an end in itself. It had been won through various post-independence power struggles in order for the victor to implement his own vision for the newly independent state. Bourguiba, Boumedienne and Hassan II all had quite different visions for their respective countries.

Tunisia: Modernisation

The clearest and most well-defined programme of policies was introduced in Tunisia. The relative speed with which the post-independence power struggles were resolved allowed Bourguiba to begin to implement his vision for Tunisia within months of the departure of the French. It was a vision that he and his supporters in the Neo-Destour had been able to formulate since the party's creation in the 1930s and which had been perhaps further honed during Bourguiba's repeated periods of imprisonment by the French. In short, Bourguiba's vision for Tunisia was one of perceived 'modernisation.' Bourguiba's education—particularly when studying for a law degree in Paris—had convinced him of the imperative of reform for his country, in line with the model of Europe. Experience and admiration of the West was something Bourguiba shared with many of the Maghreb's other post-independence leaders, but none pursued emulation of Europe with the same vigour and determination as the leader of Tunisia. For Bourguiba, the pursuit of this goal had been the motivation behind his defeat of the challenge from Ben Youssef and his removal of the *bey*. The *bey* personified the traditional institutions that Bourguiba believed were responsible for Tunisia's backwardness, and Ben Youssef had drawn support from the more conservative sections of Tunisian society allied with these institutions. Moreover, it also substantially explained his desire to focus all power in his own hands, in accordance with his belief that he was the only person fully aware of the need for and means of achieving Tunisia's development.

In practical terms, Bourguiba introduced a string of reforms he saw as essential to starting the process of modernisation which he believed had been stifled by several centuries of backward Ottoman influence. The most striking of these reforms concerned the Family Code, the collection of legal statutes that governed matters of marriage, divorce, child custody and inheritance, and was traditionally based on Islamic Sharia law. As early as 1956, Bourguiba introduced reforms to the Code that changed long-established practices, notably granting women the right to contract into a marriage voluntarily, making divorce subject to judicial processes (thus abolishing the practice of unilateral repudiation by a husband) and banning polygamy. The significance of these reforms was as much in their symbolism as in their substance: Bourguiba saw the status and position of women as demonstrative of the development and modernity of a society; he sought to create greater legal equality between men and women in order to signal his clear intent to modernise the country.[84]

Elsewhere Bourguiba dramatically expanded educational opportunities for the Tunisian people with the aim of achieving universal primary education by the end of the 1960s and also through establishing Tunis University. In the economic field, policy under Bourguiba saw a number of shifts in direction. Earlier liberal and *laissez-faire* policies implemented during the first five years of independence gave way in 1961 to rigorous state-led and planned socialism as a means of providing more dynamic economic growth. Responsibility for the new policy was given to the former leader of the UGTT and socialist ideologue, Ahmed Ben Salah. The perceived failure of Ben Salah's socialist strategy, which led to greater inefficiency, landed Tunisia in greater foreign debt and encountered significant resistance, led to the removal and public disgracing of Ben Salah in 1969. Although Ben Salah's removal was as much motivated by political as economic considerations, Ben Salah's policies were abandoned by Bourguiba at the same time as he was. Thereafter Tunisia followed a more liberal economic path which, although providing noticeable economic growth in the early 1970s, encountered difficulties by the end of the decade as economic disparities within Tunisian society began to grow (see Chapter 7).

Algeria: Socialism

Although the post-independence power struggles in Algeria took longer to resolve than in Tunisia, the ideological orientation of the leadership of the new state was remarkably consistent throughout. Both Ben Bella and Boumedienne were committed to transforming and extending the armed revolution that had brought the country independence into a social and economic revolution in the period that followed. The Tripoli conference held by the FLN in May 1962 had failed to produce agreement on political frameworks for the new state, but there had been little difficulty securing broad agreement on the ideological goals of the new state, which was to be socialist and revolutionary. Influenced by Gamal Abdul Nasser's revolutionary Arab socialism as well as by leftist ideas coming from Europe and elsewhere, Algeria's new leaders saw such an orientation as a natural response to and panacea for Algeria's bitter colonial experience. It needed to be revolutionary to overcome the stifling legacy of colonialism; and it had to be socialist to correct the harsh social and economic inequalities imposed by both the colonial state and the settler population for over a century.

Three months before Algeria became independent, Ahmed Ben Bella had declared that 'Algeria will have a socialist government.'[85] On assuming the presidency, Ben Bella had set about realising such an affirmation. Many of his 'socialist' programmes were aided by the chaotic state of the Algerian economy after eight years of war, or were motivated as much by political considerations as economic ones. Takeover by the state of lands vacated by departing Europeans was arguably socialism by default, and the much vaunted system of worker self-management (*autogestion*) helped bolster popular support for Ben Bella at a critical stage of the power struggle with other figures in the FLN and was later effectively abandoned in favour of greater centralisation.[86] Nevertheless, Ben Bella appeared genuinely committed to socialist goals and forged increasingly strong alliances with Marxist and far-left groups whose influence was clearly demonstrated in the leftist tone of the Algiers Charter of 1964, which was largely the work of these elements.

Ben Bella's increasingly exclusive reliance on doctrinaire leftists was one of the motivations for the *coup d'état* mounted by Boumedienne in June 1965. More religious and conservative elements within the army and elsewhere had become unhappy with the growing influence of Marxist ideas, which were viewed with suspicion because of their association with atheism. Nevertheless, over time, Boumedienne also came to espouse an explicitly socialist orientation for Algeria. Following his period of cautious consolidation in the late 1960s, Boumedienne launched his *Révolution Socialiste* in 1971 in the fields of industry, culture and agriculture. Five years later, the new National Charter produced for the country was replete with socialist terminology and analysis and established the construction of a socialist state as a primary goal. There was substance to these declarations. Although the *Révolution Agraire* resulted in the eventual reallocation of only 10 per cent of previously privately owned land, Boumedienne's industrial policy had a clearly socialist imprint.[87] It focused on the establishment of a range of heavy industries financed by massive public investment as part of a large-scale and comprehensive economic plan for the country.

Of perhaps even greater importance than the socialist element of Boumedienne's programme was the 'revolutionary' element. It had been the Council of the Revolution that had replaced Ben Bella in 1965, and in public statements following the coup, Boumedienne had stressed that Ben Bella had been toppled to 'correct' the Revolution. For Boumedienne the central idea of revolution (*thawra*) meant the development of the country's resources.[88] The official 'revolutions' initiated in 1971 were designed to achieve this objective. Rapid heavy industrialisation became the centrepiece of Boumedienne's development strategy as a means of closing the economic gap with the Western world. As in Tunisia, expanding education also became a priority for the regime as a means of promoting development. In this way, Boumedienne's emphasis on the imperative of development for Algeria shared much in common with Bourguiba's drive for modernisation in Tunisia. Although Algeria's leaders' commitment to the ideological goal of socialism was much more consistent than in Tunisia, and less emphasis was placed—for nationalistic reasons connected to the liberation struggle—on emulating European models, both sought to develop and improve their societies. As in the case of Bourguiba, Boumedienne saw consolidation of political power as a means to an end as well as an end in itself. Boumedienne and his supporters' 'primary goal was the construction of a strong state that would transcend and outlast personnel changes in government so that the state could get on with the real business of the revolution'; in other words, focus could be shifted 'from the political to the developmental.'[89]

Morocco: Survival

In Morocco, the effective exclusion of the nationalist movement from political power meant that the country did not witness any attempt at large-scale social and economic reform of the sort undertaken by Tunisia and Algeria. Revolutionary change was patently not going to be on the agenda of a fundamentally conservative monarchy that broadly wished to conserve long-standing political and economic structures. The Moroccan monarchy understood very well that preservation of these structures was important, perhaps even essential, to its own power and survival. In more specific terms, the absence of any real efforts at development and land reform in rural Morocco in the decades after independence had much to do with the monarchy's wish to protect and preserve its key allies amongst the rural nobility. It was thought that any substantial reform could potentially threaten the economic and political control of the rural nobility and stability in these areas. Consequently, taxation, industrialisation and other reform projects were either blocked or simply not pursued in order to preserve the palace's rural support base: something that was to have a hugely damaging impact on longer-term rural development in the kingdom and exacerbated differences with urban areas.[90]

The lack of an all-encompassing development strategy on the lines of those elaborated in Tunisia and Algeria did not mean that no attempts were made by the Moroccan regime to develop and bring prosperity to the country, but rather that such attempts tended to be small-scale and technical rather than broad in nature.[91] Overall, such attempts were rather overshadowed by efforts of the monarchy to entrench and protect its own political position, which remained arguably less secure than that of either Bourguiba in Tunisia or Boumedienne in Algeria for the first two decades after independence.

Conclusion

By the early 1970s all three states, despite their distinctive differences, had settled into fairly similar political patterns. As has been shown, these patterns were characterised by strong centralised systems largely focused on the personality of a single individual. Power was maintained by their respective leaders through manipulation of the elite and through the construction of formal political structures that gave nearly all meaningful political power to the leader. The role of the mass of ordinary people in politics in the three countries was limited to passive support of the existing leadership.

This pattern of politics and political power predominated from the early period of independence through the 1960s and into the 1970s. However, from the late 1970s this pattern was forced increasingly to confront a series of mounting and often mutually supporting challenges to its continuation. These challenges came from four main sources and directions. First of all, there was the failure in all three states to achieve the sort of economic and social progress that had been hoped for at independence. The vast increases in population that all three states experienced in the early decades of the post-independence period exacerbated this problem and led to a net decline in socio-economic conditions for—and thus greater unhappiness among—large parts of the population in all three states. Secondly, there was the fading in importance of the memory of the independence struggle, not only amongst those who experienced it, but more importantly amongst the rapidly expanding percentage of the population who had no memory of the period, having been born after its conclusion or being too young to remember it. As a result of this, rhetorical references to the anti-colonial struggle by leaders and regimes in order to shore up their own popular legitimacy and support became less and less effective. Thirdly, new political and social forces began to emerge that criticised and challenged the existing political order and which succeeded in attracting often substantial levels of support among the population. Finally, changes in the regional and international environment meant that the regimes of the Maghreb were less and less able to insulate themselves from external events and pressures that increasingly impinged on the workings of their own political and economic systems.

These four factors were clearly all interlinked and together worked to put increasing pressure on the regimes in all three states so that they were forced to react to preserve the established status quo.

3

THE MILITARY

A common feature of many of the states that won their independence from colonial rule across Africa and Asia during the 1950s and 1960s was the prominent role the military came to play in domestic politics. In an increasing number of states, army commanders seized power from initially civilian regimes based on national liberation movements, taking control of the leadership of the state either to further their own particular interests or to prevent the country from sliding into civil conflict. In Africa, the *coup d'état* of 1963 in Ghana heralded a wave of similar developments across the continent. In the Arab world, the coming to power of Gamal Abd al-Nasser and the Free Officers in Egypt in 1952 set an even earlier precedent that was repeated in Iraq, Syria and Libya. Even when the military did not seize power itself, its influence as the wielder of ultimate force within nearly all states supplied it with an often decisive influence in domestic politics.

The Maghreb provided no general exception to this pattern, but the precise role that the military as an institution has played in Algeria, Tunisia and Morocco has varied markedly between them and is thus illustrative of the differences in the political evolution of the three states. In broad terms one can say that the role played by the military in the politics of the three countries has varied from marginal in one state, to central in another and somewhere in between in the third. Specifically, it has been of pivotal importance and indeed embodied the state itself in the case of Algeria; was carefully and deliberately excluded from politics for many years in Tunisia; and played a varying role in Morocco.

The centrality of the role of the military in Algeria is demonstrated by the fact that every one of the seven presidents the country has had since independence in 1962 has succeeded to the post because of the backing of the military. Moreover, most have also been removed by the military. Three of Algeria's four longest-serving presidents—Houari Boumedienne 1965–78, Chadli Benjedid 1979–92 and Lamine Zeroual 1994–8—were senior military officers when they assumed the presidency. This has led the veteran Algerian leftist commentator Mohamed Harbi to quip memorably that Algeria 'was not a state with an army, but an army with a state.'[1] By contrast, during Habib Bourguiba's long presidency in Tunisia no military figure could be found in the upper echelons of the regime, and members of the armed forces were prevented from joining the ruling party and even voting in elections. In Morocco, the military's influence in politics has waxed and waned over time, with elements within it twice coming close to seizing power from the ruling monarchy.

Many of the differences between the three states have their origins in the varying ways the armies of the states were created in the aftermath of the achievement of independence in the 1950s and 1960s. Both Morocco and Tunisia received significant help from the departing French in assembling their militaries, as part of an agreement between them and the colonial power, which sought to bolster support for the more moderate factions that seized power in the struggles that the two states experienced after independence. Indeed a large part of the new armies of the two states was made up of native North African troops that had formed part of the French (and in Morocco's case, also the Spanish) colonial army. The post-independence leaderships of both countries relied heavily on the influence of the former French troops to instill a loyalist and apolitical ethos in the new armies.

Morocco: A Very Royal Army

In Morocco, the monarchy under Mohamed V made a point from the outset of forging strong links with the military, recruiting it as an ally in his power struggle with the nationalist Istiqlal party. The king was clearly aided in this task by the involvement of the French in the construction of the new army, the formal colonial power being explicitly committed to the establishment of a specifically 'royal' army, fearing the emergence of a radical nationalist force that would threaten its post-colonial interests.[2] Thus shortly after the formal achievement of independence, in May 1956, the birth of the 'Royal Armed Forces' or FAR (*Forces Armées Royales*) was announced. In his speech marking the occasion, King Mohamed V took care to emphasise the royal nature of the new force, speaking of it being 'placed under our guide' and 'our supreme command.'[3] It marked the beginning of a deliberately close association between the monarchy and the military, with senior members of the royal family regularly appearing in military uniform. The king also took more practical steps to ensure control over the new institution. Not only did he assume the role of supreme commander of the FAR, but also ensured that Morocco's first minister of defence was the ultra-royalist Ahmed Reda Guedira. More significantly, the king appointed his eldest son, Hassan, chief of staff of the FAR when the latter became crown prince in 1957.[4]

Having secured control over the FAR, the palace sought to ensure the new force's loyalty. It was aided in this task by a number of factors. The integration of large numbers of men—particularly at the officer level—from the former French and Spanish colonial armies had a number of beneficial effects in this regard. Firstly, transferring some of the more professional and apolitical values of particularly the French military to the new force made it less likely to be prone to political penetration by nationalist and leftist elements and ideas.[5] Secondly, and more importantly, although the colonial background of these troops left them vulnerable to accusations of collaboration and involvement in colonial oppression from both the nationalist movement and even the ordinary population, this vulnerability meant that by embracing and bringing these elements into the system, the palace was able to provide protection for them from questions over their role in the colonial period and possible purges that might follow from this.[6] In return, the king was rewarded with loyalty from a group who were deeply grateful and thus thereafter dependent on the palace.[7] A third factor that served to reinforce the new army's loyalty to the throne was its ethnic and regional make-up. The bulk of its officer corps came from large rural notable families. This reflected the rural—and thus Berber—bias that recruitment to the French colonial army had shown and which was transferred to the FAR on its creation. A largely rural and Berber officer corps in the FAR suited the palace, since it provided the perfect counterweight to the overwhelmingly urban and Arab character of the nationalists of the Istiqlal party.[8] As has been shown (see

Chapter 2), there was considerable antipathy to the Istiqlal in a number of rural areas after independence, and this provided the palace with natural allies in its struggle with the Istiqlal for pre-eminence.

The appointment of Crown Prince Hassan to the position of chief of staff of the FAR further consolidated links between the palace and the armed forces. From the outset, Hassan became actively involved in the organisation, leadership and even military campaigns of the FAR, which served to strengthen the military's links and loyalty to the palace and particularly the crown prince.[9] Hassan also worked to integrate the FAR's senior officers into the expanding royal patronage network, promoting them and giving them additional positions as well as more direct gifts of land and property that had belonged to Europeans who had left at independence.[10]

Hassan was aware that control of the army was vital in the uncertain political atmosphere of the early years of independence. The political parties—notably the Istiqlal and the UNFP—still represented a political threat to the dominance of the monarchy into the 1960s. The fact that the military's deployment after independence was very similar to that of the colonial army under the French before 1956 was indicative of how it served the same essential function of internal security.[11] Indeed, from 1960 the FAR provided many of the governors for key and sensitive regions.[12] Within the military itself the loyal French-trained officer corps worked hard to root out leftist and nationalist elements.

Once he became king in 1961, Hassan increasingly began to view the army itself as his link with the Moroccan population. He believed that the broad cross section of society that was represented within the ranks of the military meant that he had contact with all sections of Moroccan society. As he stated in a speech extolling the virtues of the FAR:

The fact that you can see there a farmer rubbing shoulders with a shopkeeper, with someone from the bourgeoisie, or a craftsmen through to someone close to the King himself, is tangible proof that the FAR represents the height of democratic principles.[13]

Significantly, this view led Hassan to view other forms of democratic representation—notably the political parties and the parliament—as being increasingly redundant. Not only did the FAR and his close relationship with it give him the means of ultimate political control, but also its make-up ensured that he would never lose touch with his ordinary subjects. This belief goes some way to explaining the confidence

Hassan felt in suspending the constitution and dissolving the national parliament in 1965.

Throughout the 1960s the Moroccan military began to grow steadily in political influence and significance. Most of the influence the military exercised was hidden from general view, but the FAR was not averse to assuming more public political roles, and in 1964 two generals assumed ministerial posts in an otherwise civilian government. The role the military played in the suppression of riots in Casablanca in March 1965 raised its profile and further impressed upon Hassan its loyalty and importance to him. Elements of the FAR even began to eclipse the civilian government and administration. In 1968 the direct supervision of links between the FAR and the palace was taken over by the Royal Military Household, which fully sidelined the civilian Ministry of Defence and effectively separated the government from any involvement in military affairs.[14] The size of the army also continued to grow throughout the 1960s, as did its budget, with the FAR consuming one-fifth of the Moroccan national budget by 1970.[15]

Algeria: The ALN as Kingmaker

In Algeria there was not the same need to create an Algerian military after independence, one having already been created in the long and bloody fight for national liberation. The eight-year-long struggle had by necessity transformed the nationalist movement into an armed force to evict the French. The FLN had created its armed wing, the ALN, just weeks before it launched its insurrection against the French colonial state in November 1954, and it was military figures who progressively saw their influence increase within the FLN as the struggle wore on. The external 'Army of the Frontiers' based in Tunisia and Morocco came to be of increasing political importance within the *political* leadership of the liberation struggle, which increasingly had to meet and function outside Algeria. In 1960 the new GPRA relinquished military powers to the new General Staff of the ALN, created and led by Colonel Houari Boumedienne, who had already established full control over the 'external' forces of the ALN in Morocco and Tunisia.

Once independence was achieved, Boumedienne and the ALN exercised decisive influence in the ensuing power struggles. In deciding which faction to back, the conclusive factor was undoubtedly the GPRA's decision to try to sideline the ALN General Staff, which prompted the latter to support Ahmed Ben Bella's challenge to the GPRA. Once president, Ben Bella recognised the role the ALN had played in bringing him to power by appointing Boumedienne minister of defence, and by giving several of the ALN commander's key allies ministries and other important positions in the new state.

The military in both Morocco and Algeria thus played a critical role in the power struggles that took place after the achievement of independence, their support being arguably decisive in the securing and consolidation of power by the monarchy in Morocco and Ben Bella in Algeria. These experiences stood in stark contrast, however, to that of Tunisia, where the military was remarkable for its near total absence from the political scene following independence.

Tunisia: The Fear of Coup d'Etat

The absence of the military from Tunisian politics is explained by the attitude of President Habib Bourguiba, who made the strategic decision from the outset that the military in the new Tunisian state would be formally excluded from politics. He not only constructed the new state's military around former members of the French colonial army in order to instil a loyalist and apolitical ethos, but also largely excluded members of the rural anti-colonial militia, or *fellagha*, whom he distrusted.[16] Moreover, he placed a civilian politician at the head of the Defence Ministry, and as early as January 1957 he officially banned all political activity or association within all ranks of the military—even withdrawing the right to vote in elections. Unlike Algeria and Morocco, where military figures played central and high-profile roles in the regimes, senior military figures were 'conspicuously absent from the elite' that ruled Tunisia under Bourguiba. Throughout most of Bourguiba's time as president, no generals played an active role in public life and little was known about the army more generally.[17]

Bourguiba set out the reasons for his policy in a speech in 1965. He declared that 'Members of the military are not free to have political opinions like other citizens,' otherwise they would become involved in the 'struggle for power' and would 'use their weapons to impose solutions of their own choosing.'[18] In making this charge, Bourguiba was undoubtedly influenced by the experience of other Arab states where the army had constantly intervened in politics at the expense of civilian politicians and which he had been able to observe at first hand during his periods of exile in the Arab east.[19]

THE MILITARY

Bourguiba's early fears were confirmed by military involvement in two unsuccessful attempts to oust him. The first, in 1957, involved officers supportive of Salah Ben Youssef; and the second, in 1962, brought together figures with a mixture of motivations.[20] The wide cross section of military officers involved in both plots—including personnel from the president's own personal guard—clearly alarmed Bourguiba.[21] It further confirmed his resolve to set the country's military apart from politics through the establishment of a professional and apolitical army on the model of the armies of Western European states.

From the creation of the Tunisian military in June 1956, Bourguiba took care to establish a clear institutional separation between the military and the country's new political structures. In contrast to many other newly independent states, Bourguiba did not seek to bring the military into the structures of the ruling party, the Neo-Destour. Indeed the ban on political activity in the military extended to membership of the Neo-Destour/PSD. As a consequence, Tunisia's first and subsequent ministers of defence were civilian members of the ruling party rather than military officers. Bourguiba even sacked one civilian defence minister in the 1970s for involving a military officer in preparations for a PSD Congress.[22]

Further forestalling any putschist ambitions that the Tunisian military might possibly harbour, Bourguiba put limits on the military's size and funds. In so reducing the army, Bourguiba potentially deprived both himself and Tunisia of the important and very necessary tasks an army is called upon to perform, namely the maintenance of internal order and the defence of the country's frontiers from external attack. However, Bourguiba believed that these essential tasks could be performed by forces other than the Tunisian military. A powerful internal security apparatus focusing on the Ministry of Interior and including the National Guard and the gendarmerie was established. This apparatus, which also relied on the strong and extensive structures of the Neo-Destour to detect and deal with challenges to internal order, played a further major role in acting as a rival and a counterweight to the Tunisian army. For the more serious task of defending the country against external attack, Bourguiba placed his confidence in Tunisia's good relations with powerful Western states—notably France—on whom he relied to come to Tunisia's defence in the event of attack from either of its two larger neighbours: Algeria and Libya.[23]

The Reality of the *Coup d'état*: Algeria and Morocco

Bourguiba's view that a strong military presented a significant potential threat was borne out by the experiences of Algeria and Morocco, in spite of the efforts that the new power holders in both states had made in forging links with their militaries.

Algeria: The Ousting of Ben Bella and the Assertion of the ANP

In Algeria it was Ahmed Ben Bella's attempts to cut himself free from the influence of the army that resulted in his ousting in the bloodless *coup d'état* of June 1965. Although prompted to act by the increasingly chaotic and leftist drift of Ben Bella's rule, Boumedienne and the army had also been motivated by a desire to preserve its own influence. This had been threatened by Ben Bella's attempts to create 'popular militias' that were to report directly to the president and were rightly seen by the army as an attempt to undermine and sideline its influence; and also by the president's progressive removal and replacement of Boumedienne's allies from their positions of power (see Chapter 2).

The success of the army's strike against Ben Bella and the lack of any organised resistance to it owed much to Boumedienne's work as head of the army and minister of defence in the period immediately following independence in transforming the wartime ALN into a new national army: the *Armée Nationale Populaire* (ANP). The core of this task consisted of integrating the guerrilla *maquisards* of the internal *wilaya* commands into the structures of the ALN of the frontiers, many of the former being highly suspicious and resentful of the predominance of the external army which many of them had briefly fought against in the power struggles of the late summer of 1962. It was notable that the new ANP did not break apart, not only when Ben Bella was removed from power but also when armed insurrections were attempted in 1963 and 1964 by disillusioned former *wilaya* figures. These rebellions were easily crushed by the ANP which remained united, as it also did, more crucially, when the ANP chief of staff appointed by Boumedienne, Tahar Zbiri (another former *wilaya* leader), attempted a coup in December 1967. The failure of all these putsches was attributed to Boumedienne's success in integrating disparate elements and also in beginning the process of turning the army into a more professional force. To achieve this, Boumedienne not only weeded out untrained and uneducated personnel and sent others to prestigious military academies abroad, but also relied on the professional expertise of some 250 former Algerian junior officers from the French colonial army who had defected to the ALN during the latter stages of the liberation struggle.[24] The progressive recruitment of younger and better educated men into both the ranks and the junior officer corps also aided this process of professionalisation, these younger generations being less politicised in outlook than the previous generation that had grown up in the revolutionary atmosphere immediately preceding the liberation struggle.[25] The clear potential danger of regionalist tendencies, which many felt had manifested themselves in the political positioning of *wilaya* commanders both before and after independence, was reduced by the shifting of army units around the country in times of crisis as well as by the introduction of political commissars into army units with the object of forging a unified national identity.[26]

The martial complexion of the regime that replaced Ben Bella was apparent in the make-up of the Council of the Revolution, which included the whole of the General Staff, the commanders of the five military regions and four former *wilaya* commanders. Only two members of the initial twenty-six member Council had not occupied active military roles during the liberation struggle.[27] However, as has been seen (in Chapter 2), Boumedienne thereafter progressively slimmed down the Council, concentrating more power in his own hands to alter the role of the military in the decision-making processes. He used the opportunity of the failed *coup d'état* of 1967 not only to ease out many of the remaining *wilaya* leaders from positions of influence, but also to formally suppress the General Staff and thus concentrate control of military affairs in the Defence Ministry, a portfolio he personally maintained through the ousting of Ben Bella and right up until his own death. Organisationally, Boumedienne's creation of a Council of Ministers separate from the Council of the Revolution created some degree of separation between the military and everyday government.[28]

The organisational distinction between military and bureaucratic structures partially reflected Boumedienne's efforts to create a less overtly military regime. Not only was a largely civilian Council of Ministers charged with the daily business of government, but those senior military officers who did hold public political office took care never to appear in uniform in public: Boumedienne himself only ever wore civilian dress after 1965. At the same time the regime worked hard to reinforce the popular view that the internal peace the country began to enjoy from the late 1960s was the result of the military's stabilising influence. It strongly promoted the view that the ANP was the direct inheritor of the wartime ALN, whose role it emphasised at the expense of other actors, and was thus a principal repository of the massive popular legitimacy that the struggle enjoyed. In this way, both rhetorically and constitutionally, the ANP portrayed itself as the 'guardian of the revolution.'[29]

In spite of the organisational changes, it would be a mistake to underestimate the continuing importance and indeed centrality of the institution of the army in Algerian political life. The ANP participated in the 'Socialist Revolution' of the early 1970s (see Chapter 2) and the army's journal, *El Djeich*, became a key forum for the new leftist official discourse of the period. Even within the new structures that Boumedienne established through the new constitution of 1976, the ANP retained a central position. In the constitution itself the army was accorded an important position, and along with the more normal duties of national defence it was charged with defending the 'Socialist Revolution' and contributing to 'the development of the country and the construction of a new society.'[30] Even the formal revamping in 1976 of the moribund FLN—viewed in the Ben Bella era as a potential rival to the power of the military—was placed under the supervision of a senior military officer. When Boumedienne died in December 1978, a full third of the Council of Ministers were military officers.

Morocco: Failed Coups and their Aftermath

In Morocco, King Hassan's aim during the 1960s had been to make the FAR completely dependent upon himself. However, it did not escape the notice of some observers that the reverse was arguably equally true: Hassan himself became completely dependent on the military. Confident of his close knowledge of and relations with the senior officers of the FAR, Hassan felt able to ignore warnings that came from leaders of the political parties that he had become 'a prisoner' of the military.[31] Hassan's confidence in his military received a rude shock with two attempted *coups d'état* organised and launched from within the FAR itself that occurred in quick succession over a thirteen-month period in 1971–2. Although both were ultimately unsuccessful, together they served to

THE MILITARY

change profoundly the nature of both the king's relationship with the military as well as the wider political landscape from which Hassan had arguably increasingly cut himself off during the previous decade.

The first coup attempt took place at the Royal Palace at Skhirat during a lavish party that Hassan had thrown to mark his 42nd birthday on 10 July 1971. The party was stormed by over a thousand military cadets. Although nearly a hundred of the guests at the party died in the attack, King Hassan survived due to a combination of luck, judgement and confusion amongst the attackers. Within a matter of hours loyal troops were able to re-establish control and arrest or destroy the rebel elements.[32]

In the aftermath of the failed coup it was discovered that the attack had been primarily the work of General Medbouh, head of the powerful Royal Military Household, who managed relations between the palace and the FAR. Other senior officers were also officially implicated in the plot, the motivations and objectives of which are contested. It does seem clear that Medbouh was primarily motivated by a desire to bring an end to what he saw as the widespread and endemic corruption that had gripped the upper echelons of the Moroccan regime. The objectives of the attempted coup, since it failed, were also not fully clear. It is argued by some that Medbouh did not plan to try to kill the king but merely wanted him to abdicate or even keep him as a figurehead at the head of a military regime.[33] However, the subsequent discovery of an aborted plot by Medbouh and his conspirators to blow up the king and his entourage near the town of El Hajeb the previous May casts doubt on this theory.[34]

Hassan appointed his interior minister, Mohamed Oufkir, to the posts of minister of defence and chief of staff with the task of reorganising the military and safeguarding against any further attempted coup. A trusted individual, close to the palace and the king and himself from the military, Oufkir had been instrumental in suppressing opposition (such as the Casablanca riots of March 1965) and breaking up the challenge from the political left in the 1960s.

The second attempted *coup d'état* came just over a year after the attack at Skhirat and this time occurred in the air. The king's personal airliner was attacked by F5 fighters from the Moroccan air force over Tetouan as Hassan returned from a trip to Paris on 16 August 1972. Although damaged, the royal airliner was able to land and the king escaped unharmed.[35] As in the previous year, although most of those involved in the coup itself were relatively junior officers, the ultimate blame for the attempt was placed at the feet of a senior military figure. This time it was none other than Mohamed Oufkir—the very man Hassan had entrusted with the task of protecting him against future coup attempts. Once again, the circumstances and explanations of the coup were rather murky. Oufkir himself died in mysterious circumstances at the king's palace at Skhirat on the evening of the failed attack on the royal airliner: official sources claim he committed suicide, whilst many others maintain he was summarily executed. Most evidence, nevertheless, pointed to Oufkir being behind the coup.[36]

Oufkir's motives for the plot were less certain. There were some claims that, like the 1971 plotters, Oufkir acted out of unhappiness with the perceived corruption of the monarchical regime, whose mistakes had not been corrected even in the aftermath of the Skhirat attack. He was also said to have believed that Hassan wanted to remove him and tried to kill him in a helicopter 'accident' in Agadir in May 1972.[37] He thus perhaps plotted the coup to 'forestall his own downfall by eliminating his master.'[38] It was possible that Hassan had grown suspicious of Oufkir, believing that he was implicated in the Skhirat plot. Indeed it is difficult to believe, given Oufkir's formidable intelligence network as interior minister, that he had been unaware of—if not actually implicated in—the plot of July 1971. Oufkir's plans for Morocco after the removal of Hassan were as unclear as those of the Skhirat plotters. Some believed that he planned to install a regent, others that he wished to establish a republic, possibly with support of the leftist parties.[39]

Whatever the motivations and objectives of the two failed coups, the political effect they had on both the monarchy and the Moroccan political system was profound. In broader political terms the coups prompted Hassan to expand dialogue and contact with the political parties, whom he had effectively ignored since the suspension of parliament in 1965, in an attempt to recruit allies and widen the base of support for the regime (see Chapter 4). In terms of the military itself, Hassan embarked on a thorough overhaul of the FAR's leadership, organisation and duties. There was a substantial purge of the officer corps and heavy punishment for elements implicated in the coups.

William Zartman usefully summed up Hassan's strategy towards the military after 1972 as aiming to keep it 'busy, dependent and divided.' He kept it busy by making Morocco a significant contributor to UN peacekeeping forces in places such as Zaire and by sending troops to Golan in Syria where they fought in the war of October 1973 against Israel. He kept the FAR dependent by first of all drawing in all-important military powers to himself. He assumed the positions of minister of defence, and chief and deputy-chief of staff, and the Ministry of Defence was reduced to a National Defence Administration for logistics and procurement. He dissolved the military regions and moved all decisions on operational initiatives to himself in Rabat. In more material terms, the military was tied more closely to the system through gifts of land and privileges to senior officers, thus compromising them as potential critics of a system from which they themselves were benefiting.[40] Indeed Hassan explicitly encouraged senior officers in the FAR to focus henceforth on making money rather than involving themselves in politics, telling them 'Don't involve yourselves in politics, there are people for that. Think, rather, of enriching yourselves.'[41]

Hassan kept the military divided after 1972 by reorganising the structure of the FAR and diversifying its composition. Different units were kept separate and rivalry was encouraged. The practice of regularly rotating army commanders through posts to avoid the establishment of powerful regional or administrative fiefdoms, already in place before 1971, was extended and accelerated. Auxiliary and paramilitary forces were created and existing ones expanded as potential counterweights to the FAR, their numbers virtually doubling in the period from 1973.[42] Ammunition dumps were put under the authority of civilian provincial governors controlled by the Ministry of Interior and were guarded by members of the auxiliary forces.[43] Hassan also sought to diversify the make-up of the FAR by appointing personnel from outside the traditionally rural and Berber elements that had dominated the officer corps of the military. Recruitment for the royal guard switched to the Tafilalet region, the predominantly Arabophone ancestral home of the Alawite dynasty. There were even efforts to attract sons from old established Fassi families into the officer corps.[44]

The role of the military in Moroccan politics changed dramatically again with Morocco's campaign from 1975 to regain what it saw as its rightful territory in the former Spanish Sahara (see Chapter 8). The military campaign there against the Polisario Front and its backers did more than meet Hassan's aim of keeping the FAR busy and away from Rabat. It was also popular with the leadership of the FAR, who were happy to demonstrate their strength to their military rivals in Algeria, and who were similarly content to see the military budget increase four-fold between 1974 and 1978 to fund the conflict.[45] The FAR's poor performance in the early years of the war against the Polisario, however, revealed the difficulties of fighting a war with the new organisational structures introduced into the military after 1972. Divided and competing units, with all operational decisions being taken by the king more than a thousand kilometres away from the front in Rabat, were not a suitable structure for fighting a war where a local unified command structure would have been much more effective. As a result, in 1980, after several significant reverses on the battlefield, full operational command of the Saharan campaign and three-quarters of the units of the military were put under the command of a single FAR general, Ahmed Dlimi. Thereafter, Morocco's military performance was seen to improve substantially. However, General Dlimi's death in a mysterious 'road accident' just three years later appeared to prompt questions as to whether this reconcentration of power in the hands of the military had once again raised the spectre of a potential *coup d'état* from within the FAR. The arrest of several other FAR officers both before and after Dlimi's death, together with the lack of public pomp with which the general was buried, seemed to confirm the rumour that Dlimi had been killed to forestall another attempted *coup d'état*. As in 1971 and 1972, the motives for the planned coup are not clear, although they appear to be primarily connected to the Saharan war.[46] Whatever the explanation, Hassan responded by breaking up the concentration of powers that had briefly been given to Dlimi and dividing them up amongst other more trusted military figures close to the Fassi bourgeoisie. In 1985 Hassan officially charged his eldest son, Crown Prince Sidi Mohamed, with coordinating the affairs of the FAR General Staff, thus repeating the action of his own father nearly thirty years earlier when he himself had been crown prince.[47] Hassan, however, retained tight personal control over appointments to the FAR, and in 1984 he rewarded those officers who had proved themselves in the Sahara conflict by ending the freeze on promotions in the military, which he had imposed in 1972, and appointing a number of new generals.[48]

Turbulent Years: Tunisia and Algeria

In comparison to Morocco, Algeria and Tunisia experienced relatively peaceful periods from the late 1960s through the 1970s, during which the military played little public role in the politics of either state. This

THE MILITARY

situation changed with the growing social and economic tensions that the whole region began to experience from the late 1970s. These problems led to outbreaks of unrest that the army was increasingly drawn into dealing with as the conventional forces of order failed to cope with the rising tide of popular unrest. In both countries, the army became even more concerned with dealing with the more political problem that grew out of this social discontent, namely the rise of powerful Islamist organisations that sought to channel and represent this dissent.

Tunisia: The Rise of Ben Ali

The more disturbed regional and domestic climate that Tunisia found itself in from the late 1970s began to put pressure on the system established by Bourguiba. In 1980 an attack by Libyan-backed Tunisian dissidents on the town of Gafsa (see Chapter 8) tested the capabilities of a Tunisian army which L. B. Ware describes as having drifted into becoming a 'bureaucratized garrison force.'[49] More seriously, the series of outbreaks of widespread social unrest that occurred in 1978, 1981 and 1984 put huge strains on the forces of the Ministry of Interior. As a result, units from the military were called in to help quell the disturbances. Although they returned promptly to their barracks following the resolution of each of these incidents, some of the opponents of the regime—notably the UGTT trade union—detected a rise in profile and political influence for the army with these crises. The budget for the military began to increase significantly from the late 1970s and a number of military personnel were appointed to positions in the Interior Ministry. Although many of the new appointments were to prove temporary and Bourguiba was later to sack the defence minister widely associated with them, the blurring of the distinction and personnel between the military and the internal security apparatus deprived Bourguiba of the security that such a separation and rivalry between the two gave him.[50] Some believed that this development proved to be the his eventual undoing.[51] His appointment of a military figure, Brigadier Zine al-Abdine Ben Ali, to the post of director of national security at the Ministry of the Interior in 1984 was remarked on even at the time.[52] The fact that it was Ben Ali who was to remove and replace Bourguiba as president three years later in November 1987 has inevitably prompted questions as to whether the accession to power of a figure from a background in Tunisia's military led to a far greater role or even supremacy for that military within the post-Bourguiba political system. The evidence for this charge is mixed.

Zine al-Abdine Ben Ali was a career military officer who had spent time training in both France and the United States. His first significant appointment had been to the position of head of Military Security which, although a much more mundane body than its Algerian namesake, allowed Ben Ali to get to know the workings of the Tunisian army well. Following his appointment to the Directorate of National Security in 1984, he was successively promoted to the positions of firstly, secretary of state for national defence, then minister of interior and finally to the post of prime minister. His entry into the politbureau of the PSD on appointment as interior minister broke for the first time Bourguiba's ban on military figures in the ruling party.[53] Ben Ali's meteoric rise owed much to the trust that a progressively senile and paranoid Bourguiba put in him, together with Ben Ali's solid background in security and intelligence that the ageing president increasingly valued.[54] Ben Ali's rise and the formidable array of powers he was able to accumulate by 1987 led some to make comparisons with Mohamed Oufkir in Morocco.[55] However, unlike Oufkir, Ben Ali's attempt to remove his master was to prove successful.

To outside observers, Ben Ali's decision to move against Bourguiba in November 1987 and remove him in a swift and bloodless *coup d'état* might have appeared like a de facto takeover by the country's military. However, the reality was more complex. Firstly, Ben Ali's action enjoyed support well beyond the military. Bourguiba's declining health and increasingly erratic leadership meant that there were few in Tunisia who opposed his eventual removal. The timing of the move had been determined by Bourguiba's urge to escalate the regime's conflict with the country's powerful Islamist movement by deciding to overrule court judgments and execute leaders of the movement (see Chapter 5). Ben Ali thus intervened to avert the uproar and civil strife that such a course of action would have inevitably provoked. Secondly, there is the strict constitutionality with which Ben Ali acted, carefully following provisions laid out in the national constitution that provided for the removal of the president: seven medical doctors overseen by the prime minister signing a document confirming that the president was no longer fit to continue in the post. The fact that Ben Ali waited until he was prime minister indicated his possible regard for legality, since it is argued that Ben Ali had already been powerful enough before he became prime minister in October 1987, and even as early as 1985, to overthrow Bourguiba by force.[56] Finally, there is evidence that Ben Ali did not act on behalf of the military in removing Bourguiba. Ben Ali only met with the country's senior generals to secure their support in the hours *after* he had acted,[57] although the fact that the commander of the presidential guard and the chief of the General Staff were contemporaries of Ben Ali's at the Saint Cyr military academy in France clearly facilitated this.[58]

Algeria: Chadli, the FIS and the Palace Coup of 1992

The likelihood that much was to change after the death of Boumedienne in Algeria in 1978 was apparent long before his eventual, if unforeseen, demise. This was no less true for the military and its political role than it was for the rest of the Algerian political system. The very personal and centralised hold that Boumedienne had been able to exercise over the army (and thus over Algeria as a whole) was unlikely to be replicated after his departure from the scene.

The centrality of the ANP as the veritable backbone of the Algerian regime was amply demonstrated by the dominating role it played in managing the succession to Boumedienne following the president's death after a short and unexpected illness in December 1978. The startling smoothness of what might have been expected to be a potentially very destabilising period for the country—given Boumedienne's immense personal power as well as the suddenness of his death—said much about how powerful and how institutionalised the military as a veritable institution itself had become. During the period of Boumedienne's illness, the Ministry of Defence took administrative control. The ANP also played a major role in organising, in accordance with the procedures set out in the constitution of 1976, a party congress for the FLN to select a new candidate for the presidency. It was in the selection of that candidate that the army most clearly demonstrated its influence by ensuring that it was a senior military figure, Colonel Chadli Benjedid, who was chosen and subsequently endorsed by national plebiscite as presidential successor to Boumedienne in January 1979.

The selection of Colonel Benjedid—or 'Chadli,' as Algerians universally came to call him—had not simply been a matter of the ANP imposing its candidate. At the time Chadli had been viewed as an acceptable 'compromise' candidate, given the deadlock that existed between those who had been considered as the two main contenders for the succession: Salah Yahiaoui, the director of the FLN, and Abdelaziz Bouteflika, Boumedienne's long-standing foreign minister. Nevertheless, the fact that the military was able to ensure that it was *its* compromise candidate that was adopted is significant, an achievement that was aided by the 20 per cent bloc of representatives that the ANP formally wielded in the FLN congress. As Entelis observes: 'Chadli's nomination reflected the army's determination to protect its own place at the very center of Algerian politics by preventing a marked shift to either the party or the civilian administration.' It was noteworthy that Chadli's first appointments, the heads of the potentially rival bodies, the positions of FLN party coordinator and of prime minister, were both military figures.[59] Chadli himself assumed the new position of general secretary of the FLN.

It is probable that any successor would have struggled to fill the void left by Boumedienne, a man with a level of personal authority and legitimacy established through leadership during the hard years of the liberation struggle and its aftermath. The fact that Chadli Benjedid was adopted as the compromise candidate for the presidency is perhaps indicative in itself of the fact that he was not a figure of the stature of his predecessor. Whilst being technically the most senior figure in the ANP by virtue of his early participation in the liberation struggle and having been commander of the Oran military region since 1964, Chadli was a man of limited education lacking the drive, judgement and organisational flair of Boumedienne. His grip on both the army as an institution and thus, by extension, the Algerian political system as a whole was thus far less firm and directed. The net result of this was a progressive fracturing and factionalisation of the Algerian polity, a polity that had only been held together by Boumedienne's resolute leadership during thirteen years. As the backbone of this polity, the Algerian military did not escape this process. The net result is summed up very brutally but very accurately by Hugh Roberts, who observes that in comparison to Boumedienne, 'Chadli had no such moral authority over the army, and therefore resorted to a strategy of divide and rule, playing off the various coteries within the officer corps against each other in an increasingly vicious game of musical chairs.'[60]

This factionalisation signalled a return to a situation of intense competition between various factions or 'clans,' a phenomenon that had first been observed during the period surrounding the achievement of independence (see Chapter 2). The formation and make-up of these clans was not based primarily on factors such as region or family, but more on connections and loyalties forged during the liberation war.[61] This was particularly true of one group or clan that began to exercise more and more influence during the 1980s and whom Chadli began increasingly to favour. Over time Chadli progressively brought members of the group of junior officers that had deserted from the French army to the nationalists relatively late in the war of independence into senior positions. Their promotion was seen as part of the president's efforts to move towards a more modern and professionalised military on the European model, of which these individuals had had experience and of whom Boumedienne had himself made use in the 1960s for his original construction of the ANP. The advancement of this group came at the expense of officers who had served most of the liberation war in the ALN and who favoured the retention of a more 'popular' broad-based army that had wider social, political and economic functions in addition to the more usual professional functions related to national defence.[62]

The ANP was not itself the public forum for the 'war of the clans' that began to emerge again under Chadli's presidency; rather it was the FLN, which had been revived by Boumedienne in his final years and which was further expanded under Chadli. Possibly conceived by Chadli as a potential rival to the ANP and thus part of his 'divide and rule' strategy referred to above, the FLN actually became little more than an institutional shell for these competing clans. The FLN party structure became the avenue for advancement of both personal and factional interests in the regime, with struggles over appointments to the bureaucracy and the ministries as well as the party apparatus itself at stake. The army remained the dominant institution in this new system, and increasing numbers of officers began to move into formally 'civilian' positions as it began to expand its influence still further. As a mark of this expanded power, in 1984 Chadli re-established the General Staff which had been suppressed since 1967 following the failed coup attempt by Tahar Zbiri. Moreover, for the first time he promoted officers to the rank of general: a new position that the original ALN had avoided (colonel being its highest rank) to prevent the creation of an elite corps of generals. For the same reason, the ALN had limited the number of colonels created to just twenty-five, but by 1993 there were to be no fewer than forty-three generals in the ANP.[63] Chadli hoped to use these changes to provide further spoils for the increasingly factionalised military to fight over and thus bolster his position above the fray, but the re-establishment of the General Staff ultimately served to weaken his control by giving more independence to the military leadership.[64]

The pattern of political power that became established through the 1980s, of struggles for influence between contending clans within the army and the FLN, appeared to be broken with the dramatic events of October 1988, when widespread and sustained civil unrest broke out in nearly all of Algeria's major cities. The exact causes of both this explosion of popular unrest and President Chadli's equally dramatic and unforeseen reaction in opening the way to multi-party elections in the aftermath of the riots and demonstrations are the subject of much debate (see Chapter 4). However, the impact this momentous series of events had on the Algerian military and its role in politics appeared initially to be significant, amounting to a formal withdrawal from the political foreground. Not only did the ANP formally pull out its representatives from the Central Committee of the FLN, but the new constitution of 1989 that enshrined Chadli's multi-party and 'democratic' reforms redefined the role of the armed forces. It reduced the ANP's role down to the simple defence of the country, thus depriving it of some of the more grandiose roles related to society and the 'Revolution' that the constitutions of 1964 and 1976 had set out for it.

The reasons for the change in the formal role and status of the military were directly linked to the events of October 1988. The scale of the unrest had led to military units being deployed on the streets to quell the unrest. The violence with which these units dealt with what were often largely peaceful demonstrations—resulting in the deaths of an estimated 500 people—damaged the ANP in the eyes of the population and seemed to signal the beginning of the end of the 'revolutionary myth' of the ANP in the public mind.[65] This withdrawal was, however, more temporary and tactical than it initially appeared. As Hugh Roberts argues, the new constitution of February 1989 was 'introduced with the conditional agreement of the army, not over its head or at its expense.'[66] The swiftness with which the army was to return to the forefront of Algerian politics was evidence of this.

What prompted the 'return' of the army to the political foreground was the dramatic way in which Chadli Benjedid's programme of political reforms began to evolve following the introduction of the new constitution of 1989. The new constitution allowed for the creation of a multi-party system and provided for multi-party elections to be held at local, national and eventually presidential level. The fact that one political party came to dominate these elections and, moreover, was from outside the circles of the regime created unease within the regime and, by extension, the military. This unease was increased by the fact that the dominant party was one appearing to espouse a fairly radical Islamist agenda with promises to make a fundamental overhaul of Algeria's established economic, political and social structures.

The challenge that this new party—the *Front Islamique du Salut* (FIS)—appeared to be making to the established order in Algeria was one to which the military felt bound to react. The challenge was primarily in the form of a direct threat to its pre-eminent position, should the party win political power through elections. Significant elements in the military also felt honour-bound to defend the state and institutions established by their founder Boumedienne which the FIS were threatening to dismantle should they come to power. It was thus inevitable that the ANP began to raise its public profile and show its teeth as the FIS made dramatic political and electoral gains through the period 1990–91 (see Chaper 5). From early 1990 senior military figures made it known through interviews with the press and through the army journal, *El Djeich*, that the army would be willing to 'respond to any organised excesses that might jeopardise the national unity of the country....[and] would not hesitate to intervene and to re-establish order and unity so that force remains in the hands of the law.'[67] These 'warnings' did not specify the FIS, but the party recognised that they were the target and for much of 1990–91 engaged in a war of veiled threats and counter-threats with the ANP through statements and the media. The party indicated that it would resist any attempt on the part of the army to intervene and restrict or confiscate its electoral gains; it would even be willing, if necessary, to provoke party supporters within the military to mutiny.[68]

The return of the Algerian army to the forefront occurred in stages, firstly with the appointment of General Khaled Nezzar as minister of defence in the aftermath of sweeping victories for the FIS in local elections in 1990. This appointment was significant not just in terms of the appointment of a senior military officer to a hitherto civilian cabinet, but also because it marked the re-establishment of Defence as a ministerial portfolio in its own right, something that had not existed since the *coup d'état* of June 1965, Boumedienne and then Chadli preferring to retain control of the key position within the presidency. The second and more dramatic stage came with the army's sudden physical intervention on the streets of the capital in June 1991 to breakup occupations of Algiers' two main squares by supporters of the FIS, who were protesting at changes in the electoral law for the upcoming national legislative elections that they perceived to be aimed at electorally handicapping the FIS (see Chapters 4 and 5). The subsequent arrest and imprisonment of most of the FIS's senior leaders was seen as the ANP acting decisively to counter and remove any possible threat from the party.

The appointment, in the aftermath of this crackdown, of a second senior military figure, General Larbi Belkheir, to the post of interior minister was not just an indication of the military's wish to establish a firmer grip on political developments through control of the two key security portfolios of Defence and now Interior. It also represented the rise to further prominence of the group of former French army officers who had defected to the nationalist side in the latter stages of the liberation war—both Nezzar and Belkheir coming from this group. It was argued that the rise of this group that had begun under Chadli in the 1980s continued after October 1988 when Chadli had used the aftermath of the unrest to sack several figures associated with the old ALN and bring in more figures from the favoured group of former French officers. However, by 1991 the nature of the relationship between President Chadli and these figures, and the ANP in which they were now the dominant faction, became more complex. Many of the senior figures in the army began to have profound misgivings about the president's control of events. The more Francophone and secularised background of the new leaders of the ANP, due largely to their time in the French army, made them even more hostile and wary of the FIS's Islamist agenda than other officers in the military. The acceptance of Nezzar and Belkheir in the ministerial cabinet was therefore perhaps as much a condition for the army to allow Chadli to continue with his multi-party experiment as a desire on the part of Chadli to promote like-minded allies.[69] Chadli only narrowly managed to persuade the ANP not to dissolve the FIS fully in June 1991, arguing that the party would not perform as well at upcoming legislative elections.[70]

Sweeping gains for the FIS in the first round of the legislative elections in December 1991 finally and definitively persuaded the army that Chadli had once again miscalculated. All the senior leaders of Algeria's military, the General Staff, the commanders of the military regions and the heads of the gendarmerie and intelligence met in the aftermath of the first round of voting and concluded that it was imperative to act, certainly before the second round of voting which was due to take place in mid-January and looked likely to confirm a huge FIS majority in the National Assembly. Such an eventuality was not to be countenanced by most of the senior figures in the military, who clearly feared that the FIS would use their new power base to strike at their enemies in the military. There was also the fear that the army might split if the FIS were to win a majority and thus have some legal legitimacy in the eyes of some of the troops.[71] Nezzar and other senior generals met with President Chadli and persuaded him to resign on 11 January 1992. The resignation triggered the cancellation of the elections and a few weeks later, following inevitable clashes between the security forces and supporters of the FIS, the FIS was finally, formally banned.

Consolidation: the 1990s and After

Despite the military origins of the new leaderships that assumed power in Tunisia in 1987 and Algeria in 1992, their nature and the military's role in them was rather different.

Tunisia

The extent of the involvement of the military in the regime Ben Ali established in the aftermath of the coup against Bourguiba in Tunisia was initially unclear. The National Pact of November 1988—which Ben Ali appeared to use as a forum for discussion with opposition forces regarding the transition from Bourguiba's rule—was in keeping with the former president's policy in explicitly subordinating the Tunisian military to civilian control and stipulating its political neutrality. However, the ruling party congress that witnessed the transformation of Bourguiba's PSD into the new *Rassemblement Constitutionnel Démocratique* (RCD) saw no discussion of the role of the army, the issue being avoided, in the view of Toumi, by the 'tacit agreement' of all present.[72] Nevertheless, four of the nine members of the politbureau that Ben Ali restructured in the wake of the adoption of the new constitution of 1989 came from either the Interior Ministry or the Tunisian military itself.

As Ben Ali began to consolidate his new regime in the 1990s, the shape of the new system and the place of the country's military within it became more apparent. Whilst it was certainly true that the military enjoyed a higher profile and greater involvement in the running of the country than they had under Bourguiba, this did not equate to an effective assumption of power by the military as an institution. Rather these developments were the result of the designs of President Ben Ali. It rapidly became clear that the man who had ousted and replaced Bourguiba was set on recreating the same sort of highly personalised power base that had been established by his predecessor. Thus the post-Bourguiba regime was one focused on Ben Ali as an individual rather than the military as an institution. This was evident in Ben Ali's personal assumption of the Defence portfolio from 1987 to 1989 and by his gradual replacement of many of the senior military officers initially appointed to important positions in the regime after his assumption of the presidency in November 1987 with loyal civilian personalities from within the newly created RCD. Even those officers that Ben Ali had brought into the regime were notable for being contemporaries of Ben Ali at St Cyr and thus owed their position more to their closeness to the new president than to their position in the military.[73] Moreover, Ben Ali was anxious to portray the regime he created as a fully civilian one lacking any khaki tinge, presenting himself as a fully civilian president and ensuring that he was never referred to again as 'General Ben Ali.'[74]

The undeniable growth in the military's budget under Ben Ali was explained not by an increase in influence of the leadership of the military but by the president's preoccupation with the issue of internal security. Ben Ali's decision to crackdown upon and eventually eliminate all public manifestations of the country's powerful Islamist movement from 1991 required significant resources. His determination thereafter to prevent any re-emergence of the movement, or indeed any other meaningful opposition to his rule, necessitated the maintenance of a formidable internal security apparatus of which the army was an increasingly junior part. Between 1987 and 1999 the budget for the police grew fourfold, much faster than that for the military.[75] This reflected the fact that Ben Ali's background in the military was not nearly as significant as his more specific experience in matters relating to maintenance of order and intelligence in which he 'specialised in an almost exclusive manner' and which went a long way to explaining the

THE MILITARY

continued preoccupation of Ben Ali's regime with these issues.[76] The focus of resources and attention on the police, internal security forces and intelligence services at the relative expense of the official military also reflected Ben Ali's wariness of the latter. A series of purges of senior and junior officers suspected of Islamist sympathies was carried out in both the wake of the ousting of Bourguiba and when the repression of the Islamist movement gathered pace in the spring of 1991.[77] Senior military officers found their room for manoeuvre and activities curtailed and increasingly controlled by the police, resulting in the growth of a climate of suspicion and even fear within the institution.[78]

Algeria: The Black Decade and the Rise of Bouteflika

The events of the early weeks of 1992 in Algeria represented the final move by the military to the very forefront of national politics, with there being no doubt that it was the army as an institution that was now fully in control of the government and regime. The announcement on 9 February of a state of emergency allowed the army to take full and effective control of the streets and everyday life. However, despite being manifestly in control of the country, the military's senior leaders felt a need to give a civilian face to the new political regime they had hastily constructed in the aftermath of the ousting of Chadli and the termination of the elections. Although these military leaders had been the essence and backbone of the Algerian regime since independence, they demonstrated a marked reluctance to assume public political power, there being a preference for civilian figures to front the regime. This need of the military for what Abdelkader Yefsah calls a '*hedjab*' (*hijab*), or covering, had for many years been provided through the existence of the FLN.[79] This had clearly come to an end with the advent of multi-party politics in 1989: Hugh Roberts has argued that the ANP's withdrawal from the institutions of the FLN after 1989 meant that 'the collapse of Chadli's pluralist experiment in 1991 left the army commanders answerable to no-one but each other.'[80] As a result, a ruling High Council of State was created consisting of mainly civilian figures and fronted by one of the original founders of the FLN, Mohamed Boudiaf, who was invited back from long-time exile abroad.

That it was the senior generals in Algeria's military who were in full control of Algeria from 1992 was illustrated by the fate of the series of figurehead presidents that the military progressively selected and then discarded in an attempt to find a suitable and reliable 'front man' for the regime. The most dramatic example was Mohamed Boudiaf, whose revolutionary credentials as one of the nine historic founders of the FLN in 1954, together with his long absence from the domestic political scene (thus disassociating himself from the failings and unpopularity of the regime), appeared to bestow on the military-dominated regime the sort of symbolic legitimacy that was much needed in the aftermath of the abandonment of the elections. However, the independence of spirit that Boudiaf demonstrated once appointed president by the High Council of State was clearly at variance with the largely figurehead role that the senior generals had envisaged for him. Attempts by the new president to appoint his own staff and even create a new political party were viewed with suspicion by the military leadership. Suspicion then changed to alarm with the announcement by Boudiaf in April 1992 of the launching of a rigorous anti-corruption drive in an effort to undercut one of the main campaigning themes of the FIS, which had similarly promised to root out corruption at the heart of the regime. The military's place within this historic core meant that any genuine anti-corruption campaign was bound to implicate many senior military figures who had benefited massively and illegally from the system, particularly during the years of clan warfare over the spoils of power under Chadli in the 1980s. Rumours began to circulate in June 1992 that the president planned to use the thirtieth anniversary of the achievement of independence on 5 July to announce the dismissal of five senior generals; this seemed then to confirm that Boudiaf was set for a showdown with the leaders of the country's military.[81] Therefore when Boudiaf was assassinated at a meeting in Annaba on 29 June, there were few people who believed official claims that the president had been killed by a bodyguard with Islamist sympathies: Boudiaf had clearly been removed by those who had originally appointed him less than six months earlier.[82]

Boudiaf's place as president was temporarily assumed by Ali Kafi, head of the war veterans association and a member of the High Council of State created in January 1992. A more long-term replacement was found in the person of General Lamine Zeroual, the minister of defence, who was appointed president in January 1994. The appointment of a senior military officer to the presidency was clearly significant, although Zeroual's record of long service in the ALN during the liberation war once again gave the sort of revolutionary legitimacy that figures such as Khaled Nezzar and Larbi Belkheir lacked (having spent most of the war in French uniforms). Zeroual's announcement of his premature retirement from the presidency in September 1998 indicated that he, like Boudiaf and Chadli before him, had fallen foul of the more senior group of generals at the head of the regime. More specifically, Zeroual had become embroiled in a renewed bout of clan warfare inside the upper echelons amongst the generals and had found himself on the losing side. Zeroual was in turn succeeded at the presidency by Abdelaziz Bouteflika, Boumedienne's long-time foreign minister who had been passed over for the presidency twenty years earlier in favour of Chadli Benjedid. Once again it was Bouteflika's association with the country's revolutionary past that persuaded the leaders of the military to propel him to the leadership. Although formally 'elected' to the presidency in April 1999, Bouteflika's 'victory' was marred by the withdrawal of all the other rival candidates the day before the ballot in protest at alleged manipulation of electoral procedures by the Algerian army—it having been evident that Bouteflika was the ANP's anointed candidate despite formally running as an independent. Like Boudiaf (and to a lesser extent Zeroual) before him, Bouteflika tried to present himself as someone rooted in Algeria's heroic revolutionary past but with a fresh reforming vision for the future.

Beyond the presidency, the Algerian military's civilian '*hedjab*' (*hijab*) extended through to civilian ministers, political parties, elections and a pluralistic press. Civilian politicians, whilst charged with the day-to-day management of the country, came to be ultimately controlled and manipulated by the generals. As Hugh Roberts explains, 'ministerial mandates have in reality been granted informally by the various factions of the army as the ingredients of complex political package-deals devised at intervals as the agreed outcomes of vigorous factional conflict and bargaining behind the scenes.' With regard to the press and the majority of the political parties, Roberts observed that the army commanders 'have also tended to invest in and manipulate the various political parties and the so-called independent press, and use them as proxies and cats paws in the factional struggle within the army.'[83]

It is important to note that the manoeuvrings at the top of the Algerian regime took place against a backdrop of sustained conflict and violence that developed throughout Algeria in the aftermath of the abandonment of the legislative elections in January 1992 and continued throughout the 1990s. This period saw the emergence of armed resistance to the regime from groups of radical Islamists incensed by what they saw as the confiscation of the Islamist electoral victory in the elections. The leaders of the Algerian military, from 1992 fully in charge of security issues, naturally moved to extinguish this resistance. However, the significant, if largely passive, support the armed groups enjoyed amongst the large sections of the Algerian population that had voted heavily for the FIS in 1990 and 1991 ensured that violent resistance to the regime endured.

Through 1993 and 1994 the conflict grew not only more violent and widespread but also more complex. Algeria's security forces, both police and military, became engaged in increasingly bloody and often highly localised guerrilla conflicts with armed groups across the country. The complexity of the conflict was not, however, restricted to just the profusion of armed Islamist groups of varying ideologies and objectives that emerged (see Chapter 5). The precise role played by the security services also became increasingly opaque. As in many such counter-insurgency conflicts, stories of deaths in custody, disappearances and torture emerged. However, as the conflict endured, evidence began to appear indicating that the forces of the state were engaging in far more extreme and unusual ways of combating the enemy. Opposition groups and deserting members of the security forces alleged that elements of the security services had not only succeeded in infiltrating some of the armed Islamist groups but had possibly actually gone as far as manipulating them into committing acts of extreme violence in order to undercut public support for the Islamist opposition. There were even suggestions that the security services had carried out atrocities themselves and blamed them on the Islamists.[84]

It was also alleged that the conflict provided a convenient cover for the settling of scores by various groups within the armed forces, not only against third parties, such as businessmen, journalists and politicians, but also within the ranks of the military itself. There was evidence that the conflict had come to be manipulated by the various factions and clans within the generals, turning them against each other as part of their ongoing struggle for dominance. This manipulation varied from the management of news releases about atrocities in the conflict to coincide with (and thus overshadow) a rival general's speech or initiative through to the physical elimination by assassination of minor allies of a rival clan.

Given the severity of the clan warfare within the upper ranks of the military, it was perhaps surprising that the ANP did not split apart and collapse, bringing down the whole Algerian regime with it. This manifestly did not happen, and as the violence receded from the late 1990s, the position of the ANP and its leaders looked as strong as ever. Part of the reason for this resilience was undoubtedly linked to the senior army leaders' willingness and ability to put aside their conflicts when confronted with a common external threat such as domestic political opposition or criticism from the international community (see Chapter 9). The securing of unity in the lower ranks of the military was another important factor. The ANP constantly defied predictions that it would eventually succumb to large-scale desertions, mutinies or even a *coup d'état* by junior officers. This was partially due to the rigour with which the army ensured that any groups or individuals with radical or dissident opinions—such as Islamists in the early 1990s—were ruthlessly weeded out from within the military. The continued loyalty of particularly the lower ranks was shored up by the military being able to offer secure employment and physical protection in times of severe economic and physical insecurity.[85] Also, the nature of the conflict that developed after 1992 produced a dynamic of revenge which, whilst pushing many young men into the armed Islamist groups to avenge the deaths of friends or family, pushed many others into the army for similar reasons.

The army's economic basis of power was also significant. Through the government, the military was able to exercise control over the income generated by the exploitation of the country's substantial oil and gas resources. Individual senior officers were also able to establish control over sectors of the vigorous import business that developed as a result of both this income and also the shortage of domestically produced goods due to the conflict (see Chapter 7).[86] It was control of these sources of income that fuelled the clan warfare raging inside the Algerian regime and army from the 1980s. It also explains the tenacity with which the senior generals struggled to maintain their positions. However, as Luis Martinez points out, 'The view of the ANP as a simple instrument of plunder lies behind many errors of analysis concerning its stability in the war.' Martinez argues that the extensive networks of patronage that the army was able to build up over the years also helped it, stating that 'Since independence it has accomplished the training, placement and consolidation of various economic actors, who owe it a debt today.'[87] These actors, together with the significant section of the population that vigorously opposed the Islamist movement and its agenda and saw the army as the ultimate bulwark against this threat, helped the military broaden its base of support in Algerian society more generally during the 1990s.

Another dimension to the military's continued strength and determination to hold onto power, often cited, relates to the similarity in backgrounds of the senior generals at the top of the ANP and the regime. Virtually all the top generals who came to the fore in the 1990s came from the group of Algerian junior officers who deserted from the French colonial army relatively late on in the liberation struggle to join the nationalists. As has been seen, they were promoted by both Boumedienne and Chadli as allies and agents of modernisation within the ANP. The appointments of two senior members of this group, Khaled Nezzar and Larbi Belkheir, to ministerial positions in 1990–91 signalled the movement of the group to the forefront of power, and it was they who pushed Chadli from power and effectively took control after 1992. From this year, nearly all the senior positions in the Algerian military came to be held by members of this group. Indeed all but two of the eleven most senior generals in the regime ten years later in 2002 came from this group.[88] This remarkable ascent to power by a relatively small group of men has been put down by some to the considerable *esprit de corps* that was forged amongst them in making the original and difficult decision to desert the French army in which they had trained and served as soldiers.[89] However, many more people attribute their achievement of power to altogether more covert and sinister factors. It is argued that it was not common circumstance that made this group work and rise together and that it was no coincidence that they all deserted from the French army late on in the liberation struggle: their 'desertion' was in fact planned and stage-managed by the French colonial authorities with the objective of retaining secret allies within Algeria who could protect French interests in the event of Algeria becoming independent. It is thus argued that when Algeria did gain its independence in 1962, this group of 'deserters' carefully planned their rise through the army and regime, taking advantage of weak figures like Chadli Benjedid, and finally achieving full political power in 1992; at which point this small group or *Hizb-Fransa* (party of France) proceeded to rule Algeria both for their own material benefit and according to the wishes of the former colonial power, France.[90]

Hizb-Fransa is, of course, a conspiracy theory. Significant circumstantial evidence for large parts of it exists, but the close links that many senior generals maintained with France may have had more to do with common cultural affinity (nearly all are primarily Francophone) and, more importantly, hostility shared with France to the phenomenon of Islamism. Nevertheless, many well-informed observers were firm advocates of the *Hizb-Fransa* conspiracy theory.[91] What perhaps matters even more than the genuine substance of the theory was that a large swathe of the Algerian population actually came to *believe* it, thus making it very powerful as a concept.[92]

The pattern of military involvement in Algerian politics established in the 1990s began to mutate again with the arrival of Abdelaziz Bouteflika to the state presidency in April 1999. Although he was the clear choice of the military leadership to front the regime, Bouteflika began to establish a much higher profile and more active role, both domestically and externally, than his immediate predecessors. Using his experience and contacts developed during his long tenure as foreign minister under Boumedienne, Bouteflika became much more active on the international scene, reinvigorating Algerian diplomacy which had become largely moribund during the crisis of the 1990s. On the domestic front the new president launched a vigorous process of 'national reconciliation' aimed at bringing to a final close the violence of the preceding decade through a series of laws and referenda aimed at persuading the remaining armed groups to give up their struggle. These initiatives were fundamentally endorsed by the Algerian army leadership and were indeed part of a deal that saw Bouteflika take the lead on these issues whilst leaving security policy to the generals.[93] Any autonomy enjoyed by Bouteflika beyond these domains appeared initially fairly circumscribed, and it seemed that any hopes he may have fostered of freeing himself from the controlling strings of the generals were destined to be as futile as those of his predecessors. As his presidency progressed, however, Bouteflika seemed able to assert himself more and more, securing further terms of office in 2004 and then again in 2009.

Part of the reason for Bouteflika's longevity as president was the success he enjoyed in the domains where he had been given leadership: levels of violence declined markedly under his presidency and new alliances were forged abroad. In these areas he had been substantially aided by fortuitous events beyond his control: most notably the sharp rise in the international price of oil and the events of 11 September 2001 in the United States. Bouteflika was also able to strengthen his negotiating position with the generals by presenting himself to them as someone who could shield them from domestic and international criticism and allegations relating to the military's role in the bloodshed of the 1990s. The president secured domestic legal immunity for the army through the Charter of Peace and National Reconciliation, passed by referendum in 2005, which criminalised critical discussion of the army's role.[94] Bouteflika was also aided, more importantly, by changes within the upper echelons of the military, most notably the progressive retirement and death of many of the senior generals who had dominated the regime from the early 1990s.

Morocco: M6 *and the Military*

The issue of the military's role in Moroccan politics was revived with the death of Hassan II in July 1999 and the accession to the throne of his son Sidi Mohamed, now Mohamed VI. The 1980s and 1990s had seen little apparent evolution in the political role of the Moroccan military. Its leadership remained busy in the Sahara even after the declaration of a ceasefire in 1991. The rise of the civilian Ministry of Interior under the powerful and loyal Driss Basri during this period helped act as a counterweight and a watchdog on any political ambitions the military might have. The vigilance of Basri and his control over the intelligence services of the kingdom were credited with the thwarting of Dlimi's plans to overthrow the monarchy in 1983.[95] Control of the FAR itself passed to a clutch of loyalist generals drawn from the Fez bourgeoisie.[96]

Speculation that the FAR might enjoy an expanded level of influence under the new king was not just due to the fact that as crown prince—like his father before him—Mohamed had built up close links with the military through his role since 1985 as chief of staff. The dismissal of Driss Basri from the Ministry of Interior in October 1999 clearly removed the counterweight to the military that Hassan had put in place. Indeed, control over the formidable array of intelligence networks that Basri had built up passed from the Interior Ministry and into the hands of individuals from the military. An expansion in the number of generals and a raised profile for the military on state occasions, most notably in 2006 with the first military parade since 1972, further fed these perceptions. Yet such moves could equally be interpreted as signs of confidence on the part of the new king.[97] Moreover, more concrete indications of greater military influence in the running of the country were difficult to identify. Any apparent signs related more to the FAR seeking to protect and define its own established interests rather than to efforts to expand these interests. One example was the prison sentence handed out to a whistle-blowing FAR captain, Mustapha Adib, who gave an interview to the French newspaper *Le Monde* to highlight the clandestine trade in petrol at his military base. Adib's imprisonment demonstrated not just the FAR's unhappiness with an officer speaking to a foreign newspaper, but also revealed its sensitivity about the issue of corruption within the military. There were accusations that the fraud and corruption revealed by Adib was the tip of a very large and growing iceberg. King Hassan's decision to grant material privileges to the military elite and his invitation to focus on making money in the wake of the *coups d'état* of the 1970s were seen as the root cause of this corruption. By 2000 it was claimed that senior figures in the FAR and the Interior Ministry accounted for half of the wealthiest individuals in the kingdom, senior generals having profited from healthy commissions on arms purchases and their domination of lucrative sectors of the economy such as fishing.[98]

The failure of the former opposition parties in the new *alternance* coalition government appointed in 1998 to intervene in the Adib affair was seen in some quarters as a clear indication of the political parties' wariness of the military.[99] Another sign of this fear was the decision to ban a family of three newspapers in December 2000 for publishing a list of individuals identified by a human rights organisation as being responsible for human rights abuses in the 1970s. The inclusion of the names of two very senior military figures on this list and the demand that they be put on trial was clearly seen by the FAR as a direct attack on itself that could not go unanswered. Significantly, the decision to ban the newspapers was taken by the civilian government and was defended by the USFP prime minister Abderahmane Youssoufi, who stated to a French newspaper: 'These newspapers dared to attack the army which is an institution respected throughout our country. This is unacceptable.'[100] These incidents, however, occurred in the early cautious years of the *alternance* government, and by the middle of the decade there were signs that the parties were more willing to challenge at least some of the privileges of the military. In May 2006 Driss Lachgar, leader of the USFP group in the national parliament, publicly demanded that the long-established practice of passing the budget of the army without discussion in the chamber be ended. With a telling reference to Morocco's neighbour, Lachgar declared: 'We are not Algeria…the budget of the army must be discussed in Parliament. Like all the other budgets.'[101]

One similarity Morocco did share with Algeria was the gradual replacement of the senior ranks of the military through retirement and death during the 2000s: a process that was achieved much more smoothly and consensually under King Mohamed than it was under Bouteflika and, moreover, often involved the replacement of military figures with civilian ones.

The future role of the military in Moroccan politics could take several different forms. The evolution of the Western Sahara issue is often seen as being crucial in this regard, given the FAR's heavy involvement there. Failure on the part of the palace or civilian politicians to achieve the full integration of the territory into Morocco would clearly go down badly with the military, which has committed so much and lost so many of its personnel in the campaign. It is therefore possible that the FAR, or figures within it, could turn against those in Rabat whom it might perceive as having betrayed and sold out what they had fought for over the past thirty years. Even if the Western Sahara conflict were to be settled in Morocco's favour, the substantial demobilisation of troops into an economy with high unemployment, and the inevitable cuts in the FAR's budget that would follow, could also lead to dissatisfaction within the military.[102] There is also the accusation that the withdrawal or scaling back of the FAR's presence in the Western Sahara would deprive its senior officers of the hugely profitable clandestine trade with the nearby Canary Islands, which has been built up since the 1970s and to which King Hassan at least had turned a blind eye.[103]

The fear still held by many in Rabat of a simple return to the era of the *coup d'état* of the early 1970s is, however, largely unfounded. Times have clearly changed. As William Zartman pointed out as early as the mid1980s:

Unlike the early 1970s, the military is not alone among organizations and institutions, and any political move by the military would have to deal with a whole system of political forces in place, each with a stake in preserving the polity as the king had restructured it.[104]

This judgement is arguably even more applicable twenty years on, with three new constitutions and various other reforms having strengthened further still the role of the other actors and institutions such as the parliament, the press, political parties and non-government organisations (NGOs). In addition, the military's potential to act as a single cohesive bloc is limited by the retention of organisational divisions put in place by Hassan II. Differences and rivalry, for example, exist between the FAR and the gendarmerie, the latter becoming more powerful after the removal of Driss Basri.[105] Despite King Mohamed's dismissal of Basri, he has also maintained a civilian counterweight to the military in the form of a long-standing technocrat as deputy minister for national defence and, more substantially, the appointment in 2005 of the first ever civilian to the head of the external security services (DGED), Yassine Mansouri, one of whose tasks is to oversee the procurement practices of the FAR and thus prevent corruption.[106]

Another scenario sees the military increasing its influence and coming to the fore to combat the growing threat from the country's Islamist movement as occurred in Algeria. This scenario appears unlikely, given the nature of the Islamist movement in Morocco, notably its divisions, its caution, its predominant attachment to non-violence and the reluctance on the part of the bulk of the Moroccan population to see a repeat of the Algerian case through lending it their support in elections or on the streets (see Chapter 5). Nevertheless, senior figures from Morocco's main Islamist organisations remain wary of the FAR and are far more reluctant to be critical of or challenge the military as an institution than they are even of the monarchy.[107] The focus on the issue of corruption by the main Islamist movements is clearly a source of concern to the FAR, given the extent of corruption within its own ranks, and this might even encourage Islamist sentiment amongst junior officers and lower ranks who, like Mustapha Adib, are fully aware of and disgusted by these practices.[108] An alleged plot by Islamists to infiltrate the airforce was officially uncovered in the summer of 2006, leading to the king declaring to the FAR in an address in May 2008 the need 'to immunize its members against different influences that go against our Malekite rite, our values of moderation and tolerance.'[109]

The most probable future scenario for Morocco's military is that it will continue to have a political presence and influence, but that this will wane with time as senior figures retire, die and are replaced by younger, increasingly civilian figures, and the memories of the putschist past gradually fade.

Tunisia: The Army, the People and the Revolution

If changes to the political role played by the military in both Algeria and Morocco occurred gradually during the first decade of the twenty-first century, that of the military in Tunisia transformed suddenly and dramatically with the popular uprising that overwhelmed the country at the beginning of the second decade. The failure of the Tunisian army to support the state's increasingly desperate efforts to contain the unrest as it expanded in the second week of January 2011 proved crucial to the toppling of the Ben Ali regime. Specifically, it was the refusal of General Rachid Ammar, the head of the army, to comply with the president's request to intervene and fire on the crowds of demonstrators that appears to have been pivotal in persuading Ben Ali to flee the country on 14 January. The leaking of that information to the demonstrators not only encouraged and galvanised the crowds in Tunis and elsewhere but also made popular heroes of the army and its leadership. The appearance of soldiers and armoured cars on the streets was applauded and cheered by the ordinary Tunisians, who saw the army as their allies and defenders in clashes with the fast disintegrating units of police and internal security services. Pictures and film footage of soldiers saluting the demonstrators and being kissed and thanked by them were some of the most striking of that remarkable week.

The failure of the Tunisian army to back Ben Ali in his hour of need was explained by a number of factors. It was partly a result of the president's distancing himself from the military and his favouring, expanding and relying on the police and intelligence services. More importantly, there was the resentment at the purges of the 1990s and the police control exercised over senior military officers. Ben Ali's distancing of the military from the regime also arguably allowed it to return to the role it had been designed to play under Habib Bourguiba: that of the apolitical guardian of the state and the constitution. Most of the senior officers in the Tunisian army were raised under the ethos of strict political neutrality established under Bourguiba, and moreover were aware of this when they chose a military career over a potentially more politically influential one in the ruling party.[110] Unlike Algeria and Morocco, a career in the military was traditionally not seen as a route to political power and influence. Evidence for the attachment to this 'republican' ethos was demonstrated by the minimal political role the military played in the weeks and months that followed the revolution of 14 January. General Rachid Ammar declined the sort of prominent political role that his popular adulation would have allowed him to play in the aftermath of the flight of Ben Ali, making only one public sortie into the centre of Tunis ten days after the fall of the president to assure the public that the military would not move beyond the role ascribed to it in the constitution. At the same time he declared that the national army would be the 'guarantor of the revolution,' which was furthermore, he said, 'Our revolution, your revolution, the revolution of the youth.'[111]

Conclusion

The role of the military in the Maghreb has varied significantly from state to state. Nevertheless, certain similarities exist. The regimes in all three states have viewed support from the military as being essential to their survival. This is seen firstly in terms of the army's ability to protect the regime from its enemies and challengers, particularly those on the domestic scene. In all three states the army has not only been involved in intelligence and security matters, but has actively intervened on several occasions in each state to restore control on the streets during times of unrest. Across the region, the military is seen as the main bulwark against the incursion of Islamism. Secondly, support from the military is seen as crucial for the regime because of the army's own ability to overthrow the political leadership. This has led the civilian leaders of the three countries to attempt both to tie the military closely to them through patronage and to create counter-balancing forces, largely in the field of domestic security. Indeed, another key similarity between the three countries has been the rise to importance of the intelligence and security services. Often grouped in with the military, these elements within all three states have arguably become increasingly distinct from the military proper and now actually overshadow it in terms of power and influence. This was most clearly apparent in Tunisia where it was Ben Ali's background in internal security and intelligence, rather than in the military, that explained both his rise and the nature and resilience of his regime. In Morocco, it was the control of these same aspects that underpinned the rise and power of both Mohamed Oufkir and Ahmed Dlimi, and which placed Driss Basri at the right hand of King Hassan in the 1980s and 1990s. The appointment by King Mohamed VI of a trusted civilian adviser to the head of the external intelligence services in 2005, in place of a general, further confirms this trend. In Algeria, the demands of the counter-insurgency campaign of the 1990s expanded the work and influence of the intelligence service of the *Département du Renseignement et de la Sécurité* (DRS), previously known as *Sécurité Militaire*, which had had a fearsome reputation as a powerful and increasingly independent counter-insurgency agency from its creation in 1962.[112] The DRS's head from 1990, General Tewfiq Medienne, became increasingly powerful and distinct from the rest of the generals at the summit of the regime, emerging as the chief power broker between the General Staff and Bouteflika by the mid 2000s.[113] This growth in influence even led to a revision of Mohamed Harbi's famous quip about the army, so that it was the secret services rather than the army that possessed its 'own country.'[114] To underline this pre-eminence, it was notable, as Zemri Benheddi has observed, that promotion for figures such as Oufkir and Ben Ali occurred *from* the military *into* the intelligence and security services, rather than the other way round.[115]

One final similarity between the three states is the way in which the engagement with the world outside the region affected the role of the military. The events of 11 September 2001 and the subsequent 'War on Terror' increased cooperation between the militaries of Morocco and Algeria and their counterparts in the United States. It led to greater sympathy and tolerance being shown to regimes that were seen as allies, be they civilian or military (see Chapter 9). The stated willingness on the part of all three Maghrebi regimes to cooperate with the US in the 'War on Terror' not only reduced American and European criticism about issues such as human rights and lack of democracy that were more audible in the 1990s; the fact that intelligence and security matters were handled by the military and related structures arguably also helped secure the place of these elements within the three states. Thus the generals in Algeria and the security- and intelligence-obsessed Ben Ali in Tunisia were able to find a new place in the sun in Washington alongside the more established US ally, Morocco.

At the same time it might also be argued that increased military cooperation has also helped accelerate processes of professionalisation and depoliticisation present in the national militaries of all three states. Robert Mortimer suggests that in Algeria this led the generals to adopt a lower profile at the time of Bouteflika's re-election as president in 2004, in order to facilitate greater cooperation with NATO.[116] It has even been suggested that Rachid Ammar's crucial decision to defy President Ben Ali in January 2011 in Tunisia was influenced by the contacts he had established with the United States through military cooperation.[117] Whether this link will have a genuinely transformative effect in the coming years, or whether the military's role in the region will continue to be determined by domestic political developments, remains to be seen.

4

POLITICAL PARTIES

Political parties came to play as high-profile a role in the politics of the Maghreb states as they did in most other states. Despite appearances, however, their influence was much slighter than in many states, and was not as important as has often been commonly assumed. The constitutional exclusivity granted to the so-called 'ruling' single parties in Tunisia and Algeria from independence obscured a reality in which other forces and actors ruled. The introduction of multi-party politics in both countries in the 1980s ultimately failed to change this reality, and created the sort of controlled and manipulated formal political system that had operated in Morocco since its own independence.

The Single-Party Regimes

The decision by the ruling elites in both Algeria and Tunisia to formally establish 'single-party states' in the wake of independence was in keeping with the pattern of most other states that became independent in the 1950s and 1960s in Africa and Asia. Across the newly decolonised world, it was accepted wisdom that only a system based on a single political party could provide the sort of dynamism and direction that could produce the necessary impetus for the kind of social and economic change needed in many of the impoverished former colonial possessions. The role of the single party was nearly always assumed by the movement or party that had led the independence struggle.

Both Algeria and Tunisia established single-party systems based on the nationalist movements of their respective liberation struggles, but the roles that these parties came to play were markedly different. This was in large part a result of the very different natures of the nationalist movements and subsequent liberation struggles in the two countries.

Tunisia: From Neo-Destour to PSD

As was seen in Chapter 2, the Neo-Destour party became one of the cornerstones of the political system created by Habib Bourguiba in Tunisia. Bourguiba made sure that the strong, pyramid-shaped party structures established in the 1930s and modelled on the parties of the French left were retained after independence, and set about creating a party state that strongly resembled the classic communist model.[1] A large centralised party structure that mirrored and soon fused with parallel structures in the state apparatus was thus established. The whole system was dominated and controlled by the person of Bourguiba himself who, as state president and party leader, ensured that both structures were subordinated to his directives and worked to achieve the clear set of objectives he had established for Tunisia. This meant that many of the formal 'representative' structures of the party, such as the party congress, played an increasingly marginal role, and by the 1970s Bourguiba was appointing all the members of both the Central Committee and the politbureau.[2] The overall party structure was, nevertheless, important to Bourguiba as a means of both control and mobilisation of the population: roughly one-third of adult Tunisians belonged to the party during the 1960s.[3] He recognised that there were things that could not be achieved simply by the force of his own, admittedly colossal, personality. A well-structured party of the state not only supplied him with the institutionalised mechanisms to push through his policy programme but also provided him with institutional ballast, legitimacy and protection that allowed him to weather difficult periods in the early part of his rule. Some even attribute the ultimate longevity of his rule to the role played by the party.[4] In 1964 the Neo-Destour was officially renamed the *Parti Socialiste Destourien* (PSD) to reflect the ideological direction adopted through the economic programmes of Ahmed Ben Salah (see Chapter 7).

Algeria: The Transition from Revolution

Despite enjoying the same constitutional status, the FLN's role in the post-independence Algerian state was hardly comparable to that of the

Neo-Destour/PSD in Tunisia. As explained in earlier chapters, the FLN was formed on the very eve of the launch of the liberation struggle in 1954, and therefore did not have the well-established institutional framework that the Neo-Destour had been able to create gradually since its formation two decades earlier in 1934. As a consequence, the FLN was not really a party in any meaningful sense, constituting instead more of an umbrella organisation for different groups united to fight against the French. Nevertheless, such a description belies the ruthless and exclusive manner with which the FLN sought to take full control of the liberation struggle, and largely succeeded, absorbing or destroying any competing groups. In the view of Hugh Roberts, this unusual form that the FLN took owed little to Western conceptions of political parties and organisations and much to the traditional political organisation of the Algerian countryside, which remained the wellspring of the Algerian resistance throughout much of the liberation struggle. It explains, in his view, why attempts during the liberation struggle to turn the FLN into a more European-style party (like the Neo-Destour) met with little success; and why individual figures who tried to assert personal leadership over it similarly failed, since this went against traditions of collective leadership of the rural tribal council or *jama'a*.[5]

The bitter and violent struggle for power that erupted between the various constituent parts of the FLN in the summer of 1962 following the achievement of independence (see Chapter 2) was testimony to the fact that the FLN was not a coherent political party. As shown in Chapter 2, the wartime FLN's eschewal of debates over ideological issues and its failure to produce a single dominant leader like Bourguiba in Tunisia were an intended function of the movement's desire to avoid potentially distracting and divisive issues which could detract from the central objective of achieving independence. However, the absence of a single leader at independence served to sharpen the power struggles that followed the departure of the French. These struggles marked the effective death of the wartime FLN and its transformation into something different. During Ben Bella's brief presidency, under which the FLN's status as the sole political party was constitutionally confirmed, there were divided views over what should become of the party. Mohamed Khider, the official secretary general of the FLN, was of the view that the FLN should be 'maintained' as a broad front of nationalists. Ben Bella, by contrast, influenced by more doctrinaire socialist ideas, believed that the party should be transformed into a much smaller and narrowly based vanguard socialist party. Despite

Ben Bella's eviction of Khider in 1963, the president failed to implement his vision for the party in the early heady and chaotic years of the post-independence period, and by the time of the *coup d'état* of June 1965 the FLN as an organisation remained in a state of limbo.

Boumedienne's reliance on the military for his institutional base (see Chapter 3) meant that he made no attempt to revive the FLN as an organisation after the ousting of Ben Bella. Throughout the late 1960s and early 1970s it was allowed to atrophy, with no party congress being held and no party central committee being constituted throughout the entirety of his leadership. It decreased to little more than a symbolic institutional shell, surviving only because of its association with the all-important liberation struggle. Boumedienne even went so far as to rely on the semi-clandestine former Algerian Communist Party (reconstituted as the *Parti de l'Avant-Garde Socialiste*, or PAGS) to provide the organisational and ideological impetus for the 'Socialist Revolution' of the early 1970s (see Chapter 2).[6]

The death of Boumedienne in 1978 and the accession of Chadli Benjedid to the presidency led to a rejuvenation of sorts for the FLN. A new article inserted into the party statutes, stipulating that officials of Algeria's mass organisations (such as the official trade union and the youth organisation) should henceforth be members of the FLN, contributed to an expansion in the membership and profile of the party. The party also began to hold party congresses again and its central committee met on a more regular basis. This attempt to revive the party came at the expense of the dominance hitherto exercised by senior figures in the military, who moved to reassert themselves in the wake of the events of the Kabyle Spring in 1980 (see Chapter 6) by strengthening the powers of the presidency.[7] As under Boumedienne, effective political power then returned to the hands of the president, with the FLN's congress and central committee having little meaningful input into the decision-making process. Instead the FLN became the forum for renewed clan warfare within the regime that had been successfully suppressed by Boumedienne but which became the hallmark of the internal politics of the Chadli presidency, in this way ironically reviving the collective leadership traditions of the wartime FLN. As Arun Kapil comments of the post-1980 period:

Far from taking on the character of a political party, the FLN remained little more than a network of clans within the power structure whose sole objective was to colonize the state apparatus with their clients.[8]

POLITICAL PARTIES

As was explored in Chapter 3, real power remained, as it had since 1962, in the hands of the country's military, whose strength and influence merely increased under the less dominating hand of Chadli Benjedid and whose senior figures participated with renewed gusto in the internal clan warfare of the 1980s.

Morocco's Stop-Go Multi-partyism

Morocco was an exception to the general pattern of single-party systems, largely due to the fact that the main nationalist party during the colonial period did not become the dominant political force after the achievement of independence. As shown in Chapter 2, the assumption by the monarchy of this role relegated the Istiqlal party to a position of subservience to the royal palace, following the latter's decisive victory in the peaceful power struggle with the Istiqlal in the years immediately following independence. This development not only worked against the institution of a single-party system, because of the threat such a party would potentially pose to the monarchy's dominance; the absence of a commitment to wholesale social and economic change (which could threaten the power bases of the monarchy) also meant that there was no perceived need, on the part of the monarchy, for a dynamic single party to implement such change.

Morocco's first constitution in 1962 enshrined the principle of multi-partyism, formally imposing party-political competition on the Istiqlal party and sealing a process that had already begun with King Mohamed V's recognition of the royalist *Mouvement Populaire* and the leftist scission from the Istiqlal, the UNFP, in 1959 (see Chapter 2). Other political parties were legalised in time for the first national legislative elections taking place in May 1963, allowing palace officials to construct a bloc of royalist parties that attempted to prevent the domination of the parliament by representatives from the Istiqlal and the UNFP, which had both performed strongly in municipal elections. Harassment of the two opposition parties and blatant intervention by local administrators only succeeded, though, in securing an exact balance in representation in the new parliament between the Istiqlal and the UNFP on the one hand and the royalist alliance (known as the *Front pour la Défense des Institutions Constitutionelles*, or FDIC) on the other. The political gridlock which ensued contributed to the sense of political polarisation and crisis that had been growing inside the kingdom, fanned by mounting social and economic problems. Arrests and imprisonments of leading members of the UNFP increased as they began to take an increasingly militant stance towards the monarchy, and led to the decisions by King Hassan to suspend both the constitution and the parliament in the wake of social unrest in Casablanca in March 1965 and to declare a 'State of Exception.'

The State of Exception, during which King Hassan ruled by decree, lasted five years and placed the political parties in a state of abeyance. Thereafter repeated attempts by the palace to resume normal multi-party elections largely foundered on the reluctance of the Istiqlal, and especially the UNFP, to involve themselves in formal political processes that they perceived to be fully rigged against them, especially following a revision to the constitution in 1970 that greatly strengthened the role of the monarchy at the expense of the parliament. Immediately after the approval of the new constitution by an officially recorded 98.7 per cent of the voters in a referendum, the two parties formed a formal pact—the National Bloc (*al-Kutla al-Watanniyya*)—which called for the establishment of full democracy and the freeing of the economy from capitalism.[9]

King Hassan's persistence in trying to bring the National Bloc parties into formal politics was something of a reversal of his stance in 1965, when he had declared the State of Exception because of the 'contradictory and irreconcilable demands of the parties,' and reflected the growing political isolation the monarch felt, especially following the two narrowly unsuccessful *coups d'état* of 1971 and 1972 (see Chapter 3).[10] It was a political isolation that ended fairly rapidly when the issue of the Western Sahara came to the fore, swinging the parties of the National Bloc rapidly behind the campaign led by the monarchy and crystallising in the Green March of 1975 (see Chapter 8). The nationalist tone of Morocco's claim on the territory elicited an enthusiastic response from the Istiqlal, which as the historic nationalist party had led calls for the integration of the territory into Morocco from the 1950s. As an offspring from the Istiqlal, the UNFP was also supportive and the issue even contributed to a formal split in the party, out of which came the more pragmatic and nationalist *Union Socialiste des Forces Populaires* (USFP), soon to eclipse the UNFP. Nationalist fervour gripped virtually the full political spectrum in the kingdom and facilitated the legalisation of even more political parties as they joined the campaign headed by the palace. These included, most notably, the remnants of the banned Moroccan Communist Party (*Parti Communiste Marocain*, or PCM) which had rebranded itself the Party of Progress and Socialism (PPS). Its leader was sent to Eastern Europe in an attempt to persuade communist states to support Morocco's claim, while leading figures from the USFP and Istiqlal were dispatched to other parts of the globe to argue Morocco's case.[11] The one exception to this trend was the revolutionary Marxist left which suffered brutal oppression from the authorities in this period, as much for its failure to join the nationalist consensus on the Western Sahara as for its republican and revolutionary objectives.

The re-entry of the National Bloc parties into the formal political system, essentially on the palace's terms, signalled the beginning of a new phase in Moroccan party politics that would persist for the next two decades. This saw the opposition parties participate in elections and institutions but accept—albeit not without protest—a heavily circumscribed role in parliament and local government. Irregular elections produced significant and clearly manufactured royalist 'majorities,' often for equally manufactured newly formed parties. The palace hoped these new parties would either unite existing supporters of the regime (as in the case of the *Rassemblement National des Indépendants*, or RNI, created by Ahmed Osman, King Hassan's brother-in-law, in 1978), or attract new social groups and classes into the formal political system (as in the case of the *Union Constitutionnel*, or UC, established in 1983 to appeal to the expanding younger generation of Moroccans). The number of political parties contesting elections continued to grow, mainly as the result of splits in existing parties—both royalist and opposition. Such scissions were frequently encouraged and aided by Hassan's powerful interior minister, Driss Basri, who sought to ensure that no one party ever became too big or too powerful; his role in the birth of new political parties led to him becoming known as Morocco's premier party-political midwife. The Istiqlal and the USFP were reborn as the 'loyal opposition,' continuing to be critical of what they saw as the lack of democracy in Morocco but no longer willing to confront the monarchy explicitly.

The Move to Multi-partyism: Tunisia and Algeria

In spite of the big differences that existed between the one-party systems in Tunisia and Algeria, both states chose to move away from the one-party model and allow other parties to form and contest elections during the 1980s. In both cases the primary motivation for this shift was the mounting political and economic crises that began to hit the Maghrebi states from the late 1970s. Once again, Tunisia and Algeria took rather different routes to the abandonment of the single-party model.

Tunisia: Staged Opening

Tunisia made the move to multi-partyism in two stages. In the early 1980s three opposition parties were accorded formal legal recognition and were permitted to contest elections. Bourguiba's motivations for formally breaking the party-political monopoly held by the PSD were largely linked to the problems Tunisia had begun to experience from the 1970s. Increasing economic problems in this period (see Chapter 7) had led to outbreaks of serious social unrest in 1978 and 1981. That this unrest had begun to develop political dimensions was particularly worrying for the regime. Bourguiba's abandonment in 1969 of the state socialist economic initiative under Ahmed Ben Salah had not only contributed to growing economic inequalities (which had fuelled the unrest) but had also deprived the PSD of much of its dynamism and *raison d'être* since 'development no longer justified the party monolith.'[12] As a result, dissident voices had begun to emerge within the PSD in the early 1970s calling for more pluralism both within the party and in Tunisian political life more generally. Outside the formal structures of the party, youth, trade union and religious groups began to make similar demands on the regime, a number of them involving themselves in the unrest of 1978 and 1981.

Several senior figures in the regime came to the conclusion that some limited degree of political pluralism should be permitted, to act as a safety valve for the clear political and economic pressures that were building in society and, more worryingly, appeared to be contributing to a growth in support for Islamism in the country. Bourguiba was unconvinced of the merits of such a response, but consented firstly to competition between PSD candidates in elections and then the legalisation of three opposition parties.[13] The president's lack of commitment to any genuine political opening was reflected in the fact that it was only three of the least threatening parties that were legalised; applications from the party formed by Ahmed Ben Salah in exile and the emerging Islamist movement were rejected out of hand. Moreover,

POLITICAL PARTIES

Bourguiba ensured that the political space the legalised parties were allowed to operate in was so restricted that they presented no possible challenge to his and the PSD's dominance. Financial and organisational constraints, together with harassment from the authorities, effectively neutralised any impact the parties might have. Blatant ballot-rigging also ensured that, despite being allowed to contest elections, no opposition party ever secured any form of representation at any level throughout the remainder of Bourguiba's presidency.

Habib Bourguiba's ousting by Zine al-Abidine Ben Ali in November 1987 opened the way for a further broadening of the party-political landscape. From very early on, Ben Ali appeared to make it clear that further political liberalisation was part of his new agenda for Tunisia. In May 1988 a new law on political parties was introduced, which improved the status of the existing political parties and allowed for and prompted the formation and legalisation of new parties. In September 1988 the representatives from both the existing and new political parties joined with other groupings in Tunisian society (including a representative from the country's main Islamist movement) to draw up, in concert with Ben Ali's government, a new document that mapped out a consensus for the post-Bourguiba era. The National Pact that emerged from these meetings, announced on the first anniversary of Bourguiba's removal from power in November 1988, included commitments to greater political freedom and the holding of multi-party elections.

Algeria: The Rush to Pluralism

The transition to multi-party politics in Algeria was more sudden and more dramatic than in Tunisia. Like Tunisia, it came in the wake of serious social unrest. Following the rioting and demonstrations that swept across Algeria's major cities in the first week of October 1988, President Chadli Benjedid announced a series of significant political reforms that culminated in the unveiling of a new constitution in February 1989, permitting the formation of 'associations of a political character.' Over the next three years nearly fifty political parties applied for and received legal recognition and were granted the right to contest multi-party elections held at local (1990) and national (1991) level. These included long-established political parties created by dissident former members of the FLN in exile, most notably ones led by two of the nine historic leaders of the original FLN: the *Front des Forces Socialistes* (FFS) led by Hocine Ait Ahmed, and the Movement for Democracy in Algeria (MDA) led by former president Ahmed Ben Bella. The former communists of the PAGS were also legalised after a long period of semi-legality. Many more new parties were created and legalised representing a full range of platforms from secular to Islamist, leftist to conservative.

The scale and speed of the transition to multi-party politics inevitably raised questions as to the motivation for the reform. In contrast to the experience of Tunisia in 1978, where unrest had grown out of a general strike organised by the UGTT trade union, there had been no identifiably political dimension to the unrest of October 1988: the rioting and demonstrations were driven fundamentally by more visceral grievances about declining social and economic conditions. The unrest had no apparent political direction or leadership and articulated no clear political demands. Thus, in introducing multi-party politics and greater political liberalisation, Chadli Benjedid was not responding to a clear and irresistible demand for democratisation on the part of the Algerian population. It was possible that Chadli wanted to use political reform to distract the restive population from the parlous state of the Algerian economy. It was considerably less likely that the president had become a sudden convert to the values of liberal democracy, some months before the collapse of communist regimes in Eastern Europe provoked a renewed interest in democratisation worldwide. Chadli's background and personality hardly qualified him as an Algerian Gorbachev—as many of his associates confirmed.[14]

The real reason behind Chadli's decision to reform lay, as ever, in the complex internal politics of the Algerian regime. The latter part of the 1980s had seen Chadli progressively lose ground in the interminable clan warfare that resumed following the death of Boumedienne. By early 1988 there were strong rumours circulating that Chadli would not be reconfirmed as president when his second formal term in office came to an end in November 1988 and that he would be replaced by another figure. It appears that Chadli took full advantage of the upheaval and shock caused by the events of October 1988 to pose as a unifying and reforming figure and to secure endorsement for a third term in office in the turbulent weeks that followed the unrest. It also allowed him to dismiss several of his many enemies inside the regime and portray that as a grand reforming gesture. Chadli's decision to go even further and introduce a multi-party system in the new constitution of February 1989 also represented a blow against his enemies. The structures of the FLN had become the main battleground for the clan warfare of the 1980s, and by suddenly depriving the party of its party-political monopoly, Chadli at once distracted rival clans, some of whose members left to form new parties, and personally cut himself loose from the fray by posing as a president above party politics.

The Reassertion of the State: Tunisia and Algeria

The opening up of the political systems in Tunisia and Algeria to apparently genuine multi-party competition in the closing years of the 1980s was hailed as evidence of the beginning of Western-style democracy in the two states. Such a view came to be questioned, however, as within a short period this opening was increasingly restricted as the established regimes sought to reassert their previous control over the political system.

Ben Ali Űber Alles

In Tunisia the earliest signs that fully-fledged democracy was not on the official agenda came with the first national legislative elections following Ben Ali's takeover from Bourguiba, held in April 1989. Despite the participation of a number of opposition parties and independent candidates, the ruling party won every single seat in the parliament. Official results from the election showed that the ruling party—renamed the *Rassemblement Constitutionnel Démocratique* (RCD)—had apparently secured the overwhelming majority of the votes cast (81 per cent) and that a 'winner takes all' rule in the multi-member voting constituencies ensured that no other party or individual secured representation. The results dismayed the other parties, who claimed they had been falsified and that, despite the likely overall dominance of the RCD, certain opposition parties had received most votes in several constituencies and thus deserved representation. One leading member of one of the opposition parties compared the election to the notoriously rigged elections of the limited opening of the early 1980s, stating 'I saw the same system in 1989 as I had seen in 1981.'[15]

The opposition parties tried to maintain a common front to protest the clear restrictions on the political system, but were weakened by divisions between and within them about the extent to which they should confront or cooperate with the regime. Many opposition figures saw Tunisia's large Islamist movement as a greater danger and threat than the regime, and when Ben Ali moved against the Islamist An-Nahda party in the early 1990s (see Chapter 5) they felt they should side with the president. This, together with the lure of state subsidies and benefits, persuaded most of the main opposition parties to abandon plans to boycott the formal political process and put up candidates in the second set of legislative elections held in 1994, despite the retention of the winner-takes-all rule. The one concession they received was that nineteen seats in the parliament would be reserved for the opposition parties and divided up on a quota basis. This provided only limited comfort when the RCD was officially credited with receiving nearly 98 per cent of the votes in the 1994 election.

The marginalisation of the opposition parties was the corollary of the reassertion of the ruling party. Following his assumption of the presidency in November 1987, Ben Ali moved swiftly to reform and renew the PSD whose presidency he also assumed. Aware that the party had become progressively less engaged with the wider Tunisian population during the 1970s and 1980s, as Bourguiba aged and it had become absorbed with intrigues concerning who would succeed him as president, Ben Ali announced in February 1988 that the party would change its name. The rather anachronistic reference to socialism was dropped and replaced with one to democracy whilst continuity was ensured through the retaining reference to constitutionalism. Change of greater substance came with the recruitment drive the new party launched attracting in former opponents of Bourguiba from human rights organizations and even the other political parties. More importantly, the party worked hard to recruit significant sections of the population that had become alienated from the regime under Bourguiba: businessmen, intellectuals, professionals, women and the young. Encouraged by the promise of reform and the benefits of involvement and concerned by the rise of the Islamists, many Tunisians responded positively and membership of the party expanded rapidly reaching 1.6 million by the time of the RCD's second Congress in 1993 and surpassing 2 million by the time of the third in 1998.[16]

The expansion of the RCD and its dominance of the formal political scene led many commentators to argue that Tunisia had succeeded in swapping the single-party rule of the PSD for the hegemonic rule of the RCD.[17] Camau and Geisser, however, argue that this overstates the role of the RCD at the expense of that played by the President. After an initial period of keeping a certain separation of the party from the institutions of state, from 1993 Ben Ali began to reinstate the integration of the two structures that had existed under Bourguiba. Rather than the party controlling the state as in the classic socialist model, it was the government, directed by the presidential palace, that came to control and supervise the party. Indeed it has been argued that throughout the 1990s both power and patronage moved increasingly away from the party and into the hands of the government and the president. RCD party congresses witnessed not only less discussion than had occurred during the PSD period but also less with each successive congress. This left the RCD largely with the task of mobilising the population in support of the regime through liaising with local elites and managing local associations.[18]

The centrality of Zine al-Abdine Ben Ali to the new political constellation became increasingly apparent. In addition to its progressive monopolisation of political power, the presidency also came to dominate the public symbols of power. Elections to the presidency quickly overshadowed those to the national parliament—which were deliberately held on the same day to emphasise the leadership of the president—and legal restrictions ensured that the first two presidential elections were not contested by other candidates.[19] Huge public portraits of Ben Ali began to appear across Tunisia; his daily official activities came to dominate television news bulletins and the front pages of the country's increasingly tame press, evoking the public profile of the Moroccan monarchy or, much more tellingly, Habib Bourguiba. Indeed Clement Henry's description of the latter's rule as 'presidential monarchy' came rapidly to fit his successor equally well.[20] If Ben Ali had initially decried the cult of personality that Bourguiba had built around himself, pulled down the statues of the 'Great Combattant' and renamed many of the streets and public places still honouring the republic's first president, his ubiquitous reference to the date of 7 November 1987 (the day he succeeded to the presidency) and its similar over-use in naming public places spoke of a comparable, if subtler, ambition to dominate the public political sphere.

Ben Ali's domination of political life, supported by the RCD, left little room for the other political parties. Several of them willingly accepted a marginal role in return for a degree of official patronage. Some of them even became official cheerleaders for the president, openly supporting his presidential election campaign, even whilst putting up candidates against the RCD. When legal restrictions on running candidates in the presidential election were relaxed from 1999, this resulted in the bizarre spectacle of several parties' presidential candidates openly proclaiming that Ben Ali was the best candidate for the office.[21] Such a stance prompted one disgruntled member of parliament for one of these parties to proclaim of his own party 'The UDU is not an opposition party but a support party!'[22] Even given this complicity, these 'support' parties were given little political space and were largely reduced to fighting against each other to secure seats within the small quota set aside for 'opposition' parties in the parliament; even their most obsequious of presidential candidates never officially secured more than a handful of percentage points at elections.

Those political parties that chose to take a less supine and more confrontational approach to Ben Ali suffered for their efforts. This was not just through the denial of official patronage, but also from the heavy hand of the state that sought throughout the 1990s to punish dissent in increasingly harsh ways. The aftermath of the 1989 legislative elections had witnessed a growing confrontation between the Tunisian regime and the Islamist An-Nahda movement, which openly accused the authorities of electoral fraud but in return was accused of resorting to extremist rhetoric and ultimately violence to achieve political power. This culminated in a comprehensive crackdown against An-Nahda by the authorities, which arrested thousands of its members and supporters and broke up all institutional manifestations of the movement (see Chapter 5). As stated earlier, many of the opposition parties shared the regime's misgivings about the Islamists, notably those from the ideological left who were alarmed by the Islamists' perceived theocratic tendencies and desire to reduce the legal rights Bourguiba had granted women. Initially siding with the regime in its attempts to rein in the movement, a number of opposition figures were subsequently unsettled by the brutality of the crackdown against An-Nahda. As the leader of one leftist party put it, 'We were opposed to An-Nahda…and early on we sided with Ben Ali against the violence of An-Nahda. By 1991 we realized what was happening and broke with Ben Ali over the repression and criticized him for having only a security response to the problem and for not leaving a door open to moderate Islamists.'[23]

Those parties that criticised the regime found themselves marginalised and increasingly harassed by the authorities. Attempts to put up candidates at elections were repeatedly blocked through a variety of pseudo-legal measures.[24] The authorities also regularly seized and banned party newspapers and election literature and prevented parties from holding meetings. As a result neither of the two most critical parties—the *Rassemblement Socialiste Progressiste* (RSP) (which became the Progressive Democratic Party, PDP, in 2001) and the *Forum Démocratique pour le Travail et les Libertés* (FDTL)—ever succeeded in having a single representative elected at any level during the whole period of Ben Ali's presidency. Even those parties with representation suffered harassment. In 1995 the two most senior leaders of the largest opposition party, the *Mouvement des Démocrates Socialistes* (MDS), were arrested and charged with espionage immediately after launching public criticisms of the Tunisian regime.[25] Thereafter the MDS refrained from criticising the regime and supported Ben Ali at subsequent elections, thus entering into the ranks of the other 'support' parties. Those opposition parties that avoided co-option regularly cooperated with each other in campaigns protesting against the regime's excesses, but were not able to forge any more enduring alliance due to regime pressure and also differences between them, often over establishing links with the banned An-Nahda movement.

Algeria: Crisis and Confrontation

The reassertion of the regime over party politics in Algeria was much more dramatic than in Tunisia. This was largely because the original liberalisation of the party-political landscape had itself been far more dramatic and much more extensive. Whilst the Tunisian regime succeeded in tightly controlling the framework and results of the move to multi-party politics, virtually from the outset, this was not the case in Algeria. Unlike Ben Ali, President Chadli Benjedid made no attempt to reform and rejuvenate the FLN in the manner of the PSD/RCD. In fact Chadli tried to distance himself from the FLN in the hope of removing himself from the perceived failings of the regime that had contributed to the unrest of 1988. Moreover, he even sought to ensure that the former single party shouldered the blame in the public eye for these failings, which he hoped would handicap his enemies within it who had reasserted themselves in the party in the wake of the unrest of October 1988.[26]

Chadli was aided in his task by the emergence of a new and well-supported party that presented a clear threat to the former single party's dominance of the new party-political landscape. As in Tunisia, the main social and political opposition movement that emerged in Algeria in the late 1980s had been that of Islamism. Unlike Tunisia, though, where the regime had declined to allow the movement to create a formal political party, the Algerian authorities granted legalisation to the party created by several of the country's leading Islamist activists in 1989 (see Chapter 5). It is unclear why they chose to legalise the party when there were constitutional provisions like those in Tunisia that appeared to rule out the granting of official recognition to a party based on religion. It does seem likely, though, that a desire to provide a competitor to the FLN was at the root of the decision. This seems to be borne out by evidence that Chadli and his allies in the government tacitly encouraged the *Front Islamique du Salut* (FIS) in its early months.[27]

The spectacular success achieved by the FIS in the first multi-party elections held for regional and communal assemblies in June 1990 showed that the new party had done far more than provide a check on the FLN. The Islamist party received over half the votes cast and more than twice those won by the FLN, which trailed in a distant second. It was clear that whilst the FIS had a large and active support base, many Algerians were voting for the new party to punish the regime which in their eyes was embodied by the FLN. This was quite symbolic. Many of the FIS's leaders explicitly claimed that the new party was in fact the inheritor of the FLN's revolutionary tradition: the FIS's leader, Abassi Madani, stated that 'The FIS wants to save the experiences of November [1954] which have been lost.'[28] The party's decision to call itself a Front was seen by many as underlining and confirming that the party had the same hegemonic ambitions as the original FLN.[29]

The rise and success of the FIS dramatically changed the political landscape and took Algeria in a very different direction to that taken by Tunisia in the same period. Attempts by Chadli and his government to curb the electoral advance of the FIS by altering the electoral law, legalising competing parties and arresting the main leaders of the party ultimately failed with the FIS's sweeping victories in the first round of national legislative elections held in December 1991. This failure led to the progressive re-entry of the Algerian military into the political scene and the forcible abandonment of the national legislative elections before the decisive second round could be held and the victory of the FIS confirmed (see Chapter 3).

POLITICAL PARTIES

The cancellation of the elections put the political parties into limbo as a new military-dominated regime sought to assert itself. The decision to impose a formal ban on the FIS in March 1992 not only removed the largest political party from the legal arena but also engendered a period of violence that prolonged the suspension of normal political life. The political parties that had won seats in the first round of the 1991 elections protested at the cancellation and abandonment of the electoral process. These parties not only included the now proscribed FIS but also, to the surprise of many, the FLN. The criticism by the FLN of the palace coup of January 1992, which it described as 'anti-constitutional,' demonstrated the extent of the former single party's detachment from the Algerian regime following Chadli's decision to distance his government from the party.[30] The parting of regime from party had allowed figures from the reformist wing of the FLN to take control of the leadership from 1989 and attempt to turn the former single party into a 'normal' political party.

The distancing of the FLN from the regime presented something of a dilemma to the Algerian political leadership as it looked to restart some form of electoral process in the mid 1990s. The party's poor performance in elections had had no real impact on the Algerian state because the bureaucratic intelligence and especially military elites stayed in place; Hugh Roberts has argued that the military was even strengthened by what he sees as the disabling of the regime's civilian wing represented by the FLN.[31] The alienation of the FLN did, nevertheless, deprive the regime of a vehicle for its interests in elections, even if it intended a close control over these processes. The authorities helped engineer the replacement of the leadership of the FLN by figures much more closely aligned with the regime in 1996, but the party remained suspect in the eyes of many in the dominant military establishment. Together with concerns that the party was still tainted in the public eye with the failings of the Algerian state in the 1980s, this led to the regime contemplating finding an alternative vehicle for the representation of its interests in elections. As in Morocco with the creation of the RNI and the UC, the Algerian leadership saw the creation of a new political party as the solution to its problem. Thus in March 1997 the *Rassemblement National Démocratique* (RND) was created. To the surprise of few, the new grouping went on to become the largest party in the elections to the National Assembly held three months later and then won control of the largest number of local and regional councils in elections the following October. Algerians joked of the new party, 'the baby is born with a moustache,' in a reference to both the military genesis of the party as well as its seemingly instant maturity. Such immediate success echoed that of the UC in Morocco in the early 1980s, and in a further evocation of its Moroccan counterpart the party incorporated most of the existing members of the pre-election government of apolitical technocrats. Thus the 'new' post-election government was made up of re-appointments from the previous government: the existing justice, interior and foreign ministers having simply joined the RND on its creation and been confirmed in their posts three months later by the new RND-dominated National Assembly, supporting the view that the new party was 'never more than the state bureaucracy in disguise.'[32]

The emergence of the RND did not, however, signal the death of the old FLN. The party continued to have its uses. Although losing support and members to the new party, the FLN made use of its long-established institutional network to win a substantial number of seats in the elections of 1997 and was invited to join the RND in the post-election governing coalition in the National Assembly. The FLN was credited with much stronger results at the two subsequent elections, making it the largest party in the Assembly, but it continued to share government with the RND. This revival was seen by some as the result of the continued symbolic significance of the FLN for those Algerians who had participated in the independence struggle. The party's established structures and more traditional and religious leanings provided a useful complement to the RND's relative youth and more secular outlook in the coalition, even if the parties were indistinguishable in most other ways, as indicated by the flow of activists between them.[33] The FLN's 'revival' was also seen as a product of the unpopularity the RND had experienced when introducing economic reforms (see Chapter 6). For others, however, the return did not represent a 'groundswell of public opinion' but rather 'a decision from on high' to shift representation between the two parties, as the FLN was finally brought back under the full control of the regime.[34] The electoral processes that were revived from the latter half of the 1990s in Algeria appeared with each set of elections to produce results that reflected less and less the currents and shifts in public opinion and more and more the wishes of the senior leadership of the state.[35] Evidence of electoral fraud grew and official figures for turnout rates appeared to bear diminishing resemblance to the observed realities on the ground.[36]

POLITICAL PARTIES

The restart of electoral processes in the mid 1990s was met with mixed reactions from the other political parties in Algeria. Whereas all welcomed the return to elections, many were doubtful about the degree of official control that would be exercised over them. In a similar way to Tunisia, the parties were divided between those that were sceptical and even hostile to the regime and those that sought to cooperate with it. This divide was clearly demonstrated in 1995 when a number of parties collaborated to issue what became known as the 'Rome Platform,' signed under the auspices of the St Egidio Community in Rome, constituting a proposal for resolving the crisis inside the country. The three main signatories were the FLN, still at that point under reformist leadership; the *Front des Forces Socialistes* (FFS), Algeria's oldest opposition party; and the FIS itself, whose rehabilitation was seen as crucial to the ending of widespread violence and the restarting of elections. They were joined by a range of parties from across the political spectrum, including leftists, nationalists and Islamists, indicating that the initiative cut across formal ideological lines.[37] This impression was further reinforced by the range of parties that refused to participate in the platform, which similarly drew together an almost identical ideological range of parties.

The restarting of electoral processes saw a strengthening of the parties that had declined to join the Rome Platform and a parallel weakening and division of those that had signed it. The regime not only secured the effective defection of the FLN through the party's change of leadership in 1996, but also the dissolution of another party that refused to change its statutes in line with a much more restrictive political parties law introduced the following year.[38] The remaining signatories to the Platform were credited with barely 15 per cent of the seats in the first elections to the National Assembly in 1997 and thereafter were further reduced through regime-sponsored scissions within the parties and disagreements between them over whether to boycott the progressively less credible polls. At the same time, other parties' representation grew. This was most notably the case with the Movement of Society for Peace (MSP), an Islamist party that had rejected the Rome Platform; it not only became one of the best represented parties in the national parliament after the FLN and RND, but actually formally joined the government coalition as its third member.

The creation of a multi-party government represented a departure from the single-party model established in Tunisia. Another important distinction was the role played by the presidency which, rather than being a hegemonic actor, fell very much under the control of the dominant military hierarchy (see Chapter 3). As a result, political parties had very little influence on either the choice or the actions of the president. Algeria's first contested presidential election held in 1995 gave victory to a former general, Lamine Zeroual, who had no formal party-political affiliation. His successor in 1999, Abdelaziz Bouteflika, similarly stood as an independent but received the backing of the FLN and the RND and was universally acknowledged to have been the choice of the senior echelons of the military, which actually used the party-political system to control the president. As Bouteflika approached the end of his first term as president, a current emerged within the FLN that urged the selection of a presidential candidate to run against Bouteflika. Although this challenge ultimately failed and Bouteflika was re-elected and subsequently chosen as the FLN's official candidate for the 2004 election, the move was widely interpreted as having been orchestrated by the military to remind Bouteflika of his dispensability and thus keep a check on any appetite for greater power and independence. The closeness and effective control of the leadership of all of the parties in the formal government coalition has also been used to constrain and hem in the presidency.[39]

By the mid 1990s the party-political systems of both Tunisia and Algeria had experienced a similar evolution, moving from an initially promising period of openness and apparent competition to a situation where the regimes began to assert increasingly tight control on the parties, elections and the overall system; this was to facilitate the dominance of parties that were supportive of the regime and concomitantly squeeze the space allowed to critical parties. In this way, both systems had come to resemble that of Morocco, which similarly gave limited legal space to opposition parties within the framework of manipulated elections and occasional harassment, with elections giving formal and usually deeply dubious 'victories' to tame pro-regime parties.

Morocco's Alternance Experiment

At the point when the evolving party-political systems of Algeria and Tunisia were coming to resemble the more established system in Morocco, the kingdom itself appeared to embark on changes to this set-up that seemed to open up rather than restrict the role and influence of opposition parties.

POLITICAL PARTIES

The early 1990s witnessed a series of overtures by the royal palace to the parties of opposition, including two modest revisions to the constitution to strengthen the role of parliament as well as invitations to join the governing coalition of parties. King Hassan's motivations in seeking a rapprochement were varied, but principally related to his desire to widen the base of his regime in preparation for the eventual succession to the throne of his son and crown prince, Mohamed, and to lessen social and political pressures in the kingdom that had shown themselves most dramatically in political protests and unrest during the time of the Gulf crisis and war of 1990–91. Hassan was also conscious of the need to improve Morocco's image abroad and particularly in the West, since its damage by high-profile allegations of human rights abuses in Morocco. These had weakened Morocco's campaign for recognition of its claim on the Western Sahara, for which support from the West was seen as crucial (see Chapter 9). There was also an awareness that Morocco's political system, which had looked relatively liberal in the region during the 1970s and 1980s, had begun to look decidedly less so in the light of the initially positive liberalising changes occurring in Algeria and Tunisia in the late 1980s and early 1990s.

The opposition parties were initially wary of the palace's invitation to join the government coalition of parties, fearing that it was trap that would simply co-opt and de-fang their criticism of the regime. In 1992, sensing the political vulnerability of the palace, the Istiqlal and the USFP revived the Kutla Alliance of the 1970s, bringing in a number of small leftist parties into the grouping. The Kutla parties were credited with a significant increase in the number of seats in the national parliament in elections in 1993, but they were unhappy that one-third of the seats were not directly elected and went largely to allies of the palace. They therefore politely declined an offer to join the government in 1995 but, following a constitutional change that created a fully directly elected chamber in the national parliament a year later and another respectable showing in the elections in 1997, they reconsidered and in 1998 after some internal debate consented to come into government.

The move was heralded both inside and outside Morocco as a significant step forward. This was mainly because the Kutla were led into the alliance by the USFP, which had won the largest number of seats in the election. The entry of the USFP into government appeared to symbolise the final rapprochement between the palace and the political left, which had spearheaded opposition to the political hegemony exercised by the monarchy since the latter had triumphed in the power struggles of the immediate post-independence period. More symbolic still was the appointment of the USFP's leader, Abderrahamane El Youssoufi, to the post of prime minister: El Youssoufi was a long-time and respected critic of the lack of democracy in Morocco and had not only sent himself into voluntary exile in protest at the outcome of the 1993 elections but, moreover, had been imprisoned by King Hassan in the 1960s for his activism in the UNFP and had even once been condemned to death *in absentia* when in exile in the 1970s. The appointment as government ministers of El Youssoufi, together with other formerly dissident figures from the USFP, the Istiqlal and ex-revolutionary Marxists in the smaller leftist parties, seemed to indicate that a genuine shift of power—or *alternance*—seemed to be occurring in Morocco.

The reality of *alternance* was inevitably more nuanced. To begin with, the Kutla parties were not given full control of every government ministry. The alliance did not command a parliamentary majority and was therefore obliged to accept ministers from other parties, largely from 'former' royalist parties or their overshoots, notably the RNI, which had led royalist governments in the 1970s, and a party led by the former leader of the *Mouvement Populaire*. Moreover, several key ministries (Justice, Foreign Affairs, Islamic Affairs and the all-important Interior) remained in the hands of non-party appointees of the king. Fully aware of these drawbacks, El Youssoufi and his colleagues took up their posts in the government believing that, through controlling ministries such as Finance, Health, Education and the premiership itself, they could still enact meaningful changes. More importantly, they believed that Hassan's reforms were genuine and, whilst not as far-reaching as they would have liked, represented a real opening that would only be expanded when the king was succeeded by his son. Indeed, when Hassan died just a little over a year after the appointment of the *alternance* government, it appeared to give even more impetus to the reformist and liberalising project as the new and youthful King Mohamed seemed to endorse and indeed embody the liberalising changes. The new king's swift decision to dismiss his father's long serving interior minister, Driss Basri, who had long been responsible for controlling and manipulating the country's political parties and the elections in which they competed, was seen as particularly important: his departure having long been a demand of the opposition parties.[40]

Optimism that the pace of liberalising reform would be sustained gradually faded over the decade that followed, as King Mohamed failed to continue the rhythm of reforms initiated by his father. Whilst the new king made bold and eye-catching reforms in the fields of women's rights, recognition of former human rights abuses and the economy, few measures were instituted to increase the power and influence of the political parties through increasing the power of parliament and the ministries. The main lines of policy continued to be determined by the royal palace, and the king's advisers remained far more powerful and influential than government minsters. El Youssoufi's government also failed to make notable headway against the multiple social and economic problems of Morocco. Some left-wing members of the Kutla parties began to fear that *alternance* had indeed been a deliberate trap designed to shoulder them publicly with the blame for the failings of the Moroccan state and so undermine their credibility and thus their support amongst the electorate. El Youssoufi was replaced as prime minister by a non-party technocrat in 2002, which seemed to confirm that any hope of a genuine shift of political power had now disappeared. Despite these disappointments, the Kutla parties stayed in the governing coalition, encouraging popular perceptions that the former critics of the government had been thoroughly co-opted and sought only to hold onto their plush offices and ministerial limousines for their own personal benefit. These perceptions appeared confirmed when declining support for the USFP at elections led to the Istiqlal taking the leading place in the government from 2007. Although the party's leader, Abbas Al Fassi, was appointed prime minister, his declaration that 'His Majesty's speeches will provide my [government's] programme' seemed to recognise that *alternance* had reached a definitive end.[41]

The full co-option of the Kutla parties through the *alternance* period brought to an end the party-political system that had operated since the early 1960s, in which the parties from the traditional nationalist movement set themselves in opposition to the political hegemony of the monarchy. The effective removal of the Kutla parties from political opposition did not, though, leave a complete void in party-political opposition. The *alternance* period had also witnessed the spectacular rise of a new political party that appeared to position itself as the new opposition force. The Party of Justice and Development (PJD) had been created by one of Morocco's main Islamist organisations, following a decision by King Hassan to allow its members to join and eventually take control of a small existing political party in 1996. Having secured affirmations of loyalty to the monarchy, Hassan hoped to use the party as a safety valve for growing Islamist sentiment in the kingdom and as a means of undercutting support for more radical and confrontational groupings (see Chapter 5). He also hoped to use it as a pressure point to persuade the Kutla parties to enter into government.[42] The party made steady and significant progress at successive parliamentary elections, moving from having a small presence in the 1997 parliament to being the third and then the second largest force following the 2002 and 2007 polls.

Many both inside and beyond Morocco saw the PJD as the new face of the Moroccan opposition and the effective inheritor of the Kutla's historic mantle. Some, thinking of the experiences of Algeria and Tunisia in the early 1990s, saw the party as a serious potential threat to the palace and indeed the whole Moroccan political system. Such fears were, however, overstated. Aware that the party's presence in the political system was on the sufferance of the palace, the PJD proceeded very cautiously, initially only putting up limited numbers of candidates in elections. The party avoided any criticism of the monarchy and was headed by a succession of leaders who were either known to be close to the palace or who were very deferential towards it (see Chapter 5).

The late 2000s also saw another attempt to establish a political party to represent a vehicle for the interests of the palace. Following the established pattern seen with the creation of the RNI in the 1970s and the UC in the 1980s, King Mohamed's closest adviser, Fouad Ali El Himma, contested the elections of 2007 and led a group of independents in the parliament that eventually transformed itself into a political party, the Party of Authenticity and Modernity (PAM) in 2008, which went on to dominate elections to local councils in 2009.

The New Multi-partyism

Morocco's apparent return to the pattern of party politics established before the advent of *alternance*, which Jean-Claude Santucci has described as 'authoritarian pluralism,' closely resembled those patterns that had consolidated in Tunisia and Algeria by the end of the 1990s.[43] These were characterised by the dominance of the formal political system by the true wielders of political power in each state: the presidency in Tunisia, the senior military leadership in Algeria and the monarchy in Morocco. All three had multi-party political systems, but these were closely controlled and manipulated to ensure that parties loyal to the leadership of the regime controlled often nominally elected institutions. Only a small and strictly circumscribed space was allowed to political parties that were critical or not fully supportive of the regime.

Regime Control and Legitimation

The reasserted dominance of the regimes in the region over the political parties prompts assessment of why political parties and a multi-party system continued to exist despite their increasing marginality. The main reason was that they provided a number of different functions for the regimes.

One of the primary functions was to supply the regimes in the region with a greater degree of perceived domestic and international legitimacy. By creating and maintaining a system in which many different political parties operated, the leaders in each country endeavoured to give the impression that their countries were effectively reproducing the multi-party democratic systems of Europe and North America. Thereby it was hoped that the ordinary populations of the three states would feel that they had a genuine say in and impact upon the political process, through support of and involvement in political parties, thus bolstering a popular sense of legitimacy which would lead to greater overall support for the wider regime and so aid stability and social peace. Legitimacy in the eyes of the outside world was similarly important to the Maghrebi states, as they were frequently heavily dependent on foreign trade and loans for which periodic consideration of the development towards internal democratisation was given by powers such as the European Union and the United States when examining trade and aid relations with the Maghreb (see Chapter 9).[44]

Allowing greater party-political proliferation also had the benefit of creating for the political power holders more avenues of contact with the ordinary population in each state. This contact was important for several reasons. Firstly, shifting patterns in popular membership and support for different political parties allowed the regime to monitor the views and reactions of the population and thus be aware of any particular and especially threatening trends. The regime could react to these trends either by adapting policies to placate them or by selectively repressing those threatening elements that had come to express themselves through individual political parties. In this way political parties brought potential dissent out into the open much more quickly than would be the case if no plurality of political parties were permitted. Once in the open such dissent could be observed, controlled and, if need be, repressed. Secondly, political parties' contacts with the ordinary population could be useful to the regime as a tool of popular mobilisation: the regime using the parties to rouse people behind a particular cause or in reaction to a perceived threat. The perfect example of this was King Hassan II's close involvement in all of Morocco's political parties in the hugely successful attempt to channel and raise support for the country's claim to Western Sahara.[45]

It was notable that the functions which Maghrebi parties provided for the state—mobilisation and a 'transmission belt' for popular opinion—were remarkably similar to those provided by the classic single-party regimes. In this way the multi-party political systems that developed in the Maghreb intentionally recreated some of the features of the single-party era in Tunisia and Algeria. As Emma Murphy has argued in the case of Tunisia, Ben Ali hoped 'to create a new state-multi-party alliance in which a number of parties acted in much the same way as the PSD had acted previously—as organically linked allies of the state' and that 'a multiplicity of parties can ultimately fulfil the function that previously fell to the single party; they provide legitimacy, credibility and the imagery of popular participation.'[46] Similarly, Hugh Roberts says that the move to party-political pluralism in Algeria merely replaced 'a monolithic façade with a fragmented one' for the ruling military-dominated leadership.[47]

The Perils of Control: Delegitimation, Disillusionment and Radicalisation

The control exercised by the regimes over the political parties became the predominant characteristic of the region's political parties and the party systems in which they operated in the opening decade of the twenty-first century. Regime control and interference took many forms, including establishing and manipulating legal frameworks governing parties; the sponsorship and encouragement of splits and divisions in, and competitors to, existing parties; controlling elections and their outcomes; and straightforward punishment and repression of critical or uncooperative parties.[48]

This control had a number of effects on the parties themselves, some of which damaged the very objectives of the regimes. Both official patronage and repression led to parties becoming largely focused on their relations with the regimes in order to preserve and sustain themselves. This meant that most parties in the region became increasingly detached from any meaningful popular base of support among the ordinary population. As Lahouari Addi commented of Algeria, 'the party system is integrated into the state and not society' with parties catering, in the view of Andrea Liverani, to 'various factions in the state, which retain control over their activities to seek legitimacy.'[49] In the case of Tunisia, one opposition member of parliament argued that 'the new parliamentary pluralism is in reality the direct result of the political will of the Head of State. It is not the product of political pluralism and ideology based in society and the public sphere.'[50] In both countries parties had little incentive to strengthen and broaden their popular bases and campaign widely for votes at elections, since they realised that any popular support they might attract had only a limited relationship with the formal representation they would receive in elected institutions. This representation was largely determined by the regime through the manipulation and close control exercised over elections.

A slightly different dynamic emerged in Morocco, where official interference in elections and parties declined noticeably from the 1990s. There the constitutional weakness of parliament encouraged parties and members of parliament to focus on the material rather than political benefits of involvement in official political processes. This only served to reinforce strong existing traditions of clientelism, particularly in rural areas which were over-represented in national elections. Significant salaries and the possibility of jobs in multi-party coalition governments resulted in most political parties becoming little more than large-scale interlinking patron-client networks. Success in elections in Morocco thus became much more closely linked to parties' efforts to mobilise these local patron-client networks than to their ability to mobilise broad sections of society around a coherent and distinct policy platform.[51] This largely explained how the Istiqlal party was able to emerge as the largest single party in the parliamentary elections of 2007 and also how spectacularly the new PAM was able to grow. Although particularly marked in Morocco, similar trends could be found in Tunisia and especially Algeria, where even participating in elections could attract substantial flows of resources from the state.[52] This served to increase the relevance of parties at the local level, but it also meant that they had little incentive to put forward comprehensive and coherent political platforms that appealed to the wider electorate at the national level.

Some opposition parties were able largely to shun clientelism and articulated a reasonably distinct platform, but the pressures exerted on them by the regime often inhibited their ability to propose a broad and coherent set of policies capable of attracting a wider support base. In some cases this meant that an opposition party's platform consisted predominantly of opposition to and criticism of the regime, rather than a set of policy proposals. Indeed the position adopted towards the holders of power in the state became not only the main ideological identifier of often otherwise ideologically diverse political parties, but also the principal dividing line between parties: those that supported the existing regime and those that opposed it.[53] In Algeria this meant that the biggest and most enduring opposition party, the FFS, largely devoted itself to contesting the legitimacy of the current regime.[54] In Tunisia the main legal opposition party, the PDP, focused on protecting and expanding its own severely limited political space, with the party viewing elections as 'a battle for political rights rather than for seats in the parliament.'[55] In other cases opposition parties felt intimidated by the regime into changing their platforms. This was the case with the PJD in Morocco, where fear that the regime might use terrorist attacks there by Islamist extremists in 2003 as an excuse to ban the party led it to curb the more distinctive aspects of the party's agenda at the 2007 elections.[56] Harassment and repression meant that opposition parties also felt obliged to look increasingly beyond the state's borders for support and protection from Western governments, foreign media and international organisations. This often succeeded in creating more space for the high-profile leaders of these parties, but it further contributed to their distance from the domestic populations.[57]

The consequence of the political parties' detachment from society was a growing alienation of the general public from political parties and elections. The Maghrebi public saw less and less reason to participate and vote in elections, which they saw as either rigged or without impact. Although official figures on the numbers of those voting were unreliable, both informal and formal indicators showed falling levels of participation in elections. In Morocco, the state where lower levels of official interference made election data most reliable, only 37 per cent of those registered to vote did so in the 2007 parliamentary elections; and of those who voted, one-fifth cast spoiled or invalid ballot papers, bringing the percentage who cast a valid vote down to barely 30 per cent.[58] Turnout in parliamentary elections in Algeria the same year officially fell to 35 per cent, with some informed observers claiming it was in reality nearer 25 per cent.[59] In Tunisia, the official rate of participation in the tightly controlled legislative and presidential elections of 2009 was recorded at 89 per cent, but other observers consider it to have been around 20 per cent.[60]

Evidence of declining rates of participation in elections caused some unease in the ruling circles of all three regimes and explained the particular hostility that was shown to groups in society advocating boycotts of elections. Both King Mohamed in 2007 and President Ben Ali in 2009 made speeches in the run-up to legislative elections warning and condemning those who questioned the relevance of the elections. The Moroccan king proclaimed failure to vote as a form of 'nihilism'; and the Tunisian president threatened legal action against anyone calling into question the validity of the election.[61] In Algeria, parties that advocated boycotting the 2009 presidential elections were vilified in the press and by other parties.[62] Turnout at elections was of particular importance to the regimes, since it demonstrated both domestically and internationally the public engagement and thus legitimacy of the political system.

Elections thus came to fulfil the same role that they played during the single-party eras in Tunisia and Algeria, where despite a lack of any real choice or influence the population was still called upon to express allegiance to the candidate chosen by the regime, meaning that elections became in essence about 'remobilization of allegiance to the state.'[63] This was a concern even in Morocco, where the regime had no formal party-political allies during the *alternance* period but still made huge efforts to persuade people to vote. When they failed massively to do so, the regime blamed the failings of the existing political parties to engage and mobilise the population sufficiently. Widespread resentment towards the corrupt and self-serving nature of many party politicians was certainly partly to blame for the failure of most Moroccans to vote, but the powerlessness and thus irrelevance of elected institutions also played a significant part.[64] As one critical PJD member of parliament argued: 'For political parties to mean something they have to be able to do something.'[65] The palace therefore still felt the need to establish the PAM to try to reinvigorate party politics and involve alienated sections of the population.[66] It remains to be seen whether the monarchy will seek once again to make active intervention in the electoral process, either to ensure the dominance of the PAM or to obscure the weak turnout in elections, and in this way remove the main distinction existing between the closely controlled and manipulated party and election systems that operated in Algeria, and especially Tunisia, and the much less constrained ones present in Morocco since the advent of *alternance*.

The failure of political parties to channel and articulate public grievances led other organisations to step into the breach. One consequence of the relative eclipse of political parties was the enhanced political role for local associations and elements of civil society. In Algeria, Liverani argues that associations became more important than political parties.[67] This has also been argued for Tunisia where, as Camau and Geisser observe, state monopolisation of the public sphere effectively rendered all independent forms of associational life political and where various associations, usually linked to civil and political rights, formed alliances with opposition parties on campaigns protesting against abuses of state power.[68] Particularly prominent, in all three countries, was the role played by human rights associations. In Algeria, associations such as the *Ligue Algérienne pour la Défense des Droits de l'Homme* (LADDH) were credited in some quarters with preparing the ground for multi-party politics from 1989. Thereafter the LADDH also associated itself with various attempts made by the opposition parties (most notably the Rome Accord of 1995) to resolve the political crisis in the country. In Tunisia, the National Council for Liberties in Tunisia (*Conseil National pour les Libertés en Tunisie*—CNLT) became a high-profile critic of the regime, and it and the Tunisian Human Rights League (*Ligue Tunisienne des Droits de l'Homme*—LTDH) became closely involved in mediating in incidents of social unrest as well as cooperating with opposition political parties. In Morocco, the *Association Marocaine des Droits de l'Homme* (AMDH) came to play a similar role, and arguably became the most trenchant critic of the Moroccan regime. Significantly, many of the AMDH's most prominent activists were members of outlawed leftist political parties in the 1970s and 1980s. This led to speculation that politically engaged Moroccans preferred to focus their activities in associations rather in the moribund political parties. One prominent member of the AMDH, however, argued that associations could never replace the proper role of political parties, since the latter were capable of putting together a full and comprehensive agenda for society in a way that more narrowly focused associations could not.[69]

Whilst human rights organisations became thorns in the side of the Maghreb regimes, the latter were far more concerned by the prospect of more populist and radical organisations moving in to fill the role usually played by political parties. This was exactly what occurred in Tunisia and Algeria in the 1980s with the rise of the Islamist movements, which clearly responded to a public desire for organised opposition to the regime. It is likely that the presence of legal opposition parties in Morocco during this same period, in the shape of the Istiqlal and the USFP, prevented the emergence of a significant Islamist movement in the form of those in Algeria and Tunisia. The decision to allow the Islamists of the PJD into the system in the 1990s arguably also helped undercut support for more radical and critical organisations. The PJD's ability to continue to perform this function was, however, damaged by the general decline in public faith and interest in the political parties and the representative institutions of which the PJD's was seen as an integral part.[70] This raised the possibility that these more radical and critical organisations, especially of an Islamist orientation, might see their support rise. Dris-Ait-Hamadouche and Zoubir observe that the compromising and co-opting of the country's Islamist political parties could have a similar effect in Algeria and reinforce popular memories of the FIS as having been the only political party to have mounted a genuine challenge to the regime.[71]

The Arab Spring of 2011

The dangers posed to the regimes by the failure of political parties to act as agents for the mobilisation of the public were dramatically demonstrated by the waves of popular protest that swept across the region in the opening months of 2011. The near complete absence of established political parties from the mass demonstrations in Tunisia and Morocco and the unrest in Algeria during that period was striking. It was a trend that Addi had already noted in 2006 in Algeria, commenting that 'The armed violence, the sporadic rioting in various local areas, the civil unrest in Kabylia since April 2001 and the general discontent that betrays a lack of civic spirit and a political apathy, indicates that the gap between the State and the population has not been filled by the political parties.'[72] Indeed, in the absence of effective political parties, cyclical riots had 'become one of the principal channels of social contestation' in Algeria.[73] Such indications of the population finding alternative means of expressing themselves were also to be found in Morocco and Tunisia, with both countries experiencing unusually serious outbreaks of social unrest in the periods either before or after their respective elections in 2007 and 2009.

The fact that the popular unrest of 2011 had the most profound repercussions for the state with the most controlled and stultified party-political system was clearly no coincidence. Within weeks of the popular revolution of 14 January, the party-political landscape in Tunisia was transformed beyond recognition. Not only was the formal political arena opened up to a plethora of new political parties that secured legalisation from the interim government, but, much more importantly, the hitherto all-powerful RCD was broken up and banned. This third opening up of the Tunisian political system promised to be the most far-reaching yet after the false dawns of the liberalisations of 1981 and 1988. This was mainly because the dominant political party was now explicitly excluded from the political arena, but also because it was an opening fully forced from below rather than conceded from above, which also marked it out from the 'democratic' opening in Algeria in 1989.

In Morocco, the succession of mass demonstrations in favour of political reform that began on 20 February 2011 featured members of political parties and organisations, but notably ones that were on the fringes or formally outside the official political processes. These notably included the leftist *Parti Socialiste Unifié* (PSU), which had just a handful of elected deputies in the national legislature, and the Islamist *Al-Adl wal Ihsan* (Justice and Spirituality) movement and marxist *Annahj Addimocrati* (Democratic Way) party, which were not officially recognised and formally boycotted elections.[74] The overwhelmingly youthful character of most of the demonstrations in Morocco illustrated the movement's ability to mobilise a section of the population that had been massively absent from the voting booths at the previous legislative elections. It was a trend also present in Tunisia, where the participation of large numbers of young Tunisians in the movement that brought down Ben Ali led to the creation of significant numbers of new political parties specifically appealing to the youth of the country.[75]

The destructive protests that large parts of urban Algeria experienced in the opening week of January 2011 involved none of Algeria's political parties, a reflection largely of the protests' much more anarchic and less politically orientated nature. Political parties were, however, heavily involved in weekly demonstrations that began to be organised in Algiers from 12 February in explicit response to the events in Tunisia. The limited public support these demonstrations were able to attract, however, in comparison to Tunisia, Morocco and indeed most of the rest of the Arab world in this period, was in part a result of this involvement and also of the specific political orientation of the parties involved. The leading role played by the *Rassemblement pour la Culture et la Démocratie* (RCD) and the former communists of the *Mouvement Démocratique et Social* (MDS) clearly alienated many Algerians, particularly the young, through their previously close links with the regime and their espousal of a militantly secularist agenda. Both, for example, had openly applauded and supported the abandonment of the electoral process in 1992. The absence of the kind of broad-based youthful protest movement that emerged in most Arab states in the early months of 2011 was therefore quite marked in Algeria. It was perhaps explained by a popular wariness of and weariness with the violent political resistance and resultant bloodshed that had characterised the 1990s, and also by the more localised and more socio-economically driven outbreaks of unrest that had become a regular feature of provincial Algeria over the previous few years and of which the unrest of the opening week of the year had possibly been an example writ large. In this way, the dramatic events of the opening months of 2011 seemed set for a total remake of the Tunisian political system, and with it its party-political constellation. They threatened to reform that of Morocco, as King Mohamed VI was prompted to revise the kingdom's constitution in July 2011 to bring about a modest strengthening of the role of parliament and that of the political parties within it. They appeared to have little effect on the sclerotic and divided party-political scene in Algeria. The holding of elections in Tunisia in October 2011 and then Morocco the following month promised to reveal the impact of the Arab Spring on the two states. The emergence of the Islamists, in the shape of An-Nahda in Tunisia and the PJD in Morocco, as the dominant force in both elections, appeared to herald a new phase in the role of political parties in both countries. It was rapidly clear, however, that the Moroccan Monarchy would not allow the PJD anything approaching the level of influence that An-Nahda came to exercise in the wake of its superficially comparable electoral victory and that the party ran the risk of suffering the same frustrated fate as the USFP had during the alternance period.

5

ISLAMIST MOVEMENTS

Of all the developments that have impacted on the politics of the Maghreb states in the post-independence era, none has equalled that of Islamism. Although a social movement and political force that arose first in other parts of the Arab and Muslim worlds and then spread to the Maghreb, the effect it had there was arguably greater than in nearly every other Arab state. Islamist movements became key elements of the political landscape in Algeria, Tunisia and Morocco from the 1980s, and their presence is crucial to understanding many of the political shifts and developments in the region during this period. They came to represent the main opposition force in all three countries, eclipsing all others, and constituted the most significant political challenge the three regimes had faced since independence. In contrast to the military, the nature of the challenge posed by Islamism was principally through the movement's ability to mobilise vast numbers of the ordinary population in each state.

In Tunisia in the 1980s and early 1990s the Islamic Tendency Movement and its successor group, An-Nahda, became the main opposition force, clearly contributing to the fall of Habib Bourguiba and his replacement by Zine al-Abdine Ben Ali. In Algeria in the early 1990s the Islamic Salvation Front, or FIS, not only similarly became the largest opposition force in the country but dominated elections at the local and national level before being banned following the palace coup led by the military in 1992. This move then opened the way for a decade-long period of civil strife, in which armed Islamist groups played a major role. In Morocco in the 2000s the largest opposition force in the national parliament became an Islamist party, the Party of Justice and Development (PJD), which attracted the largest number of votes in the legislative elections of 2007. An even larger unlicensed Islamist organisation operated outside the formal political sphere in the kingdom. In national elections in both Tunisia and Morocco in 2011, Islamist parties emerged as the clear victors.

As shown in Chapter 1, the religion of Islam had a long-established political role in the Maghreb, providing the basis for political authority and legitimacy dating back to the first arrival of it there in the seventh century. In the modern period, all three states had experienced the influence of the *salafiyyah* movement at the turn of the nineteenth and twentieth centuries, with the key Egyptian *salafi* thinker, Mohamed Abdu, visiting both Algeria and Tunisia during this time. In political terms the ideas of Abdu and the other *salafi* thinkers had greatest impact in Algeria and Morocco, where they were instrumental in establishing respectively the Association of Algerian Ulema and the religious wing of what became the Istiqlal party (see Chapter 1). In this way *salafi* ideas, with their emphasis on a return to the teachings of Islam as a means of combating the European colonial incursions, provided a vital ideological and organisational strand to the anti-colonial movement in both countries.

All three states in the region witnessed the growth of Islamist movements within their borders in the 1970s. The governments initially tolerated and even encouraged these movements as a counterweight to the radical left—particularly on the university campuses. The leadership of these Islamist movements, distinguished by their relatively high levels of education, were initially inspired and motivated by unhappiness with what they perceived as the secular orientation and policies pursued by the governments in all three states. As the movements grew in the 1970s and 1980s, they drew support primarily from the education sector: from teachers and professors as well as students. Although all three states, particularly Algeria and Tunisia, developed in time large dominant movements, all also saw a range of different organisations and groups emerge within the wider Islamist movement. These ranged from apolitical preachers, through reformist associations, through to radical and even revolutionary elements. Sections of the movements in all three states attempted to form political parties at various points to participate in formal political processes. Equally, groups have emerged in all three states that have been prepared to use violence to achieve their ends. The governments in all three states have similarly responded to the challenge these movements have represented with varying mixtures of compromise and repression. All have often sought to impose close control over the religious sphere and also paint themselves and the wider regime in more 'Islamic' colours to undermine the Islamists' appeal.

Islam and the State

To understand the context in which Islamism began to emerge in the Maghreb states, it is important in turn to understand the role that Islam, as a religion, was assigned by the state in the aftermath of the achievement of independence. Across the region there was an attempt by the state to co-opt, control and use religion for official purposes.

Islam had been established as the official religion of state in all three countries at independence. However, this represented more of an affirmation of independent national identity than anything else. The new rulers of Algeria, Tunisia and Morocco were very aware of the unifying and mobilising power of Islam and Islamic symbolism that had been used so effectively against the colonial authorities—even by fairly secular figures such as Bourguiba in Tunisia and Ferhat Abbas in Algeria (see Chapter 1). Thus, following independence, Islam was used by the governments to justify and legitimise policies to their populations. At the same time, and despite this official emphasis on religion, significant areas of life came to be 'secularised' during this same period, with the state taking control over issues and tasks that had traditionally been the preserve of independent religious institutions. Control over education, for example, came fully under the ambit of the government and religious personnel, buildings and property were formally absorbed into the state in the years that followed independence. In doing this the governments were motivated by a mixture of intentions, including a desire to harness the legitimacy and resources of religion to the service and objectives of the state and a wish to restrict independence and criticism in the post-independence period. In all three states the leaders of the religious establishment—the *ulema*—were absorbed into the state apparatus, usually as employees and functionaries of newly created ministries of religious affairs, which provided them with an income in return for their loss of independence. These state-controlled *ulema* were then often called upon to issue fatwas to justify government policy. However, such a role was as frequently filled by the political leaders themselves, who increasingly used their own authority to interpret and rule on religious texts as and when it suited them.

In Tunisia this process was most profound, partly because of Bourguiba's belief in bringing all aspects of society under his control, and partly as a result of the antipathy the Tunisian leader felt towards the religious establishment. This antipathy was grounded not just in the clear influence that French secularism had had on him during his studies in Paris; but, more importantly, derived from the fact that the majority of the country's *ulema* had sided with Salah Ben Youssef in the post-independence power struggles.[1] As well as taking control of the mosques and their personnel, Bourguiba introduced a secular family code (see Chapter 2), integrated the sharia courts into the secular legal system, and merged the famous mosque-university of Zaytouna into Tunis University. Significantly, however, and despite his instincts, Bourguiba did not attempt to introduce a formally secularised system in the way that Mustapha Kemal Ataturk had done in Turkey. Aware of both the mobilising functions of Islam and the parallel difficulties of obtaining public acceptance for such a move, Bourguiba continued to make public reference to Islam—using a fatwa to establish the new republic and making a show of attending public prayers every Friday. Moreover, Bourguiba was reminded of the limits to his de facto secularising policies when he famously failed to incite the population to abandon the Ramadan fast in the interests of economic productivity during the early years of his rule, notably through drinking a glass of orange juice following a public rally during the fast in 1964.

A similar pattern was followed in both Algeria and Morocco. In Algeria, Ben Bella and Boumedienne were aided by the fact that colonial rule had restricted and in some cases swept away the role played by the sharia and the traditional *ulema*. Abdelhamid Ben Badis' Association of Ulema had formally thrown in its lot with the FLN during the independence struggle, and after independence Ben Bella officially dissolved the Association and gave most of its members jobs in the education and religious affairs ministries. In Morocco, an important and different dimension was added through the religious role and character of the monarchy—notably the sharifian quality of the king as a descendant of the Prophet Mohamed. In the post-independence period, the Moroccan monarchy moved to establish a full institutional monopoly over the religious sphere. Not only were the *ulema* absorbed into government ministries, as in Tunisia and Algeria, but other potential challengers to this monopoly, such as the sufi orders and the *salafiyya* reformers, were also marginalised. The former were tainted with their association and collaboration with the French during the colonial period, whilst the latter's identification with the Istiqlal party ensured their eclipse when the Istiqlal lost out in the post-independence power struggles. As a result the monarchy was able to place itself at the top of the religious hierarchy, both legally as well as symbolically: the king taking on interpretative powers with regard to religious law. Moreover, as has been seen (see Chapter 2), the monarchy began to employ and surround itself with greater religious symbolism.

The full and effective control that the state was able to establish over the religious sphere in all three states came to be challenged in the late 1970s by the rise of the new phenomenon of the Islamists, who claimed that they, rather than the state, embodied and advocated true Islam. The rise of the Islamists across the region has been directly attributed to the takeover of the religious sphere by the state authorities. Firstly, the neutralisation and co-option of the official *ulema* deprived them of their traditional role as arbiters between the state authorities and the people. This created a vacuum between state and society into which the Islamists moved.[2] Secondly, the secularising reforms enacted led to the state moving into realms such as family and religious law in a way that it had not done before and which produced unease in significant parts of society. Finally, these factors combined with wider economic and social problems that served to reinforce the essentially religious critique articulated by the Islamists.

Origins

Tunisia

The origins of the Islamist movements of all three states can be found in the 1960s, but it was in Tunisia that the movement emerged earliest and strongest. The founders of what was to become the main Islamist movement in the country first met each other in the mid 1960s in discussion groups that began to meet in the Zaytouna mosque in Tunis. These figures 'all shared a profound alienation to post-independence Tunisian society,' which they felt had become overly secularised and Westernised through the sweeping reforms of the Bourguiba regime.[3] The profound nature of these reforms undoubtedly explains why it was in Tunisia, rather than Morocco or Algeria, where Islamism first began to develop strongly. As one of the founding figures was later to explain:

I remember we used to feel like strangers in our own country. We had been educated as Arabs and Muslims, while we could see the country being totally moulded in the French cultural identity.[4]

Members of these discussion groups began to organise themselves and tour mosques and secondary schools, giving talks on religious themes in an effort to counter what they saw as the increasingly secular drift of society. Calling themselves the *Jamaa Islamiyyyah* (Islamic Group) they accepted an invitation in 1969 to join an officially sponsored organisation entitled the Society for the Preservation of the Quran. This organisation had been set up by the authorities in the aftermath of the end of Ahmed Ben Salah's socialist period (see Chapters 2 and 7) and aimed to combat remaining leftist sentiment, particularly on the country's university campuses. The Islamic Group not only took advantage of the institutional and structural cover the society gave them, but it also enabled them to exploit the genuine ideological vacuum that had been left by the collapse of Ben Salah's socialist experiment.[5]

By 1973 the authorities had become suspicious of the growth and activities of the Islamic Group and expelled them from the society. The members, nevertheless, continued their work, recruiting supporters particularly in the schools and universities. However, the objectives and orientation of the Islamic Group began to change as it began to take on board some of the wider issues and developments occurring in Tunisia in the 1970s: particularly the declining socio-economic conditions in the country and the widespread dissent and unrest it produced in society. These developments—most notably the riots of 1978—had the effect of politicising the hitherto more narrowly religious and apolitical nature and vocation of the Islamic Group, which had largely followed the model established by the Muslim Brotherhood in Egypt but was increasingly influenced by the ideas and approaches of the leftist student organisations on the campuses.[6] Not only did the leadership of the Islamic Group become more convinced of the religious imperative of social justice, but it also realised that the regime's suppression of the main sources of political dissent—the student and trades unions—left a political vacuum that they could fill. Although some leading religious and intellectual figures split from the group because they were unhappy with it's increasingly political orientation, the bulk of the leadership began to reorganise the group on a more political footing, a process that involved establishing links with other political forces, including the trade union movement. The process culminated in a special conference in 1979 that restructured the movement and elected Rachid Ghannouchi as its 'Emir.'[7]

Algeria

In Algeria, the first identifiably Islamic group that began to emerge after independence was the *Al Qiyam* (Values) association which emerged to protest primarily at the leftist drift of the government of Ahmed Ben Bella. Headed by several former members of the now dissolved Association of Algerian Ulema, the new association attracted significant support. However, the overthrow of Ben Bella by Boumedienne and the army in 1965 removed much of the *raison d'être* of *Al Qiyam*. Moreover, Boumedienne sought to eradicate any potential threat to his regime from the group by an adroit mixture of repression and co-option which saw the organisation banned in 1966, with the government absorbing some of its personnel, and more importantly its rhetoric, by painting the regime in more Islamic colours.[8]

The effectiveness of Boumedienne's policy meant that by the early 1970s there was virtually no identifiable manifestation of what could be described as an Islamist movement. However, as the 1970s progressed, the first shoots of one began to show. As in Tunisia, it was in the universities that the first such groups began to emerge. As in Tunisia, again, the authorities tolerated and even encouraged these groups as ideological and organisational counterweights to the more threatening radical left. A number of these groups, both on and off the campuses, began to build and create their own independent mosques outside the ambit of state control and regulation that had been established after independence.[9] These small groups received a further boost through the effects of the regime's policy of Arabisation that began to be felt by the 1970s. The effect was twofold. Firstly, the lack of qualified Arabic teachers in Algeria led to the recruitment of such teachers from abroad, many of whom came from Islamist circles and backgrounds. Secondly, the slower pace of Arabisation in the Algerian administration compared to the education system led to the creation of a growing number of Arabised school and university graduates who were unable to find jobs in the still largely Francophone administration. Despite these supportive developments, no single organisational trend developed, as it had in Tunisia, to bring together the various groups that began to emerge on the university campuses and through the independent mosque associations. Thus, in probable reflection of Algeria's far greater size and diversity, its nascent Islamist movement was a rather atomised and fragmented affair, both geographically and even doctrinally, as different groups in different parts of the country followed specific local leaders and varying external influences.[10]

The death of Boumedienne in 1978 and his replacement by Chadli Benjedid signalled a slight lessening of the firm grip the authorities exercised over political and social life. In parallel with other groups in the country (most notably the Berberists and the women's movement) the country's Islamists began to adopt a much higher and vocal profile, particularly at the universities.

Morocco

The first emergence of identifiably Islamist trends in Morocco did not deviate significantly from the pattern of both Algeria and Tunisia, but was closer to the latter. As in Tunisia, small groups began to emerge during the course of the 1960s which eventually formed themselves into a single association—*Shabiba Islamiyya al-Maghribiyya* (Moroccan Islamic Youth)—in Casablanca. Once again the main recruiting milieu was education, with teachers and students becoming the backbone of the group. The main leading figure to emerge from the group was Abdelkrim Mouti, a schools inspector and former member of the UNFP who had become disillusioned with the failure of the political parties to arrest the decline in social and economic conditions inside the kingdom and had come to believe that the answers to Morocco's problems lay in religion. As in Tunisia, the authorities sought to use the group to combat leftist influences in the schools and universities and formally legalised the group as an association in 1972.[11]

Official sponsorship and tolerance of the group came to an end when the authorities became suspicious of its strength and objectives. The rupture with the regime, though, was much more dramatic than in Tunisia. The association was banned and broken up following the assassination of a senior member of the USFP in 1975, which was officially blamed on members of the group. Islamic Youth strenuously denied being behind the killing, which many suggested had been the work of the authorities with the aim of striking a blow at both the USFP and Islamic Youth—a suspicion shared by many in the USFP. Official antipathy towards the USFP and its forerunners was well-established at this time, but the reasons for the sudden falling from grace of Islamic Youth were less clear. Emad Shahin suggests that the group made the 'fatal mistake' of failing to declare its support for the campaign to regain the Western Sahara, which by 1975 (the year of the assassination) had become the centrepiece of the monarchy's campaign to re-establish control over the fractured domestic political landscape (see Chapters 3 and 8).[12]

Islamic Youth was not the only identifiably Islamist force to emerge in Morocco during this period. Another trend came from a very different ideological and organisational direction that had little in common with either Algeria or Tunisia. It developed from the hitherto resolutely apolitical milieu of sufism and also, in keeping with the orientation of the sufi *zaouia*, from the ideas and activism of a single individual. Abdeslam Yassine was a schools inspector from Marrakech. In 1965, after apparently experiencing a personal spiritual crisis, he joined the Boutchichiyya sufi order where he remained for six years before breaking with it in 1971 because of its refusal to engage with political issues.[13] After leaving the order, Yassine began to write a series of tracts and books on what he perceived to be the problems of Morocco and how Islam should be employed to deal with them. In 1973 he took the audacious step of addressing one of these tracts to King Hassan, which he publicly sent to the king and distributed widely. In addition to the direct and familiar language Yassine used to address the king, the catalogue of criticisms of the monarchy he incorporated in the 114-page letter—criticising his wealth, closeness to the West and even questioning his Islamic faith—caused shock and outrage in the royal palace. The religious nature of the criticism, however, saved Yassine from what even he had expected was almost certain execution, earning him instead a sentence in a secure mental hospital—an indication of the authorities' wish to portray the letter as the act of a madman devoid of any political or religious significance.[14]

Entering the Political Field

In spite of the increasingly hostile attention they attracted from the state authorities, Islamist movements in all three countries continued

163

to grow into the 1980s, taking advantage of the swelling popular discontent with the regimes that began to develop, especially amongst the young. When the governments in Tunisia and Algeria and, more latterly, Morocco sought to offset this discontent by liberalising their political systems in the 1980s and 1990s, the countries' main Islamist movements sought to enter the formal legal political field.

Tunisia: the MTI and An-Nahda

The much more organised and less fragmented nature of the Islamist movement in Tunisia meant that it was the first to take steps to enter formal politics. Having reorganised itself in 1979 to prepare itself for a more political role, a debate had taken place within the organisation as to the wisdom of abandoning its still predominantly clandestine activity and structure and assuming a more public identity. Prompted by the belief of its leader, Rachid Ghannouchi, that suddenly coming into the open would wrong-foot the authorities' plans to clampdown on the movement, the Islamic Group organised a press conference in June 1981 where its leaders announced their intention to become a formal political organisation.[15] Renaming itself the Islamic Tendency Movement (better known by its French acronym, MTI), the group used the conference to release a communiqué setting out the new organisation's agenda, which focused on restoring Tunisia's Islamic identity.

The creation of the MTI in such a formal and public fashion was also indicative of the original Islamic Group's apparent preference for legality and involvement in society. The MTI's founding communiqué formally rejected the use of violence and called for the establishment of a multi-party system in the country. In contrast to the movements in both Algeria and Morocco, and despite having long had a clandestine existence, no acts of violence had been attributed to the organisation. It had also already attempted to establish links with other groups, notably the UGTT and opposition parties such as Ahmed Ben Salah's MUP, with which it shared a press conference.[16]

The official reaction to the MTI's creation was swift. Within a matter of weeks the leadership of the new party was arrested, charged with forming an illegal organisation, publishing false news and defaming the president and was imprisoned.[17] In spite of the fact that 1981 had seen the first tentative steps towards multi-partyism with the legalisation of a party other than the PSD, Bourguiba had no intention of genuinely opening up the political system and certainly not to a group so well-organised and opposed to his secularising ideas as the MTI. He and others in the regime had been particularly alarmed by the growth in support for the movement on the country's university campuses, where they had supplanted the once dominant political left.[18]

The MTI leaders were released from prison in August 1984, and debated what should be the next step for the movement. Ghannouchi was aware that the Tunisian regime was progressively sliding into crisis and decay with Bourguiba's advancing age and senility and a parallel refusal to cede power. He believed that the situation represented a potentially historic opportunity for the MTI. The early 1980s had seen the movement continue to expand its agenda from the more narrowly religious to one encompassing issues of human rights, social justice and calls for democratisation. As a result, the movement worked hard to reorganise and build and strengthen its support and organisation, which had remained remarkably intact during the imprisonment of the leadership. The MTI also strengthened links with the UGTT and other opposition parties.[19]

The regime soon hardened its line against the movement and in March 1987, Ghannouchi was arrested for preaching in a mosque without a license. Shortly afterwards, most of the rest of the MTI's leadership was also arrested. More arrests followed in June when the government press published photographs of what were alleged to be weapons caches found near Tunis. Worse still for the movement was the involvement of Islamists in a series of bomb attacks that occurred in hotels in Sousse and Monastir in August.[20] Although the government never directly alleged MTI involvement in the August bombings, it charged the MTI's leaders with forming an illegal organisation, plotting acts with a foreign state (Iran) and attempting to overthrow the government.[21] The authorities put both the MTI leaders and those individuals charged with the August bombings on trial at the same time in a clear attempt to conflate the two groups in the public and international eye.

When the State Security Court finally delivered the verdicts on both groups of defendants in late September, seven death sentences were handed down including three *in absentia* to MTI members. Those condemned to death notably did not include the senior leaders of the MTI; Ghannouchi received life imprisonment, principally because the court failed to link the MTI leadership to responsibility for violence, but also because Ghannouchi made a passionate denunciation of violence during the trial. The verdicts and sentences of the court received a furious reaction in the presidential palace. Increasingly obsessed with the MTI, which Bourguiba perceived to be an ideological nemesis threatening to roll back all his reforms, he ordered not only a retrial but stipulated that the accused be found guilty and executed in the hope of fulfilling his promise that 'The eradication of the Islamicist poison will be the last service I'll render Tunisia.'[22] As has been seen (see Chapter 3), this decision prompted a chain of events resulting in the eventual and final downfall of Bourguiba through the constitutional removal of the president by his prime minister Zine al-Abdine Ben Ali on 7 November, just two days before the scheduled retrial of the MTI leaders.[23]

Ben Ali's constitutional coup was received positively by the MTI leadership, who believed that the prime minister had not only acted to avoid a showdown with the movement but also wished to development a less confrontational relationship with it. These hopes were borne out by Ben Ali's freeing of the several thousand MTI activists who had been imprisoned in the run-up to the coup and his release of Ghannouchi and the movement's leaders in May 1988. As further evidence of the new president's goodwill, he granted a meeting with Ghannouchi, included an MTI representative in the National Pact concluded with opposition parties in November 1988, appointed another senior MTI figure to a new Higher Islamic Council, and repealed several of the more symbolic secularising reforms of Bourguiba.[24]

Encouraged by the new *démarche*, the MTI reiterated its commitment to constitutional processes and non-violence and dropped its demands for the reversal of certain of Bouguiba's secularising reforms.[25] It also began to reorganise itself and profit from its newfound freedom, establishing a newspaper. The next challenge presented to the movement was the issue of participation in multi-party elections to the National Assembly scheduled for April 1989. Opinions in the movement were divided as to whether it should act with caution or take advantage of a potentially promising political opportunity. Those advocating a bolder approach—specifically seeking to put up a vigorous contest and possibly even win the election—triumphed over those believing that a limited and more symbolic participation would be better advised.[26] Although Ghannouchi led the advocates of a bolder approach, he tempered his ambitions for the movement with concessions to the regime. He stated that the most the MTI wished to gain from the election was ten seats in the Assembly and he toned down its references to Islam, notably in its title through renaming itself the *An-Nahda* (Renaissance) party in early 1989 in its application to be recognised as a formal political party.[27] The new party did not receive official recognition by the time of the legislative elections, but decided to put up candidates as independents in nearly all the electoral districts. References to Islam in its election literature and speeches were reduced but, pushed by an increasingly energised and ambitious rank and file, the movement campaigned hard across the country.

The first signs of official displeasure with the robustness of An-Nahda's campaign came during the campaign itself, with hostile coverage of the party in the government-controlled media. A more overt indication came with the announcement of the results of the election, which gave every seat to Ben Ali's RCD and not a single one to any An-Nahda member. An-Nahda cried foul, claiming then and subsequently to have even won a majority of the votes.[28] Although this was unlikely, given the strength of the RCD's organisation and the popularity that Ben Ali enjoyed for having ensured a peaceful succession to Bourguiba, it is suggested that An-Nahda probably attracted at least 30 per cent of the popular vote—twice what it was officially accorded.[29] Nevertheless, even the 15 per cent officially recorded by independent candidates (in practice all An-Nahda members) was a significant achievement, particularly when the other opposition parties contesting the elections collectively scored less than 5 per cent. This clearly positioned An-Nahda as the main opposition force in the country. Moreover, its attitude towards the election and its subsequent protests against the results clearly led Ben Ali to believe that the movement wished to issue a direct challenge to his newly constituted authority. It was from this point that relations between the regime and An-Nahda began to decline. In May 1989 Ghannouchi left Tunisia for voluntary exile in Algeria and later Britain, in ostensible protest against what he described as electoral fraud. At the beginning of June An-Nahda's application for recognition as a political party was officially rejected on the grounds that many of its leaders had served prison terms and many were still technically under sentence.[30] More telling, though, was Ben Ali's statement at the end of July in which he said, 'We say to those who mix religion and politics that there is no way of allowing them to form a political party.'[31] In the view of Mohamed Elhachmi Hamdi, this rejection was in response to An-Nahda's breaking the 'unspoken understanding ...that in return for official recognition al-Nahda would avoid any form of challenge for political power.'[32]

For its part, An-Nahda felt that the regime had reneged on its unspoken pledge to open up the political system and allow in their party. A tense but calm period followed, but relations between the regime and the movement began to deteriorate rapidly over the summer of 1990 as a series of events tested them. The crushing victories of the Islamist FIS in local elections in neighbouring Algeria in June alarmed the regime; still worse, a few weeks later An-Nahda members demonstrated against the arrival of US troops in Saudi Arabia following Iraq's invasion of Kuwait in August. In the view of some, this persuaded the Tunisian regime to move decisively against An-Nahda.[33]

The following months saw a gradual tightening against the movement, with restrictions on the party's activities, the closure of its newspaper and eventually the arrest of large numbers of its activists and supporters. In justification the regime cited the increasingly hostile rhetoric directed towards it by Rachid Ghannouchi in exile abroad. Much more seriously, the regime pointed to the growing evidence of the violent and insurrectionist nature and ambitions of the movement. A number of violent incidents involving members of An-Nahda were reported by the authorities, culminating in the death of a security guard at an RCD office at Bab Souika in Tunis in February 1991. In May the interior minister announced that a plot to overthrow the regime had been discovered, prompting sweeping arrests of An-Nahda activists over the months that followed, netting an estimated 8,000 party supporters by the following March.[34]

Algeria: The Emergence of the FIS

The entrance of Algeria's Islamists into formal politics occurred at the end of the 1980s as a result of the political reforms introduced in the aftermath of the riots of October 1988. The new constitution of 1989 permitted for the first time the formation of political parties other than the FLN and their participation in multi-party elections. As in Tunisia, Algeria's Islamists were divided as to how they should respond to these developments. Since they came from geographically and ideologically disparate organisations (unlike Tunisia's Islamists), no single decision was reached over the issue of participation in the new political opening. As a result, a number of Algerian Islamist figures decided to proceed and create a new political party, whilst others declined to participate. Thus in March 1989 the Islamic Salvation Front was formally launched.[35]

The new party had to wait to receive official recognition, but, in contrast to An-Nahda in Tunisia, this was formally accorded in September 1989. Having achieved recognition, the party moved quickly to organise and mobilise support for itself. Despite not persuading all of the country's leading Islamists to join the party, the FIS rapidly succeeded in attracting the vast majority of Islamist activists. An estimated 10,000 supporters attended the party's formal launch in March 1989, and by the close of the year the party was attracting crowds of over 100,000 to its rallies. By the spring of 1990 that figure had grown to an estimated 500,000.[36] The startling scale and speed of the new party's growth was attributable to several factors. Using a large and highly motivated core of activists, the party began to organise and recruit supporters across the country. Making use of the network of several thousand mosques that had come to be controlled by Islamists since the late 1970s, the party also incorporated into its activities the expanding network of medical clinics and social services that Islamists had established in some of the country's poorest areas during the 1980s.[37] In this way the urban poor, whose numbers had grown substantially with the economic crisis of the 1980s, became a bedrock of support for the FIS. Indeed the perceived failures of the regime became probably the most important factor in the spectacular growth of support for the party. Popular disillusionment with the regime had grown throughout the 1980s, boosted by the rapid fall in living standards that occurred after the collapse in the international price of oil in the middle of the decade (see Chapter 7). The explosion of unrest in October 1988 was evidence of this, and the severity of the reaction of the regime in how they quelled it further alienated large sections of the population. The FIS adroitly moved to exploit this disaffection by posing as the most effective vehicle for expressing disillusionment and alienation, making much of the evident corruption of the regime to stoke popular anger still further. It was aided in this by the vague and strongly populist agenda it adopted as a party, notably failing to spell out a policy platform as clearly as the MTI had done in Tunisia; a result not just of the party's desire to attract as broad a support base as possible, but also of the party's speedy creation and heterodox and heterogeneous composition.

Such was the success of this approach that the party rapidly moved from being a vehicle of protest to a political juggernaut, presenting itself as a political alternative to the regime itself. This was made evident in the first set of multi-party elections held in June 1990 for the country's regional and communal assemblies. In both sets of polls the FIS took over half of the votes cast—nearly double that of its nearest competitor, the FLN. As in the elections in Tunisia in 1989, no other single party featured in any meaningful way. This allowed the FIS to present itself as the sole challenger to the discredited and unpopular regime electorally embodied in the FLN, and in this way differed from An-Nahda in Tunisia whose leadership had always been at pains to deny any ambition simply to supplant the regime and so had worked with other parties from its earliest days.

The success of the FIS awoke the Algerian regime to the very real challenge that the party was posing. Up until 1990 the rise of the party had been viewed through the lens of elite infighting and clan warfare that had characterised Algerian politics since the death of Boumedienne. The original decision to legalise the FIS, which had surprised many, was itself partly a product of the internal politics of the regime. Legalisation of the party served the purpose of bringing the Islamists into the open, in order to observe and control them and prevent further radicalisation, but the Islamists also served as a potential weapon in the internal power struggles of the regime. As explained in Chapter 4, President Chadli Benjedid had seen the adoption of multi-party politics as a means of distracting and wrong-footing his enemies in the regime who had strengthened their presence in the FLN. He saw the legalisation of an Islamist political party as a means of depriving the former single party of victory in the multi-party elections he was planning, and even hoped that with no one party dominant he, as president, could dominate a future National Assembly. Once legalised, Chadli and his allies notably refrained from criticising the party in the hope of strengthening it, a favour the party appeared to return by shunning direct criticism of the president and vocally supporting his economic reforms, leading to strong suspicions that a mutually beneficial deal had been struck between the FIS and the presidency.[38]

The stunning victories the FIS achieved in the local and regional elections of 1990, which saw them take control of 55 per cent of the communal councils in the country and nearly 80 per cent of the regional (*wilaya*) councils, prompted the regime to begin to take measures to head off a similar victory in the elections to the National Assembly. New Islamist parties were legalised, headed by figures who had declined to join the FIS, opening up the possibility of splintering the Islamist vote. New electoral laws were introduced that sought to reduce the FIS's chance of securing a majority in elections, chiefly by gerrymandering electoral districts to under-represent the overwhelmingly urban strongholds of the FIS. Street protests against the new election laws organised by the FIS allowed the authorities to crackdown on the party and arrest and imprison most of the party's senior figures in June 1991.

Ultimately, the measures aimed at preventing the FIS from dominating the elections to the National Assembly proved unsuccessful. The second tier of leaders who took control of the party following the arrest of the original leadership decided to contest the elections, despite the arrest of their leaders and an unfavourable electoral law. Fears that the party might be marginalised if it boycotted the elections and its votes taken by the smaller Islamist parties strengthened the argument within the FIS for participation made by the party's new group of leaders, who represented a younger, more educated and more pragmatic approach. In the first round of voting held on 26 December 1991, the FIS took 47 per cent of the vote and received a majority of the votes in 44 per cent (188) of the (430) electoral districts. This left it just short of achieving an overall majority in the Assembly. FIS candidates had, however, finished top in a further 143 districts without achieving a majority. This meant that when the second ballot took place in the remaining 199 districts that had not seen one candidate achieve a majority of the votes, the FIS would be virtually assured of achieving a substantial majority of the seats in the National Assembly.[39] This prospect ensured that the second round of voting, scheduled for two weeks after the first, never occurred as elements of the regime dominated by senior figures in the military (see Chapter 3) intervened to cancel the second round and annul the results of the first. Within weeks the FIS was formally repressed and banned by the regime on the grounds that it had 'pursued through subversive means objectives that put at peril public order and the institutions of the state.'[40]

Repression and Resistance: The Contrasting Experiences of Algeria and Tunisia

By the middle of 1992, the authorities in both Tunisia and Algeria had succeeded in banning and repressing their countries' main Islamist movements, which a matter of months earlier had appeared to present serious challenges to the rule and legitimacy of the existing regimes. Thereafter the experiences of the two states sharply diverged. In Tunisia, the Ben Ali regime rooted out what little remained of An-Nahda, making Tunisia one of the only states in the Arab world in which Islamism had no real institutional or organisational presence. By contrast, the new High Council of State in Algeria faced a mounting tide of unrest and violence against it led by armed Islamists. By the middle of the decade this had claimed tens of thousands of lives and appeared to threaten the very survival of the regime.

Algeria's 'Black Decade'

The descent into violence in Algeria was not immediate but grew gradually. The leadership of the FIS made great efforts to avoid any physical confrontations between its supporters and the authorities in the weeks that followed the cancellation of the elections and the official annulment of its victories in the first round, fearing that the authorities were looking for an excuse to strike against the party. The party issued a communiqué instructing its supporters not to respond to the provocations of the security forces, and one senior figure pleaded with crowds outside the Al-Sunna Mosque in Algiers not to 'furnish them with the opportunity they are waiting for.'[41] Even before the move to end the electoral process, the party's leadership had been aware that elements within the Algerian military in particular wanted an excuse to crush the party. The FIS's victories in the first round of voting had been met with joy by the party's rank and file, but the party's leadership was aware of the dangers of the development; the FIS's interim leader, Abdelkader Hachani, warned supporters that 'victory is more dangerous than defeat.'[42]

The arrest of the FIS's main leaders in the weeks that followed the cancellation of the elections removed any restraining hand on those supporters of the party who wished to protest more directly at the confiscation of the FIS's certain victory. Clashes between supporters of the party and the security forces escalated, leading to the declaration of a state of emergency and then the formal banning of the FIS in March. The structures of the party were rapidly dismantled: its newspapers and offices were shut down, its control of local authorities was ended and thousands of its militants were arrested and transported to prison camps in the desert. Attempts at protests and demonstrations were ruthlessly and efficiently crushed by the security forces.

More organised and violent forms of resistance to the regime nevertheless began to grow, and throughout 1992 groups of armed Islamists formed. The leaders of these groups came from a mixture of backgrounds. Early to emerge were more radical elements who had never been part of the FIS, having disagreed with its electoral strategy and viewing the armed overthrow of the Algerian government as the correct path to political power. Many of them had been involved in a small group that had briefly led a guerrilla campaign against the authorities in the mid 1980s. Others had fought as volunteers alongside the mujahidin in Afghanistan during the same period and had brought back with them radical ideology and military training when they drifted back to Algeria following the departure of the Soviets at the end of the 1980s. Some of these figures had even joined the FIS: two former Afghan volunteers, Said Mekhloufi and Kameredine Kherbane, even became members of the party's guidance council (*majlis shura*), but were pushed out of the party in 1991 because they advocated a more confrontational stance towards the regime and proposed to establish a covert armed wing for the party.[43]

The nature and extent of links between the armed groups and the FIS itself were initially unclear, mostly because the FIS itself was in turmoil, its leadership broken up and divided between exile, hiding and imprisonment. The incarceration of several thousand FIS activists in detention camps in the Sahara during the repression of the party broke up the party's structures, but also served to embitter and radicalise an even larger section of the FIS's supporters. Links began to be established between elements of the leadership of the dissolved party and some of the main armed groups in an effort to develop a strategy, but attempts at coordination were hampered by ideological divisions and suspicions among them as well as the success of the security services in combating and breaking up the groups. This created a fractured and often atomised pattern of resistance. Connections with the FIS were explicitly spurned by a more extremist trend that began to emerge amongst some of the armed groups, known as the Armed Islamic Group (*Jammat Islamiyya Mousalaha*) or more widely by its French acronym, GIA (*Groupe Islamique Armée*). The GIA adopted a much more extreme and violent agenda and approach than the other armed groups, most of which targeted their attacks at the security forces and the institutions of the state. The GIA, by contrast, began targeting a wider range of people including journalists, local administrators, secular intellectuals and foreign nationals living in Algeria, whom they accused of supporting the regime.

The emergence of the GIA had a number of effects. Focusing its activities in urban areas allowed it to recruit from the huge pool of young poor unemployed, meaning that it was constantly able to replace members killed by the security services. The death and rapid turnover of leaders also meant that the GIA became more fractured and less coherent, leading to the creation of what in reality became a number of GIAs functioning in different areas. This in turn contributed to the activities and focus of the groups becoming increasingly local and, as Luis Martinez has shown, more economic as initial attempts to raise funds through control and extortion of local businesses developed a dynamic of their own.[44] The recruitment of progressively younger members and leaders also led to the further radicalisation and intensification of levels of violence which grew through 1993 and 1994 as whole neighbourhoods began to fall under the control of armed groups. The GIA also had a mixed impact on the remnants of the FIS and its allies in the other armed groups. Whilst horrified by the extremist and indiscriminate ideology and methods of the GIA, which many former FIS members unequivocally condemned, others were aware of its strength and influence and periodic attempts were made to co-opt and restrain it. In an effort to regain the initiative from the GIA, armed elements allied to the FIS regrouped themselves into the Army of Islamic Salvation (AIS), which they proclaimed to be the armed wing of the FIS and which set itself the objective of pressurising the regime to relegalise the FIS and restart elections. By setting this much more limited agenda and by focusing their attacks solely on the security services, the AIS hoped to distance itself and the FIS from the GIA's extremism, which it felt was alienating both ordinary Algerians and potential sympathy abroad. In fact, many members of the FIS were increasingly suspicious that the violence of the GIA was serving the ends of the regime far too well and that the group was not all that it seemed; they feared it was infiltrated, manipulated and perhaps even run by elements from within the Algerian intelligence services (see Chapter 3).

The Destruction of An-Nahda

The failure of the Tunisian Islamist movement to react to and resist the regime's attempts to crush it in the way that Algeria's Islamists did is one of the puzzles of modern Maghrebi history. As Hermassi comments, 'No-one, including those in power, thought that the movement could so easily dissipate.'[45]

The absence of the mounting of an effective armed resistance was particularly marked. Tunisia's much smaller size and less extreme geography clearly worked against the creation of a rural guerrilla resistance or *maquis* on the model of Algeria, but this had not prevented the emergence of violent resistance to the French in the countryside in the closing years of colonial rule, and much of the activities of Algeria's armed groups focused in the country's towns and cities. Tunisian Islamism was not without its more radical elements who were willing to use violence. The bomb attacks on hotels in Sousse and Monastir of August 1987, which in many ways precipitated the crisis of late 1987, were carried out by a group calling itself Islamic Jihad, who had also been responsible for acts of violence the previous year. These and a number of other similar groups, though, were very small and were successfully broken up by the authorities in the wake of the 1987 attacks. The government made great efforts to link those responsible for the bombings to the MTI, but they denied any meaningful links to the larger movement and no formal case was made in court.[46]

The existence of an armed wing of the MTI itself became a hugely controversial issue, given the charges of attempted armed insurrection that the Tunisian regime laid at the door of An-Nahda in the 1990s. It also potentially threw into question the sincerity of the movement's, and particularly Rachid Ghannouchi's, continued and passionate insistence on its attachment to exclusively peaceful and legal means for the achievement of political power. From the various accounts that have emerged, it appears that the MTI did clandestinely develop what became known as a 'Security Group' during the bouts of official repression that occurred through the 1980s, whose aim was to protect and preserve the movement's structures during crackdowns by the authorities. Whether this occurred with the full knowledge, blessing and direction of Ghannouchi is less clear, and probably unlikely given the fact that this group seemed to grow in strength when the MTI's senior figures were in prison and more hard-line figures took control of the day-to-day running of the movement.[47] It is alleged that it was following the sentencing of the MTI's leaders to long terms in prison in September 1987 that members of the Security Group hatched a plot to launch a coup to remove Bourguiba. It was the discovery of this plan, it is argued, that then prompted Ben Ali to bring forward his own plans to move against the president and put them into operation the day before the Security Group plotters had planned to strike. When this occurred the Security Group then abandoned their own planned coup and were arrested later that month.[48] They were released in 1989 following Ghannouchi's disavowal of their methods, which he described as 'not part of the movement's orientations, in spite of the exceptional circumstances surrounding them' and this paved the way for the MTI leader's own release and the rehabilitation of the movement by the regime.[49]

The Tunisian authorities subsequently alleged that the MTI did not abandon a military and insurrectionist option following these concessions, arguing that the movement set up a 'Special Apparatus' to infiltrate the government and security services as early as March 1988 and that a clandestine military wing for An-Nahda was reconstituted upon the release of the Security Group prisoners in 1989. The violence that subsequently occurred in 1990–91 was therefore part of a campaign by the Islamists to achieve power, having failed to do so by the ballot box, and culminated in the attack on the RCD office in Bab Souika in February 1991. In September 1991 the government announced that it had discovered that An-Nahda had planned to acquire a stinger missile from Afghanistan via Algeria, with which they planned to shoot down President Ben Ali's plane.[50] The movement, it was argued, therefore did indeed have a plan to resist and overthrow the government, like their Algerian counterparts, but the competence of the intelligence and security services nipped these plots in the bud.

The reality of these allegations is difficult to assess, especially when even those observers broadly supportive of the Tunisian government's claims acknowledge that the evidence presented at the subsequent trials of An-Nahda members was probably 'exaggerated,' and that the trials themselves were condemned by Amnesty International as 'unfair,' with many of those on trial 'sentenced on the sole basis of uncorroborated confessions allegedly extracted under torture and consistently denied in court.'[51] It seems fairly clear that if such plots existed, they were largely outside the knowledge of the MTI/Nahda leadership. Rachid Ghannouchi was still in prison when the 'Special Apparatus' was established and had left to go into exile before the Security Group was reconstituted.[52] The authorities linked him to the supposed radicalisation of An-Nahda through hard-line speeches he was alleged to have made from exile, notably about the presence of US troops in Saudi Arabia during the Gulf crisis in which he supposedly called for Muslims to rise up.[53] Ghannouchi himself subsequently argued that the attributed statements were simple fabrications of the regime and appeared only in documents produced by the Tunisian government.[54] Moreover, he argued that the speed and success of the authorities' repression of An-Nahda and the minimal violence that occurred when compared to the attempt to repress the FIS in Algeria actually confirmed the pacific and democratic nature of the movement. In his view the international climate, with the growing crisis in Algeria and the spreading fear of Islamism, also helped facilitate the crackdown by the regime.[55]

The success of the Tunisian regime's repression of An-Nahda was in all probability due to a number of factors that Murphy useful summarises as 'the combination of the scale of its assault, the weakness of the Islamists to withstand it and the latter's own tactical mistakes.' These tactical mistakes included Ghannouchi's departure from the country at a critical juncture, a failure to condemn the Bab Souika incident unequivocally and Ghannouchi's adoption of a more radical tone from abroad that alienated ordinary Tunisians.[56] Indeed, irrespective of the truth of the allegations against An-Nahda, many Tunisians, including those in other opposition parties (see Chapter 4) were unnerved by events unfolding next door in Algeria and chose to side with the regime and tacitly support the repression of the Islamists. Evidence of use of violence by Islamists had a far bigger impact on public opinion than they had in Algeria, quite possibly because of the very different memories of the experiences of the two countries' liberation struggles and the levels of violence that occurred within them.

Morocco: The PJD and Al-Adl wal Ihsan[57]

In contrast to Tunisia and Algeria, Morocco did not witness the emergence of a large popular Islamist movement of the dimensions of the MTI or FIS in the late 1980s. Many reasons were put forward for this absence. One was Morocco's traditionally more pluralistic religious and political complexion. The existence of a multi-party political system virtually from independence was seen as providing an outlet for political protest and opposition that was not afforded in most other Arab states, which had overwhelmingly adopted single-party political systems upon independence. As a result, opposition sentiment did not end up becoming channelled, as it did in Tunisia and Algeria, into one single large movement that was almost invariably Islamist in orientation. On the religious front, the strength and persistence of sufi practices and organisations in the kingdom was felt to present a bulwark against the spread of Islamist ideas: the more mystic and apolitical aspects of sufism undercutting support for the more literalist and political impulses of most Islamist movements. Moreover, it was also argued that the broader tradition of pluralism in Morocco also served to inhibit the development of a single, dominant, unified Islamist movement of the type seen in Algeria and Tunisia—Islamic Youth and its successor organisations failing to unite and make common cause with Abdeslam Yassine and his supporters.[58]

Whilst some explanations for the weakness of Islamist movements stressed the pluralism of religious and political life in Morocco, others emphasised the unity, strength and resolve of the regime. The regime and its supporters in Morocco were traditionally unanimous in expressing the view that the real reason behind the relative lack of strength of Islamist movements in Morocco was the religious standing of the monarchy. It was argued that the Moroccan monarchs' claim of descent from the Prophet Mohamed, together with the King's official status as *Amir al-Muminin* (Commander of the Faithful), gave the monarchy a religious authority and legitimacy that effectively undermined the religiously-based discourse and criticism of the Islamist groups. Charges of being too secular or of neglecting Islam could be more easily made against presidents and regimes that had no clearly religious dimension, but were much harder to make stick against a relative of the Prophet and a monarchical institution that traditionally clothed itself in religious imagery and symbolism.

For some observers the religious dimensions of the Moroccan monarchy's power and control were in reality overstated and were only given credibility because of the tenacity with which they were reiterated by state officials. Henry Munson points instead to the much more tangible tools and dimensions of royal power and control to explain the success of the Moroccan state in controlling the expansion of the country's Islamist movements.[59] Under the supervision of King Hassan II, the kingdom developed effective security structures that successfully headed off a number of attempts from the political left in the 1960s and 1970s to marginalise or overthrow the monarchy. These successes left the security services well equipped to deal with the type of challenge potentially posed by the Islamists from the 1970s and into the 1980s. Surveillance, infiltration, detention and periodic repression of these groups worked well in preventing their growth and spread.

In more specific terms, the challenges presented by Islamic Youth and Abdeslam Yassine in the 1970s were easily dealt with and the kingdom did not witness the emergence of a strong vocal Islamist movement as did its neighbours in the 1980s. By the early 1990s, however, there were the first signs that the situation might be changing. In May 1990 some 2,000 Islamists protested outside a court in Rabat during a trial of supporters of Abdeslam Yassine. Nine months later, in February 1991, there was a heavy Islamist presence in the mass demonstration that took place in the capital against the Gulf War.[60] This show of strength by the kingdom's Islamists convinced King Hassan and his advisers of the importance of responding effectively to this potential challenge. In looking for possible examples to follow, the Moroccan king was presented with two very different models: that of an unrestricted opening to the Islamists, followed by Algeria from 1989; and that of total repression and exclusion, followed by Zine al-Abdine Ben Ali's regime in Tunisia from 1991. Neither model was appealing. The unravelling of Algeria's experiment in the early 1990s and the descent into conflict after a belated attempt by elements in the regime to close the door on the Islamists highlighted the shortcomings of this approach. The total repression operated by Ben Ali in Tunisia not only went against Morocco's more pluralistic history and impulses, but also was arguably unfeasible in a country several times the size and with three times the population of Tunisia.

As an alternative, Hassan turned to a middle course of action that had a deep-rooted tradition in Moroccan politics: that of co-option. Since independence, the palace had consistently undermined and defanged opposition to the regime through the selective co-option of certain groups and individuals. The regime thus resolved to remove the threat posed by the Islamists by attempting to bring them into the political system. Official contacts with Islamist organisations had already begun in 1989 through religious events organised on the country's campuses by the minister of religious affairs, Abdelkebir Alaoui Mdaghri, who was charged by Hassan with managing relations with the movement.[61]

It was clear to the regime that by far the biggest and best organised movement in the country was that which had come to form around

Abdeslam Yassine. Although Yassine had acted alone when he sent his infamous letter to the king in 1973, from the early 1980s he had begun to attract growing numbers of supporters who formed themselves into a well-structured organisation that by 1987 became known as *Al-Adl wal Ihsan* (Justice and Spirituality). Significantly, the movement's growth had not been interrupted or inhibited by the imprisonment of the members of its *Majlis Irshad* (Guidance Council) in 1990. As a result, the Moroccan authorities began to put out feelers to the movement, approaching the members of the Guidance Council in prison in an attempt to persuade them to come to some accommodation with the regime. According to members of the council, officials offered the movement legal recognition, the right to form a political party and contest elections and even substantial sums of money. The sole eventual condition was that the movement publicly and explicitly recognise the authority and legitimacy of the monarchy.[62] The offer was, however, rejected, not least because *Al-Adl wal Ihsan* recognised that a significant part of its legitimacy and popularity as a movement was linked to its stance against and criticism of the monarchy's pre-eminent position in Morocco.

Having failed in their overtures towards Yassine and *Al-Adl wal Ihsan*, the authorities decided instead to see if any other Islamist groups were open to co-option.[63] The obvious candidate was a small organisation made up of former members of the Islamic Youth organisation of the 1970s who had regrouped themselves in the early 1980s and rejected the radicalism of Abdelkrim Mouti, requesting recognition as an official association and also the right to form a political party. These requests had been consistently denied by the authorities throughout the 1980s and early 1990s. However, following the failure of the attempted opening to *Al-Adl wal Ihsan*, the regime turned a more sympathetic ear to this group, which now called itself *Al-Islah wa At-Tajdid* (Reform and Renewal). Still wary of allowing the movement to form its own political party, the regime gave an effective green light to the members of *Al-Islah wa At-Tajdid* to join an existing but small and effectively moribund political party, the *Mouvement Populaire Démocratique et Constitutionnel* (MPDC). The fact that this party was led by an old established politician, Abdelkrim Khatib, who had close links with the royal palace, satisfied the requirements of co-option. To make doubly sure, Khatib stipulated that members of *Al-Islah*, before joining the MPDC, affirmed their renunciation of violence, their acceptance of constitutional and political methods and—most crucially of all—recognition of the authority and legitimacy of the monarchy.[64] Having publicly endorsed these principles for some years, the members of *Al-Islah* had no problem in making this commitment and in June 1996 they formally entered the political party.[65]

Once inside the party, the Islamists of *Al-Islah* worked to transform it into an Islamist one: a task facilitated by the fact that they substantially outnumbered existing members of the party. The party put up a limited number of candidates in the national legislative elections of November 1997 and were rewarded with victories in nine constituencies, mainly in Morocco's big cities. Within a year of the elections, the party changed its name to the Party of Justice and Development (PJD) in effective recognition of the transformation of the old MPDC. Despite its small size, the PJD soon developed a reputation for effectiveness in the parliament, thus raising its national profile. Other small Islamist groupings were brought on board and as a result *Al-Islah* (which retained its identity as a religious association distinct from the MPDC/PJD)[66] renamed itself *At-Tawhid wa Al-Islah* (Unity and Reform).[67]

In allowing these developments, the Moroccan authorities hoped to co-opt successfully at least part of the Islamist movement into the legal political processes and thus prevent the coalescence of a large radicalised opposition Islamist movement of the sort witnessed in Algeria and Tunisia. A desire to prevent *Al-Adl wal Ihsan* assuming such a role was clearly present in the authorities' calculations. Although *Al-Islah wa At-Tajdid* was far smaller than *Al-Adl wal Ihsan*, it was hoped that the presence of Islamist deputies in the national parliament would serve to undercut and siphon popular support away from the larger organisation.

As a legal political party contesting elections and sitting in the national parliament, the PJD was able to present its views and stances on issues in public fora. The party was, nevertheless, acutely aware that it had been afforded access to the legal political arena only on the sufferance of the authorities and was conscious that, should it be seen to overstep any 'red lines,' it could lose the place it had been given. As a result, the party trod a difficult line between being faithful to its Islamist agenda and supporters whilst being careful to avoid attracting the ire of the authorities. It thus steered clear of any criticism of the wider political system and the place of the monarchy and focused on more low-profile and less political, social and 'moral' issues such as corruption, education and the place of women. The PJD's clear stance on these issues, together with its reputation for hard work and honesty—not least in the local areas in which its members had been elected—contrasted markedly with most of Morocco's other political parties, who were notable for their vague ideologies and often complete lack of contact with the voters between elections (see Chapter 4). As a result, the party grew in both stature and support. Yet, the PJD's leadership acknowledged that if the party grew too quickly it could provoke unease both inside the regime as well as amongst Morocco's allies in Europe and the United States, who were wary about the rise of Islamism. As a consequence, the party's spokesmen were wont to be modest about both the party's achievements and its future prospects. As the party's deputy leader, Saad-Eddine Othmani, explained in 2000: 'We are frightened of frightening people.'[68]

Such a stance presented a dilemma when it came to contesting elections: the party clearly wanted to increase its representation in local and national government, but did not want to be seen to do well and raise the fear of an Islamist-run or -dominated government. In this regard the experience of Algeria loomed large in everyone's minds: the strong performance by the FIS in elections having prompted elements in the powerful military to intervene and ban the party. The violence and chaos that this chain of events unleashed was something that everyone in Morocco, including the PJD, was anxious to avoid. As one senior member of the PJD acknowleged in an interview with a French newspaper: 'The Algerian scenario is the fear of all Moroccans.'[69]

To head off such a scenario, the PJD voluntarily decided to put limits on the numbers of candidates it put up in elections. In the 1997 national legislative elections (as the MPDC) it fielded candidates in only 43 per cent of the electoral districts. At the next set of legislative elections in 2002, the party only slightly increased their participation to 60 per cent—a lower total than most other parties contesting the elections. In spite of these self-imposed restrictions, the party, having performed respectably in 1997, performed extremely well in 2002, winning 42 seats and becoming the third largest party in the parliament.

The reasons behind this advance were varied. The PJD had certainly helped itself through a well-organised and simple campaign that made good use of the party's strong grass-roots organisation and the high calibre of the candidates it fielded (81 per cent of whom held university degrees).[70] It had also been helped by external factors. At the national level, the party encountered little competition from the other parties, most of whom had no clear ideology, no grass-roots organisation and fielded poor quality (sometimes illiterate) candidates who relied more on patron-client networks and occasionally vote-buying to attract votes. The more established and better organised parties such as the USFP and the Istiqlal suffered from a lack of credibility, having been the major partners in the *alternance* government that had disappointed many with its failure to tackle major social and economic problems facing the country. These parties' passage from traditional opposition into the government left a clear gap for the PJD to fill. At the international level, the international 'War on Terror' proclaimed by the United States in the wake of the attacks of 11 September 2001, the pending invasion of Iraq and, most importantly of all, the continuing violence between the Israelis and the Palestinians had clearly strengthened sentiments of Islamic solidarity from which the PJD as an overtly Islamic party benefited.[71]

The PJD was therefore tipped to do well in the third set of legislative elections it contested in September 2007. Although no one expected the party to win the sort of crushing victories achieved by the FIS in Algeria, not least because of the use of a more proportional electoral system, there was near universal expectation that the PJD would emerge comfortably as the largest presence in the lower house. There was therefore widespread surprise when this did not occur: the party achieved only a modest increase in its representation, leaving it the second largest party in the parliament. Explanations for this relative failure were varied. The party itself blamed corrupt practices amongst other parties and gerrymandering from the authorities.[72] These factors, however, did not fully explain the scale of the PJD's disappointment, since these would only have had a limited impact on the party's performance. Whole-scale fraud and vote-rigging by the authorities was unlikely, given the largely transparent way in which the elections had been run, as monitored for the first time by international observers.[73]

The real reason for the PJD's setback was its failure to distinguish itself sufficiently from the other political parties and the wider political system, which had become massively discredited in the eyes of most Moroccan voters (see Chapter 4). Turnout at the election had been exceptionally low and was weakest in the areas in which the PJD was traditionally strongest, in the major cities and towns. It appeared that in its anxiety not to offend the regime and present a moderate image, the party had rid itself of its distinctive appeal.[74] Whilst some figures in the party lamented this setback, others were less perturbed. This revealed a divide in what was still a fairly heterogeneous movement between those who saw the achievement of political power as the main objective of the party and others who sought simply the achievement of a political space within which the party and its associational wing would be able to propagate its ideas.[75] Significantly, it was a representative of this latter group who was elected leader of the PJD the year after the election: Abdelilah Benkirane, having long been the leading advocate of a more accommodationist line towards the palace and having even argued that the party's setback in 2007 had been the result of it still being too distinctive and isolated from the other parties.[76]

In spite of its overall electoral successes, the PJD remained Morocco's second largest Islamist organisation; Abdeslam Yassine's *Al-Adl wal Ihsan* continuing to grow despite its formal exclusion from the political system. Yassine was finally released from house arrest in May 2000 as a gesture of goodwill by the new King Mohamed following his accession to the throne the previous year, but Yassine continued to refuse overtures from the authorities. *Al-Adl wal Ihsan*'s exclusion from the formal mechanisms of politics such as elections and the parliament meant that it had to articulate its message and agenda in different ways. From the beginning of the 1990s the movement focused on building its organisation and spreading its message, resulting in the creation of a large, well-structured and well-supported organisation with branches throughout the country. New members of the organisation were inducted in a methodical manner through groups where they studied some of the major writings of Abdeslam Yassine.[77]

The fact that the group was constructed around the ideas and writings of a single man was unusual and meant that the challenge mounted by *Al-Adl wal Ihsan* to the status quo in Morocco was of a rather different sort to that of more classic Islamist movements found in most other Arab countries, of which *At-Tawhid wa al-Islah* and the PJD were more typical. Also unusual was the clear influence of sufi ideas on the movement. Yassine spent six years in the Boutchichiyya sufi order and the legacy in his writings and the philosophy of the movement was evident. Much emphasis was placed by *Al-Adl wal Ihsan* on the inner transformation of the individual—a distinctly sufi idea. The movement stressed the importance of changing people first before attempting to change society. This stood in contrast to the more legalistic approach of other Islamist movements that emphasised the importance of law and behaviour. Indeed, *Al-Adl wal Ihsan* was openly hostile to more literalist and genuinely fundamentalist groups and ideas. Nadia Yassine, the daughter of Abdeslam and a prominent spokesperson for the movement, criticised the PJD for having rather rigid views and condemned Wahhabism as a dangerous 'virus' in the Muslim world that breeds 'violence and exclusion.'[78]

The main difference between the PJD and *Al-Adl wal Ihsan* was, however, political and principally related to the latter's continued refusal to recognise the authority of the monarchy. In this way the movement was, in the view of Nadia Yassine, 'politically extremist' rather than religiously so.[79] Abdeslam Yassine himself was unafraid to challenge explicitly the officially asserted religious legitimacy of the Moroccan monarchy, stating to the author shortly after his release from house arrest in 2000:

> You foreign journalists and academics are mistaken when you say that 'The Moroccan Monarchy's legitimacy is based on descent from the Prophet Mohamed.' This is wrong. If you think about it, there must be thousands of people in Morocco, including me, who are blood descendants of the Prophet. Why shouldn't any one of them be King?'[80]

In challenging the monarchy so directly, Yassine consciously placed himself in a long historical tradition in Morocco which had seen lone pious individuals confront the sultan.[81] How aware most ordinary Moroccans were of this tradition is uncertain, but Yassine's popularity was undoubtedly tied up with his courage in being willing to break a taboo and directly confront what he saw as the failings of the Moroccan state and the monarchy.

The support Yassine garnered did not, however, prevent a growing debate within *Al-Adl wal Ihsan* concerning its rejection of formal political processes in Morocco. Excluded from the official arena, the movement had long affected disdain toward these processes. There were, however, voices within the movement arguing that it should try to become involved in formal politics, should it be offered the chance to form a political party. Many, particularly younger, figures worried that the movement risked marginalisation if it continued to stand on the political sidelines. Older figures pointed to the frustrated expectations of the PJD, which they said underlined the dangers of co-option by the monarchy.

The Moroccan monarchy has therefore appeared to have successfully contained the political challenge represented by the kingdom's main Islamist movements. Avi Spiegel has argued that the political challenge has not been the main concern of the monarchy, which has rather sought to maintain control of the religious challenge to its authority, which King Mohamed has sought to bolster through a series of reforms aimed at reasserting official control of the religious sphere. He argues that the successful monopolisation of what he terms 'sacralised public space' by the monarchy did not allow the Islamists of either the PJD or *Al-Adl wal Ihsan* to argue effectively that the Moroccan state was non-religious, as the FIS and MTI were able to do in Algeria and Tunisia. This pushed both movements to articulate an increasingly political rather than religious agenda.[82] Emilie François, however, has argued that the king's dominance of the religious sphere explains why some in the PJD, most notably the party's leader from 2008, Abdelilah Benkirane, opted for a highly accommodationist stance towards the monarchy, believing that alliance and thus influence with the royal palace was a more likely way for the movement to get its agenda implemented than attempting to win elections.[83] The view that the monarchy and its religious standing could be an opportunity rather than a hindrance for the Islamists was one that had existed for some time and was revealed in a statement made by another senior figure of the PJD in an interview in 1994, which at the time had been seen as simply a statement of reassurance to the regime: 'Our problem in Morocco is not in establishing an Islamic state. Theoretically and constitutionally, this state already exists. We, on the contrary, support this legitimacy and consider it an asset that should not be given up or disputed.'[84] Other members of the PJD, however, viewed such an approach as naive and saw the entrenchment of the rule of law and democratic institutions as the best route to achieving the party's agenda, which they believed should increasingly focus on issues such as democracy and social justice rather than on the more narrowly religious agenda sought by Benkirane and his supporters.

Algerian Islamism After the Black Decade

Islamism's relationship with politics in Algeria appeared to enter a new phase with the marked decline in the levels of violence that occurred at the end of the 1990s. A number of factors appeared to have contributed to this relatively peaceful phase. Most obvious was the ending of operations by a number of the armed Islamist groups that had been fighting the regime. Negotiations between the regime and certain armed groups led to a ceasefire between the ANP and the Army of Islamic Salvation, the armed wing of the FIS, in October 1997, and culminated in the promulgation of a Law on Civil Concord in 1999 offering a qualified amnesty to members of the groups, which most of the fighters in the AIS together with some other smaller armed groups accepted, laying down their weapons and returning to their homes.

Both a cause and consequence of the AIS's ending of the armed struggle against the Algerian regime was the continued fragmentation of the armed groups. The emergence of the GIA had created both strategic and increasingly ideological tensions with those groups allied to the FIS, and by the mid 1990s this was leading to direct violent clashes between the two trends. Attacks on the AIS contributed to the group's decision to negotiate an end to its struggle with the regime, particularly the massacres of some of its civilian supporters in late 1996 which marked the beginning of a horrific series of similar incidents that lasted until 1998.[85] Responsibility for the massacres was never fully established, but accusations ranged from the GIA to elements of the security services. Involvement of the regime in the killings was alleged from a number of quarters, most notably defectors from within the security services themselves (see Chapter 3), who argued that the authorities profited from the wave of revulsion that the massacres provoked, thus strengthening support both domestically and internationally for the regime and undercutting support for Islamism, which was seen as developing in unacceptably extreme directions.[86]

Irrespective of the truth of these allegations, it was apparent that elements of the armed groups were becoming progressively more extreme in both their ideology and their methods. Aided by the high turnover of leaders and by the low average age of members, elements of the GIA came to be dominated by the *al-Muwahiddun* tendency, which adopted an increasingly exclusive ideological stance that saw Algerian society as un-Islamic and apostate and thus a legitimate target for violence. This doctrine of *takfir* served to increase the violence practised by these groups, but it also worked to alienate less extreme trends which repeatedly broke away from the main organisation, often after significant internal bloodletting.[87] The net effect of this was further fragmentation of what remained of the armed Islamist groups and reduction of the

GIA to a small, fanatical core which became more preoccupied with its internal feuds than with struggle against the regime. The extremism of the GIA also served to undercut support for the armed groups amongst wider Algerian society. Although the armed resistance had only managed an active mobilisation of a fraction of the millions of ordinary Algerians who had voted for the FIS in the elections of 1990 and 1991, it enjoyed clear initial sympathy from large sections of the FIS's support base. As violence escalated through the mid 1990s this sympathy was rapidly eroded, particularly amongst the party's more middle-class supporters, leading to what Gilles Kepel has seen as the break-up of the powerful coalition of the devout middle class and the urban poor that had supported the FIS, many of the former suffering at the hands of the latter through practices such as extortion of local businesses, which became a main source of fundraising for the armed groups.[88]

As the violence of the armed groups tailed off, this revived the question of the involvement of Islamism in formal political processes. The ceasefire and laying down of weapons by the AIS was widely expected to lead to some form of rehabilitation for the FIS. Negotiations between the AIS and the regime had been conducted in secret and details of the agreement were never made public by the regime; it never formally acknowledged the agreement, which had been conducted exclusively by the military.[89] Senior figures in the FIS claim that the AIS leadership was promised that some form of rehabilitation of the FIS would be permitted once the AIS laid down its weapons and dissolved itself.[90]

The FIS, however, never succeeded in formally rehabilitating itself and securing readmission to the legal political arena, despite the repeated attempts of its former members and leaders. The dissolution and repression of the party after 1992 had fragmented the party both organisationally and ideologically. Its leadership became divided between exile, prison and the armed resistance and disagreed over issues such as the use of violence and negotiations with the regime. Imprisoned leaders of the party began to be released from the mid 1990s, eventually culminating in the release of the two most senior leaders, Abassi Madani and Ali Belhadj, in June 2003. An official ban on political activism imposed on the former FIS leaders, together with the firm grip the regime had established on the political scene, ensured that FIS activists were unable to reorganise. Official hints at the possibility of the FIS being able to reconstitute itself—probably under another name—were made, but many FIS members suspected this was simply a means of creating divisions between the former leaders. Attempts to establish a successor political party to the FIS—most notably by former Algerian foreign minister Ahmed Taleb Ibrahimi—were blocked by the authorities on the grounds that the proposed party (WAFA) represented a 'reconstitution of the dissolved party' (the FIS) through its inclusion of several senior members of the FIS.[91] This led to accusations from FIS leaders that they and the AIS had been tricked into ending the armed struggle in 1997.[92]

The blocking of attempts to rehabilitate the FIS did not equate to a total absence of Islamism from formal political processes after the cancellation of elections and banning of the FIS in 1992, as it had with the repression of An-Nahda in Tunisia. The other Islamist political parties that had been created by leading Islamist figures who had refrained from joining the FIS, and which the regime had hoped would pull votes away from the FIS in elections, were allowed to continue and joined the contest when multi-party elections were reintroduced from 1995. The official intent behind this was clearly to use the parties to attract the support of former FIS voters and thus try to stem support for the armed Islamist groups. In doing this, the regime was careful to make sure that neither of the two remaining Islamist parties would reproduce either the FIS's electoral success or its radicalism. Both parties were forced to change their names to drop references to Islam, and both were subject to official attempts to control them.

In the case of the *Harakat al Mujtama As-Silm* or Movement for a Society of Peace (MSP) led by Mahfoud Nahnah, the party's established hostility towards the FIS and ostensibly more moderate social and political platform made it a natural ally for the regime. Members of the party were appointed to positions in government from 1994 and the party itself became a part of the governing coalition alongside the FLN and RND later in the decade.[93] Critics of the party, especially from within the FIS, portrayed the MSP as a simple co-opted tool of the regime. The party itself argued that it was able to retain a degree of independence and to influence government policy in some areas and thus had chosen 'a third way between regime and opposition.'[94] The party had a fairly solid base within Algerian society, particularly amongst the bourgeoisie and small businessmen, and there was evidence to suggest that these groups transferred their support from the FIS to the MSP during the 1990s as they became alienated by the violence of the armed groups and were encouraged by the free market reforms of the regime.[95] The regime was clearly aware of the importance of these groups to the national economy, and this helped further facilitate the MSP's alliance with the regime and integration into the system. It was noticeable that, although only minor ministries were allotted to MSP ministers in the coalition governments, most of these were in economic fields in recognition of the economic weight of the party.[96] The party nevertheless remained on the fringes of real power in Algeria and wielded nowhere near the influence of its coalition 'partners,' the RND and the FLN. Privately its senior figures complained of official interference in the party's internal affairs, notably in its selection of candidates for elections. Its leader, Mahfoud Nahnah, was prevented from standing in the presidential elections of 1999 through the application of a new rule that seemed designed purposefully to exclude him and was undoubtedly related to his relatively strong performance in the previous presidential election of 1995.[97]

The second Islamist party allowed to continue in the system after the exclusion of the FIS, An-Nahda (not to be confused with its Tunisian counterpart), took a more critical line towards the regime. It allied itself with other more hardline opposition parties in demanding greater democracy and the strengthening of elected institutions, and even called for the re-legalisation of the FIS.[98] This led the Algerian regime to adopt a more coercive approach towards the party which involved engineering its takeover by pro-regime elements. This led to the party's leader, Abdallah Djaballah, leaving An-Nahda and in 1999 setting up a new party—*Islah*—with the majority of the original party's supporters. The new party subsequently continued to suffer from officially sponsored splits and divisions.

Doctrinally the MSP and An-Nahda/Islah differed very little from each other; their differences were mainly political rather than religious and, as with the PJD and *Al-Adl wal Ihsan* in Morocco, largely related to their relative willingness to criticise and confront the regime.[99] Both were, however, explicitly committed to legal and non-violent methods and had historically kept their distance from the FIS because of what they both saw as the excessive populism of the party, pushed by its undereducated base and spurred on by its early successes.[100] The MSP, An-Nahda and Islah all performed respectably at elections from 1995 and often finished in second place to regime-backed parties and candidates, but never came close to winning or dominating elections in the way the FIS had been able to. The utility of both parties to the regime was clearly in attracting former supporters of the FIS into formal political processes. The fading of the memory of the FIS over time and the decline in levels of violence from the armed groups weakened this utility and began to call into question the importance of these parties to the regime. This explained the increased willingness of the regime to undermine and marginalise Abdallah Djaballah and the indications that it was preparing the same fate for the MSP, which began to be wracked by internal disputes resulting in a formal scission in the party in 2009.

The Shadow of Al Qaeda

The evolving place of Islamist movements within the Maghreb came to be substantially affected by the attacks on the United States of America of 11 September 2001. The attacks gave encouragement both to those elements within the regimes that sought a harder line against the movements as well as to those individuals and groups within the wider movement that sought to use violence to achieve their ends. Overall it had the effect of internationalising the issue of Islamism in the region.

At the international level it allowed the regimes, especially those in Tunis and Algiers, to portray themselves to the United States and Europe as seasoned bulwarks against the threat of Islamist extremism (see Chapter 9). Domestically, it meant that local Islamist groups could be depicted as part of some sinister wider global trend. In Tunisia, the events of 11 September facilitated the resurrection of the Islamist scarecrow that had been used so effectively by the Ben Ali regime to marshal support internally and externally behind it in the early 1990s, but whose effectiveness had declined by the end of the decade with the success of the repression of An-Nahda.[101] An-Nahda's leadership in Europe was obliged to redouble its efforts to distance itself rhetorically from violence and exclude more radical elements from the party, in order to maintain its networks in a now much more wary environment in Europe. It was aided in this by Rachid Ghannouchi's long-standing criticism of violent and extreme groups and his vocal differences with these elements within Islamist circles in London, with whom he pointedly refused to establish formal links.[102] This together with his endorsement of most elements of liberal democracy led some Islamists to question his attachment not just to Islamism but to Islam itself.[103] In

Morocco, both the PJD and *Al-Adl wal Ihsan* felt the tightening of restrictions on them in the wake of the attacks, Nadia Yassine saying in their immediate aftermath: 'If it is indeed Ben Laden who has done this, then he has done us Islamists a bad turn.'[104]

Pressures on Islamist movements increased further with incidents of violence occurring in the region itself in the period that followed September 2001. Seven months after the attacks in the US, twenty-one people, predominantly European tourists, were killed when a truck carrying gas canisters was rammed into a synagogue in Djerba in southern Tunisia in April 2002. A year later, in May 2003, forty-five people were killed in a coordinated series of suicide bomb attacks in Casablanca in Morocco. Evidence indicated that both attacks were the work of local Islamists. Direct links of command and control back to international organisations such as Al Qaeda were less clear, but those locally involved in the attacks were at the very least inspired by the organisation.[105] The attacks in Casablanca had a direct and adverse effect on the political position of the PJD, whose existing concerns about the precariousness of its position were confirmed in the aftermath of the bombings. Although the party had no links to the small group found to be responsible for the attacks, and explicitly rejected the use of violence for political purposes both before and after the bombings, the PJD came under severe political pressure in the weeks that followed. Opponents of the party in the leftist and secularist press and political parties accused it of having helped prepare the ground for the attacks through their sustained and intemperate rhetoric against the West and Israel (all the targets of the bombings had been Western or Jewish establishments) in the party's newspapers and official statements. The deputy leader of the USFP, Mohamed El Yazigh, called publicly for the PJD to 'apologise to the Moroccan people' for its contribution to creating an atmosphere that resulted in the bombings.[106] More ominously for the party, it became clear that there were important elements within the country's security establishment who wanted to ban and dissolve the party. The party was not, however, banned, quite possibly because of fears that such a move might radicalise the party's supporters in much the same way as the proscription of the FIS had in Algeria. Significantly, the counter-example of Tunisia, which succeeded in dissolving and repressing its Islamist movement, was not followed. Nevertheless, the atmosphere was sufficiently hostile to the party to necessitate some sacrifices on its part. The authorities made it clear to the PJD that the price the party had to pay to escape a formal ban would be a dramatic reduction in the party's participation in the September 2003 elections for local government and the removal of more radical figures from positions of influence in the party. Although the party survived and contested the 2007 elections, the continued delicacy of its own position in the legal political arena was underlined, perhaps intentionally, by the authorities' dissolution of two much smaller Islamist parties in 2008. The arrest and conviction of the leaders of these parties, for fairly tenuous past links to individuals allegedly involved in terrorism, was seen as a warning to the PJD, not least because several of the imprisoned figures had been former members not only of Islamic Youth but of the various forerunner organisations to *At-Tawhid wa al-Islah* and the PJD.[107]

Although neither Tunisia nor Morocco experienced attacks of a similar impact to those of the 2002–3 period in the years that followed, both moved to break up extremist groups apparently planning further attacks. In Morocco, the authorities regularly broke up cells of alleged violent extremists across the country, most of whom appeared to follow the model of the group responsible for the May 2003 attacks. This featured small networks of disillusioned youths in poorer parts of the kingdom's cities falling under the influence of local extremist preachers and ideologues and seeking to put together small, usually homemade, explosive devices; this was the pattern followed in a bomb attack on a café in Marrakech in April 2011. A more substantial grouping appeared to be uncovered by the Tunisian authorities in late 2006, producing a battle between armed militants and the Tunisian security forces in a Tunis suburb in January 2007 that resulted in 15 deaths. The Tunisian government alleged that the group of militants, who were a mixture of nationalities, had crossed over from Algeria to launch attacks on Western targets in the country. The fact that this followed on from a series of bombings in Algeria in the closing weeks of 2006 suggested that hitherto declining levels of violence from Algeria's remaining armed groups were not only rising again but also taking on a more international dimension. This seemed confirmed when one of the armed groups, the Salafist Group for Preaching and Combat, known by its French acronym GSPC, announced that it had renamed itself 'Al Qaeda in the Islamic Maghreb' (AQIM) in January 2007.

The struggle by the armed Islamist groups against the Algerian regime in the 1990s had had few external links beyond fundraising amongst the Algerian diaspora in Europe. The decline and increasingly local and economic focus of the remaining groups inside the country, however, contributed to Algerian Islamists in exile strengthening their links with similarly exiled Islamists from other states and forging ideological connections between the struggle in Algeria with those of Palestine, Kashmir and Chechnya. It was therefore in the diaspora that the links between Algerians and groups such as Al Qaeda began to grow, building on existing connections between those Algerians that had served in the Arab mujahidin in Afghanistan alongside figures such as Osama Bin Laden in the 1980s.[108] Although supportive of the campaign of the armed groups against the regime, Ben Laden and his followers had been angered and alienated by the growing extremism and *takfirist* ideology of the mainstream of the GIA. When elements of the GIA became similarly unhappy and broke away in 1998 to continue the armed struggle against the regime rather than Algerian society more generally, forming the GSPC, links were established with Ben Laden and his group. Although initially intent on focusing on the domestic struggle against the regime, it was argued that a diminishing presence and influence in Algeria increased the attractiveness to the GSPC of establishing external links with organisations such as Al Qaeda, especially after a change in leadership in 2003.[109]

Although internal developments within the armed groups remained as opaque as during the 1990s, there was both a qualitative and a quantitative increase in the violence officially attributed to the armed Islamist groups from the beginning of 2007, coinciding with the announcement of the GSPC's formal affiliation with Al Qaeda. These constituted a series of large-scale bombings targeting important locations in Algiers in April 2007 and again the following December; several of these were suicide operations, which marked a departure for the Algerian Islamists and appeared indicative of the influence of Al Qaeda. The new AQIM also appeared to extend its activities beyond the populated north of Algeria into other regions and into neighbouring states. There were growing reports of activities by armed Islamists in the vast Saharan south of the country, notably involving the kidnapping and holding for ransom of foreigners. For some observers, these new developments were in reality the result of the manipulations and internal politics of the regime, with figures in the upper echelons seeking to use the violence against each other politically in the same manner as they had been alleged to have used it during the 1990s (see

Chapter 3). Others asserted that the upsurge of violence, particularly in the south, was a deliberate ploy on the part of the Algerian intelligence services, the DRS, to attract Western and especially US support for the regime (see Chapter 9).[110] Yet others saw the kidnappings in the south to be more likely the product of mere criminality in a region where smuggling and banditry had long been common.[111] Whatever the respective truths of these theories, it did appear by the end of the first decade of the twenty-first century that genuine Islamists had come to be increasingly involved in activities in the Saharan south, perhaps being drawn to the area through the publicity given to the supposed presence of Al Qaeda in the Islamic Maghreb there. But as Camille Tawil has observed, despite these activities, 'nothing could disguise the fact that AQIM was a shadow of its Algerian forebears.'[112]

Islamism and the Arab Spring of 2011

The pattern of Islamist involvement in politics in the region was, along with much else, shaken up and recast by the dramatic developments of the opening months of 2011. To the surprise of most observers outside the region, and indeed also of some within it, Islamists were not the driving force behind the popular demonstrations and unrest that swept the region. They were not absent, but rather constituted just a part of the much broader social and political coalition that came onto the streets to demand political change.

The future role that Islamists would play in post-Ben Ali Tunisia inevitably attracted most attention, given the ferociously anti-Islamist stance adopted by the deposed president during most of his twenty-three-year rule. The success enjoyed by the Ben Ali regime in repressing Islamism in Tunisia from the early 1990s had prompted speculation that Tunisia subsequently enjoyed a 'post-Islamist' environment envied by other states in the region. In contrast to Algeria, where Islamist movements other than the FIS were allowed to continue to operate, the authorities frustrated the hopes of An-Nahda members who had left the movement in ostensible protest at its radicalisation in the 1990s and expected to be allowed to form a new political party. Instead all institutional and organised manifestations of Islamism were ruthlessly broken up and repressed by the authorities.

The dissolution and rooting out of the An-Nahda movement led it to relocate its structures and leadership abroad, notably in London where Rachid Ghannouchi lived in exile from 1990. There the movement focused on maintaining its structures, providing support for the large numbers of its imprisoned members in Tunisia and campaigning to highlight the lack of democracy and abuses of human rights by the Ben Ali regime. To these ends, it established charitable networks, an internet site and even a satellite television channel. From exile it maintained and strengthened links with other opposition parties, cooperating with them on campaigns; Ghannouchi called for the creation of a 'Democratic Front' to oppose the regime.[113] He continued to argue that social and economic pressures inside Tunisia would eventually lead to social unrest: an 'intifada' of the sort witnessed in the late 1970s and 1980s.[114]

The belated arrival of this intifada at the very end of 2010 re-opened political possibilities for An-Nahda and Tunisia's other Islamist groupings. Two weeks after the departure of Ben Ali, Rachid Ghannouchi left London to return to Tunisia, ending twenty-two years of exile abroad. He was greeted by large crowds of supporters at Tunis airport, indicating that, despite the years of official repression, he and the An-Nahda movement still clearly had a substantial support base. Quite how large this was, how the movement would use it and for what ends became major subjects of debate in Tunisia in the months that followed the fall of Ben Ali, as the country sought to recast its whole political system. The movement was quick to reassure the substantial part of the Tunisian population and outside opinion that were highly wary of its intentions. It restated its long-established position of seeing itself as only one part of the political scene; it wanted to cooperate with other forces and had no intention of dominating or monopolising whatever new political system would emerge. Rachid Ghannouchi reasserted that, 'We are ready to accept the outcome of the elections in a fair democratic regime. This is beyond question even if the adversaries of the Ennahda Movement took power as a result of the elections.'[115] To reinforce this, the movement, which received official recognition from the interim government on 1 March, declared that it would not field a candidate in any presidential election; Rachid Ghannouchi himself stepped down from the leadership of the movement in order to allow a younger figure to stand. Whilst some doubted the sincerity of these statements and steps, the movement's history both before and especially after its repression strongly suggested that of all the main Islamist movements in the Muslim world, it was possibly best suited and most accepting of the sort of pluralist democratic system that most Tunisians claimed they wanted to introduce following the fall of Ben Ali.

The mass demonstrations that began in February in Morocco in direct response to the events in Tunisia were met with a mixed reaction from the kingdom's main Islamist movements. As a long-time advocate of thorough-going political reform, *Al-Adl wal Ihsan* welcomed and participated in the marches and sit-ins but, fully aware that too heavy or obvious a presence might alienate other supporters and allow the authorities to characterise and thus repress the 20 February Movement as an Islamist one, it limited both its participation and profile within them. The PJD, for its part, was severely split in its response to the movement. In keeping with his accommodationist stance towards the palace, the party's leader, Abdelilah Benkirane, declared that the party would not participate or support the movement, a response that angered many in the party who disputed not only this view but also Benkirane's apparent lack of consultation with the party on the issue. Three senior members of the party resigned from the executive of the PJD to participate in the marches and demonstrations. One of them, Mustapha Ramid, who had long been an advocate of thorough constitutional and democratic reform, claimed that the party's position was 'unacceptable' and stated that all political parties and actors should involve themselves in the movement.[116] Thus the existing division within the party opened even wider, between those who saw support for the monarchy as the best means of advancing the party's agenda and those who viewed the establishment of fully democratic institutions as the way forward. The leadership of the party, nevertheless, formally endorsed the modest constitutional reforms introduced by the palace in July 2011 which sought to placate the demands of the protesters.

Islamism was notable by its apparent absence from developments in Algeria in the opening months of 2011. No organised political grouping was associated with the destructive unrest of the first week of the year in the country, and the small-scale demonstrations that began on February 12 were organised and led by the avowed ideological and political opponents of the Islamists; they chased away the former deputy leader of the FIS, Ali Belhadj, when he tried to participate on the first day.[117] As noted in Chapter 4, this absence was perhaps most readily explained by a reluctance on the part of both Algeria's Islamist movements and its wider population to see a return to the sort of confrontational street politics that had culminated in the prolonged bloodshed of the 1990s.

Conclusions

The varying experiences of Islamism in the Maghreb revealed a number of things about the region as a whole but also about the distinctive features of individual states. In many respects these distinctive features were reflected in the characteristics of the Islamist groups and organisations that developed in each country. Tunisia's reformist and constitutionalist tradition was clearly present in the agenda and thrust of the mainstream of the MTI and An-Nahda. Similarly, the populist, hegemonic and ultimately insurrectionist traditions of the FLN and its nationalist forerunners were unmistakably reproduced in the FIS and its offshoots, which consciously and explicitly laid claim to the nationalist party's historic and revolutionary legacy.[118] The more cautious and plural nature of the Islamist organisations in Morocco also followed established historical patterns in the kingdom. Abdesalam Yassine's challenge to the monarchy had, as has been seen, clear and conscious roots in Moroccan tradition, and *Al-Adl wal Ihsan*'s focus on the individual leadership of Yassine has been seen to have had echoes of the position of the king in the Moroccan political system.

In spite of their differences and particular historic traditions, the Islamist movements in all three states also had clear similarities and followed similar trajectories. The slight differences in timing of the emergence of substantial movements can be explained by differences in circumstances. The early emergence of a substantial Islamist movement in Tunisia undoubtedly had much to do with reactions to the more secular direction taken by Habib Bourguiba in the decades that followed independence. The comparatively late emergence of similar movements in Morocco was attributable to many of the specifities of Morocco explained earlier, but also to factors such as the kingdom's slower rate of urbanisation and less precipitous periods of economic crisis: factors that had provided a boost to Islamist movements in Algeria and Tunisia.

The distinctions between the states were both reduced and sharpened by increasing awareness of each other's experiences. The crisis and violence that unfolded in Algeria was followed closely in Morocco and Tunisia, and both the regimes and the Islamist movements there sought, often in sharply differing ways, to avoid reproducing such upheaval. Whilst elements within the security establishments and secular parties in Morocco and Algeria looked for lessons to be drawn from Tunisia's successful repression of Islamism, Islamists drew other lessons from Tunisia and from each other. Abdeslam Yassine praised the Tunisian movement's attachment to the issue of justice, which he said had been often neglected by Islamists; and An-Nahda itself looked to what were seen as the positive elements of Morocco's handling of Islamism.[119] In an interview in 2002, Rachid Ghannouchi called on Tunisia to follow the positive example of Morocco which had been able peacefully to incorporate the PJD into formal political processes.[120] On another occasion the leader of An-Nahda stated that his party in Tunisia and the FIS in Algeria had made the same mistake in seeking to move too quickly to achieve majority support within their respective countries. This was because the domestic and international contexts had not been ready for it and, as a consequence, 'we paid a high price for our mistake.'[121]

The international context in which the Maghrebi Islamist movements operated is dealt with elsewhere (see Chapter 9). The domestic situation is often overlooked. Opposition to Islamist movements came most obviously from the regimes in the region, but this opposition was often strongly supported by not insignificant parts of the ordinary populations in all three states that were wary and frequently hostile to the Islamists and their perceived agenda. Much of this hostility came from sections of society that had strong connections and affinities with Europe, and particularly France. These saw the Islamists as threatening important efforts to reproduce the sort of liberal, stable and prosperous social and political models that existed in the continent through their rejection of Western influence and advocacy of a 'return' to more 'authentic' models found in the Middle East—a prospect that these groups viewed with horror. Although such opinions were most commonly to be found amongst the elites in all three states, this was not always the case. They were also present in leftist circles, among much of Tunisia's large middle class and also among minority groups, notably in many Berberist associations (see Chapter 6).

In spite of these significant pockets of opposition to Islamism, Islamist groups nevertheless retained a significant potential purchase on the majority of the population of certainly Algeria and Morocco and a substantial minority of Tunisians, who still felt primarily defined by an Arab and Islamic identity and alienated from the ruling elite of the state through economic and political as well as cultural marginalisation. A noted feature of all three states in the early part of the twenty-first century was the growth in outward manifestations of religious piety, such as attendance at mosque and the wearing of beards and headscarves. To what extent this indicated a growth in potential support bases for Islamist movements was unclear. Some research suggests that the phenomenon is a largely apolitical and pietistic one. Leila Nadir Jones, who conducted research in 2005 in some of the areas of Algeria most affected by the violence of the 1990s, found that whilst most people rejected the violence of that period they recognised that the emergence of the FIS had allowed them to become more aware of Islam and that this had led to levels of increased religious awareness.[122] Other observers conclude that the emphasis on social justice in Islam suggests that personal piety will eventually become political, given the social, political and economic circumstances prevailing across the Maghreb.

One feature of Maghrebi Islamism has been its increased internationalisation. In their early stages, most of the Islamist organisations were clearly influenced by ideas and forms of organisation that originated outside the region—most notably the Muslim Brotherhood in Egypt. Yet although events like the Iranian revolution of 1978–9 provided initial inspiration to a number of these groups, they became increasingly focused not just on the Maghreb but on the individual national contexts in which they operated.[123] The repression of both the FIS and An-Nahda in the 1990s pushed large parts of the leaderships of both organisations into exile, predominantly in Europe, bringing them into contact not just with European society but also with other exiled and migrant groups, most notably from other parts of the Arab and Muslim worlds. They also strengthened links with the huge Maghrebi diaspora in the continent. The cumulative effect of all of this has been mixed. Whilst, as has been shown, it has clearly had a radicalising effect on some aspects of the movements, it has arguably had a rather different impact on other parts, with figures such as Rachid Ghannouchi becoming a vocal advocate of Western liberal democracy. This has led to his critics accusing him of simple opportunism, whilst others argue this endorsement built on the movement's existing commitment to peaceful and constitutional methods. It is a debate that is likely to be substantially resolved following Ghannouchi's return to the country in January 2011 and An-Nahda's legalisation as a political party.

A further driver for internationalisation has come through Islamism's engagement with and commitment to pan-Islamic causes. Protest marches in the run-up to the Gulf War of 1991 were critical of the development and expansion of these movements in both Algeria and Morocco. The huge popular support that causes such as that of the Palestinians enjoy among the vast majority of ordinary Maghrebis serves in turn to bolster support for Islamist parties, which are perceived to be the strongest and most authentic supporters of Pan-Islamic causes. In the 2002 elections in Morocco, some of those voting for the PJD claimed to be doing so primarily because of the party's position on the Palestinians.[124] The events of early 2011 demonstrated, though, that pan-Islamic causes were not, after all, the only ones capable of mobilising huge numbers of Maghrebis to take to the streets. Nevertheless, the victories for An-Nahda and then the PJD in the national elections of October and November 2011 in Tunisia and Morocco demonstrated the continuing appeal of Islamism. Evidence from both countries suggested, however, that much of the electoral support for the two parties was due to them being the main beneficiaries of the appetite for change and reform amongst the population that was a major product of the events of 2011. The degree to which they would be able to deliver such change and reform would therefore be a major test for both parties in government. Yet despite these apparently parallel experiences, there were important differences between the positions the two Islamist parties found themselves in after winning the elections. While An-Nahda became the leading and most powerful player in a political landscape that had been totally remade by the fall of the Ben Ali regime, the PJD in Morocco continued to operate in a system still very much under the control of the monarchy inviting comparisons with the position of the USFP and kutla parties in the *alternance* government that came into government in 1998. The complete failure of Algeria's Islamist parties to make comparable advances in the legislative elections held in May 2012 spoke of the absence of a similar popular demand for significant change as well as of the continuing sclerosis of formal politics within the country.

6

THE BERBER QUESTION

Political issues and conflicts around questions related to ethnicity became a feature of most newly independent countries in post-colonial Africa and Asia. The Maghreb was no exception to this trend, but what was remarkable was that ethnicity only became a significant political issue a generation after independence, rather than in its immediate aftermath.

One of the reasons for ethnicity failing to become an immediate political issue in the Maghreb states in the years following the achievement of independence was the relative homogeneity of the region. In religious terms over 95 per cent of the region's population at independence was not only Muslim but also Sunni of the Malekite rite. Significant Jewish populations had long been present across the region, but these declined dramatically with large-scale emigration to Israel and Europe both before and immediately after the independence of the three states. Although individual Jews remained prominent in all the states after this period, particularly in Morocco, the small size of the remaining Jewish populations, numbering a few thousand, left little scope for meaningful politicisation. Similarly small minority Ibadite Muslim communities existed in Algeria in the Mzab region and Tunisia in Djerba but were too small and remote to be of real political significance.[1]

Another major marker of ethnicity is language, and here there was comparatively much more diversity in the Maghreb than there was in religion. Although significant localised patterns of speech existed, and the presence of the colonial languages of Spanish and especially French had an impact, virtually all of the Maghreb's populations at independence spoke a variant of one of two main languages present in the region after independence: Arabic and what was generally known as 'Berber.' It is the real or perceived differences between speakers of these two languages that came to be a politicised issue in the Maghreb in the decades after independence, notably from the 1980s.

Historical Evolution

The politicisation of the issue of Arab and Berber language and identity has inevitably complicated attempts to examine the realities of the differences and divisions between speakers of these two languages. This is particularly true of discussion of the historical evolution of this issue since two widely differing narratives have emerged: one emphasising historical differences, the other long-standing unity between Berber and Arabic speakers.[2] There is, nevertheless, agreement that both languages coexisted following the arrival of the Arabs from the east from the seventh century to live amongst Berber-speaking populations that had been present in the region during the previous two and a half millennia. Berber languages remained predominant in the more rural, mountain and desert areas of the region; and Arabic became prevalent in the cities and the plains. The various ruling dynasties that rose and fell across the region over the following centuries emerged from both Berber- and Arabic-speaking areas, and language appeared not to be an issue of major division, especially given the unifying presence of Islam to which the Berber communities almost universally converted within a few centuries of its arrival with the Arabs.[3]

French Colonialism and the 'Berber Myth'

There is also general agreement that the establishment of European colonial control of the Maghreb from the nineteenth century is crucial in understanding the origins of the politicisation of the Arab-Berber issue. There is clear evidence that elements of the French administration that progressively took control of what would become Algeria over the middle decades of the nineteenth century took a particular interest in the issue. Already aware of the presence of Arabs and Arabic before their arrival in 1830, the French, notably the military administration, were intrigued to encounter local populations that spoke a different language—notably the Kabyle tribes in the mountainous areas to the east of Algiers whom they encountered early on in their conquest. An assumption was progressively made that not only did the Kabyles speak a different language—a form of Berber—from the Arabs of the cities and the plains, but also they represented a fundamentally distinct people or 'race.' Influenced by the expansion in pseudo-scientific interest in issues of race that was a feature of the period, a theory began to develop that not only were the Kabyles a *separate* people, but they were also a fundamentally *superior* people to the Arabs. There was even the suggestion that they were European in origin and that they had converted under duress, and therefore superficially, to Islam. Much of the supposed evidence to support these ideas was largely spurious, but it gave birth to something that became known as the 'Kabyle Myth.' Opposition from European settlers in the region prevented any attempt at treating the Kabyles on a par with Europeans, and as a result no thoroughgoing pro-Kabyle policy was ever applied by the colonial authorities. However, through migration to both Algiers and France itself to escape the privations of Kabylia, Kabyles became more exposed to France and, in particular, French education.[4]

The 'Kabyle Myth' nevertheless persisted within elements of the French administration and informed aspects of subsequent French colonial policy elsewhere in the Maghreb. Tunisia had only a very small Berber-speaking population, but in Morocco the French encountered large Berber-speaking communities. The most famous example of the influence of the Kabyle Myth in Morocco came with what became known as the 'Berber' Dahir of 1930, which was a French initiative that sought to institutionalise local customary law, rather than Islamic sharia law, in many of the main Berber-speaking areas of Morocco. Although historians are divided as to whether the Dahir sought to introduce or preserve this distinction, all agree that the Dahir became a major rallying cry for the emerging nationalist movement in Morocco, which interpreted it as an assault on the Islamic identity of Morocco by attempting to use religious issues to divide Arab from Berber.[5]

Nationalism and the Liberation Struggles

It was the emergence of the nationalist movements across the Maghreb in the mid-twentieth century that appeared to show that French colonial policies aimed at differentiating between speakers of Arabic and Berber had ultimately proved fruitless in terms of recruiting the Berber-speaking populations as allies for the colonial power. Even before the emergence of the nationalist movements in the 1930s, Berber-speaking areas had played a leading role in resisting European colonial rule. The great revolt against the French in 1871 in Algeria had begun in the Kabyle region and in Morocco the Berber tribes of the High Atlas had been the last to submit to the French campaign of 'pacification.' The most significant revolt against European colonial rule in Morocco occurred against the Spanish in the Berber-speaking Rif in the 1920s. When the organised nationalist movements did appear, Berber speakers were not only present in these movements but, moreover, came to play a major role when the struggle against colonial rule turned to violence in the 1950s. In Morocco the French were attacked in the rural Berber-speaking areas as well as in the towns; and in Algeria Berber-speakers arguably dominated and led the opening years of the liberation struggle. The Army of Liberation that began a campaign against the French in parts of rural Morocco from 1955 was overwhelmingly Berber in composition, and its attacks 'ensured rapid, total and irreversible independence' from the French.[6] Berber-speakers were disproportionately represented amongst the nine historic chiefs of the Algerian FLN and on the CNRA (*Comité National de la Révolution Algérienne*), and Kabyles dominated the core of the FLN's organisation in Algiers and in the Front's structures in France.[7]

Independence

The manifest failure of the French to prevent Berber-speakers joining with their Arabophone compatriots in ejecting France from the Maghreb was one of the main reasons cited in the immediate aftermath of independence for the remoteness of the possibility of any politicisation of the Arab-Berber divide in the post-colonial era. Such a view was not limited to nationalist politicians but was similarly endorsed by Western academics, many of whom expressed this view in an edited volume entitled *Arabs and Berbers*, published in the early 1970s. The contributors to this volume argued that identity in the Berber areas of the Maghreb was linked to tribe and clan and, beyond that, to Islam rather than to any notion of being ethnically Berber, the latter remaining abstract and fundamentally meaningless to the various geographically dispersed and relatively isolated Berber-speaking populations across the Maghreb.[8]

Given this consensus it was therefore strange that within less than a decade of the publication of *Arabs and Berbers,* Berber identity should become a significant political issue. Rival explanations for this development have portrayed it as either the culmination of centuries of struggle by Berbers against repression of their language and culture; or, alternatively, the deferred fruition of the original French colonial plan to differentiate and divide Arab from Berber. The reality, however, was that the emergence of Berber identity as a political issue was due much more to developments that occurred in the post-independence period in the region.

Algeria and Kabylia

The politicisation of the issue was witnessed initially and most dramatically in Algeria. In April 1980, a decision by the authorities to cancel a course on Berber poetry at Tizi Ouzou University in the Kabyle region led to large-scale demonstrations and unrest across Kabylia. Although this reaction took many by surprise, it was neither truly spontaneous nor unexpected in Kabylia itself and was the result of a number of different factors that had emerged over previous decades.[9]

Kabyles had dominated the FLN in the early years of the liberation struggle against the French, but early setbacks in the armed struggle had resulted in the deaths of many in the disproportionately Kabyle leadership—particularly in the capital during the Battle of Algiers in 1956–7. These defeats had led to the elements of the FLN based outside the country taking control of the struggle.[10] There were far fewer Kabyles represented in this new leadership and, more crucially, many of the new external leadership had spent time in and developed strong ties with the Arab world, which they recognised as a major source of external support. Egypt's Gamal Abd al-Nasser was a vociferous supporter of the FLN's struggle and his Arab nationalist ideology had strongly influenced many of the FLN's leaders. Although providing a strong unifying theme in the more religiously heterogeneous Mashreq, the message of Arab nationalism was bound to be more divisive in the Maghreb where significant parts of the population were not Arabic-speakers.[11]

It was after the final achievement of independence by the FLN in 1962 that the potentially divisive effect of Arab nationalism was felt. Ahmed Ben Bella's declaration of 'We are Arabs! We are Arabs! We are Arabs!'[12] on returning to Algeria at the end of the struggle was meant more as an assertion of national liberation than of ethnic supremacy, but it was a clear indication of the impact of Arab nationalist ideology not only on the man who would become independent Algeria's first president but also on the declared identity of that state. The formal and constitutional decision to declare independent Algeria to be an explicitly Arab state was intended, as Ben Bella's statement, to be a riposte against 132 years of French colonialism. It certainly did not amount to an attempt to marginalise and exclude Kabyles or other Berber-speakers from the circles of power. Individual Kabyles, in particular, continued to occupy senior positions in the state throughout the period after independence. The desire to rid independent Algeria of the nefarious effects of colonialism did, however, impact upon the Berber aspects of the new state, both indirectly and directly.

The decision to Arabise the country's Francophone education and administrative systems had an indirect effect. The mass exodus of the European population from Algeria in the run-up to independence in June 1962 had left a huge void in the structures of government which the new Algerian government struggled to fill. Francophone Algerians were thus appointed to fill these positions and Kabyles, being frequently the most accomplished Francophones by virtue of their greater exposure to French education and France itself (through migrant labour), made up a disproportionate number of those appointed. The advent of Arabisation, the impact of which began to be felt in the 1970s, posed a direct threat to the numerous Kabyles in the education and administrative systems who did not master Arabic. Unable, for obvious political reasons, to defend the use of French, these Kabyles, it is argued, resorted to a defence of their mother tongue—Kabyle Berber—to make a stand against Arabisation.[13] Arabisation not only threatened the livelihoods of Kabyle teachers and administrators, but also riled many ordinary Kabyles who were forced to learn what was for many of them a completely new language. Jane Goodman points out that it is no accident that the unrest of 1980 in Kabylia coincided with the coming of age of the first educational cohort that had been Arabised.[14]

More direct attempts were made to reduce the role and profile of Berber language and identity. Under the governments of both Ben Bella and Boumedienne—who shared the same Arab nationalist influences—radio broadcasts in Berber and Berber cultural festivals and music concerts were reduced and cancelled throughout the 1960s, and it became illegal to give Berber names to children.[15] This quite specific repression of expressions of Berber identity also had its roots in the official desire to reverse the effects of colonialism: the post-independence regimes viewing such expressions as a divisive legacy of the colonial Kabyle/Berber myth. The policy was also clearly in line with attempts in other newly decolonised states in Africa and Asia to impose a unified—and thus unifying—national identity. The irony that this model drew heavily on French Jacobin traditions of cultural and linguistic unity was not missed, especially by those seeking to defend against official policies.[16]

France also played a role in the development of another, external, factor that contributed to the politicisation of the issue of Berber identity. In 1967 the *Académie Berbère* was established in Paris to study Berber history, culture and language. Although decried by some as a neo-colonial effort to revive the Berber Myth and sow division in the societies of the newly independent Maghreb, the *Académie* and other similar initiatives over the following decade were part of a broader trend in Western academia during this period that took greater interest in and placed more emphasis on diversity and differences in societies. Previous emphases on themes of commonality and unity gave way to a trend towards rediscovering and preserving diverse and minority cultures and traditions. The long-standing educational and migratory links between France and Kabylia ensured that this was a trend that found influence amongst the large numbers of Kabyles studying and teaching at French universities, some of whom began to take greater interest in studying Kabyle language, history and culture.[17] In parallel with these developments in academia, there was also a growth in Berber associations in Paris amongst the large expatriate Kabyle community there.

Within the Kabyle region itself the combination of these various factors led to a steady growth in organisations and associations dedicated to the protection and promotion of Berber culture and language, spearheaded by student organisations at Tizi Ouzou University.[18] The very term 'Berber' itself was rejected by these groups (because of its supposed etymological links to the term 'Barbarian') in favour of the word *Amazigh*, the singular form of *Imazighen* being the name of a Berber tribe from southern Morocco meaning 'free man.' The first signs of this new 'Berberist' trend began to emerge in the early 1970s, with an explicitly Berberist riot occurring in Larbaa n'Ait Irathen in Kabylia in May 1974.[19] It proved to be a foretaste of the substantial upheaval that would follow six years later in Kabylia in April 1980. It also showed that the events of that month were less of a spontaneous explosion (as they were subsequently widely characterised) but were more a result of a convergence of factors of which the new Amazigh associations were a very conscious, crucial and active part.[20] Nevertheless, the events of April 1980 came to assume enormous significance for the emerging Berberist/Amazigh movement at a number of levels. The participation of large numbers of ordinary, particularly younger, Kabyles in the strikes, demonstrations and confrontations with the authorities during that period marked the transmission of Berberist ideas from the Kabyle intelligentsia to the wider Kabyle population, and this would prove enduring. The development of a strong Kabyle 'consciousness' amongst the youth in Kabylia was also significant, Jane Goodman arguing that the parents of the youths who spearheaded the protests of 1980 would not have thought of themselves as distinctly Kabyle.[21] At the national level, the Kabyle Spring of 1980 was also significant as the first incidence of large-scale popular unrest in independent Algeria, and as such the first major popular challenge to the regime.

A notable feature of the events of 1980 was that they were confined to the Kabyle region. Despite being popularly labelled the 'Berber' Spring, the protests and unrest were not replicated in Algeria's other Berber-speaking regions. Indeed, the emergence of Berberist sentiment witnessed through the 1960s and 1970s had also been absent in these regions. This serves to underline an important point: that the development of Berberist sentiment in Algeria by 1980 was an almost exclusively Kabyle affair. Quite why this was the case is explained by important differences between Kabylia and Algeria's other principal Berber-speaking areas: the Aurès and the Mzab. The dual facts that Kabyles constituted roughly two-thirds of Algeria's Berber-speakers and that Kabylia was geographically closer to Algiers than the more remote Aurès and Mzab were clearly significant. Historical factors, notably in the colonial period, are also of importance. Kabylia's geographical proximity to Algiers meant that its population was exposed to French colonialism from early on, following the French takeover of Algiers in 1830. As stated earlier, one of the results of this was proportionately greater exposure to French education, partly as a result of official French efforts inspired by the Kabyle Myth but also through migration to Algiers and to France itself. The development of a large and influential Kabyle community in France played a crucial role in the development of Berberist sentiment. The failure of these factors to obtain in the Aurès and the Mzab is due to a combination of both geography and religious tradition. The Chaouia Berbers of the Aurès mountains were more geographically dispersed and nomadic than the Kabyles in Kabylia and proved less open to French educational efforts—possibly because of the greater influence of the Association of Ulema in the 1930s and 1940s. For the inhabitants of the Mzab, their long tradition of independence and isolation as a (Ibadi) religious minority, together with their location on the northern fringes of the Sahara, insulated them from outside trends.[22] Nevertheless it was significant that the movement in Kabylia articulated itself as a movement for Berber rather than specifically Kabyle rights, for reasons that will be explored later.

Morocco: The Royal Alliance

The specificities of the Kabyle experience and the absence of any resonances in other Berber-speaking areas of Algeria suggested that the prospects for the development of Berberist sentiment or consciousness beyond Algeria's borders were likely to be very limited. This was something that appeared to be borne out during the early decades in the Maghreb state that contained the largest number of Berber speakers—Morocco.

As in Algeria, the issue of Berber identity had become politicised in Morocco in the colonial period through the furore surrounding the Berber Dahir of 1930. Leading the protests against the Dahir were embryonic nationalist organisations that would consolidate themselves into the Istiqlal party by the 1940s. Developing out of intellectual and religious circles in Rabat and Fez in the 1920s, the Istiqlal was an overwhelmingly urban movement that drew relatively few adherents from the rural and Berber-speaking *milieux*.[23] Although the latter played their own part in the eviction of the French from the country in the 1950s, the Istiqlal itself remained a fundamentally urban and Arab party. The recruitment by the French colonial authorities of notables from Berber areas to help them run much of rural and southern Morocco created certain cleavages in Moroccan society, which although predominantly urban-rural in nature could not avoid developing an Arab-Berber dimension as well. This divide was exacerbated upon the achievement of independence as Istiqlali officials not only moved into rural areas in an attempt to take control but also embarked on a campaign to root out former French allies amongst the rural nobility.[24]

It was the entrance of the Moroccan monarchy into the developing conflict between the rural nobility and the Istiqlal that changed the situation. Mohamed V's need for allies in his struggle for political supremacy with the Istiqlal in the years after independence led him to recruit significant allies from the rural world to counterbalance the power of the nationalist movement (see Chapter 2). This was done through appointments to the Ministry of the Interior but, most notably, the newly created military (see Chapter 3). The king also sanctioned the legalisation of the new rural and Berber-based political party—the *Mouvement Populaire*—as a bulwark against Istiqlali ambitions in the parliament and at elections.[25]

The common desire to protect themselves from the ambitions of the Istiqlal and its allies helped consolidate the strategic alliance between the royal palace and the rural Berber nobility in the decades that followed independence. The palace gained valuable and loyal allies in the military and the parliament, whilst the rural notables, in addition to positions of influence in the state, were able to maintain traditional power structures and ways of life in the countryside.[26] It would be mistaken, though, to think that this alliance translated into any tangible 'Berberisation' of the Moroccan state. There were no official initiatives to protect or further Berber language, culture and identity. In common with Algeria, Morocco affirmed its Arab identity in the first post-independence constitution and began to introduce Arabisation measures from the 1960s. The fact that the *Mouvement Populaire* was part of the royalist coalition government that introduced the Arabisation law in 1965 was an indication of the monarchy's control over a party that had originally called for the introduction of education in the Berber languages.[27]

In spite of the official emphasis on the Arab identity of the kingdom, there was not the same official hostility to expressions of Berber culture as witnessed in Algeria during this period. This was largely due to the fact that, unlike Algeria where Arab nationalists took control of the government and policy, Morocco's Arab nationalists concentrated in the Istiqlal and its allies were shut out of power from the early 1960s. As Salem Chaker has pointed out, whereas Algeria adopted Arab nationalism as a major part of its national identity at independence, this role was filled by the monarchy in Morocco. As a result, the monarchy proved willing to tolerate low-profile expressions of Berber culture so long as they did not develop any political dimensions.[28]

The more permissive official policy in Morocco facilitated the emergence of small numbers of Berber cultural associations from the 1960s. These associations were explicitly cultural in character and were not permitted to use the word Berber in their titles.[29] The numbers and membership of these associations gradually expanded during the 1970s, often for many of the same reasons that Berberist/Amazigh activism had begun to grow in Kabylia in Algeria in this period: antipathy towards Arabisation policies and the growing influence of new ideas about identity affecting the intellectual and diaspora communities.[30] More specifically Moroccan factors also played their part. Ideological shifts with the repression and decline of the political left and the beginnings of the rise of Islamism also helped expand the support of the Berber cultural associations.[31]

In spite of similarities with Algeria, Morocco did not experience anything akin to the upheavals of spring 1980. This was largely because, as Brett and Fentress point out, Morocco 'has no Kabylia.'[32] Geographically, Morocco's Berber-speaking regions are all more dispersed and remote than Kabylia, being concentrated in the mountainous areas of the Rif and the Middle, High and Anti Atlas regions, as well as the Souss Valley. None of these regions was affected in quite the same way as was Kabylia during Algeria's much longer period under French colonial control. Whilst it was true that the French drew heavily on the Berber populations for their colonial army and gave local control to Berber chieftains in a number of regions, the French education that came to have an important influence in Kabylia was limited in Morocco's Berber areas.[33] In spite of these important differences, Morocco was not unaffected by the events of spring 1980 in Kabylia. It emboldened the kingdom's growing number of Berber Cultural Associations to develop a more political agenda.[34] The first edition of a new revue entitled *Amazigh* appeared in Morocco in 1980 and contained articles that sought to challenge official positions on Berber identity—most particularly an article on history that described the first Arabs to arrive in the Maghreb as 'conquerors' who had oppressed the native people. The fact that the revue was banned within months of appearing, and the author of the offending article on Moroccan history arrested and imprisoned for a year, was clear evidence of the limits of the tolerance of the Moroccan regime.[35]

Berberism in the 1990s: Concessions from the State

The end of the 1980s and the advent of the 1990s marked a new phase in the development of Berber identity in Morocco and Algeria, with both countries increasingly moving in step on the issue. The 1990s witnessed both states making significant concessions to their respective Berberist movements, largely in response to internal and external pressures to democratise and also to the domestic challenge of Islamism.

Berberism and the Multi-party Opening in Algeria

The tumultuous events of October 1988 in Algeria and President Chadli Benjedid's decision to introduce multi-party elections changed the political context and outlook for the Berber Cultural Movement (*Mouvement Culturel Berbère*, or MCB) that had developed out of the Kabyle Spring of 1980 and had grown through the following decade. Many Berberist activists took credit for the reforms of 1989, arguing that the Kabyle Spring had paved the way for a democratic opening by presenting the first genuine popular challenge to the Algerian regime. It also provided activists for a new and more vibrant civil society which focused not just on Berber culture but also on human rights: most of the stalwarts of the first human rights organisations to emerge in the 1980s being Kabyles.[36] Although the reforms of 1989 had more to do with internal regime politics (see Chapter 4) than any pressure from Kabyle civil society, the perception of being at the vanguard of change in Algeria was an important one for Kabyles. It explains why there was no attempt to launch a regionalist Kabyle political party to take advantage of the regime's decision to permit the formation of independent political parties. Instead, Kabyles lent their support, to two political parties which, despite being created and based in the region and led by Kabyles, had national political scope and ambitions. The *Front des Forces Socialistes* (FFS) had been set up in 1963 by Hocine Ait Ahmed, one of the nine historic chiefs of the FLN, to combat what Ait Ahmed regarded as Ben Bella's attempt to establish dictatorial rule in Algeria. Following a failed uprising during the year of its creation, the FFS had been repressed and functioned largely in exile until the opening of 1989. The second party, the *Rassemblement pour la Culture et la Démocratie* (RCD) was, in contrast to the FFS, a new political party created in 1989 by activists from the MCB, a number of whom had previously been members of the FFS. Both parties campaigned on a national level in subsequent elections.

Morocco: Royal Concessions

The dramatic introduction of pluralism in Algeria from 1989, and the change of leadership and apparent opening of the political system in Tunisia, led to attention being focused on Morocco's failure to follow suit. Pressure from both within and outside the kingdom led to the beginning of a process of gradual political reform from the early 1990s. Morocco's emerging Berberist movement sought to take advantage of this changing situation, but not by forming a political party. This was because of the existence of the *Mouvement Populaire* and the fact that the political opening was not as dramatic or as initially promising as in Algeria. Instead six associations came together to draw up a set of demands which they subsequently presented to the regime. The Agadir Charter of August 1991 called essentially for the Berber language to be officially recognised and given a greater place in Morocco. Specifically it called for the Berber language to be given national status alongside Arabic and for it to be integrated into the education system and the national media.[37]

The Agadir Charter further galvanised Berberist activism in Morocco. Associations began to grow in number and in the scope of their activities, both inside and beyond Morocco, and began to coalesce under the broad banner of the Amazigh Cultural Movement (*Mouvement Culturel Amazigh*, or MCA) and created a National Committee for Coordination in 1994.[38] The regime, however, remained wary of any activism that moved beyond academic and cultural circles. In May 1994 seven members of the Berber cultural association *Tilleli* (Freedom) in Goulmima in the south-east of the country were arrested and charged with disturbing public order and threatening the security of the state after they unfurled banners calling for the Berber language to be officially recognised. The event proved to be a catalyst for a remarkable series of concessions from the regime. Not only were the initially harsh sentences imposed on those arrested at Goulmima subsequently reduced or dropped, but on 14 June the prime minister, Abdelatif Filali, announced that the national media would begin broadcasts in the three main Berber dialects. More remarkably, in a speech on 20 August, King Hassan himself announced that plans were to be drawn up to teach the language in schools.[39]

The shift in policy by the royal palace can be explained by a number of factors. The arrest of the activists in Goulmima had attracted significant publicity, not least abroad where Berberist activists had begun to become increasingly active in lobbying and making their cause known at international fora where their argument for expanded minority rights was well received. In the context of the early 1990s, when the Moroccan regime was attracting significant international criticism over its human rights record and perceived intransigence over the Western Sahara and lack of democracy, the regime was anxious not to worsen things by appearing to oppress ethnic minority rights. By seeming to concede to some of the main demands of the MCA, the palace was also using one of its oldest and most well-established strategies in dealing with political opposition: that of co-option. King Hassan was aware that the movement posed no real immediate threat to the regime and that by selectively implementing parts of its agenda he could at once prevent the sort of radicalisation of the movement that had occurred in Kabylia in Algeria and also recruit a potentially valuable political ally in a way that his father had succeeded in doing with the Berber notables in the immediate aftermath of independence. The perceived need for allies had arguably grown in the early 1990s, as King Hassan observed the rise of Islamism next door in Algeria.[40]

The Regime Concedes: Algeria

In Algeria, the rise of Islamism, in the shape of the FIS, had left the regime feeling increasingly embattled and isolated, particularly with the rising tide of violence that followed the decision to cancel elections and ban the FIS in 1992. In a reversal of the trend hitherto for Algeria to set the pattern for Morocco, the Algerian authorities followed Morocco's lead in seeking to recruit an ally in the Berberist movement by making significant concessions to it. The MCB, in particular, had shown itself capable of mobilising significant numbers of people for non-Islamist causes—most notably through a school strike organised in Kabylia in 1994–5 in support of the introduction of Berber language into education. Thus a matter of months after Morocco declared its intention to integrate Berber language into education and the national media, Mokdad Sifi, the prime minister of Algeria, made an unprecedented speech in November 1994 in which he affirmed the Berber elements of Algeria's identity and called for the launch of efforts to integrate the use of the Berber language, *Tamazight*, into everyday life. The following year, on the fifteenth anniversary of the Kabyle Spring, the Algerian government announced that it would be creating a *Haut Commissariat à l'Amazighité* (HCA) which would be attached to the president's office and charged with the rehabilitation of Berber culture and the introduction of *Tamazight* into the education and communication systems. A year after that, in one of a series of constitutional amendments, Berber/Amazigh was officially recognised as one of the elements of Algeria's national identity, alongside the existing Arab and Islamic elements.[41]

The Challenge of Islamism

The belief amongst the leaderships of both Algeria and Morocco that the Berberist/Amazigh movement would be an ally against the Islamists was founded on an awareness of the significant ideological differences between the two movements. Islamism's vision of a unified society based on a single source of identity—Islam—clashed visibly with the Berberists' call for greater recognition of minority identities. More specifically, Berberists' opposition to Arabisation was regarded as highly problematic by most Islamists who viewed Arabic, as the language of the Quran, as having a special status. Islamists were also highly suspicious of the strong links the Berberist movement had in Western countries, notably France, believing that the movement was largely a product of the neo-colonial ambitions of the former colonial power. There were also more tangible demonstrations of these differences. In the local and national elections of 1990 and 1991 in Algeria, the Kabyle region had been one of the few in the country to have not voted heavily for the FIS, preferring instead to vote for either the FFS or the RCD. Indeed the RCD had adopted a more or less explicitly secular political platform and was extremely hostile to Islamism. In Morocco, Abdeslam Yassine, the leader of the country's largest Islamist movement, published a book in 1997 detailing conversations he had had with one of Morocco's leading Berberists, in which he set out his main ideological differences with and objections to the Berberist movement.[42]

Kabylia 2001: The Berber Spring Revisited?

Islamism dominated Algerian politics in the 1990s, first through the electoral victories of the FIS and subsequently through the bitter civil conflict of the 1990s. In spite of the concessions made by the regime, the issues of both Berber identity and the Kabyle region slipped from the headlines. It was significant that it was as the violence of the 1990s began to abate that the issues returned to centre stage with the eruption of violent protests in Kabylia in April 2001. That the protests grew out of events to mark the twenty-first anniversary of the Kabyle Spring of April 1980 led many, particularly in the international media, to conclude that they marked a renewal of the campaign for Berber linguistic and cultural rights in the region. The precise cause of the unrest had, however, been public unhappiness with the actions of the police in the region: specifically the death in police custody of a young Kabyle and arrests of Kabyle high school students for supposedly insulting the police, rather than anything explicitly related to Berber identity.[43] This reading also overlooked the fact that many of the demands of the Berber Cultural Movement had been met by the regime during the previous decade. When the initially largely uncoordinated unrest developed institutional structures and was able to put forward a set of demands, it was noticeable that out of the fifteen demands presented, only one (that *Tamazight* be made an official language) related to cultural and linguistic rights.[44] The other fourteen demands were related to efforts to defuse the crisis and, more significantly, to proposals for reforms for Algeria as a whole. The latter category included demands to place 'all executive functions of the state and security corps under the authority of democratically elected bodies' and for 'a state that guarantees all socioeconomic rights and freedoms.'[45]

The national scope of the demands coming out of the 2001 protests was striking and clearly related to Kabylia's view of itself as being in the vanguard spearheading political change for the rest of the country. The demands were also related to more specific economic and political problems in Kabylia. Economically, the region had suffered throughout the 1990s, as a decline in state investment across Algeria combined with a reduced flow in workers' remittances. Politically, the region had become more and more isolated through its consistent support for opposition parties such as the FFS and the RCD which enjoyed little support outside Kabylia and areas populated by Kabyles.[46] As the International Crisis Group (ICG) observed, this meant that the population of Kabylia had 'been excluded from the routines of party-political clientalism that operate elsewhere.'[47] Nevertheless, the general grievances expressed by the protesters in Kabylia related to issues such as police brutality, declining socio-economic conditions and lack of democracy that were common to all Algerians.

In its initial stages the impact of the unrest was significant. Not only did protests and demonstrations continue into the weeks and months that followed the initial outburst, but the organisations produced by the unrest that came together in what became known as the 'Coordinations Movement' proved capable of articulating the grievances of the unrest in a written document, the El Kseur Platform, and then mobilising support for it. The Coordinations Movement organised mass marches, culminating in one held in the capital Algiers in June which attracted over one million people, making it easily the largest march in Algerian history—bigger even than the rallies organised by the FIS at its height. Over time, however, the movement born out of the unrest of spring 2001 lost momentum as the regime's 'oblique and partial' approach to negotiations led to it splintering into factions.[48] This splintering was aided by the Algerian regime's decision to concede the one demand in the El Kseur Platform that related to Berber culture and identity: that *Tamazight* be recognised as a national language. This had the effect of encouraging elements within Kabylia to push more heavily on this issue and demand *Tamazight*'s recognition as an official language alongside Arabic. More significantly, conceding this demand permitted the regime the opportunity to portray the unrest as essentially ethnic and particularist in nature and thus prevent the spread of unrest and protests to non-Kabyle areas of the country.[49]

Morocco: New King, New Openings?

King Hassan's apparent endorsement of a number of the demands of the Amazigh Cultural Movement in Morocco greatly encouraged the movement, which felt it had been given a 'green light' by the palace for its agenda.[50] There was disappointment, however, about the slow and superficial introduction of the promised reforms. News bulletins in the three main Berber dialects were introduced into the national broadcast media, but these were very short and Berber activists complained that they were of poor quality and focused on events in the Arab world.[51] No progress had been made on the introduction of Berber languages into schools by the end of the 1990s. The appointment in 1998 of the *alternance* government dominated by opposition Kutla parties raised the hope of greater democratisation amongst the general population but was viewed with mixed feelings by the Berberists, because of the historic attachment to Arab nationalism of the principal Kutla parties.

The arrival of a new king in 1999 carried the promise of a renewed impetus for reforms on the issue of Berber identity, and to this end, Berberist activists drew up a document that became swiftly known as the 'Berber Manifesto.' Signed by nearly 200 intellectuals, businessmen and academics, the Manifesto called principally for Berber to be made an official language, the introduction of Berber language into the administrative and educational systems, a greater place to be given to the Berbers in official history and economic development programmes for marginalised Berber-speaking regions.[52] The Manifesto was announced on 1 March 2000 and a copy was sent to the royal palace. Two months later the signatories of the Manifesto met at Bouznika to elect a council.[53] The Berberist movement became more visible and vocal in other ways too. The events of the spring of 2001 in Algeria were followed closely by Amazigh associations, who published communiqués and organised meetings in solidarity with the protesters in Kabylia.[54] At a march organised on 1 May 2001, Berber activists chanted 'No to an Arab Morocco.'[55]

King Mohamed responded to these new calls by announcing at the end of July 2001 that he intended to create an institute of Amazigh culture; less than three months later he announced a decree (*dahir*) establishing the *Institut Royal de la Culture Amazigh* (IRCAM). The new institute would contain six different centres, each dealing with different areas concerned with the promotion of Amazigh culture: including the development of a unified form of Berber language to be used in education. Prominent Berberist activists were invited to join the institute. Its formation, however, split the Berberist movement, with some seeing it as an opportunity to further its agenda whilst others viewed it as a classical Makhzen strategy to co-opt and defang the Berberist movement.[56] Consequently, whilst many Berberist activists accepted the palace's invitation to work within IRCAM, others kept their distance.

The palace's motivations in creating IRCAM were a continuation of the mixture of reasons that had prompted the concessions made on the issue of Berber identity from the mid 1990s. King Mohamed was aware of the continued growth in popularity of the movement and clearly sought to co-opt it further before it developed too oppositional a stance.[57] In doing this he was very conscious of the experience of Algeria: his announcement of his intention to establish IRCAM coming a matter of months after the unrest in Kabylia of spring 2001.[58] The new king's wish to portray himself in the eyes of Western governments as a young reformer promoting cultural rights and civil society also clearly played its part, with him pointing out in an interview with the French press that his mother came from a Berber family and that he regretted never having been taught the Berber language.[59] Perhaps most importantly of all, the continued rise in support for the kingdom's Islamist movements reinforced the need to foster the Berberist movement as both a counterweight and an ally for the palace. By championing its cause, the palace knew that it could gain the loyalty of the Berberist movement, which was aware that the promotion of the Berber language enjoyed little support amongst the main political parties in the country, which were largely Arab nationalist or Islamist in orientation. This realisation made some Berberists cautious about pushing for further political reform and democratisation, since this would inevitably give more political power to these parties.[60] Within a short time of IRCAM's establishment there were complaints from both outside and within the institute that, despite royal endorsement, the institute's efforts were being frustrated and delayed by elements of the administration, even at the ministerial level, allied to the Kutla parties. In 2005 a number of members of IRCAM left the institute in protest at what they saw as attempts to block the integration of Berber into education and the media.[61] In spite of this, a unified form of Berber—*Tifinagh*—was formally introduced into a number of Moroccan schools from September 2003, and this was seen as an important step forward and evidence of the political will existing at the top of the state even if the number (317) and proportion (5 per cent) of schools it was initially introduced into were quite low.[62] Nevertheless, critics pointed out that the reforms were introduced by administrative circular only, and that no changes had been made to either the education law or the constitution to reflect these new initiatives.[63]

Those members of the Amazigh Cultural Movement that had stayed out of IRCAM viewed the problems it encountered as an inevitable result of co-option. The more radical wing of the movement believed that a more independent and political approach was needed in order to move beyond the cultural dimension within which the Moroccan state wished to contain the Berberist movement. Since the 1990s there had been talk of the need for the creation of a Berber political party. Berberist activists had an established contempt for the *Mouvement*

Populaire, which they viewed as a loyalist sinecure to attract Berber votes, devoid of any ideology. Some even accused it of being sustained and paid by the Makhzen to recuperate and thwart the Berber elite.[64] In 2005 radical activists announced their intention to create a new party entitled the *Parti Democrate Amazigh Marocaine* (PDAM). Aware of the legal ban on political parties referring to ethnicity in their name, statutes and agenda, the PDAM sought to get round this by arguing that the party was open to all Moroccans, and that since everyone in Morocco was at least partly of Berber descent, the use of the term Amazigh could not be seen as ethnically divisive.[65] This argument was not accepted by the authorities, and in April 2008 the Administrative Tribunal of Rabat annulled the constitution of the PDAM because of its formal references to Amazigh identity.[66]

The creation of IRCAM and the PDAM took place against a backdrop of continued growth in support for the MCA. The Agadir Charter of 1991 had involved just six associations, but by 2005 the number of associations belonging to the MCA totalled an estimated 300.[67] Within two years of its appearance, the Berber Manifesto of 2000 had been signed by two million supporters.[68] This dramatic expansion drew in activists from new backgrounds, expanding the movement from its original core of urban intellectuals in the universities that had been the mainstay of associations from the 1970s. Large numbers of younger activists began to be drawn into the movement, with growing representation of students and individuals from Morocco's increasingly politicised unemployed graduates.[69] For its part, the PDAM, despite its fundamentally intellectual make-up, was proud to claim that 80 per cent of its officials were aged below thirty.[70] Popular music played a significant role, as it had in Kabylia, in the spread of Berberist ideas amongst the young. One group, Izenzaren, that promoted awareness of Berber identity sold in excess of 160,000 cassettes of their latest album in 2005.[71] There was also evidence that the movement was beginning to make inroads into rural areas where the overwhelming majority of Berber speakers lived but had hitherto had no involvement with the movement.[72] In contrast to Kabylia where the events of the spring of 1980 had succeeded in spreading a Berber consciousness to the mass of ordinary Kabyles, no such process had occurred in Morocco. Many Berberist activists hoped that with the spread of both media and education in the Berber language, to these areas this might eventually come to pass.

THE BERBER QUESTION

The Dilemmas of Nationalism, Regionalism and Particularism

One of the major issues confronting the Berberist movement in both Algeria and Morocco is whether to perceive its goals and agenda in national or in regionalist and particularist terms. Until very recently, the movement has very much had national ambitions and perspectives. This has partly been due to the fact that regionalism and ethnic particularism have been not only technically illegal but also officially repressed in both states. Recent developments have, however, seen the first shifts in this position with the emergence of voices within the Berberist movement arguing for ethnic particularism and regional autonomy.

Algeria: The Challenge to the National Agenda

In Algeria, the Berberist movement has had a long and established history as a movement with a perspective and vision for the whole of the country rather than for one or more of its Berber-speaking regions. Berberists have pointed as evidence of this to the involvement of Berber-speakers in the struggle to eject the French from the *whole* of Algeria, dating from the Kabyle revolt of 1871 through to the strong presence of Berber-speakers in the revolutionary FLN (which, after all, was the *National* Liberation Front). Even when a Berberist movement emerged in Kabylia after independence, it was noticeable that its leaders did not argue for independence from the Algerian state and viewed the events of 1980 and their aftermath as spearheading change for the whole of Algeria. Even the focus of the movement on linguistic and cultural rights was seen as a strategy for transforming the wider Algerian state: recognition of such rights being an acceptance of greater pluralism and thus a step on the road to greater democracy. Moreover, the cultural and linguistic demands of the movement were for *Berbers* generally, rather than specifically for *Kabyles*. For although the events of 1980 were limited to Kabylia and were absent from Algeria's other Berber-speaking areas, they did not produce a 'Kabyliest' movement.[73] For the International Crisis Group, this attachment to a national vision can be explained with reference to the significant Kabyle contribution to the liberation struggle: 'The collective memory of Kabylia's contribution to the nationalist movement has furnished grounds for grievance over what the resulting Algerian state had become and arguments with which to legitimise the Berberist cause and de-legitimise the regime in Algerian-nationalist terms.'[74] As Hugh Roberts stated with regard to the Kabyle Spring of 1980, but which held true for the events of 2001: 'the relevant opposition is not: Kabyles versus the nation state, but: Kabyles versus the regime in power. This is a very different matter.'[75]

Following the opening up of the political system in 1989, the dominant parties that emerged in Kabylia, the FFS and RCD, whilst both overwhelmingly Kabyle in terms of origins, leadership and membership, were vociferously national in their ambitions and rebutted any suggestion that they were in some way 'Kabyle' or 'Berber' parties. It was true that the new constitution forbade the formation of parties on ethnic grounds, but a similar provision applying to religion had not prevented the legalisation of the FIS. The events of 2001 demonstrated the persistence of this trend through the El Kseur Platform's demands for changes at the national level in Algeria.

In spite of the national orientation of the demands of the movement that emerged out of the unrest of 2001, the period witnessed the first signs of a rival more regionalist trend. In August of that year the veteran Kabyle singer and cultural rights campaigner, Ferhat Mehenni, announced the creation of the Movement for the Autonomy of Kabylia (MAK). Mehenni explained his decision to launch the new movement as a result of his conclusion that the Berberist movement had failed in its attempts to change and reform the Algerian state and that the logical course of action was to try to implement these changes within Kabylia's own borders in the context of regional autonomy. In addition to the manifest failure of Algeria to democratise, he also pointed to the clear failure of the FFS and the RCD to attract non-Kabyle support.[76] He was joined by the Kabyle intellectual Salem Chaker, who argued that 'one can have no doubt that the "Algerianist" strategy of the Kabyle political elites has shown itself to be a path that has not brought and will not bring democracy to Algeria, nor freedom and security to Kabylia.' This was because, Chaker argued, the Algerianist strategy ignored the fact that the majority of Algerians were Arabophones and could not relate to the references of the Kabyles or Berbers.[77] This reference to differences in outlook between Arab-speakers, and not simply Kabyles but Berbers as a whole, marked not just a significant break with the national vision of the leaders of the Berber Cultural Movement in Kabylia (which Chaker had himself hitherto endorsed)[78] but also represented an adoption of a potentially more ethnic view of politics. Nevertheless, the focus of the MAK was to be on Kabylia and, in the view of the International Crisis Group, marked an abandonment of a vision for not just Algeria but also Berber-speakers beyond Kabylia.[79] As Mehenni himself concluded, '…there is only one solution: that Kabylia ceases to demand for others what it wants for itself. Its grievances must be applied only within its own natural frontiers.'[80] The precise strength of this trend was difficult to discern, although it was clear that it enjoyed much greater support amongst the Kabyle diaspora than within Kabylia itself, where the majority still identified Algeria rather than Kabylia as their state. Nevertheless, the MAK received significant attention from the regime. This was almost certainly because the MAK's regionalist agenda dovetailed perfectly with the regime's desire to portray the Kabyle movement of 2001 as an ethnic and regionalist one, rather than one that articulated issues that were of concern to all Algerians.[81]

A further boost to the case for Kabyle regionalism came in September 2005 with President Abdelaziz Bouteflika's statement that 'the Arabic language will remain the national language and the only official language of Algeria…there is no country in the world that has two official languages [sic] and this will never be the case in Algeria where the only language, established by the Constitution, is Arabic.'[82] This definitively rebuffed a demand from elements of the Coordinations Movement that *Tamazight* be made an official as well as a national language. Whether part of the conscious official policy to play up the MAK or, more likely, a populist gesture to Algeria's majority Arabophones in the context of the national referendum on the Charter for Peace and National Reconciliation, the effect was the same in further convincing the likes of Mehenni and Chaker of the futility of pursuing Berberist objectives within the framework of the wider Algerian state.[83]

Morocco: A Berber State in Part or in Whole?

The Berberist movement in Morocco has remained overwhelmingly national in its vision, partly because of the lack of an equivalent region to that of Kabylia in Algeria but also undoubtedly because Berber-speakers represented a much larger proportion of the population in Morocco. This has allowed Berberists to claim that Morocco is ethnically a Berber country. Ahmed Adghrini of the PDAM has argued that through centuries of intermarriage no fully genetically Arab population remains in Morocco, whilst fully genetically Berber communities clearly exist in remote mountain and desert areas. This has left a Berber population being ruled by a minority 'Arabo-Islamic' creed.[84] The PDAM's founding objectives were profoundly national in scope, with even its call for a federal structure being firmly anchored in a 'united kingdom.'[85] In spite of this, the possibilities for the emergence of ethnic nationalism and regionalism exist. David Crawford has pointed out that whilst local, national and religious (Islamic) identities remain strongest in Morocco's main Berber-speaking areas, the fact that these regions are the poorest in the kingdom opens the door to the argument that a connection exists between this poverty and the Berber ethnicity of these regions' inhabitants. Even though this poverty is clearly linked more to the remote and rural location of these populations than their ethnicity, this may prove to be irrelevant. As Crawford points out, 'Whatever the statistical reality, if rural Berbers come to see themselves as a group that is disproportionately impoverished, there will emerge the real potential for a distinctly radical Berber politics.'[86]

The potential for regionalism is perhaps even greater in Morocco for a number of reasons. Firstly, several of Morocco's main Berber-speaking areas have strong senses of regional identity—notably the Rif mountains and the Souss Valley—produced by rather distinct historical experiences, particularly in the case of the Rif where colonisation by the Spanish rather than the French and systematic disfavour during Hassan II's rule helped accentuate a feeling of distinctiveness. Secondly, migrants from both of these regions make up a disproportionate number of Morocco's expatriate community in Europe, and whilst the bulk of these migrants are far less educated and integrated into their host societies than the Algerian Kabyles have historically been in France, the European connection is still potentially influential. The fact that most migrants from the Rif live in European states such as Germany, Belgium and Spain with federal or quasi federal political structures could conceivably have an impact. In Spain, in particular, the development of individual autonomous regions based on linguistic nationalism such as the Basque and Catalan regions could provide a potential model for Rifi Berber activists.[87] (One could also speculate here whether the Kabyle presence in avowedly unitary France has influenced the national mindset of Kabyle activists in Algeria.) Thirdly, and relatedly, the Moroccan government's increasingly developed proposals for the autonomy of the Western Sahara, in an effort to secure international recognition for control over the territory, have clearly emboldened regionalist claims from elsewhere in Morocco. Indeed, in early 2008

Berberist activists from both the Souss and the Rif made the first organised calls for regional autonomy for the two regions; and in March 2011 the Moroccan government began to unveil its plans for a regionalised system of local government which included proposals for a greater role for locally elected regional councils.

Trans and Pan-nationalism

In addition to the regional and national dimensions of the Berberist agenda, there has now emerged a third aspect—transnationalism—through the emergence from the 1990s of an international pan-Berberist movement and agenda. In 1997 a first World Amazigh Congress was held in the Canary Islands, which brought together representatives from Berberist associations and groups from across North Africa, as well as expatriate organisations in Europe and North America. Subsequent congresses took place at regular intervals in Europe before the first to be held in the Maghreb itself took place in Nador in the Rif in Morocco in August 2005. These congresses represented the consolidation of Berber activism that transcended national boundaries and the concerns of individual Berber-speaking communities, and thus appeared to create a genuinely trans- and pan-'Berber consciousness.' In this way it seemed to transform early assertions that Berbers did not think of themselves as Berbers, but rather as Riffis, Kabyles or Soussis and, beyond that, as Muslims. This transformation was significantly facilitated by advances in globalised technology, most notably the internet, that enabled activists from all over the world to communicate and cooperate and thus form—albeit largely in cyberspace—a common agenda and sense of community.[88]

The development of a transnational consciousness had potentially wider repercussions for both the Maghreb as a region and its relations with the outside world. Many of the more committed and radical Berberists had developed a critique of their states that extended to foreign policy. A prominent call amongst many Berberists came to be for the teaching of Maghreb history to be revised to accommodate and give credit to the contributions made by Berbers both before and after the arrival of the Arabs, whose history many saw as having unduly dominated official histories. In this way there was an attempt to shift the Maghreb away from its long-defined orientation towards the Middle East, Arab and Islamic worlds. For some activists, the Maghreb should be redefined in its own specific and historical terms. For others, an alignment with Europe was more appropriate, given not just historic ties, but strong existing ones forged through trade and migration, which dwarfed equivalent links with the Middle East.[89]

In the process of this redefinition of Maghrebi identity, increasing numbers of Berber activists began to argue that Maghreb states should abandon their preoccupations with and loosen their loyalties to the Middle East. They argued that it was a region that was remote from the Maghreb's concerns and from which the Maghreb had unnecessarily imported problems of violence, terrorism, and political and religious extremism.[90] Official attempts to encourage solidarity with Middle Eastern causes were viewed as not only damaging to the Maghreb's relations with the West but also serving domestic political ends, such as undermining the Berberist movement and distracting from more pressing domestic concerns.[91] As one young Berber activist explained: 'Before becoming involved in faraway causes that have nothing to do with Morocco, we must first of all combat the misery that rages in this country.'[92] Such a viewpoint remains restricted for now to the Berberist movement itself. Most ordinary Berber-speakers in both Algeria and Morocco remain staunchly committed to international causes such as the Palestinians, not out of pan-Arab but rather pan-Islamic sentiment, which continues to be strong.[93] Nevertheless, if these Berberist viewpoints were to become more mainstream among Berber-speakers and subsequently in the society as a whole, then this could have significant repercussions for regional and even international politics.

Berbers in an Arab Spring?

The portentous events of the early months of 2011 appeared, at first sight, to have little direct connection or implication for the Berber question in Maghreb politics, given, not least, the fact that they formed part of a wider wave of events focused specifically on the *Arab* world. Yet the issue was very much present, largely through the Amazigh movement's belief that its agenda could best be achieved through, and was an integral part of, the demands for political change and democratisation that were at the forefront of the mass demonstrations.

Berberist activists featured very prominently in the demonstrations in Morocco, and the demand that *Tamazight* be given official status alongside Arabic in the national constitution became one of the core stated demands of the February 20th Movement. The inclusion of a clause recognising *Tamazight* as an official language in the new constitution, introduced in July as a response by King Mohamed to the demonstrations, was seen as a major victory for the movement and evidence of the palace's desire to appease the Berberist activists and possibly secure their defection from the 20th February Movement, as they continued to protest for more reforms even after the introduction of the new constitution. In Algeria, the same demand featured amongst the core platform of the movement that organised demonstrations for political change in Algiers; they were dominated by the RCD party, which explained their limited appeal, but also served to continue to underline the national, rather than particularist vision of the largely Kabyle party. Even Tunisia's small Berber population was emboldened by the fall of the Ben Ali regime to demand greater rights for itself, arguing for official recognition in the forthcoming constitution.[94]

All in all, the linkage made by Berberist activists between democratisation and a greater space being given to Berber identity, together with the continuing commitment of most of these activists to a genuinely *national* vision and agenda, indicated that the pro-democracy movement sweeping the region in 2011 was likely to advance the objectives of the movement and further raise the profile of the issue of Berber identity.

7

POLITICS AND ECONOMICS

The relationship between economics and politics in the Maghreb was one that increased in importance and intensity as the post-independence period wore on and came to shape and explain progressively political developments in the individual states. Remarkably similar patterns were seen in Algeria, Tunisia and Morocco, as the political leaderships in the three states adopted and abandoned economic approaches in a largely, if unconsciously, synchronised pattern. All three proved strikingly successful in their attempts to ensure that economic changes did not result in unmanageable or unduly threatening parallel changes in the field of politics up until the dramatic events of the opening weeks of 2011.

Economic Policy in the Immediate Post-Independence Period

The economic policies pursued by the three states followed fairly similar paths during the first two decades or so following the achievement of independence, with the state playing a dominant role in the economy. In this, the region was consistent with the pattern established across most of the newly decolonised world, which reflected a broad international consensus that freshly independent states required the strong hand of central government to correct the inequalities and exploitation of the colonial period. In the case of the Maghreb, state domination was almost inevitable given that this had been the pattern established during the colonial period and the vacuum that was left by the departing colonial administration and its European settlers was one that could most easily be filled, certainly in the short term, by the new indigenous governments. Nevertheless, despite these commonalities, there were subtle differences between the paths taken by Tunisia, Morocco and Algeria.

Tunisia: The Rise and Fall of Ahmed Ben Salah's Socialist Experiment

Although Habib Bourguiba came to power with some clear ideas about what policies he wanted to implement in the social and educational realm in Tunisia, there was less clarity about the economic path to be taken. Initially opting for a fairly liberal approach with significant space being left for the country's private sector, the failure of the latter to provide sufficient levels of investment contributed to a change of tack by 1961, with the adoption of an explicitly socialist approach under a new finance and economy minister, Ahmed Ben Salah. Motivations for this shift, though, were not fully or even mainly economic in nature, since Bourguiba recognised the political benefits of promoting Ben Salah and his powerful allies in the UGTT trade union. At the same time, the move economically undercut the last bastions of support for Bourguiba's former rival, Salah Ben Youssef (see Chapter 2), amongst small farmers and artisans.[1] For the next eight years a fairly orthodox policy of socialism was pursued, with a large-scale ten-year economic plan setting out substantial increases in state investment. As a reflection of this ideological choice, the Neo-Destour formally changed its name at its 1964 party congress to the *Parti Socialiste Destourian*, or PSD.

In 1969 the explicitly socialist path was precipitously abandoned, once again for a mixture of economic and political reasons. The policies followed under the ten-year plan not only failed to achieve the very optimistic growth rates that had been promised but caused significant disruption to a number of sectors of the Tunisian economy, notably agriculture.[2] More importantly, the wide-ranging powers wielded by the socialist path's architect and director, Ben Salah, gradually attracted the suspicion and ire of firstly many other members of the elite but also eventually of Bourguiba himself. Concerned that his powerful minister might be in a position to threaten his supremacy atop the Tunisian state, Bourguiba sacked Ben Salah in 1969.

From 1970 there was a return to a more ostensibly liberal approach, with significant encouragement being given to the private sector. This did not mean, however, that the role of the state shrank. Boosted by increased revenues from rises in price for oil and phosphates, the Tunisian state arguably expanded its role, aiding and protecting the private sector from international competition and making the private sector heavily dependent on the state.[3] The shift in economic policy also led to changes in the realm of politics. The 1970s witnessed the first signs of political dissent within both elements of the political elite and parts of Tunisian society more generally. The jettisoning of both Ben Salah and his socialist programme led to a reconcentration of power in the hands of Bourguiba himself, which culminated in his self-appointment as president for life in 1974. For Emma Murphy, this process also reflected a movement away from the essentially corporatist structures that had been established in the aftermath of independence, in which economic and social interests and actors had been able to negotiate their interests in the National Assembly.[4] This reconcentration of power unsettled other senior members of the PSD. At the popular level, the abandonment of socialism also left an ideological vacuum that came to be filled first by a dissident UGTT and more latterly and forcefully by the Islamists (see Chapter 5), who also benefited from the growing inequalities that began to emerge in Tunisian society despite overall economic growth.[5] These factors ensured that, by the time the Tunisian economy began to run into trouble in the late 1970s, there were political repercussions.

Morocco: Patronage and the Elites

In Morocco after independence, political considerations dominated economic policy to an even greater degree than they had in Tunisia. The kingdom's economic structures had survived the transition to independence relatively intact, with large para-statal enterprises constructed in the colonial period continuing to dominate the economy.[6] At the same time, the French presence had allowed an indigenous business elite to prosper and penetrate into growing cities such as Casablanca, creating a more ostensibly 'mixed' economy than existed either in Algeria or Tunisia at independence.[7]

The monarchy, particularly King Hassan, used economic policy and resources to retain key alliances. In the countryside, the monarchy shored up support amongst the rural elites (see Chapter 2) by resisting large-scale land reform and redistribution and by allowing both rural and urban elites to acquire land left by departing European settlers after independence.[8] The move was repeated in 1973 in the wake of the two failed *coups d'état* when a politically isolated Hassan introduced a policy of 'Moroccanisation' of foreign-owned business with a new law stipulating that all major businesses in the country needed to be 51 per cent Moroccan-owned. This move not only played to nationalist sentiment but, more importantly, opened up huge new sources of patronage for the monarchy to distribute to recruit and retain allies. Hassan was particularly concerned about securing support among two sections of Moroccan society whom he feared siding with any future coup plotters: the business elite and the new generation of administrators.[9] At the same time, the regime took advantage of a tripling in the international price of phosphates (of which Morocco was a major exporter) in early 1974 to expand public expenditure significantly in areas such as infrastructure, salaries and food subsidies, which served the dual purpose of expanding its role and influence in the economy and bolstering popular support.[10]

Algeria: The Consensus on Socialism

Of the three Maghrebi countries, Algeria had the most clearly established official economic policy at independence. Whilst the Tripoli Conference had failed to agree political structures for the post-independence Algerian state (see Chapter 2), there had been near-universal agreement on the adoption of a socialist approach to running the economy. Ideological concerns aside, a large role for the government in the economy was almost inevitable given the devastation left by eight years of war. Furthermore, the departure *en masse* of the near entirety of the European population at independence in 1962 effectively necessitated the takeover of European-owned farms and businesses by the new Algerian government. In spite of Ben Bella's vaunted policies of *autogestion* (self-management), the fundamental feature of the economy in the immediate aftermath of independence was the government's expropriation of former European properties and land. This initially fairly chaotic process was rationalised following the fall of Ben Bella and became a useful form of patronage for the regime in the same way as had occurred in Morocco. Land, property and private business licences were granted to former guerrilla fighters to buy their political docility in the fractious political atmosphere of the early years of independence.[11]

As in Morocco, the depletion of the resources of the immediate post-independence years left the regime searching for new sources of patronage by the 1970s, with which to buy off political opposition. Whereas in Morocco the 'Moroccanisation' law had filled this gap, in Algeria there was little foreign-owned business remaining to exploit in the same way. Fortuitously, the spectacular surge in the international price of oil in the early 1970s provided the Algerian regime with ample financial resources to continue the flow of patronage and ensure political stability soon after the nationalisation of the oil and gas industries was completed in 1971. These resources also allowed the state, as had occurred in Morocco with the rise in the price of phosphates, to expand public investment most prominently in the realm of heavy industry, which became a major feature of the Boumedienne period as part of a strategy of creating 'industrialising industries,' aimed at expanding Algeria's economic independence.[12] In this way, the management of the Algerian economy became—and would remain—fundamentally about the distribution of 'rent' from oil and gas revenues.

Crisis and the Move to Reform

By the mid 1970s, the management of the economies of all three of the Maghreb states bore significant similarities. Despite differing origins and trajectories, all three witnessed increased state involvement and control in the economy, largely financed by steep increases in the prices of commodities. None of the states had followed a consistent or pre-established policy since independence, with many of the twists and turns being dictated by events or, more frequently, political considerations. Regime security remained the priority across the region and explained both the adoption and jettisoning of Ben Salah in Tunisia and the pattern of patronage and distribution of resources in Morocco and Algeria.

It was significant, then, that all three regimes also began to experience similar economic difficulties by the late 1970s, difficulties that began to develop into full-blown crises by the 1980s. The most obvious symptom of these problems was the dramatic worsening of public finances: all three states came to find themselves progressively heavily in debt. In large part this was due to precipitous falls in the international prices of key commodities such as phosphates (in 1976) and later oil and gas (1985–6) which hit hard in Morocco and then Algeria respectively, and (to a lesser extent) Tunisia. The effects of these changes were exacerbated by the fact that all three states had not only financed huge expansions in public expenditure in the 1970s through revenues from the exploitation of these commodities but had also borrowed heavily against them in the expectation that the high prices of the 1970s would be maintained indefinitely. Other factors, such as corruption, inefficiency and—in the case of Morocco with the Western Sahara (see Chapter 8)—involvement in an expensive military conflict, all further contributed to worsening the financial state of all three countries. Particular strain was also put on state resources through the massive growth in the population that the region had experienced: all three states having more than doubled their populations in the first three decades after independence.[13]

The growing seriousness with which the regimes began to take these mounting crises was due to their realisation that the difficulties soon developed a political dimension, presenting a potential threat to the stability of the regimes. As a result, all three began to attempt to reform their economies in the same way, primarily by reducing government expenditure, encouraging export growth and decentralising economic management.[14] Significantly these were all remedies prescribed by a growing body of economists in Europe and North America which by the 1980s became orthodoxy in both the World Bank and the International Monetary Fund (IMF) and became known as the 'Washington Consensus.' Grounded in the ideal of the free market, this new consensus asserted that most of the economic ills of the world were the result of excessive government interference in the workings of the economy; ills that could be remedied by reducing the role of the state in terms of government spending, state ownership of the economy, price controls (subsidies) and tariffs, all of which distorted the proper workings of the market.

Many other states at this time were obliged to make a formal approach to the IMF and the World Bank for loans and assistance with their financial difficulties. The Maghrebi governments tried to avoid this, since this would give these institutions a say in the management of their economies. Instead the governments of all three Maghrebi states initially tried to introduce reforms by themselves to improve their finances, but the huge difficulties of doing so forced all three to turn to the international institutions which could provide the necessary funds to smooth the transition.

In Tunisia the effect of the fall in the international price of oil was compounded by the decline of the country's own oil resources. This served to worsen budget and trade deficits produced by significant increases in goods imported to feed production in Tunisia's inefficient private sector, which had become heavily dependent on and protected by the state during the 1970s.[15] A series of poor harvests in the early 1980s pushed the government—on the prompting of the IMF—into cutting back its expenditure, notably through lifting public subsidies on bread and semolina. The effect of this was to double the prices of commodities that formed a fundamental part of the expenditure of ordinary households in Tunisia. The result was two weeks of rioting across the country in January 1984 and the consequent restoration of the subsidies.[16]

The failure of Tunisia's attempt to deal with its budgetary crisis, which deepened as the 1980s progressed, led to the government formally signing up to an IMF-sponsored programme of economic reform in 1986. As before, political factors played a major role in this decision. The unrest of January 1984 had greatly alarmed the regime, which itself was increasingly riven by divisions as Bourguiba's health and judgement faltered and the Islamists of the MTI continued to garner popular support. The regime had already seen how popular unrest had led to opposition to the regime becoming better organised, with the significant unrest that surrounded a strike led by the UGTT in January 1978 which had increased links between the Islamists and dissidents within the PSD.[17] The IMF agreement was therefore felt to give the regime vital breathing space to deal with these and other challenges.

Morocco followed a similar path to Tunisia and was hit even earlier—in the mid 1970s—by fiscal crisis: the result of a fall in the price of phosphates and the beginning of the military campaign in the Western Sahara. In common with Tunisia, the government tried to impose its own home-grown austerity measures to reduce spending in the late 1970s by freezing government salaries, raising taxes and cutting public investment. As in Tunisia, these measures met with public protest in the form of strikes and workers' unrest in 1978 and 1979. From 1980, the Moroccan government turned increasingly to the IMF and other institutions, but the implementation of the programmes recommended by the Fund was regularly delayed by outbreaks of serious social unrest—most notably in 1981 and again in 1984—in reaction to cuts in subsidies on basic goods.[18]

Algeria's financial and economic situation witnessed the most precipitous decline of all the states, following the collapse in the international oil price in the mid 1980s. Even before that, the government had embarked on a series of reforms designed to rectify weaknesses in the economy. Following Boumedienne's death in 1978, Chadli Benjedid's new administration began to introduce reforms aimed at restructuring and decentralising the centrally planned national economy. These were deemed necessary in order to combat rising inefficiency and declining productivity as well as mounting international debt, which had been substantially incurred through imports of plant equipment for Boumedienne's programme of industrialisation.

The 40 per cent fall in the international oil price in 1985–6 hit Algeria far harder than its neighbours, because of how dependent its economic strategy had become on the continuing flow of revenues from both oil and natural gas. In 1986 hydrocarbons exports represented 97 per cent of Algeria's export revenues, meaning that a 40 per cent fall in the price of oil and gas translated into a comparable proportionate fall in export revenues.[19] Matters were worsened still further by the fact that a fall in the international value of the US dollar during the same period meant that even those revenues Algeria continued to receive—and which were paid in US dollars—were themselves significantly reduced. The impact of this was even greater, given that the large international debt that Algeria had built up since the 1970s to fund its heavy industry projects and import food to compensate for a neglected agricultural sector was primarily owed to European rather than US banks.[20]

The sudden impact of these changes forced the Algerian government to introduce a series of drastic measures: salaries were frozen, subsidies were removed and imports were compressed. Both the scale and swiftness of these changes hit the ordinary Algerian population hard and compacted existing problems of housing and unemployment that had been growing through the 1980s. A drought in the summer of 1988 leading to water shortages and further rises in food prices pushed the population to breaking point, and was the underlying cause of the explosion of public anger that boiled onto the streets of the country's main cities in the opening week of October 1988. At no stage, though, did the Algerian government try to turn to the international financial institutions, preferring, like Tunisia and Morocco before, to attempt to apply its own programme of reform. A resistance to the idea of foreign interference in the internal affairs of the country, founded in the nationalism of the independence struggle, prevented any recourse to the IMF until the dark days of the conflict of the mid 1990s made the country's position untenable.

Reforming Without Liberalising? Economics and Politics from the 1990s

The application firstly of what Layachi has termed 'home-made' remedies to the economic crises of the 1980s and, later, of IMF and World Bank reform programmes demonstrated a convergence of development strategies across the three states by the 1990s.[21] Designed to combat the huge fiscal crises the states were experiencing, the reform programmes were not without political risk. Firstly and most obviously, many of the reforms demanded by external institutions had effects that provoked as much—if not more—popular unrest than those produced by the original fiscal crises themselves. The unrest of the 1980s across the region presented the most serious challenge the regimes had faced from their ordinary populations, who had been noted for their relative political docility during the early years of independence (see Chapter 2). This new willingness on the part of Maghrebis to take to the streets to express their discontent with their rulers clearly owed much to the specific material deprivations that emerged, often very suddenly, in the 1980s. Such demonstrations of popular discontent also had a more political dimension with the coming of age in the 1980s of a disproportionately large section of the population who had little or no memory of the anti-colonial liberation struggles upon which all three regimes based much of their claim to legitimacy. For this new generation the legitimacy of the regime was much more closely tied to the performance of the government in terms of providing basic needs such as food, housing and jobs. Such a view of government had been strengthened by the major role the state had played in the economy in the early years of independence, encouraging the popular view that the state was overwhelmingly responsible for the provision of these basic needs, and in this way forging an effective social contract between the state and the population.

A second potential political risk that the application of the programmes of economic reform represented to the existing regimes was more subtle. Many of the architects and supporters of the Washington Consensus on economic development argued that the application of their proposed programmes would serve not only to stabilise and strengthen the economies in which they were applied but would also contribute to the establishment and strengthening of pluralistic and even democratic structures and trends in more authoritarian and undemocratic societies. Based broadly on the view that a withdrawal of the state from the management of the economy would also lead to a parallel withdrawal of the ruling elite from the exclusive control of the political system, it was argued that the increased plurality of economic ownership would inevitably lead to a greater plurality of political forces inside a country.[22] It was therefore thought that the endorsement of liberalising economic reforms by Algeria, Tunisia and Morocco in the 1980s would in time lead to a progressive liberalisation of their political structures.

What became remarkable, though, as the 1990s progressed was the way in which the individual states were able to maintain—at least in form—the economic reform programmes they had embraced in the 1980s, whilst being able to ensure that the regimes in power were able to sustain their political dominance of the country. How this was done varied from state to state.

Tunisia: Controlling Liberalisation

In common with its neighbours, Tunisia maintained its commitment to the economic reform process it embarked on in the early 1980s. Remarkably, this commitment survived the transition from Habib Bourguiba to Zine al-Abdine Ben Ali in 1987, there being arguably an intensification of this commitment under the new regime. What was even more striking was the way in which the Ben Ali regime was able not only to avoid an erosion of the monopoly of political power he and his supporters in the RCD were able to exercise, but how they were actually able to strengthen it. The primary mechanism through which this was achieved was via the state's penetration and control of the private sector, which stood to grow and benefit from the effects of economically liberal reform programme.

From the outset of his rule, President Ben Ali sought to gain the support of Tunisia's private sector to enlarge the social base of the regime, which had become worryingly narrow during Bourguiba's final years in power. There was also the realisation that an expanded private sector could serve as a future power base for opposition to the regime.[23]

Beginning by winning its confidence through the National Pact of 1988, the regime controlled the bourgeoisie by ensuring that it received the natural benefits that flow from a formal liberalisation of the economy, whilst at the same time ensuring that it was never forgotten that the regime had control over this flow and could stem it if necessary. Through appointments of senior businessmen to government positions and the selective application of laws, regulations and even taxes, the state ensured the dependency, loyalty and political passivity of this class, which consolidated itself in the early 1990s.[24] As Murphy notes:

> The economic winners of liberalization are ultimately unable to disengage themselves from political dependence on the regime—indeed their profitability in the market is enhanced by constructive relations with the state and access to arbitrarily distributed patronage.[25]

Aware of the dangers of allowing the entrepreneurial class any degree of political independence, the regime was not averse to using more strong-arm tactics to ensure support and compliance. In 1993, a leading commercial bank, the BIAT (*Banque Internationale Arabe de Tunisie*), suffered a series of damaging withdrawals of funds by several large para-statal organisations in what appeared to be a coordinated campaign by the Tunisian regime. It was suggested that the motivation for the campaign was both to undermine the strength and independence of an increasingly successful and powerful bank and also to destroy the political ambitions of the head of the bank, who was rumoured to be considering putting himself forward as a candidate against Ben Ali in the presidential elections of 1994.[26]

At the other end of the social scale, the Tunisian regime prevented a repeat of the popular unrest witnessed in 1978 and 1984 by carefully targeting resources towards the poorest sections of society. A series of funds were established for this purpose, most prominently the National Solidarity Fund (NSF), which was set up in 1992. These funds received contributions from Tunisian businesses on a supposedly 'voluntary' basis: contributions were made in exchange for favourable treatment from the government through the selective application of rules and laws referred to earlier. Those businesses that did not contribute, or contributed insufficiently, risked experiencing problems with tax demands, government bureaucracy and gaining access to public markets. The processes of both collecting and spending money by the NSF were very opaque and meant that they were often distributed in a 'clientalistic, discriminatory and inefficient way' and thus became another instrument of negotiation and control for the regime. In addition, because they operated outside the government budget, the contributions allowed the regime to circumvent IMF and World Bank pressures to reduce social spending and introduce budget cuts and in this way became a form of private taxation. Significantly, the Fund also operated under the name and auspices of the president himself rather than the government, thus serving to reinforce the image and, in Beatrice Hibou's view, the personality cult that was clearly and carefully built around Ben Ali.[27]

In rural areas, Stephen King has concluded that the effects of the programme of economic liberalisation clearly benefited larger landowners at the expense of the poorer parts of the population. These effects were partially offset by a conscious return to more traditional forms of dealing with inequality, such as ad hoc local distribution of aid to poorer families and individuals. This in turn, King argues, also led to greater political passivity as more traditional structures and forms of authority were able to reassert themselves more generally. He suggests, moreover, that the 'resurgence of traditional politics in rural areas has helped to reconfigure authoritarianism in the country as a whole,' largely because of the rural landowning origins of the RCD elite, who expanded their interests and practices into the towns and cities.[28]

In these ways Tunisia was able to ensure that the economic effects of its adoption of a programme of liberalising economic reform did not weaken the hold of the regime on power. By incorporating important sections of Tunisian society—notably the private sector, rural landowners and the trade union movement—into its structures, the regime appeared to be adopting a newly corporatist approach to both the economy and politics. Stephen King, though, believes that it is important to stress that this new corporatism was based on the *state* rather than on society, with the former playing a controlling role.[29] Although the reforms produced a larger private sector, it is one that was penetrated and controlled by the state. In this way, the distinction between public and private became blurred, which Hibou has described as a 'privatisation of the state.'[30]

There was also a parallel blurring of the boundaries between the realms of politics and economics. In the same way that businessmen were increasingly appointed to government positions, politicians and figures in the regime became increasingly involved in the economy and business. Inevitably, in a system in which clientalism had deep roots and was encouraged under Ben Ali, this led to increasing levels of corruption. In the view of Hibou, corruption became an increasingly central part of the regime's character because of the absence of any genuinely functioning political life. During Bourguiba's presidency corruption was clearly present, but essentially took the form of 'collateral damage' from the bigger political struggle to succeed the president.[31]

Substantial links between the presidential palace and business in Tunisia developed, with the family of Ben Ali's wife, Leila Trabelsi, becoming particularly involved from the late 1990s and enjoying frequently monopolistic control over larger and larger sections of the economy, and with relatives strong-arming their way into the ownership of successful independent businesses.[32]

The rampant and shameless corruption and visible excesses of Ben Ali's family made a crucial contribution to the swift collapse of the regime in January 2011: a collapse that owed much to the failings of the regime's handling of the economy, despite the outward impression of control and stability. The uprising that eventually toppled Ben Ali had its origins in the small towns of the neglected south and interior of Tunisia, where the lack of jobs and opportunities together with the nepotism and indifference to local problems of the local elites and administrations had already led to a significant outbreak of unrest in early 2008. When Mohamed Bouazizi set himself alight outside the local governor's office in the town of Sidi Bouzid on 17 December 2010 as an act of desperation and protest following the confiscation of his vending cart by the authorities, the simmering resentments present in the region boiled over, making use of the protest networks established two years earlier. A major role was played by the trade unions in the UGTT, whose local sections successfully organised a series of rolling and expanding strikes that helped push the protests out of the interior to the towns and cities of the north and the coast. On reaching the urban areas, the protests spread first through the working-class districts and finally ignited the long-suppressed resentment at the total absence of political freedoms amongst the middle classes, in particular, fed by growing rage at the rapaciousness of the president's family, meaning that the revolution rapidly took hold.

The crucial role played by the UGTT in the revolution was further evidence of the failure of the economic policies pursued by the Ben Ali regime, as well as the fragility of the hold it believed it exercised over important sections of Tunisian society. Ben Ali had been aware that the

UGTT represented a potential source of political opposition to the regime, but had come to believe that he had effectively neutralised it. Historically the most powerful trade union organisation across the Maghreb, the UGTT had been a powerful force in the anti-colonial movement, had been the original power base of Ahmed Ben Salah and was at the origin of the strikes and unrest of early 1978. Although the Union was formally detached from the RCD in 1988, it was progressively co-opted by the regime drawing it into its corporatist structures. The regime was helped in this task by the liberalising economic reforms which substantially reduced the bargaining power of the Union. Initially recruited as a powerful ally against the Islamists, the UGTT was also kept close to the regime to avoid it becoming once more a pole around which opposition to the regime could gather. The regime remained sensitive to this possibility and in 2000 engineered, through accusations of fraud, the resignation and downfall of the Union's secretary general, Ismail Sahbani, who had publicly deplored the absence of trade unionists in the Tunisian parliament at the UGTT's congress.[33] This proved ultimately insufficient to bring the union to heel, as the membership and provincial sections of the UGTT successfully revolted against the leadership imposed by Ben Ali as the revolt of 2010–11 gained ground.

Morocco: Co-opting Liberalisation

Morocco followed the same path as Tunisia in continuing to stick to a programme of economic reform. Like Tunisia, the regime worked to ensure that the economic and social changes produced by the new economic structures posed no fundamental threat to its control over the system.

As in Tunisia, the regime largely achieved this goal by penetrating and controlling the expanding private sector produced by reforms. It did so, though, in a slightly different way. Whereas in Tunisia the emphasis had been on control over penetration, the reverse was the case in Morocco. This was largely achieved by the monarchy becoming 'the premier private entrepreneur in Morocco.'[34] In 1980 the royal palace—as distinct from the government—bought a substantial interest in the major conglomerate ONA (*Omnium Nord-Africain*), making it a major player in the developing private sector. ONA took advantage of the new opportunities presented by liberalising reforms and privatisation of state-owned companies to acquire new companies and assets and expand itself until it became the largest 'private' company in the country. Thus, whilst the state was gradually withdrawing from the economy, the Makhzen was moving into it in a new way. As Clement Henry and Robert Springborg observe: 'the king regained in the private sector the influence that policies of economic liberalization were progressively eroding in government and the public sector.'[35] On a political level, this gave the monarchy several advantages. Most importantly it opened up a new flow of resources that allowed it to maintain its large network of patronage, notably through appointments to ONA and its subsidiaries—a vital part of the Makhzen's means of preserving influence. At the same time, by disengaging the state from the economy, the palace reduced its political responsibilities.[36]

The need to control the rest of the burgeoning private sector was initially less important than had been the case in Tunisia. This was because of the close and well-established links between the regime and the private sector, which remained dominated by a relatively small number of families with strong traditional ties to the palace. This link was maintained by the existence of a significant overlap between positions in the government and the private sector, with prominent businessmen holding positions in the administration. Thus, as in Tunisia, the distinction between the public and private sectors became extremely blurred.[37]

As economic liberalisation progressed, however, new economic forces and actors began to emerge over whom the palace was able to exercise far less influence. This was particularly the case with the informal black economy that began to balloon from the 1980s. Historically present but traditionally tolerated, this part of the economy began to attract the attention of the regime more because of its size and independence than its illegality. By the mid 1990s contraband alone was estimated to have reached $1 billion in value and was able to support 600,000 people. There was particular concern that the revenues it generated could fund economic and political actors outside the control of the state. The spectacular rise in the trade in hashish from northern Morocco provoked particular unease, given the Rif's established hostility to Hassan II.[38]

The desire to try to reduce and control the black economy in Morocco was one of the main factors behind a major campaign launched by the regime in the mid 1990s. Officially aimed at stamping out corruption, contraband and drug trafficking, the 'Sanitisation' campaign of 1995–6 led to the arrest and prosecution of a large number of members of the business community. The fact, though, that most of those convicted were subsequently pardoned and that uncertainty exists over whether fines imposed were actually paid and whether the campaign achieved its stated objectives indicated that the campaign had less to do with cleaning up official corruption and eradicating the black market than with a show of force by the regime in the face of an economic sphere that it perceived to be escaping from its full control. Significantly, it was a campaign initiated by the palace rather than the government or administration and was led by the king's main enforcer, Driss Basri at the Interior Ministry, who also negotiated its end with leaders of the business community in May 1996, again with no formal input from the government.[39] This show of force by the monarchy can be seen to have historical parallels and roots. It has been compared to the historic *harka* of the pre-colonial period, when the sultan would make regular sorties into the countryside to subdue rebellious tribes who traditionally expressed their resistance by refusing to pay taxes.[40]

The 'Sanitisation' campaign was finally brought to an end in June 1996 through negotiations between Driss Basri and the body that formally represented the kingdom's major entrepreneurs, the *Confédération Générale des Entreprises du Maroc* (CGEM). The so-called 'Gentlemen's Agreement' provided for a calling-off of the campaign by the regime in return for the business community putting its house in order.[41] This engagement with the CGEM, which grew in importance during this period, was evidence to some of the development of a more corporatist strategy on behalf of the Moroccan regime and an attempt to bring Morocco's new economic actors closer to the Palace.[42] Indeed, the CGEM appeared to represent a new generation of businesses that did not rely as heavily as their more established counterparts on the traditional networks and connections.[43] Such a development clearly threatened to undermine the existing system and there was evidence of attempts by the Makhzen to bring the CGEM under its control. In elections to appoint a new president of the body in 2003, however, the candidate backed by the more established corporations (including ONA) was defeated in favour of one supported by the new generation of entrepreneurs.[44] The independence of the new president, Hassan Chami, was shown in the summer of 2005 when he launched a scathing attack in a newspaper interview on the whole system of governance in Morocco, which he argued was preventing the country from developing because of the blurred nature of lines of responsibility and forms of interference that prevented the government from doing its job.[45] This proved a step too far, and Chami was made to feel the displeasure of the Makhzen. He was attacked by newspapers close to the establishment, found himself excluded from official functions and witnessed his own business suddenly suffer from a range of difficulties. Within a year he had been formally replaced at the head of the CGEM by a more conventional figure, following a campaign led by the more traditional corporations, including ONA, who hitherto had had little involvement in the confederation and who publicly declared that the confederation would henceforth be taking a far less political and confrontational stance.[46]

Although the ejection of Chami from the presidency of the CGEM bore some similarities to the heavy-handed approach taken by the Tunisian regime to political dissidence amongst business leaders, there were important differences. Foremost were the increasingly divergent political climates in the two countries. Whilst Tunisia was marked by the consistently repressive grip the Ben Ali regime was able to maintain on Tunisian political life, Morocco witnessed a clear liberalisation in this sphere from the 1990s. The relationship between this political liberalisation and the introduction of liberalising economic reforms is worth exploring, especially given the experience of Tunisia, which appeared to suggest that economic reform served to inhibit political reform. The relationship is inevitably complex. Guilain Denoeux and Abdeslam Maghraoui argue against the view that economic reform contributed to political reform, stating that 'broader socio-economic changes' had more of an impact, notably in terms of rapid urbanisation, the growth of an urban middle class and events beyond Morocco.[47] Urbanisation reduced the importance of the palace's alliance with the rural notables, which had been an important plank in the monarchy's political strategy in the decades following independence. This alliance could be replaced by one with the emerging urban middle class, which was arguably much more interested in issues of political freedom.[48] Denoeux and Maghraoui argue, moreover, that political reform actually helped facilitate the economic reforms that Morocco became committed to from the 1990s:

> The regime has been able to pursue rigorous economic reforms in part because it also has moved—albeit incrementally and tentatively—towards new political arrangements that emphasize partnership and negotiation, as opposed to patronage and allegiance.[49]

It is, however, difficult to dismiss the idea that economic change produced by the application of the structural adjustment programmes was not of any influence. The adverse effects of the programmes had led to popular unrest and repeated strikes by the country's trade unions. The latter, in particular, emboldened the demoralised political opposition, which had strong ties to the unions, to confront the regime. This probably contributed to the formation of the Kutla alliance in 1992 (see Chapter 4), which pushed for further reform in the 1990s and eventually came into government in 1998.[50]

Social changes produced by the economic reform programmes may also have had an effect on the development of political reform. Even Denoeux and Maghraoui acknowledge that King Hassan II may have seen in privatisation a means of producing a new middle class that he could recruit as allies for the regime.[51] The programmes also encouraged the development of the new generation of entrepreneurs that responded to the drive to create more export-oriented businesses and made their presence felt in the CGEM. Less reliant on the connections and networks of the old established business elite, this grouping developed new practices and ways of doing business that made greater use of more open and formal mechanisms and institutions. As Melani Cammett observes with specific reference to the textile industry:

Changes in the structure and organizational strategies of producer groups in the 1990s brought about more formal modes of interest transmission based on publicly articulated demands through professional associations and the economic press.[52]

It can be argued that these changes could contribute to the development of a more liberalised and more democratic framework in society as a whole. Nevertheless, Myriam Catusse argues that even these new entrepreneurial elites still make recourse to traditional networks and family connections. Moreover, whilst they may come from outside the small, restricted circle of the traditional business elites, they are far from being on the margins of society and have strong roots in the existing system and therefore have little interest in politically challenging it.[53] This is reflected in the fact that, whilst there has been a significant increase in the numbers of businessmen and entrepreneurs entering the Moroccan parliament since the 1990s, most have done so as members of political parties allied to the Makhzen or as independents. The few attempts by prominent business figures, including a former head of the CGEM, to create new political parties have resulted in these parties enjoying very limited electoral success, largely because of their failure to make use of the traditional networks of clientalism that have long been crucial to success in elections in Morocco (see Chapter 4).[54]

In spite of these developments it should not be forgotten that the vast majority of Moroccans in both the countryside and the poorer parts of the swelling cities remained largely untouched by these developments, and it is perhaps politicisation and mobilisation of these people that the regime most fears. It was concern about this development that led to a significant re-engagement of the monarchy in the economy under King Mohamed VI. King Hassan's interest in business had diminished towards the end of his reign, and when Mohamed came to the throne in 1999 he too indicated that he wished to withdraw from involvement in business. The reverse, however, occurred as the monarchy became progressively more involved in the economy through expanding the interests and control of holdings such as those in ONA, which came to dominate key sectors in the Moroccan economy like mining, agribusiness and financial services and soon came to hold a significant part of the stock value on the Casablanca stock exchange. What elements of the Moroccan press were wont to call the 'Alaouisation' of the economy was a complex development, but at heart represented an attempt by the palace to control and direct the economy in new and dynamic ways in order to defend against increasing numbers of foreign takeovers of Moroccan companies. More importantly, the intention was to produce levels of economic and social development that would head off socio-economic and consequently political crises. This process was driven by the appointment of younger technocratic figures close to the king to head key economic sectors in both the public sector as well as the formally private sector. This blurring of the public and private sectors led to a growth in accusations that elements of the nominally private sector were being given unfair advantages.[55]

These accusations achieved a sharpened significance following the rapid collapse of the Ben Ali regime in Tunisia in January 2011, given the similarly close links between the private sector and the circles of power in both countries. Calls for an end to corruption and, more pointedly, the disengagement of the royal palace from the economy and the dismissal of many of the king's closest economic advisers featured prominently in the slogans and official demands of the demonstrations and marches that began and grew from 20 February across Morocco. Amongst the students, leftists, Islamists and Berberists, a notable presence in the demonstrations were several major businessmen, specifically ones who had long complained of being excluded from and disadvantaged by the cosy relationship between the traditional business elites and the palace.

Algeria: Conflict, Hydrocarbons and Clientelism

Algeria represents the most complicated case of the three countries in terms of the relationship between the new policies of economic liberalisation and political change. The aftermath of the riots of October 1988 witnessed a dramatic shift to an ostensibly more liberal political system, with the introduction of a new constitution creating for the first time a multi-party system (see Chapter 4). The exact nature of the link between the events of October 1988 and the subsequent political reform later became hotly debated, particularly as to whether the unrest had been politically or economically motivated. Several commentators noted the absence of political slogans and demands coming from the rioters and demonstrators, indicating the essentially economic nature of their grievances. It therefore appeared strange that the regime should respond to economic grievances with political reforms.[56] At the same time, however, others have noted that the rioters targeted institutions and symbols of the state rather than economic targets such as private businesses, which had benefited from the de-regulation of the economy introduced earlier in the decade.[57] Thus it was the state and politicians who were being blamed for the crisis. Nevertheless, the decision to embark on a programme of political reform was an unusual and bold one and was far from inevitable or unavoidable in the aftermath of the riots. As indicated earlier (see Chapter 4) the decision to open up the political system had much more to do with the internal politics of the regime than a desire to respond to popular anger. Chadli Benjedid clearly wanted to use the change in the political rules of the game to wrong-foot his opponents within the regime.

If the role played by the economy in the political opening of 1989 was unclear, what was clear was that, as in Tunisia and Morocco, the regime stuck with the economic reform programme begun in the 1980s, despite subsequent changes in the political landscape. It is doubtful that Chadli was ideologically committed to the economic reforms, but rather saw them as politically useful. Many of his enemies within the regime harboured profound doubts about the economic reforms embarked upon after 1979, for both ideological and more self-interested reasons: socialism remaining a touchstone for some, and the personal material benefits of the Boumediennist system being more important for an even larger group. Chadli therefore saw advantages in pushing ahead with the reform programme. Firstly, it allowed him to build an alternative power base consisting of younger technocratic reformers: in 1989 he appointed a noted proponent of economic reform, Mouloud Hamrouche, as prime minister. Secondly, it enabled him to portray his political enemies within the regime—not least to external creditors and foreign governments—as reactionary and anti-reform.[58]

The new constitution of 1989 radically altered the political landscape, primarily through the legalisation of new political forces, most importantly the Islamists. As shown in previous chapters, the decision to legalise the *Front Islamique du Salut* was primarily the product of the political calculations of Chadli and his allies, who wished to create competition for their enemies in the FLN. It was also hoped that the new party would become an ally of the economic reform programme. This undoubtedly explains why Prime Minister Mouloud Hamrouche's government not only pushed for the FIS's legalisation in September 1989, but also avoided any criticism of the FIS during its early and spectacular rise, which alarmed many other figures in the wider regime.[59] In return, the FIS was not only remarkably uncritical of the Hamrouche government's economic reform programme, despite vigorously attacking most other aspects of the regime, but actually vocally supported it. The FIS's first formal policy document lambasted the failings of the previous planned economy and called for a limitation of state ownership and the encouragement of decentralisation and competition, describing the latter as the 'agent of plenty.'[60] More explicitly still, the president of the FIS, Abassi Madani, stated in an interview in January 1990 that 'The FIS is more concerned than anyone for these reforms and demands their application.'[61]

This strategic alliance built on the FIS's tacit support for the economic reform programme has been seen by Hugh Roberts as indicating the fundamental opportunism of the FIS and its lack of ideological depth.[62] Whilst it was certainly true that the FIS developed no coherent economic policy during its early years, there were, however, more solid reasons for supporting the economic reforms.[63] At the ideological level, Islamist movements worldwide had an established ideological antipathy towards socialism, due to its roots in atheistic Marxism and its violation of the Islamic principle of private property. A number of prominent Islamist figures in Algeria had publicly contested aspects of Boumedienne's Socialist Revolution of the 1970s, most notably its attempt to nationalise privately-owned agricultural land.[64] Islamists were thus open to supporting liberal economic programmes, particularly those seeking to dismantle Boumedienne's state socialist vision. The FIS's endorsement of the economic reform programme can also be explained with reference to the party's support base amongst petty traders, who resented the restrictions and control exercised by the Algerian state over their businesses. Luis Martinez goes even further and argues that such sentiments were shared with the FIS's foot soldiers amongst the mass of urban unemployed and underemployed:

Among the young FIS voters was emerging a will to change the rules of the game, to democratise the opportunities to acquire wealth ... State control over the economy was in their eyes not a way to increase the wealth of the nation, but a political instrument used to stop the emergence of private economic and political entrepreneurs.[65]

This perhaps helps explain why the FIS leadership was able to refrain from attacking the government's economic policy without undermining the party's high levels of support amongst the poorest Algerians, who might otherwise have been expected to have endorsed populist critiques of the reform programme that blamed the decline of living standards on the application of the reforms. Nonetheless, the FIS sought to alleviate some of the worst effects of the growing poverty in Algeria through the establishment of local 'Islamic souks,' which sold basic goods and vegetables at reduced prices and proved highly popular. In establishing such souks, the FIS significantly made use of the expanding parallel market which had been a by-product of some of the liberalising reforms of the 1980s.[66]

That Hugh Roberts' charge of opportunism and lack of ideological depth was not totally unfounded was demonstrated by the FIS's abrupt ending of its support for the economic programme in 1991. In May of that year Abassi Madani launched a blistering attack on the programme, stating:

These things called reforms are in fact nothing more than an operation to enable the regime to steal from the pockets of the citizens, make the poor still poorer and trying today to exhaust the money of the wealthy.[67]

The reason for the about-face of the FIS was political. Abassi's statement came shortly after the unveiling of the government's new electoral code, which threatened the party's chances at the upcoming legislative elections. Feeling betrayed by Chadli Benjedid and the Hamrouche government, the FIS no longer felt obliged to support the reforms.[68]

The FIS never got to demonstrate what economic policies it might follow in government. The forestalling of its anticipated electoral victory in January 1992 changed the political landscape, and with it that of the Algerian economy. The escalating civil conflict that the cancellation of the elections and the banning of the FIS unleashed a very new set of dynamics in the relationship between politics and economics.

For the first two years of the conflict between 1992 and 1994, the Algerian economy was put under increasing strain as the regime struggled to deal not only with the cost of the mounting violence coming from its confrontation with the armed Islamist groups but also with a further decline in the international oil price during 1993, which significantly reduced government revenues. By the beginning of 1994, the country slipped into payment arrears on its huge and ballooning international debts, as debt repayments threatened to absorb the entirety of the country's foreign currency earnings. Creditor confidence had also been undermined by the appointment in 1992 of a new government headed by a long-standing critic of the programme of economic reforms introduced in the 1980s, Belaid Abdeslam, who had been the prime architect of Boumedienne's state-led heavy industrialisation programme of the 1970s. Belaid attempted to reverse many of the liberalising reforms, reimposing state controls on foreign investment and injecting large amounts of money into state companies. The failure of this strategy to arrest Algeria's slide into debt, together with pressure from foreign donors, led to Belaid's replacement by an advocate of the economic reform programme, Redha Malek, in 1993. The programme was publicly put back on track, but continuing difficulties forced the new government finally to do what many in the Algerian regime had resisted since the 1980s when both Morocco and Tunisia had taken the option: turn to the IMF for help. In April 1994 an agreement was struck with the Fund that cleared the way for the rescheduling of the international debt and the arrangement of a substantial multilateral aid package.[69]

The agreement of 1994 relieved the Algerian regime from the immediate pressure of its crushing international debt and gave it much more room to manoeuvre financially. Specifically, it allowed Algeria to focus many more resources on the struggle against the armed groups, whose activities had expanded massively in 1993–4. It also allowed for a rebuilding of the patronage networks that were essential to maintain support for the regime.[70]

Initially, and somewhat paradoxically, the financial agreements of 1994 also served to strengthen elements of the armed opposition. During the early part of the conflict, the armed groups relied predominantly on donations from the local population in the areas in which they operated, notably in those that voted heavily for the FIS in 1990 and 1991 and felt betrayed by the cancellation of elections and the banning of the party. When these resources began to dry up, an increasing number of armed groups began to rely on extortion and protection rackets to fund their operations. The expansion in government spending, together with the liberalisation of international trade recommended by the IMF, significantly increased the resources upon which the armed groups could prey. For a period it appeared as if the agreements of 1994 had strengthened both sides in the conflict. As the 1990s progressed, however, it was clear that the regime had been given a decisive advantage. Not only did the authorities now have access to expanded resources, but the armed groups were undermined by their own attempts to take advantage of the new resources. As local groups and their 'emirs' focused more on taking control of local sources of money through extortion or by moving into forms of trade themselves, the focus of their activities became progressively more economic and local, and thus less and less political and national. It was a process that was accelerated by the high turnover of 'emirs' as they were killed or captured by the regime and were replaced by younger, less ideological individuals driven more by a desire to accumulate wealth than confront the regime. This also possibly explains the remarkable absence of attacks on Algeria's oil and gas installations during this period, which could have seriously weakened the regime but would have provided no direct economic benefit for individual armed groups. In the view of Luis Martinez, who made a detailed study of these developments, this change 'was one of the major turning points in the urban guerrilla war.'[71]

The changes from 1994 also weakened the armed groups in two further ways, by undermining support for them in two important groups. Firstly, the liberalisation of controls that the state exercised on external trade dealt a blow to the strong links many armed groups had established with the black market and smuggling networks which had provided important logistical support for the armed groups in the early years of the conflict. The liberalisation of trade greatly expanded opportunities for the black market '*trabendo*' networks, which no longer needed to rely on the armed groups for resources as they had in the early 1990s, when there had been restrictions on trade and visas. At a more subtle level, the liberalising reforms also undercut support for armed resistance amongst the petty bourgeoisie, who had been strong supporters of the FIS but now valued the new opportunities presented by a liberalised trading environment and consequently switched their support to another Islamist party, the Movement for a Society of Peace (MSP), which had roots in this part of society and formally allied itself with the regime (see Chapter 5). As Martinez comments: 'The conditions imposed by the IMF in fact fit marvellously together with the demands of the Islamist "bourgeoisie."' Privatisation, in particular, helped to recruit new allies for the regime by giving elements of the private sector a stake in the survival of the regime, whilst also protecting sectors of the economy from attack by the armed groups who deliberately targeted state-owned interests.[72]

Just as the programme of economic liberalisation was undermining the armed groups, the activities of the latter were also serving to bolster and expand the liberalisation process. Martinez argues that the attacks mounted against state-owned property and operations (such as public transport) actually speeded up processes of privatisation by forcing the withdrawal of the state from these areas and facilitating the takeover of these sectors by private interests who took advantage of trade and price liberalisation to run the operations for profit, often paying protection money to the local armed groups.[73]

Although the agreements of 1994 officially recommitted the Algerian government to the programme of economic reform it had begun in the 1980s, the progress of these reforms thereafter was—as in Morocco and Tunisia—determined more by the demands of the specific political configurations of the regime than by the hand of the market. This was particularly true for the programme of privatisations that the IMF recommended Algeria should undertake. In Tunisia and Morocco, privatisation went ahead and the regimes in both countries were able to ensure that the new owners of previously state-owned industries and operations were kept either very close or, indeed, within the regime itself. In Algeria a rather different pattern emerged. A World Bank report in 2000 noted that, despite Algeria publicly undertaking to privatise significant parts of its economy as part of the agreement struck in 1994, not one corporate public enterprise had been fully sold off to outside interests.[74]

The reasons for this failure lay in a number of political factors identified by Isabelle Werenfels. The first and most commonly cited is that privatisation was resisted on ideological grounds by elements within the Algerian regime which represented, in the view of Werenfels, 'the continuing and powerful remnant of the nationalist, *étatiste* and collectivist ideological foundations on which post-independence Algeria was built.'[75] In other words, there remained a significant part of the regime that was still committed to the ideas of Boumediennist state socialism, which saw economic liberalisation in general and privatisation in particular as anathema. This would certainly seem to help explain the significant and vocal opposition mounted by more traditional elements, particularly within the FLN, to the reform programme from its inception under Chadli Benjedid, who had articulated their criticisms in highly ideological terms.[76]

Ideology, however, whilst frequently cited, is seldom a determining factor in Algerian politics; and therefore the opposition to privatisation, especially its success, is more fully explained by other factors. As explained earlier, Algeria's domestic political economy has been largely characterised by rent-seeking and patronage since independence. Whereas the regimes in both Tunisia and Morocco were able to make sure that these mechanisms survived the transition to a more privatised economy largely intact, it seems that the Algerian regime was uncertain of being able to do the same. This was largely a reflection of the more fractured and collective leadership of the country—specifically within the military—which was unable to provide the sort of unified leadership present in both Tunisia and Morocco, as was needed to make the transition. The absence of such unified leadership has led to a resultant absence of a coherent economic strategy. This, in turn, is both a cause and consequence of the lack of consensus—which Ivan Martin characterises as 'almost total'—on economic policy, and in part explains why economic liberalisation has not enjoyed the remarkably broad support that it has amongst even the opposition in both Tunisia and Morocco. By contrast, committed reformers in Algeria only ever comprised a small group of individuals within the regime.[77]

As a result of these deficiencies, those interests and elements in Algeria who feared that privatisation would damage their entrenched rent-related interests were able to block it successfully. Privatisation was perceived as a clear threat to those interests that, for example, exercised near total control over the import and distribution networks in the country and became the dominant forms of business within an economy that produced little for either export or domestic consumption beyond oil and gas, and led to references to Algeria having an 'import-import' economy. The presence of these interests 'close to or in the army and the administration' enabled them to block and sabotage any attempts at privatisation.[78] As Werenfels concludes more generally:

...resistance to privatisation of industrial SOEs [State Owned Enterprises] results from the fact that these SOEs are deeply embedded in patron-client networks and (military) clan structures and closely linked through these structures.[79]

The small size of the reforming constituency within the leadership, together with the need to retain the support of many of the opponents to privatisation in the bureaucracy and the trades unions in the struggle against the armed groups in the 1990s, ensured that there was no concerted attempt to face down opposition to privatisation.[80]

Other aspects of the reforms advocated by the IMF were more readily accepted because they served the interests of the existing patron-client networks. Trade liberalisation, for example, 'simply moved import monopolies from industrial SOEs to oligopolies of private importers close to the army.'[81] In addition, the ability to grant import licences allowed figures in the regime to establish themselves as patrons of commercial clienteles.[82] The domination of the economy by hydrocarbons has meant that the Algerian private sector had traditionally been involved in commerce rather than productive industry, and this has eased its absorption into these clientelist networks built around the distribution of imports.[83] As Martin observes: 'The fact is that, for a large part of the private sector ... proximity to the power circles continues to be as important in order to thrive as a company's productivity and competitiveness.'[84] Traditionally the smallest in the Maghreb, the Algerian private sector has—like its counterparts in Tunisia and Morocco—thus been thoroughly penetrated by regime interests and clientelist practices. The significant rise in the international price of oil that occurred from the early 2000s served to strengthen and entrench these characteristics further as the amount of available rent increased dramatically and remained in the system long after the price had reached its peak.

In this way, Algeria—like Tunisia and Morocco—formally embraced a programme of liberal economic reforms without allowing it to alter fundamentally the structures of power. The more factionalised nature of the political leadership resulted in a more complex and opaque situation developing. The lack of a clear decision-making centre in Algeria has meant that no clear economic policy has been developed, and in its place rampant clientelism and rent-seeking have come to dominate the economy even more than ever.

Although this situation gives a certain degree of short-term stability to the political system, it does expose it to more long-term dangers, notably through the exclusion of the bulk of the ordinary population. From the 1980s the lot of the ordinary population demonstrably worsened. Between 1986 and 1999 GDP per capita per annum declined from $2,590 to $1,550.[85] Much of this was due to the collapse of the international oil price in the mid 1980s and the civil conflict of the 1990s. Significantly, though, the situation has not noticeably improved with the sharp rise in the international price of oil since the early 2000s and the corresponding decline in the civil conflict from 1999. Martin speaks of a 'growing pauperisation of broad segments of the population.'[86] Unemployment rates remain high, having been worsened by the application of structural reforms for state-owned industries in preparation for privatisation demanded by the IMF after 1994, resulting in 450,000 workers being laid off.[87] The concentration of unemployment amongst the country's youth—who continue to comprise a large share of the population—represents a powerful potential threat to the regime. It was the country's youth who took to the streets in October 1988, and it was the urban unemployed who provided the foot soldiers and core supporters of both the FIS and later the armed groups of the 1990s. The unrest that broke out in Kabylia in 2001 (see Chapter 6) was substantially socio-economic in origin and spearheaded by the youth of the region; it was symptomatic of disillusionment with the regime that spread well beyond Kabylia. The continued failure of this section of the population to gain a noticeable share in the benefits brought by the steep rise in hydrocarbons revenues that occurred from the early 2000s has only underlined the feeling that 'the hydrocarbons wealth does not belong to them, does not contribute to their well being'. It has thus worked to stoke more feelings of resentment and alienation towards the Algerian regime.[88] It clearly contributed to the outburst of unrest that occurred across the country in the first week of 2011, but significantly it did not translate into the sort of political protest movement that developed in Tunisia, Morocco and much of the rest of the Arab world in the months that followed. Much of the reason for this lay in the Algerian public's wariness of street politics, derived from the bloody experience of the 1990s, and the fact that civil society and the political parties did not coalesce to organise the kind of broad coalition mobilised in other Arab states. It was also explained by the Algerian regime's ability to draw on the large revenues accumulated by the long years of high oil and gas prices to dampen public anger through increases in state subsidies and the creation of jobs.[89]

The International Dimension

An important feature of the Maghrebi economies since the 1970s has been their increasingly external connections and orientation. Part of this has been due to processes of globalisation that have become a progressively larger feature of the world economy over this period. It is also a direct product of the programmes and policies of economic reform and liberalisation pursued by all three states since the 1980s: increased integration of the global economy being one of the major specified goals of the Washington Consensus. Free Trade Agreements were the centrepiece of the expanded relationship with the European Union that the three states entered into through the Euro-Mediterranean Partnership Agreement from the mid 1990s (see Chapter 9). This increased integration into the global economy has had a number of consequences for the political economy of the states in the region.

Most obviously, greater integration into the global economy has given outside forces greater influence over the economies of the region through increased trade, investment, loans and aid. This influence clearly opens up the possibility of the region being susceptible to external economic and political pressure. This was clearly the case economically with the striking of agreements with the IMF in order to fend off external creditors. The exertion of political pressure has largely come from foreign governments on whom the Maghrebi states are, to varying degrees, dependent for trade, investment, loans and aid. The Maghrebi governments have thus been subject to pressure to alter aspects of both their foreign and economic policies. More interestingly, pressure has also been put on states to change aspects of their internal politics. That the bulk of the Maghreb's main external partners are from the liberal democratic states of Europe and North America has meant that some of this pressure has been political, to liberalise and democratise their domestic political systems.

As the state with the traditionally most externally oriented economy, Morocco has been most vulnerable to this pressure. A desire to keep its major creditors and trading partners in Europe happy has been a major contributing factor to the political reforms introduced since the early 1990s. As Denoeux and Maghraoui argue:

Political reforms have thus become a necessity, if only because the success of Morocco's economic liberalization depends on the continued cooperation of international financial institutions; that cooperation in turn is influenced by the kingdom's international image.[90]

Accusations and revelations about human rights abuses in the kingdom that emerged in the early 1990s damaged Morocco's image in Europe and contributed to a decision by the European Parliament to vote to suspend a financial aid package to Morocco in 1992. Release of political prisoners by the Moroccan government and the introduction of liberalising constitutional amendments were the visible result of these pressures (see Chapter 9). Adverse reactions in the EU and France to reports about corruption and the drug trade in Morocco were also a contributing factor to the launching of the 'Sanitisation' campaign of 1995–6.[91]

Expectations that the Euro-Mediterranean Partnership Initiative of 1995 would increase European leverage over the Maghreb states and thus accelerate political change and reform were, however, to be disappointed. Algeria, Tunisia and Morocco developed effective methods of deflecting attempts to link economic ties to political reform (see Chapter 9). The failure of the EMPI, particularly its free trade agreements, to have any noticeable impact on the economic fortunes of the Maghreb states further weakened the leverage of the EU. Moreover, the use of economic ties to apply political pressure was not entirely a one-way street. Despite their clear disadvantage in terms of economic size, Maghrebi states developed ways of putting pressure on Western governments. All three states used fears of Islamism to ensure continued economic support from abroad. In 1998, for example, the Moroccan prime minister, Abderrahmane El Youssoufi, spoke in uncharacteristically dark terms about the dangers of Islamism in an interview with a French newspaper shortly before a trip to Europe to renegotiate Morocco's external debt.[92] Throughout the 1990s, Algeria warned foreign governments that any external political or economic pressure put on it could lead to the fall of the regime and the takeover of Algeria by militant Islamists. At the same time, the increased levels of foreign loans and investment that came into Algeria after 1994 clearly strengthened foreign governments' and international financial institutions' ties to the regime and interests in its survival.[93] The subsequent rapid rise in the international price of hydrocarbons from the early 2000s quickly reduced any pressure that external powers were able to exercise over Algeria as the country paid off its debts, built up reserves and became a significant supplier of energy to parts of Europe, allowing it to pay little attention to the concerns or criticisms of foreign governments. The onset of the 'War on Terror' after the attacks on the United States of 11 September 2001 also strengthened the position of Algeria in this regard, as it did for Tunisia and Morocco who, whilst not possessing the same natural resources, were able to argue for more advantageous economic agreements and the relaxation of any linkages that Western governments might want to make between economic relations and internal political reform (see Chapter 9).

Concerns expressed by Maghrebi governments about domestic political stability were not entirely disingenuous. The popular unrest experienced by all three states in the 1980s, which was largely a product of the attempts made by the regimes to introduce their own programmes of structural reforms, made them wary of introducing too swiftly and comprehensively the reforms demanded by institutions such as the IMF, particularly those that involved lay-offs or cuts in subsidies on basic goods. These genuine fears have led governments to try to delay and water down reforms demanded in these areas, which has led to them becoming 'engaged in an unsteady balancing act involving economic accountability to foreign creditors and political accountability to domestic populations.'[94] Concerns about public reactions were also viewed as lying behind Algeria's long-standing resistance to a formal deal with the IMF, which could be popularly perceived as a breach in the nationalist determination to avoid foreign interference in Algeria's affairs, borne out of the independence struggle against the French.[95] Nevertheless it has been argued that these essentially ideological concerns were in reality a cover for fears amongst the elite that a deal with the IMF might lead to a loss of control over the distribution of rent.[96]

Increased economic ties with the wider world have also possibly had more subtle intended consequences for the politics of the Maghreb. Economic reforms have clearly boosted the private sector and in places have led to the strengthening and expansion of the commercial middle class. Whilst most of the regimes have been able to restrict the growth of the middle class or, more usually, co-opt and control it, these restrictions have not been total and there is evidence that elements of that class have begun to forge an independent and more politically critical path. In Morocco, the progressive liberalisation of trade, bolstered by the Free Trade Agreement with the EU in 1995, has led to the emergence of a class of entrepreneurs from outside the small established economic elite who have taken advantage of the new export-orientated trade regime.[97] These entrepreneurs have begun to make their economic and political presence known, as shown with the case of the CGEM. At a more subtle level, it is also possible that, as globalisation continues, the region's middle classes will increase their interaction with other countries—notably through business abroad and the education of their children at foreign universities—and gradually import political as well as economic values that could contribute to the spread and deepening of liberal and democratic values within the region. At the end of the 1990s, Emma Murphy presciently observed of the country with the biggest middle class, Tunisia:

As Ben Ali's economic reforms encourage the infiltration of externally-derived cultural and political norms and as technology, communications and private freedoms are enhanced, it is difficult to see how the deepening *civisme* of Tunisian society can be reversed, or even kept to its current configuration.[98]

Conclusion

The interaction between economics and politics in the Maghreb states followed a remarkably similar pattern in the first few decades following independence. All three moved from a situation of state dominance in the economy, which allowed for the distribution of resources by the political elite, through to ostensibly more liberalised economic arrangements that the regimes were similarly able to manage to ensure political support. This latter development saw a slight divergence in the experiences of the states, as each used different methods to prevent the economic changes that economic liberalisation and structural adjustment brought from producing effects that challenged the essential power structures in each state. The political leaderships in all three countries successfully penetrated and controlled the new social forces and economic actors produced by the changes, with Tunisia putting much more emphasis on intimidation and control, and Morocco and Algeria on penetration and cooption.

It was always likely that the successful management of the political effects of economic change would prove more difficult to sustain over the longer term as greater economic interaction with the outside world and the development of more gradual socio-economic changes had an effect. Layachi argued that perceiving economic reform purely as a regime survival tactic ran the risk of overlooking the effects of important 'socio-demographic and political mutations in the region.'[99] Although a thoroughgoing analysis of the political economy of Tunisia in the run-up to the collapse of the political regime will be needed to analyse its precise role in the revolution of January 2011, it is clear that such mutations were indeed occurring in Tunisia during this period and influenced the subsequent course of events.

One of the difficulties in assessing the future shape of the political economy of the Maghreb states lies not just in the opaque nature of the decision-making processes within them and the lack of reliable statistics, but also in the fact that so much of the economy of the region lies outside the formal ambit of the states. According to one estimate, as much as 35–40 per cent of economic activity in the Maghreb takes place within the black or informal economy.[100] The importance of this dimension is, as has been shown, vital to an understanding of much of the dynamics of the conflict in Algeria in the 1990s. Its strength in Morocco during the same period contributed to the launching of the 'Sanitisation' campaign directed against the private sector. Its presence across the region may even have explained, through its supply of jobs and resources that were largely unmonitored, the surprising lack of large-scale popular unrest of the sort that all three countries experienced in the 1980s but was not repeated during the 1990s and 2000s, despite apparently often equally adverse economic conditions. It may or may not have been a coincidence that the Maghrebi state that had the smallest informal economy, Tunisia, was the one which experienced the most serious popular unrest in the opening months of 2011.

The future economic course plotted by Tunisia in the post Ben Ali era will potentially give some indications as to the lessons learned from the political economy of the previous period; lessons that may well be taken on board by other states, including Morocco and Algeria, who have followed a similar path and who wish to avoid the fate of Ben Ali. Whilst the adoption of a substantially democratic political system seems highly likely, given the almost universal popular demand for it within the country and especially amongst those who led the revolution; the continuation of ostensibly liberal economic policies is less certain, given their negative association with the Ben Ali period. Some argue that it was the application of these reforms and policies that sustained the former president's system for so long; others point out that they were actually at the root of his final downfall and were even a vindication of the view that economic liberalisation would eventually provoke political liberalisation. What was clear was that political authoritarianism of the sort exercised under Ben Ali had proved incapable of managing the economy in a way that compensated for the lack of political liberties enjoyed by the general population, and actually contributed to its own downfall by fostering the type of 'crony capitalism' and ultimately kleptocracy that saw the presidential family loot vast amounts of money from the national coffers.

The collapse of the Ben Ali regime also contained lessons for Tunisia's foreign economic partners and the international financial institutions. The Tunisian economic model that operated under Ben Ali had long received substantial plaudits from Western governments, the IMF and the World Bank, which saw it as a model for other countries in the region, endorsements that the regime and its supporters were quick to cite in response to criticism of the country's lack of democracy and poor human rights record.[101] The dramatic demonstration of the Tunisian model's failure to deliver for its own people through the popular uprising of 2010–11 therefore destroyed many of the assumptions that Tunisia's foreign economic partners had previously held about the economic health of the country. It remains to be seen whether the destruction of these assumptions will lead to a fundamental review of how economic health and progress in the region are measured and judged.

8

REGIONAL RELATIONS

The differences and similarities between Algeria, Morocco and Tunisia at the level of domestic politics have made for interesting and dynamic politics at the regional level. Since independence, relations have swung between conflict and cooperation—the two extreme examples of this being armed clashes between Morocco and Algeria and attempts to create a formal union between the states. Regional relations have inevitably been dominated by Morocco and Algeria, as the countries with the largest populations and territory, while Tunisia has played a much more peripheral role. Significantly, though, regional politics in the Maghreb have come to encompass not just the three states of the central Maghreb but also those of the wider Maghreb region: Libya and Mauritania, both of which have come to be heavily involved in the armed conflicts and attempts at regional cooperation that have been a feature of regional relations.

The Colonial Period and its Aftermath

As with domestic politics, it is important to look at the colonial era to understand the context in which regional relations developed in the post-independence period. The experience of European colonial rule was a common one, which had an initially unifying effect on the region. Although separately administered, Morocco, Tunisia and Algeria were all ruled by the French. This not only created links across the region but also provided a common enemy to unite against once nationalism began to gain ground in the 1940s and 1950s. Contact and cooperation between the nationalist movements in the three countries grew, and once Morocco and Tunisia gained independence in 1956, the new governments united to press for the securing of independence for Algeria. This cooperation culminated in the Conference of Tangier, held in Morocco in 1958, which brought together representatives of the Istiqlal from Morocco, the Neo-Destour from Tunisia and the FLN from Algeria. So strong were the feelings of solidarity that the conference adopted a resolution on the creation of a federal union between the three states. The fact that Algeria was still under French rule at this point meant, however, that these plans could not be put into practice. When Algeria did finally become independent four years later in 1962, other problems arose that were themselves direct products of the colonial period.

The War of the Sands

Algeria's achievement of independence in 1962 was warmly welcomed in Tunisia and Morocco, but relations between Algeria and its western neighbour cooled fairly quickly over a border dispute between the two states. The origins of the dispute lay in the decision taken by French officials following the establishment of the protectorate in Morocco to shift a substantial part of the length of the pre-protectorate border between Morocco and Algeria westwards, effectively carving off a strip of land from Morocco and adding it to Algeria. The move—accomplished in a series of gradual stages in the 1930s and 1940s—was variously explained as the result of a power struggle between French officials in Rabat and Algiers and alternatively a deliberate attempt by France to secure more territory for French Algeria, which was a formal part of France rather than just a protectorate.[1] The move did not attract huge attention or controversy at the time, since the territory concerned consisted mainly of sparsely populated desert that had never been fully demarcated and did not include the more heavily populated border area in the north. In addition, France controlled both Algeria and Morocco and looked set to do so for the foreseeable future, so the development had few immediate political effects.

After Morocco achieved its independence in 1956, and when Algerian independence began to look increasingly likely, Morocco communicated to the FLN its wish to see the territory returned. Morocco received promises in 1960 from the FLN's 'Provisional Government'

(GPRA) that the border issue would be settled after independence to avoid French exploitation of the issue. The French had already begun attempts to exploit the issue by offering Morocco the territory in return for cessation of support for the FLN—an offer Morocco rejected. Once Algeria achieved independence, Morocco again raised the issue and, after some initial stalling by the new Algerian government, was eventually informed by the Algerians that the existing border between the states was permanent and that Algeria did not intend to transfer the territories back to Morocco.[2]

Outraged at what it saw as a betrayal of both commitments made before independence and, more broadly, of Morocco's support for Algeria's liberation struggle, Morocco cried foul. However, on the first of these points at least, Algeria's new leader, President Ahmed Ben Bella, did not feel honour-bound to respect the promises made to Morocco before independence, since it was not he who had made them: the promises having been made by the GPRA, which Ben Bella and his allies had defeated in the power struggles that followed independence (see Chapter 2). On the broader issue of history and legality, Algeria cited in justification the charter of the new Organisation of African Union (OAU) of newly independent African states. This declared that, in order to prevent the unleashing of a torrent of debilitating border disputes between the decolonised states, the colonially imposed boundaries—no matter how illogical or arbitrary—should be accepted and respected as the borders of post-colonial Africa. Abdelaziz Bouteflika, Algeria's foreign minister from 1963, described the agreement between Morocco and the GPRA as a 'circumstantial political compromise,' made in the context of the demands of the liberation struggle, which was not legally binding on a now sovereign and independent Algeria.[3]

Behind the public stance, it is likely that the new Algerian government's position was motivated by a mixture of principle and opportunism. It is certainly true that many Algerians viewed Algeria's borders as having what Ben Bella described as a 'sacred character' because of the huge sacrifices of the liberation struggle that could not and should not be signed away easily on the achievement of independence. At the same time, endorsement of the OAU's position on the inviolability of post-colonial frontiers strengthened Algeria's own claim to its southern territories and borders which had little in common with any precolonial Algerian political entity.[4] It is also true that the tough stance taken by Algeria was a result of Ben Bella's belief that confrontation with Morocco would rally national support behind him in the aftermath of the divisive struggles of the immediate post-independence period. It is also speculated that the new president also mistakenly believed that the sizeable presence of deputies from the leftist UNFP in the Moroccan parliament following the elections of May 1963 would undermine King Hassan's position—especially given the good relations between the FLN and the UNFP.[5]

In response to Algeria's refusal to hand over the border territories, Morocco decided to take matters into its own hands and attempted to regain them by force: border clashes erupted into full-scale war in October 1963, in which both sides occupied parts of each other's territory on the border. Fighting was brought to an end after three weeks through OAU mediation, which persuaded the two sides to withdraw to their pre-war lines in preparation for a negotiated solution to the dispute.

Although the ceasefire held, tensions between the two states remained high throughout the rest of the 1960s. The leaderships of both states felt angry and betrayed; Morocco's resentment being countered by Algeria's belief that Morocco had unnecessarily resorted to force and timed it to occur in October 1963 when the regime was still newly established and fragile and, moreover, facing an insurrection in Kabylia. The so-called 'War of the Sands' thus set the scene for regional relations in the post-independence period that would be dominated by mistrust and rivalry between Morocco and Algeria.

Rapprochement

Attempts to heal the breach between Morocco and Algeria were made throughout the 1960s, notably through holding meetings between ministers from Morocco, Algeria and Tunisia aimed at strengthening economic ties and cooperation across the region. These culminated in the setting up of a permanent consultative commission to investigate the possibilities of economic integration following a meeting of economic ministers from the three countries in September-October 1964. This initiative did not, however, make much further progress as the coup of June 1965 in Algiers brought to power Houari Boumedienne, who took a much more sceptical approach to regional cooperation than had Ben Bella, Boumedienne believing that economic development within the individual states should precede regional unity, rather than the other way around.[6]

A more substantial thaw in Algerian-Moroccan relations occurred at the end of the 1960s when efforts to resolve tensions through bilateral negotiations culminated in the signing of a Treaty of Fraternity, Good Neighbourliness and Cooperation in Ifrane in Morocco in January 1969. This treaty paved the way for accepting the proposals made by a joint boundary commission set up by the two countries recommending the acceptance of the status quo antebellum, which basically meant Algeria keeping all the disputed territory. Agreement on the boundary was reached in May 1970 and King Hassan formally accepted it at the time of an OAU summit in Rabat in June 1972.

Morocco's surprising acceptance can been explained with reference to a number of factors. The OAU summit in Rabat fell between the two attempted coups of July 1971 and August 1972, and thus occurred at a time when the monarchy was clearly feeling vulnerable and insecure. A deal with Algeria therefore gave King Hassan security not just from an external threat from the east but also, given links between the FLN and the UNFP, from an Algerian-sponsored internal challenge from the Moroccan left. Nevertheless, from the first meetings in Ifrane in 1969, Morocco did set a price on an agreement to settle the border in Algeria's favour. It asked for joint exploitation of resources in the disputed territory (notably of the iron ore mine at Gara Djebilet), together with use of some of Algeria's substantial energy resources. More importantly and significantly for future relations, Morocco demanded Algeria's support for its claim on the territory that would become known as the Western Sahara.[7]

Morocco's Claim on the Western Sahara

Morocco's interest in and claim on the Western Sahara is the subject of much debate, not least because the claim came to be made so vigorously and was then equally ferociously disputed. It has yet to be resolved, making the Western Sahara one of the most enduring international disputes.

The territory known as the 'Western Sahara' corresponds to the area of land which was taken over by the Spanish in the 1880s, in the context of the European 'Scramble for Africa' at the end of the nineteenth century. Although fairly sizeable, the territory on the north-west coast of the continent, which then became known as the 'Spanish Sahara,' contained little more than rock and desert, and was inhabited by a few thousand, mainly nomadic, Sahrawi (Saharan) tribesman. As a result, Spanish control—which amounted to little more than the establishment of some small coastal outposts—aroused little attention or genuine controversy at the time.

The territory's nature and remoteness, together with the timing of its occupation nearly thirty years before the establishment of the protectorate by France and Spain over Morocco to the north, meant that it was not part of the protectorate. It was consequently dealt with separately and distinctly by the Spanish, who did not relinquish it when they withdrew from northern Morocco at the formal end of the protectorate in 1956. How genuinely concerned Morocco's post-independence government was about the Spanish Sahara is the subject of some debate, particularly given the fact that, although Morocco stated its claim to the territory, it did not do so vociferously and did not push for its immediate return. This may well have been due to the fact that Morocco was more concerned with its claim on other more immediately important territories, such as Tangier in the north (which had been an 'international zone' since 1924), Sidi Ifni and Tarfaya in the south (which the Spanish retained) and, of course, the disputed territories on the border with Algeria. Nevertheless, elements within the nationalist Istiqlal party did explicitly and stridently claim the territory, along with parts of Senegal, Mali and Algeria, and all of modern-day Mauritania. The Istiqlal's position on the issue prompted King Mohamed V to endorse the claim himself in 1958, out of fear of being outflanked on the issue by the Istiqlal in the context of its power struggle with the monarchy in the aftermath of independence in the late 1950s.[8] This did not, however, prevent the Istiqlal from criticising King Hassan's closeness to the Spanish leader General Franco and his perceived lack of commitment to Morocco's claim on the Spanish Sahara following his accession to the throne in 1961.[9] Nevertheless, the progressive reintegration of the territories of Tangier (1958), Tarfaya (1958) and Sidi Ifni (1969) encouraged the political class in Morocco to believe that a step-by-step approach would gradually result in the regaining of the territories it claimed, with the Spanish Sahara gradually rising to the top of that list by the advent of the 1970s.[10]

Spanish Withdrawal and the Green March

Morocco was confident in its claim on the Spanish Sahara, and during the 1950s and 1960s it stated that when Spain eventually withdrew there should be a referendum on the future of the territory. Morocco clearly assumed that the small population of the territory would recognise the historic ties it had with Morocco and vote for integration into the kingdom.

Spain remained committed to remaining in the territory, but by the early 1970s pressure began to mount from all sides for it to withdraw. The rapprochement between Morocco and Algeria in 1969, combined with urgings from the UN, led to Spain declaring its willingness to make preparations for self-determination.[11] Spanish desire to hold onto the Spanish Sahara was further weakened by the emergence in the early 1970s of a small anti-colonial resistance movement inside the territory that began to launch attacks on the Spanish in May 1973. The appearance of this resistance movement caused some unease for Morocco, which in 1974 altered its acceptance of the idea of a referendum on the territory's future to a policy of seeking a negotiated settlement with Spain for a transfer of power.[12] Spain, however, believed that a referendum should still take place, hoping perhaps that the creation of a small weak state would still allow Spain preferential access to the territory's mineral resources.[13] Morocco responded by proposing that the issue be put to the International Court of Justice (ICJ) in The Hague, a proposal that Spain agreed to on condition that the opinion of the court would be 'advisory' and thus 'non-binding.' The ICJ was asked to rule on two questions: firstly, whether the territory of the Western Sahara before colonisation by the Spanish had been *terra nullius*—that is that there had been no political authority to claim sovereignty over the territory; secondly, if it were not *terra nullius*, to establish what ties did exist between the territory and the kingdom of Morocco and the 'entity of Mauritania.'[14]

The inclusion of Mauritania in the framework was the result of Mauritania making its own claim on the territory with which it shared a border. Anxious that Mauritania's claim should not muddy its own, Morocco accepted that the two states should make a joint claim and subsequently partition the territory. Significantly, Morocco had also laid claim to the territory of Mauritania from the 1960s and had bitterly contested France's decision to create a separate state when it withdrew in 1961. Despite initially refusing to recognise the new state of Mauritania, Morocco had bowed to reality by 1969 and quietly extended recognition, thus giving up its claim.

The ICJ gave its ruling in October 1975 on the two issues. Firstly, it declared that Western Sahara was not *terra nullius* at the time of Spanish colonisation. Secondly, it ruled that legal ties of allegiance did indeed exist between the Moroccan sultan and some tribes in the region, and between the territory and the area that was to become Mauritania; but, crucially, these ties did not constitute territorial sovereignty and the population of the territory had a right to self-determination through a referendum. Morocco's response to the ruling was to take what John Damis described as a 'nationalistic and highly partisan' reading of the ruling, ignoring those parts that did not suit Morocco's case and declare that the ICJ's recognition of 'legal ties of allegiance' were tantamount to sovereignty in Islamic law.[15]

The stridency of Morocco's claim to the territory began to increase notably during this period and was due only in part to its belief in the validity of its claim. The coming to the fore of the issue of the Western Sahara coincided with a particularly turbulent time in Moroccan domestic politics, with King Hassan II narrowly surviving two successive attempted *coups d'état* from the country's military in July 1971 and August 1972, and an attempted leftist insurgency the following year (see Chapter 3). Feeling extremely vulnerable, Hassan was able to seize upon the issue of Morocco's claim on the Spanish Sahara to forge a nationalistic cause that could unite the mutinous military and the political opposition behind him: the military being anxious for prestige and the main opposition parties all being descendants of the nationalist Istiqlal party that had instigated the initial claims on the territory. It was a feat that he pulled off with considerable aplomb, transforming the domestic political landscape in a short space of time and uniting previously hostile forces behind the monarchy. This transformation substantially explains Morocco's subsequent tenacity on the issue of the Western Sahara, which is motivated by fears that defeat of its claim may unwind this unity and return the country to the instability and challenges to the monarchy witnessed in the early 1970s. Although the territory was known to contain significant natural resources and its coastal waters were some of the richest fishing grounds in the world, it was the imperative of regime security that was to drive Morocco's claim to the territory thereafter and explained why it became a priority above all others for the Moroccan monarchy.

The ICJ ruling did not, however, bring Morocco closer to controlling the territory, since Spain still held firm on the issue of holding a referendum. Morocco then made an unusual move both to underline Morocco's claim and to pressurise the Spanish into negotiating. What became known as the 'Green March' was the personal idea of King Hassan; it saw Morocco organise a mass march of 350,000 unarmed Moroccan civilians into the territory at the beginning of November 1975. As well as further mobilising the Moroccan population behind the territorial claim, the organisation of the march constituted a middle path for Hassan between the equally hazardous alternatives of military confrontation and inaction: mounting an armed attack against the militarily superior Spanish risked significant casualties and humiliating defeat, whilst doing nothing risked political challenges from the political parties and even unilateral action from the country's military.[16] Although the marchers withdrew after entering only a symbolic distance into the territory, the pressure on Spain paid off.[17] As a result, with General Franco on his deathbed and splits in the government emerging, Spain backed down on its plans to hold a referendum and signed what became known as the Tripartite Agreement with Morocco and Mauritania, committing itself to a complete withdrawal from the territory by February 1976 and the transfer of administrative control (but significantly not sovereignty) to Morocco and Mauritania. This withdrawal and transfer occurred rapidly, with Moroccan and Mauritanian forces moving in to take control of the territory in the closing weeks of 1975.

Algerian Opposition

The takeover and partition of the former Spanish Sahara by Morocco and Mauritania appeared a fairly simple *fait accompli* but was, in the event, strongly contested from at least two directions. The most important and most surprising source of opposition came from the third state with borders on the territory: Algeria. It was surprising because it had initially appeared that Algeria was supportive of Morocco and Mauritania's plan to divide up the territory between them. Morocco had made this a largely tacit condition of its settlement of the border dispute with Algeria in 1972, and on several subsequent occasions Algeria's leader, Houari Boumedienne, had privately indicated that he had no objection to this plan, most notably and latterly at an Arab heads of state meeting in Rabat in October 1974.[18] As late as July 1975, just months before the Tripartite Agreement, Algeria appeared to give a public endorsement to the plan: a visit by Abdelaziz Bouteflika to Rabat producing a joint communiqué that recorded Algeria's 'great satisfaction' with the Moroccan-Mauritanian agreement.[19] Yet, in spite of this public declaration, Algeria did not shift its diplomatic position and in the aftermath of the July communiqué restated its established position in support of the principle of self-determination for the territory.

There are several suggested explanations for what had prompted this apparently abrupt about-face on the part of Algeria. The first points to a progressive breakdown of trust between King Hassan and Houari Boumedienne. Relations between the two countries had clearly improved in the late 1960s, with the Ifrane Treaty of 1969 and the agreement on the Moroccan-Algerian border. The Algerians, however, had grown increasingly suspicious of Morocco's failure to give formal ratification to the agreement on the mutual border (Algeria had ratified it in May 1973), and saw the Moroccan explanation for this—the absence of a sitting national parliament due to internal political turmoil—as worryingly disingenuous in a state where the king manifestly held all the power and could institute whatever policy he liked.[20] Algerian fears that Morocco had no intention of ratifying the agreement and was seeking possibly to renew its claim once it had secured control of the Western Sahara therefore began to grow. These fears were significantly heightened when King Hassan appeared to adopt a much more emotive and propagandist line of rhetoric on the territory.[21] As a result of this suspected duplicity, it is argued, Algeria sought to go back on its part of the tacit agreement to recognise and not block Morocco's takeover of the Western Sahara.

Other explanations emphasise Algeria's geo-political concerns. One stresses the growing realisation inside Algeria that a Moroccan takeover of the Western Sahara would substantially increase the size of Moroccan territory and territorially surround Algeria: a potentially hazardous position for Algeria, having been invaded by its western neighbour only a decade earlier. Boumedienne was said to favour the preservation of the status quo, which he believed was a stable equilibrium and which a Moroccan (and Mauritanian) partition of the Spanish Sahara would upset. Boumedienne was also concerned by Mauritania's closeness to Morocco, Algeria's southern neighbour having previously been a close ally of Algeria. He feared that this relationship would lead to Algeria's diplomatic isolation in the region and, moreover, worried that Morocco would use the partition plan over the Sahara as a first step in making an eventual move to takeover Mauritania.[22] At the international level, the Algerians were also highly suspicious of the support being lent to Morocco's case by both France and the United States; by 1975 they feared this was part of an international effort to isolate Algeria by the former colonial power and the leading Western power, both of whom had tense relations with Algeria in this period.[23] For Morocco, Algeria's geo-political concerns were related more to ambition than fear: Algeria was clearly interested in gaining a political, territorial and economic foothold in the Western Sahara for itself. King Hassan argued that the Algerian policy demonstrated that Boumedienne wanted to establish hegemony for Algeria over the region.[24] Even if this was not the primary motivating factor of Algerian policy, there were clearly elements within the Algerian political elite who viewed Algerian regional leadership as the natural and proper regional order, given the country's size, iconic revolutionary status and its substantial hydrocarbon wealth.[25]

The reason Algerian officials themselves formally gave for Algeria's eventual policy was that it endorsed the right of the population of the territory to exercise self-determination through a referendum. Algeria rejected the accusation of a switch in policy in 1975, with Boumedienne subsequently claiming that Algerian support for Moroccan-Mauritanian partition had been on the assumption that the population of the territory would eventually have to give its support to such a plan.[26] This stance—and probably its late assertion of it—can possibly be explained by Algeria's growing awareness of the increasing strength of a national liberation movement within the territory itself. Algeria claimed that, having itself been born out of a national liberation struggle against the French, it felt duty-bound to back similar movements elsewhere. This was not simply an issue of pure principle for Algeria, but also related to the high regard in which Algeria was held across large parts of the decolonised world (see Chapter 9). As Tony Hodges observed, 'Boumedienne recognized that his government's credibility as a consistent supporter of national liberation movements would be knocked, to the detriment of its claims to third world leadership and revolutionary legitimacy, if it failed to defend the Sahrawis right to independence.'[27] Although some observers have pointed to the inconsistency of Algeria's position elsewhere on the principle of self-determination,[28] it is noticeable that Algeria did not make, and has never made, any claim for itself on the territory of the Western Sahara. Instead, it came to back and has continued to back the indigenous resistance movement that emerged inside the Western Sahara and which became known as the Polisario Front.

Polisario and the SADR

The emergence of an indigenous national liberation movement within the Spanish Sahara in the early 1970s was perhaps the factor that most changed the political landscape. It was a late-emerging phenomenon that grew out of the changing socio-economic situation inside the territory during the 1950s, when it was still under Spanish control. This saw both the settlement and urbanisation of the previously largely nomadic indigenous Sahrawi population and an expansion in education opportunities, including at university level, with a number of students being given places in Moroccan universities. These factors, together with Spain's co-option and increased use of a Sahrawi assembly or *djemaa*, combined to produce a growing nationalist movement and consciousness amongst a people who had previously thought of themselves only in tribal terms.[29] The prime instigators of the nationalist movement were students becoming radicalised in Moroccan universities by the prevailingly radical atmosphere on university campuses in the early 1970s, especially with strong support for the Palestinian national cause. These students linked up with other nascent nationalist groups to launch in May 1973 the Popular Front for the Liberation of Seguia el Hamra and Rio de Oro, known by its Spanish acronym of Polisario, which later that same month began its campaign to liberate the territory by launching armed attacks against the Spanish authorities there.

Anti-colonial nationalism was the driving force of the movement in its early stages, and it was not until August 1974 that Polisario declared itself to be in favour of the independence of the territory.[30] This explained the resistance that the movement mounted when Mauritanian and especially Moroccan troops and administrators moved in, following the signing of the Tripartite Agreement in November 1975. The heavy-handed approach and response of the incoming Moroccans prompted significant resentment from much of the population, many of whom left the cities and relocated to the desert, where many were attacked by the Moroccan armed forces. Polisario progressively took charge of both the resistance to the Moroccans and the evacuation of somewhere between a third to a half of the population of the territory across the border to Algeria.[31] There, in camps around the town of Tindouf, Polisario began to organise the refugees and help with the administration of aid that began to arrive from international agencies. Following the formal transfer of administrative power from Madrid to Rabat and Nouakchott in February 1976, Polisario proclaimed its own state and government in exile—the Saharan Arab Democratic Republic (SADR)—on 27 February 1976.

Conflict in the Western Sahara

The small scale of Polisario would have meant its early defeat, had it not been for the support of Algeria in terms of arms and—more crucially—the provision of a base inside Algerian territory. Algeria had cold-shouldered early approaches for support from Polisario, being unconvinced that the organisation carried significant weight, but changed its stance once it realised that Polisario was capable of launching modest but effective military attacks on the Spanish, and so began diplomatically and materially to support Polisario from mid 1975, Boumedienne declaring that his decision to support Polisario had been influenced by the willingness of the Sahrawi to fight like 'lions' for their ideals.[32] Algeria threatened to intervene militarily to support Polisario after the Spanish withdrew, but its troops only directly clashed with those of Morocco briefly in January 1976 and thereafter limited itself to supporting Polisario's efforts.[33]

Polisario also received early backing from Libya, due to Muammar Qadhafi's support for national liberation movements but also his opposition to the Moroccan monarchy as a form of government that he claimed to despise. The Libyan leader had enthusiastically welcomed the early success of the 1971 coup against King Hassan in Morocco and had been accused by the Moroccans of being involved in the plot the following year.[34] In an attempt to isolate and put pressure on Morocco, Algeria and Libya formally aligned themselves through a treaty signed at Hassi Messaoud near the Algerian-Libyan border in December 1975.

Polisario, meanwhile, grew rapidly in size and power, attacking the Mauritanian capital Nouakchott in June 1976 and by 1978 causing serious problems for both Morocco and Mauritania militarily. The ability of Polisario forces to retreat into Algerian territory, which Morocco and Mauritania were loath to attack for fear of a full-scale war with Algeria, gave them a huge advantage. Morocco's highly centralised military command structure, a product of the well-founded fears of the monarchy of the independence of the military, dating back to the failed coups of the early 1970s which resulted in nearly all decisions having to be authorised by Rabat, further disadvantaged Morocco (see Chapter 3). Mauritania suffered even more, especially because of the strains the conflict put on its tiny and fragile economy. In July 1978 the Mauritanian President Mokhtar Ould Daddah was overthrown in a military coup, the leaders of which made peace with Polisario and formally withdrew from its part of the Western Sahara in August 1979 leaving Morocco, which annexed the one third of the territory that had been controlled by its southern neighbour, alone.[35]

Attempts to halt the armed conflict were handicapped by the largely fixed positions of the participants, which did not allow for compromise. Polisario stated its willingness to enter into negotiations with Morocco, but Morocco refused negotiations with the liberation movement. This was because it did not recognise it and argued that Polisario was a simple creation of Algeria and therefore the conflict was in reality an Algerian-Moroccan one which could only be resolved directly between the two states. Morocco did not initially recognise the principle of self-determination, believing that the principle of territorial integrity took precedence, and argued that participation by Sahrawis in Moroccan elections and the oath of allegiance (*ba'ya*) to the Moroccan monarchy by prominent Sahrawis obviated the need for a referendum.[36] For its part, Algeria stated that it was not a party to the conflict—which it viewed as being between Morocco and Polisario—and that it was simply supporting the principle of self-determination in giving aid to Polisario and in recognising the Saharan Arab Democratic Republic (SADR).

Tunisia

The conflict over the Western Sahara put relations between Algeria and Morocco centre stage in the Maghreb during the 1960s and 1970s. This did not mean, though, that Tunisia was absent from regional diplomacy during this period.

The early years of Tunisia's independence had witnessed significant tensions with its Maghrebi neighbours. The ousting of the *bey* and the proclaiming of a republic by Bourguiba and the Neo-Destour (see

Chapter 2) in 1957 went down badly in monarchist Rabat and had led to Morocco speaking out against Tunisia's application to join the Arab League the following year. These tensions were further exacerbated by Tunisia's subsequent decision to recognise Mauritania out of solidarity with what Bourguiba saw as another Francophile moderate state and also a desire to put limits on Morocco's territorial ambitions, and prompted a recall of ambassadors. Difficulties in relations with Algeria in this period were born of Bourguiba's closeness to the leadership of the GPRA, which had lost out in the post-independence power struggles to Ben Bella and his allies and also to the latter's strong links to Salah Ben Youssef, who had himself been defeated in the parallel struggle to control the Neo-Destour and Tunisia. The difficulties took more concrete form in the alleged implication of an Algerian consular official in the failed coup plot against Bourguiba in 1962 (see Chapter 3) and a wider dispute over the border between the two states.[37]

Relations with both Morocco and Algeria were patched up by the end of the 1960s, with Moroccan acceptance of the republican regimes in both Tunis and Nouakchott and settlement of the border with Algeria on Algiers' terms.[38] Bourguiba acquiesced on the latter issue out of a concern to avoid a confrontation at a time when the country was experiencing social discontent caused by the Ben Salah economic programme (see Chapter 7) and, more importantly, when its neighbours to the east—Libya, Egypt and Sudan—were forming a political bloc following the worrying overthrow of the Libyan monarchy by Muammar Qadhafi in September 1969.[39]

Bourguiba had long been of the view that Tunisia's small size made it much more vulnerable to its neighbours than most other states in the region, and as a consequence the main thrust of Tunisian foreign policy in the region in the early decades following independence focused on balancing potential threats from its two large immediate neighbours: Algeria and Libya. Both states made separate offers of union with Tunisia in the early 1970s. Bourguiba had been tempted by the offer from Tripoli, believing that Libya's size and resources (especially in the wake of the oil boom of 1973–4) could have been used to Tunisia's advantage. Nevertheless, he saw the obvious pitfalls of such a deal and ultimately declined it, incurring the wrath of the Libyan leader who expelled Tunisian workers from Libya and began to harbour and support the opposition to Bourguiba both inside (the UGTT) and outside (Youssefists) Tunisia. The failure of the proposed union with Libya did, though, lead to a significant warming of relations with Algeria.[40] This rapprochement was, however, cut short by the developing conflict in the Western Sahara, in which Bourguiba took a robustly pro-Moroccan line. At the beginning of November 1975 the Tunisian president declared to the French newspaper *Le Monde:* 'Self-determination for 40,000 nomads?... The Western Sahara is in Moroccan territory. I advised Hassan II to share it with Mauritania.... A small phantom state will be subject to surrounding pressures.'[41] Such a stance succeeded in uniting Libya and Algeria against Tunisia and led to their cooperation in a plan to destabilise their smaller neighbour through the infiltration of Tunisian exiles from Libya via Algeria into the southern Tunisian city of Gafsa in January 1980, where they attempted to mount an—ultimately unsuccessful—armed insurrection.[42]

Regional Manoeuverings in the 1980s

The Gafsa incident marked an inauspicious start for regional relations in the 1980s. The decade did, however, see a progressive easing in tensions between the states. A significant rapprochement occurred between Algeria and Tunisia, helped by the accession of Chadli Benjedid to the Algerian presidency in 1979. The new president worked hard to mend fences with the Tunisians and succeeded in developing a much better personal relationship with the Tunisian president. Bourguiba responded to the Algerian overtures because of his perceived need for some protection against further pressures from Libya. He also believed that Chadli had been unaware of Algeria's involvement in the Gafsa operation, which had been planned by Boumedienne before his death and subsequently carried out by his allies.[43]

Relations improved to such a degree that Algiers and Tunis signed a formal 'Treaty of Brotherhood and Concord' in March 1983. Largely drawn up by the Tunisian prime minister Mohamed Mzali, the new treaty explicitly envisioned its expansion to include other Maghreb states, and the Tunisians actively sought to achieve this as a further guarantee of their own security in the region.[44] Mauritania joined the treaty later that year, but efforts by Tunisia to involve Morocco failed to persuade King Hassan, who remained suspicious of Algerian motives, possibly aware that Tunisian attempts to involve Morocco in the original treaty had foundered on Algeria's insistence that the Polisario SADR be invited to the founding summit. Hassan also felt that he had been purposefully excluded and declared to the Tunisian foreign minister, 'I do not board a moving train.'[45] The extent to which Algeria had indeed intended to exclude Morocco from the treaty is unclear, but the Tunisian foreign minister felt that, whilst Chadli Benjedid was anxious to involve Morocco, other forces in the Algerian regime prevailed against him.[46]

Hassan was suspicious that the treaty was a means of putting pressure on Morocco over the Western Sahara, but his absence from it isolated Morocco within the region. This sense of international isolation over the issue of the Western Sahara was further increased following Mauritania's decision to recognise the SADR in 1984 and the latter's admission to the OAU after its recognition by a majority of member states the same year. It goes some way to explaining Morocco's surprise rapprochement with Libya that culminated in the signature of a treaty at Oujda in August 1984. Both baffling and alarming to observers outside the region, the new alliance was in fact a product of a general thawing in relations between the two countries that had been underway since the early 1980s. Libyan support for the Polisario had been on the wane from the late 1970s and Rabat hoped to bring it to a definitive end. Hassan was also keen to exploit a growing estrangement between Tripoli and Algiers, caused by disagreements in the OAU, Libyan intervention in Chad and over relations with the Polisario. For Libya, the treaty with Morocco, beyond satisfying Muammar Qadhafi's usual appetite for Arab unity (the treaty was formally titled the 'Arab African Union'), also ended Moroccan support for the Libyan opposition and helped him save face over Libya's withdrawal from Chad.[47]

The mid 1980s thus saw the formation of two sets of alliances in the Maghreb, consisting of the tripartite alliance of Algeria, Tunisia and Mauritania and the new 'union' between Morocco and Libya. This new pattern did not last long. American unhappiness with the Moroccan-Libyan treaty led to the rather unusual agreement being short-lived and was formally ended in 1986 by Morocco.[48] Then in a further unexpected turn there was a sudden thaw in relations between Algeria and Morocco. The first formal meeting between Chadli Benjedid and King Hassan took place in May 1987 and culminated a year later in the two countries re-establishing diplomatic ties that had been broken by Morocco following Algeria's recognition of the SADR in 1976.

The impetus behind the rapprochement came predominantly from the Algerian side and occurred for a variety of reasons. The end of the

Libyan-Moroccan alliance had initially prompted Algeria to attempt to incorporate Libya into the Treaty of Brotherhood and Friendship and in this way complete Morocco's isolation in the region. When this approach foundered on Colonel Qadhafi's preference for a full union, Algeria changed tack and decided to approach the Moroccans directly. This shift in policy, which appeared sudden from the outside, had in fact been in process for some time: there had been low-profile meetings between the two countries since the early 1980s.[49] On assuming the presidency, Chadli Benjedid had gradually adopted a much more pragmatic and less ideologically framed approach to foreign policy than his predecessor, Boumedienne, including towards the Maghreb. This new approach was partly influenced by the ongoing power struggles within the Algerian regime and represented part of a strategy by Chadli to distance himself from his enemies, most of whom were partisans of Boumedienne's foreign policy. For their part, many of the latter had been in favour of the proposed union with Libya as a means of undermining the president's programme of economic reform.[50] Economics provided another more immediate and specific motivation for a rapprochement with Morocco. The collapse in the international price of oil in 1985–6 (see Chapter 7) dramatically weakened Algeria's ability to follow a more activist and even aggressive foreign policy, much of which had hitherto been funded and underwritten by revenues from the country's hydrocarbon resources. A less confrontational and more cooperative relationship with Morocco was thus now more desirable. For its part, Morocco welcomed Algeria's overtures out of the belief that it was opening the way to an eventual shift in Algerian policy towards the Western Sahara, King Hassan believing that Chadli had been a critic of Boumedienne's hardline approach to the dispute.[51]

The Creation of the Arab Maghreb Union

The rapprochement between Morocco and Algeria rapidly paved the way for closer relations across the region. The deposition of Habib Bourguiba as Tunisian president in November 1987 facilitated a final rapprochement between Libya and Tunisia: the two countries re-establishing diplomatic relations by the end of the year. A month after diplomatic relations were re-established between Algiers and Rabat in May 1988, the heads of state of Algeria, Morocco, Tunisia, Libya and Mauritania met in Zeralda in Algeria to discuss regional cooperation.

The eventual outcome of these discussions was a second meeting in Marrakech in Morocco eight months later in February 1989, which unveiled a treaty signed by the five heads of state establishing a new regional organisation: the Arab Maghreb Union (AMU). The new union united for the first time the five states into a single body and represented a move to create a coherent regional organisation which sought closer political and economic cooperation on the acknowledged ultimate model of the then European Community. This dramatic move, which represented a full swing away from the tensions and conflicts between the states of the region over previous decades, was the product of numerous factors at both the collective and individual levels.

At the collective level there were both economic and political factors at work. Economically, all five states were suffering from an increasingly adverse economic environment by the late 1980s. The already debt-laden economies of the region were hit hard by a succession of events in the later part of the decade: notably the collapse of the price of oil, a series of droughts and locust plagues that seriously damaged agriculture and the enlargement of the European Community (EC) to the north to include Spain and Portugal, giving the new members huge economic advantage over the Maghreb states which had been their main competitors in terms of agricultural exports to the EC.[52] It was believed that many of these problems could be combated through the Maghreb states coordinating their economies through an equivalent union. The experience of the EC had shown that the creation of a single regional market could significantly stimulate regional trade. In addition, it had allowed the member states to form a powerful collective bloc through which to negotiate with external trade partners. The Treaty of Marrakech thus included the creation of a single Maghrebi market as one of its main objectives.

Politically, the Maghreb states collectively faced a number of challenges that the creation of a regional union might help meet. A changing political landscape in the Middle East, with Egypt coming in from the diplomatic cold following its peace treaty with Israel, and Iraq emerging from its long conflict with Iran, provided one such political challenge, especially following Egypt's and Iraq's decision to join Jordan and North Yemen in a new regional body called the Arab Cooperation Council in 1989.[53] More positively, the rise of Mikhail Gorbachev and his policies of Glasnost and Perestroika in the Soviet Union served to reduce the importance of the Cold War and narrow differences between the traditionally more conservative pro-Western states such as Morocco and Tunisia and more politically radical ones such as Algeria and Libya.

The most important motivating factor of all, though, in the creation of the Arab Maghreb Union, which dwarfed all others, was the belief that the union might provide a means for a resolution to the Western Sahara dispute. From the Algerian side, Chadli Benjedid hoped that the AMU might persuade Morocco to adopt a more flexible stance, with the union providing ideological cover for a watering down of claims of national sovereignty in favour of broader notions of regional Maghrebi identity, in which the Western Sahara's *Maghrebi* identity would matter more than whether it were Moroccan or independent. At the very least, the Algerians hoped that the dynamics of rapprochement, together with the institutional structures of the union, might pave the way to direct negotiations between Morocco and Polisario, which began to occur from January 1989.[54] Morocco was also of the belief that the structures and dynamics of the AMU could lead to a resolution to the Western Sahara dispute. Mirroring the convictions of the Algerians, the Moroccans believed that the union would provide a framework that would allow the Algerians to retreat from their position of support for Polisario, negotiate directly with Morocco and permit the kingdom to take over the territory. Algerian overtures since 1987 had been taken as signals that Algeria was willing to change its position, as was the exclusion of any reference to Polisario or the SADR in the treaty of Marrakech.[55]

Such hopes of a resolution to the dispute were encouraged by Tunisia. After initially favouring Moroccan-Mauritanian partition of the Western Sahara, Bourguiba had shifted to a position of neutrality on the issue and had consistently tried to act as a mediator between Morocco and Algeria from the late 1970s.[56] Always a keen supporter of regional cooperation, Tunisia became an enthusiastic advocate of the idea of a Maghrebi Union, following Ben Ali's accession to the presidency in November 1987, believing that regional cooperation would give it greater security.

The Course and Decline of the AMU

The agreement signed in Marrakech in February 1989 established a secretariat for the new union and put down plans to set up a Maghreb parliament, bank, university and court, each of which would be based in a different member country. The treaty stated that decisions in the union would be made by a presidential council, composed of the heads of state of the five member states, that would meet every six months and reach decisions through consensus.[57]

The grand hopes and visions of Marrakech, however, soon ran into problems and the union did not succeed in progressing far with its objectives. Institutionally, only the secretariat in Rabat was ever formally established; no meaningful progress was made on the bank, university, court or parliament. The meetings of the presidential council were held only irregularly, often because of a lack of things to discuss. It met only six times in total—often without every leader present—with the last full summit occurring in April 1994 in Tunis. Thereafter member states began withdrawing from summits. From December 1995 Morocco ceased participating in Maghreb forums and called for a freeze of the union's activities in protest at what it saw as Algeria's continued diplomatic support for Polisario. The following year Colonel Qadhafi refused to take on the rotating presidency of the union, because of what the Libyan leader saw as an unpardonable lack of support from the other four states in the union in helping Libya stand up to the international sanctions that had been imposed on it in 1992.[58] A few years later, in 1999, Mauritania's decision to become only the third Arab state after Egypt and Jordan to recognise the state of Israel also created tensions with Arab nationalist sensibilities in Algeria, and especially Libya. Periodic attempts to hold a seventh presidential council have since been made but have foundered, usually on Morocco's unwillingness to attend whilst Algeria continues to back Polisario strongly in international forums such as the United Nations.

The reasons why the Arab Maghreb Union failed so quickly and so clearly in its objectives are several. By far the biggest obstacle was the persistence of the Western Sahara conflict. All the member states had hoped that the AMU would provide a framework for the resolution to the issue. Both Algeria and Morocco expected each other to use the union as a cover to back down from their existing positions. King Hassan had seen the exclusion of Polisario—SADR from the Marrakech treaty as a sign that Algeria was gradually withdrawing support from its protégés. When this did not occur, the *raison d'être* of the union disappeared for Morocco and it froze its participation. This development formed part of a pattern of worsening relations between Algeria and

Morocco during the 1990s. The more accommodating policy of Chadli Benjedid, which had arguably been reinforced by Algeria's domestic turmoil from October 1988, did not immediately disappear with his removal from power in January 1992 as he was replaced as president by Mohamed Boudiaf, who had close ties with Morocco having spent nearly thirty years in exile in the Moroccan town of Kenitra. The assassination of Boudiaf only six months later marked the beginning of a sharp deterioration in bilateral relations, not least because of the near-universal conviction that his killing was the work of senior figures within the Algerian military (see Chapter 3). It was also believed that one of the reasons for Boudiaf's removal was because of his closeness to Morocco and a suspicion on the part of the Algerian military leadership that he was planning to make major concessions to Morocco on the Western Sahara. This was something that the military was unwilling to countenance, perhaps because of its institutional memory of confrontation with the Moroccan military in both 1963 and 1976, and its wish not to be seen as backing down to Morocco.[59]

The reassertion of influence by the Algerian ANP from 1992 further contributed to poor relations between the two countries, as the republic descended into civil conflict. The decade progressed with the Algerians suspecting their western neighbour of seeking to take advantage of its domestic turmoil. Morocco was accused of turning a blind eye to gun-smuggling for the armed Islamist groups and attempting to secure the withdrawal of Algerian support for Polisario in return for handing over leading members of the armed groups.[60] Tensions culminated in September 1994 with Algeria closing the land border with Morocco in retaliation for the reimposition of visas for Algerians visiting Morocco; this followed an attack on a tourist hotel in Marrakech in August of that year, which had involved French citizens of Algerian origin.[61]

Although continued antagonism between Algeria and Morocco over the Western Sahara lay at the heart of the stalling of the AMU, other factors contributed to its problems. At the institutional level, there was the difficulty of getting unanimous agreement between five very different states. An early test for the union was the Gulf crisis and war of 1990–91, which saw all five states taking slightly different positions on the issue.[62] The fact that all decisions needed to be taken by the presidential council meant that progress became dependent on the individual heads of state and their personal whims and prejudices. One theory of regional integration argues that political differences between states can be mitigated and overcome by the economic benefits produced through increased cooperation. This was the central idea behind the creation of the European Community, which sought to use economic ties to reduce potential frictions between its two main founding states, France and Germany. Such benefits were not, however, forthcoming for the AMU. Intra-regional trade between member states was minimal: just 3 per cent of their total trade was between AMU member states in 1989 compared to 40 per cent between the founding states of the European Community at its creation in 1957. It was a figure that remained unchanged over ten years after the establishment of the union.[63] The weak economic links between the member states of the AMU also contrasted strongly with the links with the EC, trade with which amounted to roughly two-thirds of total Maghrebi trade. This statistic also helps explain the failure of the AMU to negotiate as a bloc with the EC as envisioned in the original treaty. In 1993 the EC became the EU (European Union), and the importance of EU trade to individual Maghrebi states persuaded first Morocco and Tunisia (1996) and later Algeria (2001) to defect from the AMU's agreed position and sign separate bilateral free trade agreements with Europe (see Chapter 9).

Resolution Attempts in the Western Sahara

Aside from the creation of the Arab Maghreb Union, the other positive development to emerge from the Algerian-Moroccan rapprochement of 1987–9 was the agreement of a formal ceasefire between Morocco and Polisario which came into force in September 1991. The military side of the conflict had declined since its peak in the late 1970s and early 1980s, following Morocco's construction of a huge fortified sand wall that largely prevented Polisario attacks on the western four-fifths of the territory that Morocco controlled. Encouraged by Chadli Benjedid's overtures and by splits inside Polisario, which saw a number of senior figures defect to Morocco, Hassan II agreed to meet members of Polisario in January 1989. This began a process which allowed the United Nations to negotiate a ceasefire and begin work on a full solution to the conflict, through getting the parties to agree to hold a referendum on the territory's future. No referendum, however, took place, largely because of disagreements about who should be entitled to vote, with Morocco insisting that large numbers of ethnic Sahrawis living inside Morocco proper should be entitled to vote: a proposal Polisario rejected.[64]

Failure to agree on the modalities for a referendum led to a search for alternative solutions, specifically a politically negotiated agreement. Hopes for this were raised by new leaders coming to power in both Algeria and Morocco. In April 1999 Abdelaziz Bouteflika was elected president of Algeria and three months later, in July 1999, Crown Prince Sidi Mohamed succeeded to the Moroccan throne upon the death of his father Hassan II. Optimism was based on the fact that the new king was less personally invested in the Western Sahara issue than his father, who had made it one of the pillars of his rule and was aware that it may even have saved his throne in the turbulent years of the 1970s. The return of Abdelaziz Bouteflika to the forefront of Algerian politics intuitively suggested that, as Boumedienne's long-running foreign minister, the new president was likely to follow his former patron's uncompromising line on the Western Sahara. A closer examination, however, of his tenure as foreign minister revealed clear indications that Bouteflika had taken a much more conciliatory line towards Morocco (where he had in fact been born). It was also widely suggested that Algeria's apparent endorsement of the Moroccan-Mauritanian plan to take over the Spanish Sahara at the Rabat summit of July 1975 had been largely the work of Bouteflika, whose initiative had been subsequently rejected by Boumedienne when Bouteflika had returned to Algiers.[65]

In spite of these positive signs, domestic pressures on both new leaders ultimately led them to take much more hard-line stances than their predecessors. As a new and youthful monarch, King Mohamed VI was aware of concerns within the kingdom that he might not be made of the same formidable material that his long-reigning father had been and that any early perceived concessions on the issue of the Western Sahara would serve to confirm this fear. For his part, Abdelaziz Bouteflika was open to compromise, but swiftly became aware that he was subject to the will of the leaders of the country's military (to whom he owed his position) and that the Western Sahara issue was very much the preserve of the military and important to its image and prestige. Thus, after an initial honeymoon, both states reverted to more entrenched positions on the dispute.[66]

The international search for a negotiated political solution to the Western Sahara dispute was led by the special envoy appointed by the UN secretary general to the issue, former US secretary of state James Baker, who produced two proposals in 2001 and 2003. The two proposals—the latter being in essence a more detailed development of the former—essentially suggested an interim five-year period of regional autonomy with a locally elected administration. A referendum at the end of the five-year period, in which Moroccans who had settled in the territory between 1976 and 1999 would be entitled to vote, would decide the final status of the territory.[67] The first part of this proposal was clearly designed to appeal to Polisario and the Algerians, with the latter part aimed at the Moroccans. Morocco accepted the first and less detailed version of this plan but then rejected the later version, largely because it explicitly listed independence for the territory as one of the options in the final referendum. This was not to be countenanced by Morocco out of principle, but also out of fear that the interim period of regional autonomy would be exploited to the maximum by Polisario to lay the ground for a vote in favour of independence in the eventual referendum. Morocco was also concerned by growing indications that ethnic Sahrawis who had been brought into the territory from Morocco proper to boost support for Morocco in any future referendum were becoming increasingly sympathetic to Polisario's cause.[68] For its part, Polisario rejected the first plan because it still held to the original plan for a UN organised referendum, which it believed it would win if Morocco were prevented from introducing Moroccan-born voters. It was prepared to have the same response to the second plan, before Algeria persuaded Polisario to endorse it following Morocco's rejection of the plan, in order for Morocco to appear as the obstacle to a settlement.

The failure of the parties to agree to either of the two proposals led to James Baker's resignation as special envoy and to the UN inviting Morocco to submit its own proposal for the territory's future. Morocco eventually submitted its plan in April 2007, which proposed a significant degree of autonomy for the territory under Moroccan sovereignty. The absence from the Moroccan proposal of any mechanism that could result in independence for the Western Sahara led to the Moroccan plan being rejected by Polisario, which presented its own proposal reiterating the need for a referendum. Mounting international pressure, however, to break the deadlock and resolve the conflict led to all the parties agreeing to a series of meetings in Manhassett in the United States from 2007, none of which was able to provide a breakthrough in a situation where none of the three main parties was prepared to make concessions on the crucial issue of sovereignty.

By the late 2000s Morocco believed that both time and momentum was on its side, through control of the bulk of the territory and the tacit support of the main external powers interested in the region (France, United States, and from 2004, Spain), and thus it should just sit tight and hold out until either Polisario or Algeria conceded. The kingdom maintained its claim on the territory as its number one policy priority subsuming all others, often to the bemusement of foreign countries. This stance was bolstered not only by the perception that victory was within its grasp but also by the continuing concern that failure to secure integration of the territory would not only result in huge loss of face internationally but, more crucially, could result in serious domestic challenges to the monarchy. Concessions by Morocco on the principle of a referendum in the 1980s had provoked public criticism from the USFP and a confrontation with the party.[69] Fears remained that this criticism could be endorsed by significant sections of the population who had experienced nearly forty years of ferocious official propaganda on the central importance of the issue and so might express their disillusionment on the streets.

For its part Polisario held out, aware that accepting Moroccan sovereignty under whatever framework would sign its own death warrant and that of the SADR, which over the thirty plus years since its creation in 1976 had developed sophisticated and entrenched institutions and, more importantly, a sense of distinct national identity amongst the Sahrawis in the refugee camps in Algeria.[70] Diplomatically, Polisario held to the UN peace plan of 1991 and to the hope of convincing external opinion of the justice of its cause. The latter objective received a boost with the growth in organised manifestations of popular protest and unrest that began to occur from 1999, and gained pace from 2005 inside the part of the Western Sahara controlled by Morocco in favour of the independence of the territory. This 'intifada' strategy had the aim of demonstrating the lack of popular support for Moroccan rule in the territory and the illiberalism of the Moroccan state as it cracked down on this dissent and unrest. Polisario's leadership was aware that the political liberalisation that had occurred in Morocco since the 1990s had partly been a product of the kingdom's desire to portray itself as a liberal and democratic state to the outside world in the hope of reducing resistance to its formal and full takeover of the Western Sahara.

With the positions of both Morocco and Polisario entrenched, attention has turned to whether Algeria may move on the issue, since withdrawal of support for Polisario could only lead to the latter's collapse. There are, however, no indications that Algeria will change its long-established position of support for Polisario. Publicly, Algerian officials explain the country's position by simply restating its support for the principle of self-determination in the territory. However, as the International Crisis Group has observed, Algeria's position on the conflict 'is arguably the most complex and certainly the most controversial,' and explanations of Algeria's stance as being one of either simple principle or strategic and material interest are 'simplistic and misleading.' The fundamental maintenance of the position established in 1975 by Houari Boumedienne is explained in terms of resentment at the ultimately unilateral way in which Morocco acted to acquire the territory and by the influence of the Algerian military in politics. Whilst the older generation of military figures identified closely with Boumedienne's policy, the subsequent generation, who might have been expected to have compromised, have allowed the matter to 'become an issue in the broader conflict between the army commanders and the presidency in Algiers,' since the accession of Abdelaziz Bouteflika.[71] Algeria's leaders are also aware that any retreat from their established position without the endorsement of Polisario would severely damage the country's admittedly tarnished international image. Much more importantly, it would be seen both as a climb down and thus a loss of face for the regime, which would be humiliating internationally, and, more crucially, potentially dangerous domestically. The more secure and stronger position of the Algerian state following the dramatic decline in the levels of violence witnessed in the 1990s, together with the increased revenues from rises in the price of oil and gas, also helped firm up existing positions and remove incentives for concessions to Morocco.

Conclusions

The pattern of Maghrebi regional relations since independence has been one of volatility between conflict and cooperation. Part of this volatility is due to the absence of a dominant regional state which could act as a 'hegemon.' Instead there are two more powerful states—Morocco and Algeria—who have tried to dominate the region to realise their own particular agendas. Both have tried to recruit the other states in the region as allies, since the other three states are either very weak (Mauritania), very small (Tunisia) or internationally isolated and erratic (Libya).

The persistence of Algerian-Moroccan rivalry can only in part be explained in geo-political terms. The very different histories and natures of Algeria and Morocco have also made for significant regional rivalry. Algeria's revolutionary origins as a fundamentally new state created through a long struggle of national liberation contrasts significantly with the centuries-old monarchy of Morocco. The socialist rhetoric and third worldism of the governments of both Ben Bella and Boumedienne in Algeria were very different from the conservatism and deference of the Moroccan Makhzen and its close alliance with the major Western powers. Such differences were played up during the Cold War, but the fact that difficult relations survived the end of the Cold War and the effective abandonment by Algeria of its 'socialist' path were indications that tensions were rooted in differences over more profound issues than ideology. The looming presence of the Western Sahara conflict certainly accounts for most of the tensions in the relationship, but difficulties between Algeria and Morocco before the dispute arose in the 1970s indicate that it does not exclusively account for the troubled relationship and that final resolution of the issue will not necessarily result in the end of tensions between the two neighbours. The relationship is clearly more complex than that and undoubtedly entwines elements of geo-politics, history, economics and personality. Nevertheless, the two states' confrontation over the Western Sahara remains the centrepiece of regional relations and the single most important obstacle to greater regional cooperation and even unity.

The impact of the events of 2011 on regional relations was not as immediately obviously felt as in other spheres. The collapse of one of the five member states of the AMU, Libya, into civil war following the uprisings had a direct effect on that country's most immediate neighbours, Tunisia and Algeria, notably through the influx of refugees into Tunisia. A less direct but potentially more profound and long-term effect came through the precedent and example set by Tunisia, not just through its successful overthrow of Ben Ali but also through the likely creation of a new substantially democratic political system to sit amongst the surviving and distinctly undemocratic regimes in Rabat and Algiers. The final collapse of the Qadhafi regime in the late summer of 2011 and its replacement by a new regime further bolstered this dynamic. It also promised to substantially strengthen the ties between Tunisia and Libya, as the two states were able to build on long-standing economic and family ties to cement revolutionary solidarity, as was demonstrated through the support shown by Tunisians for the rebellion in Libya.

9

INTERNATIONAL RELATIONS

The fact that the Maghreb is geographically and politically part of a number of different regions of the world has long been a staple cliché of diplomatic statements on the region. Interaction with Europe, Africa and the Middle East characterised much of the Maghreb's history (see Chapter 1). The colonial period inevitably privileged the European connection at the expense of others, and the achievement of independence by Morocco, Tunisia and Algeria led to a gradual re-growth of connections with other parts of the world. It also a led to a period of relative autonomy for the states where foreign relations were important but not central to their concerns as the regimes sought to consolidate themselves domestically.

The steady globalisation of the world economy, in particular, led the region, from the 1980s, to pay increasing attention to the outside world: notably to Europe and the United States, which consequently began to enjoy more and more leverage over events in the region. However, this did not necessarily lead to increased outside influence on the part of Europe and the US as the Maghreb states became progressively more adept at making sure that relations worked to their own interests. The last decade of the twentieth century and the first of the twenty-first witnessed new trends developing as domestic populations became more vocal in their views on foreign relations and challenged the monopoly of the political leaderships of the states, notably on issues of pan-Arab and pan-Islamic solidarity. Globalisation also saw the long peripheral regions of sub-Saharan Africa and Asia strengthen their connections with the Maghreb through the impact of migration and economic exchange respectively.

The Transition from Colonial Rule: Ties with France

The most important foreign relationship that the Maghreb states had in the period after the achievement of independence was naturally with France. This was largely a result of the practicalities of transferring administrative control from the former colonial authorities to the new independent governments. The persistence of the primacy of relations with France over the decades that followed, resulting in France remaining the most important bilateral relationship for all three states fifty years after Paris had conceded independence, spoke, however, of the strength and depth of ties that had been established and consciously maintained between metropolitan France and the Maghreb in the post-independence period. Indeed, France remained the state with the largest population of Maghrebis outside the region itself well into the twenty-first century.[1] Similarly, it remained the principal trade partner for all three states in the region.[2]

As the first of the states to achieve independence, in 1956, Tunisia and Morocco developed formal relations with France relatively quickly as the former colonial power sought to concentrate its efforts on retaining Algeria, then still an integrated part of France itself. The two newly independent states' support for the FLN's struggle in Algeria produced early tensions in relations with France, most notably following the bombing of the Tunisian border village of Sakiet Sidi Youssef by the French air force in early 1958. French withdrawal from Algeria in 1962 paved the way for much smoother relations, which were aided by both France's withdrawal from its remaining outpost in the Tunisian port of Bizerte in 1963 and, more importantly, French support for the victorious sides in the post-independence power struggles (see Chapter 2) in the shape of the Moroccan monarchy and Habib Bourguiba's faction of the Neo-Destour. The accession of Hassan II to the Moroccan throne in 1961 led to both countries being led by men who were not only educated in France and maintained strong personal ties there, but who, moreover, were committed to developing and retaining strong links with the former colonial power in particular and the West in general.

France's final withdrawal from Algeria in 1962, ending over a century of colonisation after a long, bitter and bloody liberation struggle, led to an 'intensely emotional and complex relationship' between France and the new state of Algeria in the post-colonial world.[3] Although Algeria itself experienced the overwhelming bulk of this trauma, the effects on France should not be overlooked, a sizeable percentage of the French population having had a direct experience of Algeria through the colonial period and especially during the war of liberation which saw two million French soldiers cross the Mediterranean.[4] Indeed, the depth and complexities of Algeria's ties to France ensured that independence in 1962 did not represent a total severing of relations between the new state and the former colonial power. For whilst Algerian rhetoric against France remained sharp throughout the post-independence period, social and particularly economic links remained strong. France provided generous assistance throughout the 1960s to its former North African *départements* and the departure en masse of the French colonial administration and the European settler population in 1962 left vast gaps in skills that the newly independent state was only able to fill through France's provision of qualified personnel (*coopérants techniques*). In providing such support, Paris aimed to make the best of its withdrawal, hoping to retain and strengthen its links with Algeria so that it could use the newly independent state as a 'strategic doorway to the third world.'[5] Although the intensity of economic links reduced by the end of the 1960s as Algeria was gradually able to replace French personnel with its own nationals, and reduced further with Boumedienne's nationalisation of the hydrocarbons industry in 1971, links still remained strong.

The Cold War

The international context into which the independent Maghreb states emerged in the late 1950s and early 1960s was that of the Cold War. The rivalry and conflict between the United States and the Soviet Union and their allies did not have as great an effect, though, as it did on much of the rest of the world, largely because of the shared view of the two superpowers that French pre-eminence in the region was preferable to the influence of each other and should therefore not be unduly challenged. The three states themselves took different stances towards the Cold War. Habib Bourguiba in Tunisia assumed a resolutely pro-Western stance from the outset, a product not just of his ideological convictions but also out of a concern for his small country's security, which he saw as largely dependent on the West.[6] Morocco initially adopted a much more independent line, becoming significantly involved in the emerging non-aligned movement of newly independent

Third World states. The retention of territory and bases in Morocco by France, the United States and Spain contributed to Morocco's stance, as did the powerful influence of the nationalist political parties in the years immediately following independence, Allal Al Fassi of Istiqlal having attended the Bandung conference of newly independent African and Asian states in 1955. Morocco also sought to mitigate the kingdom's economic dependence on the West by seeking to expand trade links with the Soviet Union and the Eastern bloc. These links, however, remained modest in comparison with those with the West, and following Hassan II's accession to the throne in 1961, Moroccan policy took a decisively pro-Western turn, a move aided by the domestic political marginalisation of Istiqlal and its allies during the early 1960s. Thereafter Morocco came to be regarded as a reliable supporter of conservative governments in the Third World and a staunch opponent of radical regimes such as those of Gamal Abd al-Nasser in Egypt. The kidnap and likely murder of the exiled UNFP leader, Mehdi Ben Barka, in Paris in October 1965 did lead to a crisis in Morocco's relations with France in the late 1960s as President de Gaulle formally severed relations with Morocco over King Hassan's refusal to respond to international arrest warrants for senior figures in the Moroccan Interior Ministry, whom a French inquiry had found responsible for the murder. Although this led to a renewed flirtation on the part of Rabat with Moscow, Hassan also sought, in parallel, to expand ties with the United States to fill the gap left by France. Washington obliged out of concern over Soviet influence, but was content to let France resume its pre-eminent role when Franco-Moroccan relations were fully restored following de Gaulle's retirement in 1970.[7]

Algeria's long and bloody liberation struggle meant that its adoption of a more radical anti-imperialist and Third Worldist policy following independence was almost inevitable. Its identification with and strong support for movements of national liberation across the globe became a central part of its foreign policy and rapidly brought it into diplomatic conflict with the United States over America's involvement in Vietnam and policy towards the Arab-Israeli conflict, the latter leading to Algiers breaking diplomatic relations with Washington following US support for Israel in the 1967 war. Differences with the United States did not, however, lead to Algeria formally aligning itself with the Soviet Union. Although the Russians became Algeria's main supplier of military hardware from the 1960s, newly and proudly independent Algeria was not about to become a client state or come within any foreign state's sphere of influence, and steadfastly resisted requests to allow the Soviets to establish military bases or have access to naval bases in the country. Algeria's support for the Palestinians also created tensions with Russia, with Algeria accusing Moscow of 'treachery' following the USSR's lack of support for the Arab states in the 1973 war with Israel. The war paved the way for the re-establishment of relations with Washington in 1974 through Henry Kissinger's involvement of Algeria in the shuttle diplomacy that followed the conflict. The improvement in relations with the US was also facilitated by internal shifts inside Algeria which saw more ideological concerns being gradually replaced by priorities related to economic development, championed by a strengthening industrial lobby that advocated expanded links with the US.[8] As a result, Algerian trade with the US, primarily in oil and gas, increased, and by 1977 America had even supplanted France as Algeria's primary export market.[9]

The Arab World and the Middle East

The regional context into which the independent Maghreb states emerged in the late 1950s and early 1960s was also one of conflict and division, due to the Arab 'Cold War' between radical and conservative states being at its height. Although the choices of alignment of the three new states proved to be fairly predictable, these choices were more nuanced than they often appeared and their commitment to the conflict was more limited. Algeria's alignment with the radical 'progressive' bloc of Arab states was unsurprising, given its revolutionary liberation struggle and its adoption of socialism. More importantly, the staunch support the FLN had enjoyed from Nasser's Egypt throughout the liberation struggle and the periods spent in Cairo by many of the senior figures in the FLN created strong ties between Algiers and the leading state in the 'progressive' bloc, ties that were cemented by the close personal relationship between Ahmed Ben Bella and the Egyptian president. Algeria's attachment to its own independence ensured, however, that Algeria did not become fully beholden to Cairo, and Algiers similarly kept its distance from both more direct involvement in the inter-Arab conflict as well as the various schemes of Arab unity that were a feature of this period. Nevertheless, many senior figures in the regime were uncomfortable about the closeness between Ben Bella and Nasser and the latter's perceived interference in Algerian domestic affairs, and this played a role in Ben Bella's removal as president in 1965, which led to a significant cooling in relations between Cairo and Algiers.[10]

Personal factors also played a role in Morocco's alignment in the intra-Arab conflict. Nasser enjoyed good personal relations with King Mohamed V but these did not transfer to his son, Hassan, when he assumed the throne in 1961. Hassan was much more sceptical and wary of the Egyptian leader, whose influence he viewed as destabilising to the region. He differed ideologically from Nasser not simply through his closeness to the West but also, more importantly, through his view of the Arab-Israeli conflict that had emerged whilst Morocco and the other Maghreb states had still been under French rule. Hassan had taken the view from the late 1950s that Israel was a reality that the Arab states would have to accommodate, and argued in Arab summits from 1965 that negotiations should be opened with the Israelis before the technological gap between the Jewish state and the Arabs became too wide.[11] These views were also shared by Habib Bourguiba, who aired them much more publicly, arguing on a tour of the Middle East in 1965 that the Arab states should seek the implementation of the original 1947 United Nations partition plan for Palestine.[12] This common stance had its origins in the pragmatic outlook of both leaders and their distaste for what they saw as the bluster and bravado of Egypt and the other radical Arab states. Both also felt concerned and threatened by Nasser's potential to interfere in the affairs of the Maghreb, particularly through his links with the Arab nationalists of the FLN in Algeria and through the domestic opposition in Morocco and Tunisia. The prevalence of military regimes amongst the 'progressive' bloc of Arab states provoked Bourguiba's antipathy through his deep-rooted suspicions about military involvement in politics (see Chapter 3).[13] Hassan's position on the Arab-Israeli conflict had arguably more profound roots in the Moroccan monarch's particular outlook, which Bruce Maddy-Weitzman has characterised as possessing 'a particular vision of renewed Semitic brotherhood based on an idyllic Jewish-Arab past in Morocco and Muslim Spain, which could contribute to an economic and human renaissance in the contemporary Middle East.'[14] It was a vision informed by the historically large size and significant influence of the Jewish community in Morocco stretching back centuries and its long-standing relationship with the royal palace. Although Morocco's Jewish community came to be hugely depleted in the decades after independence, through departure for Europe and especially the new state of Israel, Jews remained in prominent positions in the kingdom and many were crucial intermediaries in the growth of discreet relations between Morocco and Israel. This relationship saw the Israelis providing training and some military support to Morocco in return for the removal of restrictions on Jewish emigration from Morocco to Israel and the acquisition of a low-profile but valuable ally in the Arab world.[15]

The views of Hassan and Bourguiba went strongly against the public consensus of the time amongst the Arab states, which advocated the defeat and removal of the state of Israel by armed force. It was a consensus strongly supported by the Algerians, who saw in the struggle against the Israelis direct parallels with their own struggle against the French. Algeria became one of the staunchest supporters of the rights of the Palestinians amongst the Arab states, particularly as the Palestinian Liberation Organisation (PLO) began to emerge as an independent actor after the 1967 war.[16] The catastrophic defeat of the Arab states in that war, followed three years later by the death of Nasser, helped to close the gaps between the Arab states, including those in the Maghreb. King Hassan enjoyed a much better personal relationship with Nasser's successor, Anwar Sadat, which dated back to the 1950s, and this led to a weakening of ties with Israel. Both Hassan and Bourguiba sent troops to support and participate in the Egyptian and Syrian attacks on Golan and the Sinai Peninsula in 1973, Hassan viewing the campaign as an important Arab show of strength.[17]

The Western Sahara Conflict

The emergence of the Western Sahara conflict and war in the Maghreb in the mid 1970s attracted international attention and elicited mixed reactions from the outside world. Although no other state apart from Mauritania formally endorsed Morocco's claim on the territory, most of the major Western powers privately supported Morocco whilst maintaining an official stance of neutrality. French president Valéry Giscard d'Estaing provided what Daguzan has termed 'discrete military and fervent diplomatic' support for Morocco in the conflict.[18] The United States adopted a similar stance, even during the closing period of Spanish control of the territory, as it hoped to see a Moroccan takeover and its international legitimation, wishing to support a staunch ally in the region.[19] This support inevitably put renewed strains on Algeria's relations with both France and the US, Algeria having suspected the United States of covertly supporting Morocco in the War of the Sands of 1963 (see Chapter 8).[20] US support for Morocco weakened briefly under President Jimmy Carter, whose administration doubted the durability of the Moroccan monarchy and imposed restrictions on arms sales to the kingdom out of the view that their use inside the Western Sahara did not constitute self-defence. However, the spilling over of the conflict into Moroccan territory proper helped reverse this policy, a process that was also aided by the fall of the Shah in Iran in 1979, prompting US fears about undermining established allies in the broader Middle East region.[21]

After Algeria, the state that most energetically backed the Polisario Front's claim on Western Sahara was Libya; the Qadhafi regime being an enthusiastic advocate of national liberation movements and an ideological critic of the Moroccan monarchy. Together, Algeria and Libya actively solicited international diplomatic recognition for the Saharan Arab Democratic Republic (SADR), an endeavour that succeeded in large parts of Africa, Asia and Latin America, securing the recognition of fifty-four countries by 1983. This was achieved through a mixture of Algeria's diplomatic experience and prestige, identification with the Polisario cause and Libyan financial largesse. Although Moscow did recognise the Sahrawis' right to self-determination, the Soviet Union never recognised either Polisario or the SADR in spite of its usual policy of backing Third World liberation movements. This was largely explained by a desire in Moscow to avoid alienating Morocco and also to retain important contracts for the supply of phosphates and access to the rich fishing areas off the Moroccan coast.[22]

The most significant longer-term effect that the Western Sahara conflict had on relations between the Maghreb states and the wider world was the transformation in Moroccan foreign policy priorities. From the outset of the conflict, Morocco's determination to press its claim on the territory came to trump all other policy concerns for the kingdom, and Morocco began to view all its foreign relations through the prism of the conflict, which explains the complete failure of the Carter administration's efforts to use arms sales and good relations as tools to moderate Moroccan policy in the dispute.[23] The election of Ronald Reagan as US president in 1980 led to a return to a robustly pro-Moroccan stance by the US, as the new administration viewed all regional conflicts such as that in the Western Sahara as part of the broader Cold War struggle against the Soviet Union. The fact that the Algerian military was largely supplied by the Soviets was seen as evidence of where the Cold War battle lines were drawn in the Sahara—a view that Morocco did not seek to correct, as the US removed all restrictions on arms sales to the kingdom and became its main supplier after France.[24]

Peacemaking in the Middle East

The 1970s and 1980s saw the Maghreb states drawn into Middle Eastern affairs in a greater way than had hitherto been the case. In the wake of the 1973 Arab-Israeli war, King Hassan played a progressively larger role in trying to seek a more durable solution to the broader conflict. In 1974 Rabat hosted the Arab League summit that saw the Palestine Liberation Organisation (PLO) recognised as the sole legitimate representative of the Palestinian people and the following year King Hassan became chair of the Al-Quds Committee of the Organisation of the Islamic Conference that sought to represent and safeguard Muslim interests in the city of Jerusalem. More substantially, and using his established contacts with Israel, Hassan facilitated and hosted the first secret meetings between the Israelis and the Egyptians that eventually led to the Camp David accords and the Israeli-Egyptian peace treaty of 1979. King Hassan was the only other Arab leader to support Sadat's historic visit to Israel in 1977, and although pressure from the rest of the Arab world forced Hassan to distance himself from the eventual peace treaty, he believed Egypt's consequent exclusion from the Arab League to be an 'injustice' and worked throughout the 1980s to secure its readmission.[25]

Elsewhere in the Maghreb, Algeria reacted with predictable anger to the peace treaty and joined the Rejection Front group of Arab states that sought to resist any further such agreements with Israel. More surprisingly, Tunisia also joined in the condemnation of Egypt, partly a result of the increasingly erratic nature of the ageing and unpredictable Bourguiba, but also a more considered move to offset popular resentment inside Tunisia at Bourguiba's closeness to the West. Such considerations played an important part in Tunis' acceptance as the new headquarters of the Arab League, following its relocation from Cairo when Egypt was expelled from the League in 1979, and also to host the leadership and headquarters of the PLO, following its expulsion from Lebanon in 1982.[26] This led to Tunisia assuming a new and much larger role in Middle Eastern and Arab affairs, representing a break from earlier decades when Bourguiba had tended to shun the region in preference for contacts with Europe, the United States and his immediate neighbours in the Maghreb.

These developments represented a greater involvement of not only Tunisia in Arab affairs but of the Maghreb more generally. The legacy of French colonialism had resulted in the region being initially less intellectually and linguistically disposed to involvement in the Arab world, as the small number of Maghrebis in Arab institutions in the 1960s and 1970s showed. By the early 1980s, the diplomatic efforts of Hassan, the relocations of the Arab League and the PLO to Tunis, the exclusion of Egypt and the emergence of the first cohorts of comfortably Arabophone Maghrebi diplomats all contributed to the greater integration of the region into the broader Arab world.[27] As a consequence, the Maghreb hosted some of the most important inter-Arab summits of the 1980s, such as that in Fez in 1982 which sought to push a new Arab peace plan in the wake of the Israeli invasion of Lebanon that year and that of the Palestinian National Council (PNC) in Algiers in November 1988, where concerted Algerian mediation between the various Palestinian factions led to Yasser Arafat's declaration of the independence of Palestine following the end of the first year of the intifada in the West Bank and Gaza.[28]

These developments did not, however, lead to King Hassan abandoning his links with the Israelis, which he maintained throughout the early 1980s. From 1986, in an effort to achieve a breakthrough in the dispute, he started to meet overtly with figures from the Israeli Labour party, whom he regarded as much more open to reason than those in the Likud. In doing this he braved the displeasure of the more hard-line Arab leaders, including, most famously, Muammar Qadhafi, who wore a white glove to shake hands with the Moroccan monarch following Hassan's meeting and handshake with Shimon Peres in 1984.[29]

Domestic Reform and the End of the Cold War

The decline and end of the Cold War from the late 1980s did not affect the Maghreb as dramatically it did other regions of the world, but it was not without impact. Somewhat surprisingly, Algeria initially emerged as a bigger diplomatic beneficiary than Morocco. Although

Algeria witnessed the decline and ultimate demise of its biggest military supplier, the Soviet Union, Morocco experienced a weakening of US support as the fear in Washington of Soviet expansion in North Africa evaporated. US relations with Algeria had already begun to improve in the 1980s as a result of both Algerian diplomatic assistance in securing the release of the US hostages in Iran in 1980 and of Chadli Benjedid's more pragmatic and less ideological approach to foreign policy. Increasingly aware that Polisario was unlikely to be defeated militarily, the US began to nudge Morocco towards making concessions on the Western Sahara and began establishing contacts with Polisario.[30]

One reason why the end of the Cold War had a limited effect on the Maghreb was that it came to be overshadowed by events within the region itself. The moves taken by both Tunisia and Algeria at the end of the 1980s to end their one-party political systems and open up to other political forces were cautiously welcomed in the West. As the most important external power in the region, France took most interest in these developments. Initial concerns in Paris that Zine al-Abdine Ben Ali's constitutional coup against Bourguiba in November 1987 was replacing a long-standing, if increasingly erratic, friend of France with a president and regime much closer to the United States were rapidly allayed by the fundamental continuity displayed by the new president.[31] Similarly, the violence of the unrest of October 1988 in Algeria shocked and surprised France, but the political opening it led to, as with Ben Ali's launching of a dialogue with the Tunisian opposition, was viewed as a positive development.[32]

The Gulf War

Developing events inside the Maghreb came to be abruptly interrupted by the fallout that occurred following Iraq's invasion of Kuwait in the summer of 1990. The invasion and the crisis and war that eventually evolved out of it not only altered the international context in which the changes within the Maghreb were occurring but became integral parts of the evolving internal political dramas that were unfolding within the states. Indeed, it marked the first major incursion of international affairs into domestic politics in the region since its achievement of independence.

The effects of the Gulf crisis across the region were remarkably uniform. The governments of Algeria, Tunisia and Morocco all condemned the invasion of Kuwait, but rapidly all found themselves faced with a huge and unexpected groundswell of support for the Iraqi position from their ordinary populations that expressed itself through civil society, political parties and ultimately in mass demonstrations. Quite why events so geographically removed from the region should have had such an effect, and a greater impact than that found in states much closer to the crisis itself, can be explained by reference to a number of factors. Firstly, the timing of the crisis, coming in the midst of the unprecedented political openings in Algeria and Tunisia, allowed popular opinion to express itself in ways that hitherto had not been possible and which were still not possible in most other Arab states. It also presented newly legalised opposition parties with an issue they could take advantage of to mobilise popular support for themselves, which many of them did, often quite cynically. In the case of the Islamist parties, both An-Nahda and the FIS were able to set aside their established hostility to the secular nature of the Iraqi regime and become its ardent defenders when they saw the popular support that emerged for Iraq. Furthermore, for the FIS, concern that it might be outflanked by other political parties led to it being willing to forfeit valuable existing financial support from Saudi Arabia in order to align itself with public opinion on the issue.[33]

Yahia Zoubir points to three important reasons that help explain why public sentiment was so strong on the issue, particularly given the very different view taken by the regimes and even, initially, the main opposition parties in the shape of the Islamists. Analysing the various phases of the conflict, he points out, firstly, that public sentiment was not aroused by the initial invasion but by the subsequent and consequent arrival of American troops in the Gulf. This, he argues, evoked strong collective memories of colonialism which had been particularly harsh in the Maghreb and which were only strengthened by French participation in the coalition brought together to oust Iraqi forces from Kuwait. Secondly, any sympathy for the plight of the Kuwaitis and the potential threat to the Saudis was more than neutralised by deep-seated antipathy to Gulf Arabs amongst ordinary Maghrebis, who viewed them as rich, arrogant, uncultured and hypocritical and thus undeserving of protection or support.[34] Thirdly, and perhaps most significantly, the outpouring of popular anger and feeling on the streets of the Maghreb during the Gulf crisis was possibly as much an expression of discontent with conditions within the Maghreb as it was with events in the Middle East. The political openings in Algeria and Tunisia of the 1980s not only provided an avenue for political expression but were themselves reactions to growing socio-economic and political crisis and unrest in the region that had mounted since the end of the 1970s. These pressures were also felt in Morocco, there being a major outbreak of unrest linked to economic factors in Fez in December 1990 in the midst of the Gulf crisis. The importance of these domestic factors was illustrated the mass demonstrations that occurred in all three countries in the early weeks of 1991 in which participants, certainly in Algeria and Morocco, chanted slogans against the regimes.[35]

Public reactions to events in the Gulf forced the governments in all three states to change their official discourse towards the crisis. This occurred most quickly and smoothly in Tunisia, where Ben Ali and the RCD, aware of the dangers of allowing An-Nahda to exploit the issue, sensed the public shift and took the lead themselves in organising marches in support of Iraq and the Iraqi people.[36] In Algeria, the government's initially more even-handed condemnation of both Iraq and America gave way to a new position that stated that the latter's actions were 'more grave.'[37] The most dramatic change occurred in Morocco, where King Hassan's close relations with both the United States and Saudi Arabia had led him not only to take a robustly critical line towards Iraq but also to send a small force to help defend Saudi Arabia against possible attack. Morocco had long enjoyed close relations with the fellow monarchies of the Gulf states, and particularly Saudi Arabia, since the time of the Arab 'Cold War,' sharing with them both a hostility to Nasser's brand of Arab nationalism and an alignment with the West. Morocco provided security personnel for the Saudis in return for often massive financial support, which had been crucial to Morocco's campaign in the Western Sahara.[38] Taken aback by the scale of the public reaction to the crisis, which involved a national strike and a huge demonstration in the capital in early 1991, and aware that the opposition parties were seeking to use the issue to link the gap between official policy and public sentiment to the lack of democracy in the kingdom, Hassan progressively softened his line towards Iraq and refused to participate in meetings with Arab members of the US-led coalition.[39]

The swift eviction of the Iraqi army from Kuwait in the spring of 1991 brought a fairly rapid halt to the crisis and reactions of relief and stunned disbelief on the parts of the Maghrebi regimes and the general populations respectively. Although domestic politics in all three states appeared to return quickly to their status quo ante, the crisis left more long-term effects. Significantly, it marked the first major occasion when public opinion had actually managed to force changes in foreign policy, in this way effectively breaking the autonomous and exclusive grip that the countries' leaders had until that point exercised over the management of foreign relations. In the case of Algeria and Tunisia this was, as has been shown, a result of the broader opening up of their political systems. In the case of Morocco, which was not experiencing a parallel development, the crisis had the effect of helping to persuade the royal palace to embark on an extended series of political reforms over the ensuing decade to relieve the political pressures that had so dramatically manifested themselves in the crisis.

International Reactions to the Rise of Islamism in Algeria and Tunisia and the Onset of the Algerian Crisis

The refocusing on domestic politics that occurred in the aftermath of the Gulf War did not signify a disengagement from the outside world. Increasing international interest came to be paid to events in the region, particularly in Algeria, as the political openings of the late 1980s developed and began to incorporate the rising Islamist movement.

Reactions in France

The emergence and rise in Algeria of the Islamist FIS, as a consequence of the opening forged by President Chadli, attracted significant attention, notably in France where interest developed into unease. Not only did the rise of the Islamist movement in Algeria take Paris by surprise, but it represented a new and vibrant force with which France had startlingly few links and thus little understanding, drawing both its leadership and support from *milieux* far removed from the established post-independence elites with which France had long dealt with and felt it understood.[40] The growing strength of the Islamists in neighbouring Tunisia from the mid 1980s had already been of some concern to France, and although Paris had tried to dissuade Bourguiba from his path of outright confrontation with the MTI, it had done so discreetly and out of fear of the possible consequences. French support for Bourguiba's successor was strengthened by revelations that his move against the ageing president had narrowly pre-empted an alleged coup attempt by Islamist elements (see Chapter 5).[41]

French unease was further sharpened by the explicit hostility displayed by significant elements within the Islamist movements towards the former colonial power. All the main Islamist movements argued that the strong persistence of French culture and language in the postcolonial Maghreb had a distorting and corrosive effect on Maghrebi societies, which could be remedied through rigorous replacement by Islamic culture and Arabic language. Until this was achieved, it was argued, the Maghreb would remain under neo-colonial domination by France. In a further populist twist, many Maghrebi Islamists also argued that continued French influence and even domination was achieved and maintained with the active cooperation of a native Francophile elite in each of the Maghreb states. The strong links that much of the ruling—and largely francophone—elites in the three Maghrebi states enjoyed with France gave credibility to this charge and helped further strengthen support for the Islamists amongst the largely Arabophone masses. The Islamists' criticism of France became a major part of the Islamists' rhetorical repertoire.[42]

French participation in the Western-led coalition to force Iraq from Kuwait in 1991 exposed France to even more criticism in the Maghreb, particularly from the Islamists who had been a dominating presence in the mass demonstrations against the war that occurred in Morocco and Algeria in the early months of 1991. Coming on the back of sweeping victories achieved by the FIS in regional and communal elections in June 1990, French fears over Islamism were further raised by the claim in May 1991 by the Tunisian government that they had uncovered an Islamist plot for a violent overthrow of the Tunisian government.[43]

French disquiet about the rise of the FIS in Algeria was eased by reassurances from both its own diplomats and Algerian government officials that the party's popularity had more to do with its being a vehicle of protest than with its Islamist ideology, and that internal splits and external competition would rapidly reduce its strength.[44] The commanding position taken by the FIS following the first round of parliamentary elections in December 1991 came therefore as a shock to many in the French political establishment, a shock that was compounded by the palace coup that took place before the second round of voting occurred and which forestalled a likely confirmation of an FIS victory. Official reactions in Paris to the developments varied significantly and reflected the confusion and divisions within the establishment over whether Algeria's democratic opening should be supported whatever the result or whether the coming to power of a political movement that was ideologically hostile to France and perhaps even the idea of democracy itself should be blocked even if that meant the suspension of democratic processes. These confusions and divisions were not resolved as Algeria's political crisis lurched into civil violence in the months and years that followed the cancellation of the elections and the outlawing of the FIS. Opinions were divided between those who believed that robust backing for the Algerian regime against what was seen as an increasingly fanatical insurrection was the correct policy and those who viewed dialogue and inclusion of elements of the Islamist opposition as essential to an end to the bloodshed. As a result, official French policy shifted regularly in the 1990s, not only in response to events in Algeria but also to political shifts within France: a situation exacerbated by changes and rivalry between ministers within the same government, and political cohabitation between the presidency and the prime minister.[45]

Reluctance in France to adopt a more consistent and proactive policy towards the Algerian crisis was also bolstered by huge sensitivities within Algeria, stemming from the colonial period, to any perceived French interference in Algerian affairs. This applied to both the opposition and the government in Algeria. The government in Algiers had been unhappy at the lack of explicit support from Paris for the blocking of the FIS's route to power in 1992 and responded angrily to any criticism coming from France on issues of democracy and human rights, which worsened drastically as the violence escalated. For elements of the Algerian political opposition, French passivity equated to endorsement of the effective *coup d'état* and subsequent repression. Islamist groups were more trenchant in their criticism, especially after France began a crackdown on Algerian Islamists living in France following attacks on French citizens living in Algeria.[46] At the popular level and particularly in Islamist circles, the *Hizb-Fransa* conspiracy theory (see Chapter 3) of collaboration between the Algerian elite and the former colonial power gained increased currency. A series of attacks on French soil itself from 1994 appeared to indicate that extremist Algerian Islamist groups such as the GIA were targeting France for its perceived support for the regime in Algiers. Algerian opposition figures claimed, however, that many of these attacks were not in fact the work of Islamists but of elements within the Algerian regime itself that hoped to turn French opinion against the Islamists and in favour of more robust support for the Algerian regime.[47] The uncertain provenance of a number of the attacks in France, together with significant evidence of official Algerian manipulation of Islamist violence within Algeria (see Chapter 3), lent some credibility to this claim.

Reactions in the United States

Reactions in the US to the dramatic turn of events in Algeria were initially as confused and divided as those of France. Events elsewhere in the period 1989–91, notably in eastern Europe and the Gulf, meant that relatively little American attention had been paid to the rise of the FIS. The steady increase in violence that occurred from 1992 onwards did, however, begin to elicit growing US concern. As in France, official opinion in Washington became split between those who favoured confronting the Islamist threat to the Algerian regime and those who were of the view that the best route out of the crisis was through some degree of accommodation of the Islamist opposition. In the view of Zoubir and Zunes, the latter opinion held sway from 1993 as the dramatic increase in violence led to concerns that the regime in Algiers might be toppled. Out of fear of recreating the 'Iran scenario' by siding with a doomed regime against an Islamist-led opposition, Washington opened up links with exiled FIS figures and urged moderates on both sides to seek a compromise solution. The US criticised the regime's deteriorating human rights record and its failure to reinstitute democratic processes. There was even some discussion in Washington about the possible benefits of Algeria becoming a test-case for US relations with an Islamist regime. This approach, however, gave way by 1995 to one that was more explicitly supportive of the regime as actions from amongst some of the armed groups appeared to become increasingly extreme and the violence spread to France. More importantly, the threat to the immediate survival of the regime appeared to recede slightly and it seemed to be restoring elected institutions, notably through the election of Lamine Zeroual as president in November 1995, who looked to enjoy substantial popular support.[48]

Events in Algeria also helped shape American policy towards Tunisia. Until the 1990s, Tunisia had figured little in US considerations because of its small size and the pro-Western stance of its government.

Growing hostility to Tunisia's eastern neighbour, Libya, had led to increased US interest in and military support for Tunis, which came to eclipse that of France in the 1980s, and helped overcome the Tunisian government's unhappiness with Washington's knowledge and support of an Israeli air strike on the PLO headquarters in Tunis in October 1985.[49] The rise of the country's Islamist movement in the 1980s was viewed with little concern by the US State Department, due to its apparently moderate caste. The claims by the Ben Ali government that the Islamists were threatening a violent overthrow of his regime, together with the growth of violence in Algeria next door, led to a change of tack by Washington with an abandonment of links with the An-Nahda party and strong backing for the Tunisian regime.[50]

Morocco, the United States and France

Although Morocco did not experience the same internal convulsions as its Maghrebi neighbours in the late 1980s and early 1990s, its foreign relations were not unaffected by the turbulence elsewhere. It clearly benefited from the crisis in Algeria as its long-term regional rival became increasingly focused on its domestic turmoil at the expense of pursuing its foreign policy objectives. The events in Algeria also led to a reinstatement of staunch US support for Morocco, as policy-makers in Washington feared a spill-over of the violence from Algeria. Appreciative of King Hassan's support in both the Gulf crisis and war of 1990–91 and the emerging peace process in the Middle East, the US reinforced its relationship with Morocco, which remained the biggest Arab recipient of US aid after Egypt. Having urged Hassan to accept the UN Peace Plan on the Western Sahara at the beginning of the decade, Washington was reluctant to force Hassan to accept modalities for a referendum that Morocco might lose and which, in the view of US diplomats, might lead to the fall of the monarchy.[51]

Morocco's relationship with France in this period was much more turbulent. After the freeze in relations during the latter part of the 1960s as a result of the Ben Barka affair, Franco-Moroccan relations had improved significantly under de Gaulle's successors, especially Valéry Giscard d'Estaing in the 1970s, who became a strong advocate of Morocco. Giscard's defeat in the presidential election of 1981 by François Mitterrand led to a cooling of relations, in part because of the close links between Mitterrand's Socialist party and the opposition

USFP in Morocco. Relations between the two countries chilled further by the late 1980s due to the increasingly critical attention directed by parts of the French media and civil society towards Morocco. The political changes and reforms undertaken by Tunisia and Algeria in this period threw into relief the absence of such developments in Morocco. Particular attention began to be paid to the kingdom's record on human rights.[52]

Morocco bridled at this attention and relations worsened in 1990 with the release of a book in France that was hugely critical of King Hassan. *Notre Ami le Roi* (Our Friend the King) by the French journalist Gilles Perrault contained not only salacious stories about the Moroccan monarch but also, more substantively, detailed accounts of human rights abuses within the kingdom. French media coverage given to the book led to the banning of several French newspapers in Morocco and the blocking of several French television stations. The announcement at the beginning of November by the French human rights NGO *France Libertés* that its president would visit the Polisario-controlled refugee camps near Tindouf in Algeria convinced the Moroccan authorities that a concerted campaign was being launched against the kingdom in France and, moreover, one that involved the French government itself, given the fact the president of *France Libertés* was none other than Danielle Mitterrand, the wife of the French president. In response, a huge campaign of protest was organised in Morocco that involved the local press, political parties, NGOs and popular petitions. Tensions were gradually reduced through a combination of moves from both countries that included, from the French side, the cancellation of Danielle Mitterrand's planned trip to Algeria and, from the Moroccan side, a charm offensive towards the French media and public opinion and, more substantively, the release of nearly all the kingdom's political prisoners by 1992.[53]

Relations between Morocco and France improved dramatically from 1995, following the election of Jacques Chirac to succeed Mitterrand as French president. Chirac was a long-established friend of Morocco, having developed a strong relationship with King Hassan when Chirac had been mayor of Paris, and both men had identified each other as valuable allies. This led to the reactivation of what Daguzan has termed 'the networks of pro-Moroccan Gaullists' and an intensification of contact between the elites of the two countries that was already substantial, both already familiar with each other through regular mutual visits. The unabashed warmth in relations under Chirac led one Spanish newspaper to dub the French president 'Chirac El Alaoui.'[54]

Chirac's presidency also witnessed the first serious challenges being made to France's predominant position in the Maghreb by other actors, some of which the new president pragmatically gave way to whilst others he sought to resist. Most prominently there was the surge in interest and activism shown by the European Union towards the Maghreb from the 1990s that clearly challenged the leading role that France had hitherto taken in the region. In the early part of the decade, France had initially resisted this challenge and, in particular, worked hard to keep the EU from intervening in Algeria during the early 1990s. Under Chirac from 1995 France gradually gave way to these pressures as French policy became more 'Europeanised' and more coordinated with its European partners.[55]

The Rise of EU Influence: Barcelona, the ENP and Beyond

The early 1990s saw the metamorphosis of the European (Economic) Community into the European Union as member states further integrated their economies and, for the first time, began to develop a political character to their cooperation.

The strong economic ties the Maghreb states had to Europe meant that they developed relations with the EEC from an early stage. Morocco and Tunisia secured their independence from France a year before the Treaty of Rome and were initially able, with French backing, to secure preferential trading terms with the EEC. For its part, Algeria, which had formally been a part of France at the time of the EEC's creation, was initially able to maintain this status in terms of its trade with the Community. These sets of arrangements, however, soon came under pressure from other EEC members and all three countries were obliged to negotiate new arrangements which culminated in Morocco and Tunisia signing Association Agreements with the Community in 1969, Algeria holding out for an improvement on the modest advantages offered to its neighbours. In an effort to develop a more comprehensive approach, the EEC signed new cooperation agreements with all three states in 1976 which covered technical and financial cooperation as well as trade.[56]

By the beginning of the 1990s pressure had begun to mount on both sides of the Mediterranean for a new approach to relations. From the Maghrebi states' point of view, the 1976 agreements had only had modest benefits, having granted only limited and heavily qualified concessions on trade and with relatively small amounts of financial aid that the future King Mohamed of Morocco was to term 'derisory.'[57] Morocco had also been deeply insulted by a vote taken by the European parliament in 1992 to suspend a financial protocol in response to the growing international criticism of its human rights record during the early 1990s.

From the European perspective, impetus for a new approach came mainly from southern member states who were concerned that growing political instability in the Maghreb (notably in Algeria) would adversely affect them and that European preoccupations with developments in Eastern Europe—political transitions in former communist states— would lead to this issue being neglected. The economic downturn in Europe in the early 1990s also raised European concerns about unemployment and domestic political pressures to reduce or reverse flows of migrants coming from the Maghreb. By 1990 at least two million migrants from the Maghreb were believed to be living in EC countries.[58]

All of these pressures led to a series of moves that culminated in the launching of a new initiative that planned to bring together all existing EU Mediterranean policies in a comprehensive package. The Euro-Mediterranean Partnership Initiative (EMPI), launched in Barcelona in November 1995, represented a comprehensive framework with which to manage relations between the new European Union and the states of the Maghreb. Pressures from Middle Eastern states and the signature of the Oslo Declaration secured the extension of the arrangement to the states of the eastern Mediterranean, but its central focus was on the relationship between Europe and the Maghreb. According to its founding declaration, the initiative had the objective of:

Turning the Mediterranean basin into an area of dialogue, exchange and cooperation guaranteeing peace, stability and prosperity [which] requires a strengthening of democracy and respect for human rights, sustainable and balanced economic and social development, measures to combat poverty and promotion of greater understanding between cultures.[59]

It planned to do this by establishing frameworks for cooperation between the Union and southern Mediterranean states in three areas (or 'baskets'), broadly defined as partnerships in political and security affairs; economic and financial affairs; and social, cultural and human affairs.[60] The most important of these was the economic basket, the central component of which was the proposal for free trade agreements between the EU and the southern Mediterranean states. To be supported by development funds, the proposal aimed to stimulate economic development in the region, and in this way help reduce poverty and political conflict, which should in turn reduce pressures for emigration from the southern shore of the Mediterranean. All three Maghreb states were invited to Barcelona and became part of the initiative, with Morocco and Tunisia rapidly signing up to the new Association Agreement that would contain the Free Trade Agreement.

The grand hopes of the Barcelona Declaration struggled, however, to be realised in the years that followed. At the institutional level, the collapse of the Oslo Process between Israel and the Palestinians brought many of the multilateral frameworks of the EMPI and hopes for a cooperative security agreement to an effective halt. At the economic level, little transformation was experienced in the southern Mediterranean states, including the Maghreb. Unemployment remained high, and emigration to Europe continued largely unabated. Hoped-for increases in European investment in the Maghreb did not materialise, which one Moroccan academic viewed as one of the EMPI's 'most serious shortcomings.'[61]

The free trade agreements that had arguably been the central tool of the whole initiative failed to stimulate the hoped-for economic growth in the region. This was partly due to the continued rise of Asian producers that were able to undercut the Maghrebi textile industries following the end of the multifibre agreement in 2005.[62] Failure was also due to the heavily qualified nature of the free trade agreements. Pressure from southern European states, anxious to avoid having their agricultural sectors undercut by produce coming from the Maghreb, had ensured that agricultural products were excluded from any 'free' trade agreement. This removed the main potential benefit that the Maghreb states were likely to gain from a free trade agreement, given the fact that the European Union was their largest export market for agricultural products and, in the cases of Morocco and Tunisia, agriculture was a major sector of the economy. At the same time, they were left exposed to having their small and fragile industrial sectors potentially decimated by dismantling tariff barriers against European industrial goods. Although aware of these shortcomings, Tunisia and Morocco signed up for the new association agreements in the hope that they could subsequently negotiate a better deal and also because, in the light of dependence on trade with Europe, there was felt to be no alternative: two-thirds of the Maghreb's trade was with the European Union and had been since the 1970s.[63] The not-insignificant aid packages provided for were also attractive—particularly the funds that were to facilitate the adjustment of business and industry to enable them to compete once tariff barriers came down. This also explained the long delays in actually beginning to implement the agreements that were not formally launched in Tunisia until 1998 and in Morocco until 2000. For its part, Algeria held back from signing an association agreement: its internal turmoil not only distracting it from its relations with the European Union but also complicating them through Algiers' wish to incorporate into any agreement extra elements aimed at helping the regime in its struggle.

Little progress was made in achieving the essentially political objectives of the second basket of the EMPI, which had hoped to 'develop the rule of law and democracy' and 'respect human rights and fundamental freedoms' in the southern Mediterranean as a route to achieving greater stability.[64] Included in the EMPI essentially at the insistence of the European Parliament, the objective enjoyed little support from southern European countries, concerned that such measures would actually serve to undermine existing governments in the region. Funds were made available for these objectives principally through projects to strengthen civil society in the Maghreb, but as a study on the effectiveness of the EU's democracy promotion agenda concluded in 2002, 'North African governments have contrived either to nullify its impact or to reorient it towards projects compatible with their own objectives.'[65] No attempt was made by the European Commission to invoke the sanctions provided for in the Association Agreements when Tunisia and Algeria were shown to have committed significant human rights abuses.[66]

The disappointing results of the Barcelona Process prompted efforts to find new ways of managing relations across the Mediterranean. The 'big bang' expansion of EU membership in 2004 brought in ten new member states, and with them a whole new set of neighbouring states with which the EU had to manage relations. Although the expansion was overwhelmingly to the east of Europe, southern European states secured the extension of what became known as the new European Neighbourhood Policy (ENP) to the southern Mediterranean. The new policy consisted of the EU establishing bilateral relations with each of its neighbouring states. Modelled on the process by which the EU had managed the admission of new states, they proposed to establish an 'Action Plan' of reforms negotiated by the European Commission with each state, which, if fulfilled, would be rewarded with closer relations with the EU. In the case of applicant countries to the EU itself, it was seen as a means of preparing them for membership by securing their alignment with EU laws and practices. For the southern Mediterranean countries, including the Maghreb states (for which membership was not considered), it was seen as a means of securing reform through the promise of closer cooperation. The European Union was anxious to stress that the ENP complemented rather than supplanted the existing EMPI, but the new policy differed in two important ways. Firstly, the multilateral approach of the Barcelona Process was replaced by a much more bilateral approach, with every country able to negotiate its own set of relations with the EU. Secondly, the 'positive conditionality' of the Action Plans meant that progress would be rewarded with closer cooperation, but there would be no sanction for states that did not make progress or which undid reforms.[67]

Following the pattern of the EMPI, both Tunisia and Morocco signed up early for the new policy, whilst Algeria hung back. Algiers expressed its unhappiness with the new ENP, arguing that the EMPI was sufficient and that the new policy was overly Eurocentric in its approach and had been formulated unilaterally without consulting potential partner states.[68] Pleased to be dealt with individually, both Tunisia and Morocco agreed their Action Plans by 2005. Both plans identified priority areas that encompassed investment, poverty reduction, education and training, counter-terrorism, migration, transport, energy, trade liberalisation, legislative reform and human rights standards. Although this list appeared impressively comprehensive, many observers pointed out that they did not collectively represent a coherent programme and contained few specifics with regard to timeframes, actors, implementation and evaluation mechanisms.[69]

The Impact of the Oslo Process

The renewed international efforts to resolve the Arab-Israeli conflict in the 1990s also involved and impacted on the Maghreb states, particularly Morocco. Morocco was represented at the Madrid Peace Conference of 1991 and, although not directly involved in the negotiations that led to the Oslo Accords between the PLO and Israel, King Hassan hosted Shimon Peres and Yitzhak Rabin on their way back from signing the accords in Washington in September 1993. King Hassan became one of the most enthusiastic supporters of the accords amongst the Arab leaders and rapidly pushed for an upgrading of Morocco's relationship with Israel. Although Israel pressed for Morocco to open full diplomatic relations, King Hassan was conscious, in the wake of public reactions surrounding the Gulf War, not to go too far too soon. His decision to organise the opening of 'liaison offices' for Morocco in Tel Aviv and for Israel in Rabat in November 1994 encountered some apparent resistance, even within the habitually pliant Moroccan cabinet. He mitigated this unhappiness by also opening a liaison office in Gaza and by helping to develop the new airport there, which soon began to receive flights from Royal Air Maroc.[70]

The Oslo Accords were also welcomed in Tunis, where they had the added benefit of facilitating the departure of the PLO, whose presence had come to be seen as a burden for the Ben Ali government. They arranged for the establishment of liaison offices in Tel Aviv and Tunis in April 1996. In addition, Tunisia, like Morocco, hoped that the upgraded relationship with Israel would bring more tangible benefits through trade and particularly tourism. Algeria, by contrast, stood back from following the example of its neighbours, not least because of the complications of its own domestic turmoil that could only be worsened by publicly improving relations with Israel.[71]

Morocco's and Tunisia's relations with Israel followed the twists and turns of the peace process in the 1990s, entering an effective freeze during the period of Benjamin Netanyahu's hard-line premiership in the latter part of the decade. They saw a brief revival following Ehud Barak's election in 1999 and his subsequent push to reach a final deal to end the conflict.[72] Both states nonetheless resisted pressures from Barak and the US administration to upgrade their relations to the full diplomatic level as a gesture of support for the Israeli leader who also planned to involve Morocco in the final deal on the status of Jerusalem with Morocco, as chair of the Al Quds committee of the Organisation of the Islamic Conference, to share custodianship of the Temple Mount/Haram al-Sharif with the Palestinian administration.[73]

The death of King Hassan in July 1999 ironically provided a further boost to the efforts to clinch a deal through the presence of so many of the key players at his funeral, notably Barak, Yasser Arafat and US

President Bill Clinton, giving them the opportunity to speak to each other informally. More unusually, the event also witnessed a handshake and brief discussion between Barak and the newly elected Algerian president, Abdelaziz Bouteflika—the first public contact between the two states. The president promised to help mediate between Israel and the Arabs and subsequently declared that Algeria would be willing to recognise Israel in return for Israel's withdrawal from the West Bank, Gaza and Golan, the dismantling of settlements and help in the creation of a Palestinian state.[74]

The collapse of the Camp David talks between the PLO and the Israelis and the beginning of the second intifada in the autumn of 2000 ended not only efforts to advance relations between the Maghreb states and Israel, but also the formal progress that had been made since the signing of the Oslo Accords. The violence that erupted in Israel and the Palestinian territories provoked a huge public response in the Maghreb, with the Palestinians being seen as the principal victims. Massive demonstrations in both Rabat and Casablanca in October in support of the Palestinians demanded the closure of the liaison offices in Rabat and Tel Aviv. Both were duly shut by the end of the month, and although the Moroccan government stated that this was due to the deaths of Palestinians and the Moroccan king's role as chairman of the Al Quds committee, it also demonstrated, for the second time after the initial experience of the Gulf crisis, that the Moroccan public was capable of influencing foreign policy decisions. Tunisia similarly closed its own offices in Tunis and Tel Aviv that same month.

After 2000, the Maghreb became less and less involved in the affairs of the Middle East. Morocco maintained its informal links with Israel, hosting regular low-profile visits from Israeli officials. In so doing, its primary hope was not to relaunch the Middle East process but rather to further Morocco's own goals of securing Israeli investment in the kingdom, which continued to grow, and, more importantly, gain the support of Israel's powerful friends in Washington for its claim on the Western Sahara. Although Israeli officials pushed for Morocco to expand its formal links with Israel still further, public opinion retained a heavy restraining hand on Morocco doing this. Israeli offensives against the Palestinians regularly led to mass demonstrations in the kingdom and expanded political and press freedoms gave outlets to critical opinions absent in most other Arab countries. Moreover, King Mohamed VI showed markedly less interest in the Middle East than his father, often absenting himself from Arab summits, which he viewed as fruitless wastes of time. In this way he relinquished the role established by Hassan, as the main Arab initiator of Arab peace initiatives, to other states: principally Saudi Arabia.[75]

11 September 2001

The emerging pattern of relations between the Maghreb states and the outside world changed dramatically with the attacks of 11 September 2001 on the United States. The shift in US and European priorities towards combating Islamist violence, and threats to their security more generally, had a significant impact on relations. The United States made a priority of searching for allies in what became known as the 'War on Terror.' Particular interest was shown in receiving backing from states in the Muslim and Arab worlds. All three of the Maghreb states responded positively in their own ways and for their own reasons to President George W. Bush's call.

The most enthusiastic response came from Algeria, where under Abdelaziz Bouteflika's presidency from 1999 a more vigorous and active foreign policy had been pursued. This was bolstered by the decline in civil conflict in the country and a rise in the international oil price from the early 2000s. Bouteflika flew to Washington to meet with President Bush in November 2001, despite having made a similar visit only four months earlier. There he pledged his support for the US campaign against international Islamist terrorism, arguing that Algeria was 'well-placed to share in the current pain and suffering of the American people.' Explicitly linking the violence in Algeria with the 11 September attacks, he said that 'Terrorism is one and indivisible. If we are going to combat terrorism, we must do it together.'[76] Bouteflika's offer of support was warmly welcomed by a US administration anxious to learn from the experiences of other states in combating Islamist violence, and the years that followed saw a dramatic improvement and intensification in relations between the two states, Donald Rumsfeld the US defence secretary stating, 'It's instructive for us to realize that the struggle we're in is not unlike the struggle that the people of Algeria went through.'[77] Besides learning from Algeria, the US was also anxious to help the country eradicate what remained of the armed Islamist resistance to the regime inside the country. There was a fear that grew throughout the 2000s that Algeria, and the Maghreb more generally, might become a new theatre of operations for Al Qaeda, particularly in the south of the region and into the Sahel, following its effective ejection from Afghanistan. In 2004 the Department of Defense established the Trans-Saharan Counterterrorism Initiative in cooperation with Algeria, Tunisia and Morocco, as well as number of states in the Sahel and West Africa, to help control what were thought to be dangerously empty areas that could provide 'safe havens' for terrorists.[78] The extent to which these dangers were well-founded was unclear, and there were persistent suspicions that the threat was being overstated by Maghreb states to gain valuable external support for their struggle against domestic enemies and to reduce pressures for political reform and improvements in human rights. It was even argued that the very idea of an Al Qaeda presence in the Maghreb-Sahel region was a deliberate invention of the Algerian intelligence services, the DRS, the propagation of which extended to acts of terrorism and the kidnapping of foreign tourists in the region.[79]

Although Algeria was the main beneficiary from increased US interest in the region, due to its vast Saharan south, Morocco and Tunisia also sought to benefit, although less directly. Moroccan anxieties about the expansion in US-Algerian relations were at least partially offset by the US designating Morocco a 'major non-NATO ally' in 2004 and signing a Free Trade Agreement with the country the same year. Although continued attempts to persuade the US of highly improbable links between Polisario and Al Qaeda failed, the suicide bombings that occurred in Casablanca in May 2003 helped remind Washington of the vulnerabilities of what it regarded as a stable and established ally in the region.

The bombing of a synagogue in Djerba in April 2002 produced a similar affect for Tunisia, where the regime was anxious to demonstrate that the established security-oriented and anti-Islamist credentials of the regime produced a much more useful ally in the struggle against terrorism than one hamstrung by concerns about human rights and democratic rule. The US had already been publicly very supportive of Tunisia during the 1990s, praising its support for the Oslo process and portraying it as an economically liberal and secular success story, despite adverse reports from the State Department regarding human rights in the country.[80] This approach succeeded to the extent that US security aid to Tunisia in dollars amounted to more than the combined total given to both Algeria and Morocco in the period 2002–6.[81] This did not, though, prevent both President Bush and Secretary of State Colin Powell from publicly expressing their concerns about these issues in meetings with Ben Ali in 2003–4 as part of the Bush administration's brief push for political reform in the Arab world as a counter to Islamist extremism.[82] Although the initiative was effectively abandoned following Hamas' victory in the elections to the Palestinian authority in early 2006, it was, nonetheless, welcomed by the beleaguered Tunisian opposition who contrasted it with the lack of response from the French government and the Europeans more generally.[83]

The Maghreb was also incorporated within the US administration's broader response to the events of 11 September. The events of the 1990s within the region had already prompted the US to rethink its policy towards the Maghreb. Washington had traditionally not approached the area as a region but as a set of individual states with which it conducted distinct bilateral relations. The end of the Cold War and a degree of convergence between the political, economic and social conditions and challenges within the three Maghreb states led to an attempt to adopt a more regionally oriented policy. Encouraged by the decline in the levels of violence in Algeria by the end of the decade, 2000 saw the launch of the US-North Africa Economic Partnership (USNAEP) initiative, which sought to encourage greater cooperation between the states with the view of creating an integrated regional economic body.[84] This rather low-key and fundamentally economic approach was expanded and integrated into the Broader Middle East and North Africa (BMENA) initiative that the Bush administration launched in 2004 in fundamental response to the events of 11 September 2001, putting much greater emphasis on issues of governance in an effort to deal with the perceived problems of the Arab world that were seen as having contributed to the attacks of 2001.[85]

For France, the attacks of 11 September 2001 led to the removal of any remaining reservations about support for the Algerian regime against the vestiges of armed Islamist resistance. French relations with Algeria had deteriorated during the early part of the presidency of Jacques Chirac, as the new president sought to link French support for Algeria to political progress, but contact began to improve with the election of Abdelaziz Bouteflika as president in 1999.[86] Elsewhere in the Maghreb, French support for Ben Ali's regime in Tunisia had strengthened, following revelations of the alleged Islamist conspiracy to overthrow the regime in 1991 amid concerns about the situation in

Algeria. This support consisted, for the main part, of a less sympathetic treatment of Tunisian Islamist exiles in France and a reluctance to criticise the increasingly authoritarian and repressive drift of the Tunisian authorities' attitude towards even legal opposition forces throughout the 1990s.[87] Patience on the latter issue did begin to wear thin by the end of the decade and, during 2001, several French officials, including the foreign minister, Hubert Vedrine, were publicly critical of the 'increasing use of violence by the Tunisian security forces against the defenders of human rights.'[88] Within weeks, though, this new approach was washed away by the events of 11 September 2001 and six months later by the terrorist attack in Djerba, in which a number of European tourists died. Thereafter security became the main concern for the French, and concerns over human rights were explicitly relegated to a position of secondary importance. As President Chirac infamously observed on an official visit to Tunisia in December 2003, 'the first human right is to eat, to be looked after, to receive an education and to have somewhere to live,' in reference to the relative economic success and stability of the country.[89]

The events of 11 September 2001 changed EU relations with the Maghrebi states in important ways. The greatest impact was on relations with Algeria. Throughout the 1990s the government in Algiers had been unhappy about the lack of support it had received from Brussels and the scepticism that seemed to be shown towards the government role in the violence that shook the country. European reluctance to include clauses relating to counter-terrorist measures in an Association Agreement was the main reason why Algeria only signed up to an agreement in December 2001, several years after Morocco and Tunisia. In the wake of 9/11, the EU dropped its objections to the inclusion of clauses relating to terrorism, and negotiations were successfully concluded in December 2001. At the same time, the European Union appeared to drop any references to Algeria's need for political reform or democratisation out of presumed concern that this might endanger the degree of stability that Algeria had managed to regain after the turn of the century.[90]

With regard to Tunisia and Morocco, the events of 11 September 2001 served to reinforce existing tendencies in the EU for backing the current regimes as points of stability either side of Algeria. This led to the EU refraining from putting strong pressure on the two regimes over issues such as political reform and human rights, an approach that was strongly encouraged by both regimes, seeking to portray themselves as resolute allies in the struggle against international terrorism. The attacks on the United States also helped tip the balance in favour of those, predominantly southern, EU member states who sought such an approach to the Maghreb, against those mainly northern member states which had greater reservations based record on human rights and progress towards democracy.[91] As a result, the EU failed to invoke the conditionality clauses within the ENP agreement with Tunisia, despite attempts by the Tunisian authorities to frustrate certain programmes agreed in the Action Plan for Tunisia. The Tunisian regime made efforts to stress that it shared common values with the EU and faced the same common threat of radical Islamism. This led to the EU effectively excluding all Islamist actors and organisations from its democracy promotion agenda in Tunisia, despite the facts that the Islamist An-Nahda party remained arguably the most important opposition force in the country and, moreover, that it had no truly verifiable links to international terrorism.[92]

In Morocco, the EU did not seek to exclude Islamists, largely because, unlike Tunisia, the government there did not itself exclude all Islamists from the legal political arena. It did, nonetheless, breathe an apparent sigh of relief when the Party of Justice and Development failed to join the governing coalition in the wake of the legislative elections of 2007.[93] In more general terms, Morocco's perceived stability in the eyes of the EU and the steps it continued to take, in contrast to its neighbours, towards domestic reform in a number of areas led to the EU regularly praising the kingdom This paved the way for the awarding of what was commonly known as 'Advanced Status' in its relations with the European Union under the ENP in October 2008. Although the 'Advanced Status' added little of substance to what had already been agreed in its ENP Action Plan beyond more diplomatic exchanges, it was a clear public diplomacy success for Morocco and was further recognition of the EU's favour.[94] Such praise and recognition also arguably served to reinforce the political status quo within the kingdom.[95]

The overall effect of the evolution of the European Union's relations with the Maghreb states after 11 September 2001 and through the ENP, was to create a significant degree of convergence in aims which amounted to an almost tacit agreement to prioritise regime stability and continuity over—or in the cases of Tunisia and Algeria to the exclusion of—moves towards greater political liberalisation and democratisation.[96]

The bilateral approach of the ENP also served to increase tensions between the Maghreb states. Morocco revelled in the praise and privileged status it enjoyed from and with the European Union, and sought to use this diplomatic capital to pursue its key objectives on issues such as the Western Sahara. Although Algeria rejected the ENP, Darbouche argues that concerns about Morocco's favoured position were probably present in Algeria's proposal in March 2008 for a 'Global Strategic Partnership' with the EU, and even possibly in its decision to start using its position as a key energy supplier to Europe in a more political way. This appeared to be the case with Spain, Algeria's main gas client in the EU, which had steadily become an increasingly important player in relations with the Maghreb.[97]

The Rise of Spain

Spanish influence in the Maghreb had grown significantly from the late 1980s. Spain's colonial presence in the region had been much shorter and far less extensive than that of France. Nevertheless, geography alone had dictated that historical interaction between North Africa and the Iberian Peninsula had been extensive and substantially pre-dated the modern colonial period. Both the Muslim kingdoms of the *Al-Andulus* period in medieval Spain and the subsequent assaults on North Africa by Spain and the other European states throughout the centuries that followed the fall of the last Muslim kingdom in Granada in 1492 left a surprisingly vivid and lasting impact on both sides of the Straits of Gibraltar. These effects lasted into the modern period, not least in the suspicions harboured at the popular level in both Spain and Morocco, and made for potentially difficult relations in the post-independence period.

Early Spanish interaction with the independent Maghreb states almost exclusively focused on Spain's staged departure from the various territories it had held onto after Morocco formally gained its independence in 1956, culminating in its withdrawal from the Western Sahara following the death of General Franco in 1975. Absorbed with its own domestic affairs and the delicate transition to democratic government that occurred in the late 1970s, Spain did not begin to figure again as an actor of note until the mid 1980s. Boosted both politically and economically by its acceptance into the EC in 1986, Spain began to focus much more attention on the Maghreb, partly because it saw the region as one where it could exercise its newly regained influence. It also believed in the importance of stability in the Maghreb. These developments led to Madrid taking a major role in the establishment of the EMPI and hosting the founding conference in Barcelona.

More tangibly, it believed that it had a number of important interests in the region which it needed to protect. Of primary concern were the two Spanish enclaves of Ceuta (Sebta) and Melilla (Millilia) on the North African coast and surrounded by Moroccan territory which Morocco formally claimed but which Madrid had not ceded because they had been established in the fifteenth century and long before the modern colonial era. Access to the fish-rich waters off Morocco's Atlantic coast for Spain's huge fishing fleet was also of interest for Madrid, as was controlling the flow of hashish and—as Spain's growing economic wealth transformed it from a country of emigration to one of immigration—illegal immigrants coming from Morocco. As a consequence, relations with Morocco came to be accorded significant importance and an unwritten convention developed, according to which Morocco became the destination for the first foreign visit made by newly elected prime ministers of Spain.[98]

To defend these interests, Spain adopted a policy of developing what it termed a 'cushion of shared interests,' mainly in the economic field by boosting trade and investment in Morocco, in the hope of creating levels of interdependence that would prevent clashes over these issues. Commerce between the two countries quadrupled between 1980 and 1992, and by the mid 1990s Spain had become Morocco's second largest trading partner. Arms sales to Morocco also increased substantially in this period as part of a wider programme of cooperation in the military sphere. At the diplomatic level Spain offered and secured a Treaty of Friendship and Cooperation with Morocco in 1991—its first with a state outside Latin America.[99]

Morocco responded positively to the Spanish overtures, welcoming increased trade and investment, particularly for its impoverished north. Rabat was also pleased to diversify and reduce its dependence on France during its period of strained relations with Paris in the 1980s and early 1990s. King Hassan was aware of the importance of the relationship with Spain and had stated that history and geography ensured that the two countries were 'condemned' to get along.[100] Morocco was, however, concerned and suspicious about Spain's stance on the crucial issue of the Western Sahara. Spain's anxiety to achieve a swift and painless withdrawal from the Western Sahara in 1976 had led to it concluding a deal that was very favourable to Morocco in the form of the Tripartite Agreement of that year (see Chapter 8). King Hassan was therefore surprised and angered when in the 1980s the government in Madrid began to back calls for a referendum in the territory. This was the result of a growth of feeling in Spain of what Haizam Amirah-Fernandez has termed 'historical and moral responsibility' towards the Sahrawis, whom many Spaniards felt had been unjustly abandoned in 1976. Spanish concern about Spain's own interests, however, prevented it from taking too critical a line towards Morocco, although not sufficiently to mollify fully Moroccan displeasure, which often failed to distinguish between official Spanish policy and the statements and actions of the Spanish media and civil society, over which the Spanish government had much less control than Rabat often appreciated. Morocco was none the less very aware of Spanish worries over maintaining access for its fishing fleets to Moroccan waters and the status of Sebta and Mellilia, and was not averse to raising these issues to put pressure on Madrid over its stance on the Western Sahara.[101]

Tensions between Madrid and Rabat ebbed and flowed during the 1990s, but relations remained generally good. They witnessed a precipitous decline, however, in the early 2000s, deteriorating almost to the point of armed conflict. The crisis formally began with the collapse of negotiations to renew a fishing agreement in the spring of 2001. Although it was the EU that formally negotiated with Morocco, the agreement was effectively one between Spain and Morocco, given the fact that 90 per cent of the European vessels fishing in Moroccan waters were Spanish.[102] Spanish anger at the failure to secure a renewal of the agreement, which would have a significant economic impact on those parts of Spain whose economy relied on the large fishing fleet, was reflected in the Spanish prime minister, Jose Maria Aznar, warning in the wake of the collapse of the talks that 'there would be consequences for relations between Spain and Morocco.' Unhappiness on this issue added to growing tensions about the growth in illegal migration from Morocco to Spain, which had become a significant public issue in Spain and which the Spanish felt Morocco was doing little to control. Tensions mounted over the following months as Morocco, for its part, became increasingly unhappy at what it saw as hostile Spanish behaviour with regard to the Western Sahara; specifically the organising of a mock 'referendum' on the territory's future by the regional government of Andalusia and, more substantially, Spain's blocking of a French initiative to get EU backing for the idea of regional autonomy for the territory within Morocco.[103]

Tensions reached genuine crisis point in July 2002, when Madrid reacted to Morocco sending a small group of gendarmes to the disputed rocky islet of Leila (known as Perejil in Spanish) off the north coast of Morocco by sending a substantial military force to eject the gendarmes. It took the intervention of the US secretary of state, Colin Powell, to defuse the incident and secure the withdrawal of the Spanish presence and the restoration of the effective status quo ante. The crisis demonstrated a number of important factors about the relationship between Morocco and Spain. Firstly, that existing mechanisms to restrict potential conflicts between the two states, such as the treaty of Friendship and Cooperation and the 'cushion of shared interests,' had manifestly failed.[104] So too had the forum provided by the Barcelona Process, the shortcomings of which were painfully demonstrated by the intervention of the United States to resolve the dispute. Indeed, the failure of the EU and the parallel success of the US persuaded Aznar to strengthen relations with Washington at the expense of those with Europe. The crisis also saw a marked development in relations between Spain and Algeria, which was not coincidental as both parties sought to exploit their relationship to put pressure on Rabat, a development that did not go unnoticed in Morocco and which one newspaper described as a clear attempt 'to isolate Morocco.'[105] Economic relations between Spain and Algeria had developed significantly, with Algeria becoming Spain's main natural gas supplier; but Algeria's domestic turmoil of the 1990s and a desire to maintain relations with Morocco had prevented the development of more advanced political relations. With violence having declined and with relations with Morocco at an all-time nadir, Spain signed a Treaty of Friendship and Cooperation with Algeria in October 2002.[106]

Spanish approaches to the Maghreb witnessed a major shift following the defeat of Aznar's Popular Party and the election of the Spanish Socialist party to government in March 2004. The new prime minister, J. L. R. Zapatero, reversed much of the policy of his predecessor. Judging that there was much to lose and little to gain from continuing to alienate Morocco, Zapatero set about rebuilding relations with its southern neighbour, which he stated was his 'foreign policy priority.'[107] The involvement of Moroccan nationals in the group found responsible for the bombing of the Atocha station in Madrid in the dramatic run-up to the election in March 2004 provided the new prime minster with another reason to enhance cooperation with Morocco. A public charm offensive was followed up by a clear realignment in rhetoric and policy on the question of the Western Sahara. Aligning Spain very much with the established position taken by both France and the United States, Madrid backed the proposal made by Morocco in 2007 for regional autonomy for the territory within Morocco (see Chapter 8). Delighted by the change in approach, Morocco responded by agreeing to a new fishing agreement with the EU and by ensuring a significant drop in the level of illegal migrants travelling from Morocco to Spain. The new policy was not, however, without its costs, as domestically the Zapatero government faced criticism from the well-organised pro-Polisario elements of civil society.[108] Internationally Spain encountered inevitable hostility from Polisario and more importantly Algeria, whose decision in March 2007 to increase the price of the gas it supplied to Spain by 20 per cent came a matter of weeks after Madrid's endorsement of Morocco's autonomy plan for the Western Sahara.[109]

The Zapatero government also mended relations with France, which had deteriorated substantially during Aznar's premiership because of relations with Morocco. Throughout the 1990s, Spain had progressively challenged France's assumed role as the main interlocutor for the Maghreb states within the European Union; but shared concerns with Paris about the need for stability in the Maghreb, and to prevent the EU focusing its attention and efforts exclusively on Eastern Europe, led Paris and Madrid to coordinate their policies. Aznar's securing of a second mandate for the Popular Party in the election of 2000 encouraged the Spanish prime minister to pursue a much bolder and more independent foreign policy for Spain, which in terms of the Maghreb meant deferring to and coordinating with France much less. This move was encouraged by a growing feeling in the Spanish administration that France was seeking to reassert itself mainly through the influence of the Francophile advisers to the new Moroccan king, Mohamed VI, who even sought to 'maintain a degree of tension in Moroccan-Spanish relations.'[110] This, combined with the new more hard-line posture Spain took towards Morocco, led to diplomatic clashes between Madrid and Paris as France posed as the defender of Moroccan interests. In concrete terms this meant French opposition to Spanish proposals in June 2002 that aid to countries that were perceived to be insufficiently cooperative in efforts to control illegal immigration be reduced, and, more inflammatorily, France's blocking of a communiqué of support for Spain during the Perejil/Leila crisis a month later. The new approach of the Zapatero government from 2004, however, realigned Spanish policy with France and within the broader framework of that of the EU.[111]

The Realignment of External Interests

The rise of the interest and influence of both Spain and the European Union in the Maghreb from the 1990s had challenged the long-established dominance of France in the region's interactions with the wider world. France, after initial resistance, accommodated these challenges largely through finding common interests with both Brussels and Madrid. French willingness to relax its hitherto often jealous exclusive grip on the Maghreb was also explained by reference to its concern about the growing interest and influence of the United States in the region. French concerns about American involvement were long-standing but increased in the latter part of the 1990s and became acute in the aftermath of the events of 11 September 2001 as the United States began to establish much stronger links with Maghreb states as part of its 'War on Terror.' The elaboration of a regional approach to the Maghreb by the US was widely seen, despite official protestations to the contrary, as direct competition not only to France but also to the EU's EMPI and the ENP.[112] France was able to stem this drift with Chirac's stand against the US-led invasion of Iraq in 2003, which boosted France's image in the Arab world as it damaged that of the United States. This, however, proved to be only temporary as the leaderships in the Maghreb states continued to view relations with America as of more long-term importance and, as a result, were not afraid to use French concerns to their own advantage. In Tunisia the situation was used to ward off French criticism of the country's human rights record, whilst in Algeria it is possible that it contributed to President Bouteflika's increasingly critical public pronouncements towards the former colonial power.[113]

The election of Nicolas Sarkozy as successor to Jacques Chirac in May 2007 saw another significant shift in French approaches, if not necessarily policy, towards the Maghreb. In the midst of his campaign for the presidency, Sarkozy had announced his desire to establish a new 'Mediterranean Union' of the states bordering that sea. The initial proposal was short on details and was clearly primarily designed as a headline-grabbing declaration in the race for the presidency. Sarkozy did, though, clearly see his proposal as a means for France to reassert itself not only in the Mediterranean but also within the European Union. Ultimately, however, the proposal became an object lesson in the limitations of French power. The original plan was successively watered down and modified under pressure, initially from the Spanish and the Italians, and ultimately from the Germans, who succeeded in bringing it within the ambit of the European Union and ultimately under the umbrella of the EMPI.[114] The initiative had received mixed responses within the Maghreb where, once again, observers were struck by the lack of consultation there had been with the region. One Algerian newspaper complained that the Arab states had not had 'a word to say' in the project, which had been reduced to a 'Euro-European affair.'[115]

By the end of the first decade of the twenty-first century it became clear that a significant convergence in policies towards the Maghreb had occurred on the part of France, the United States, the European Union and Spain. Concerns over migration and particularly terrorism became paramount. This led to a much more conciliatory and less critical line being taken towards the regimes in place in the region, which were seen as crucial to the management of both issues. For their part, Rabat, Algiers and Tunis understood this very well and sought to reinforce this view. Moreover, they moved to exploit it by ensuring that favourable terms were secured in other areas such as trade and, more importantly, in the neutering of any official criticisms of the lack of democracy and human rights in the states. Whilst much literature on relations between Europe and North America on the one hand and Africa, Asia and Latin America on the other hand continued to argue for a core-periphery relationship in which the latter were subservient to the former, the Maghreb appeared to contradict this trend, at least as far as the leading elites were concerned, and were able to enjoy a surprising degree of autonomy in terms of foreign policy choices. Whilst Western governments became hugely cautious in their willingness to criticise Maghreb governments, the latter often had few qualms about lambasting the actions and statements of European governments. Good examples of this were Algerian protests against proposed changes to the French school curriculum in 2005 to mention the 'positive role' France had played overseas and especially in North Africa during the colonial period; Tunisian officials similarly evoking the negative side of France's colonial record in response to and protest at French criticism of a perceived worsening of human rights abuses in Tunisia in late 2009; and regular Moroccan protests against criticisms of Morocco in the Spanish media.[116] Perhaps more surprising was Tunisia's willingness to see relations with the United States deteriorate in the late 2000s.

At the same time as convergence seemed to be occurring amongst the established international actors in the Maghreb, other new and renewed actors began to enter the scene. The expanded presence and influence of China in the Maghreb formed part of a much broader pattern being felt worldwide and particularly in sub-Saharan Africa. Although the impact of this was comparatively minimal in the Maghreb than further south in Africa, it was not without importance as Chinese companies and labour became increasingly present, most notably in Algeria during the construction boom financed by the high oil price of the mid 2000s. As elsewhere, this presence was avowedly apolitical, but its continued growth unavoidably made it less likely to remain so. More generally, it exposed the Maghreb to a part of the world and a broad culture with which it was historically very unfamiliar, both politically and at the popular level.

Interaction also grew with a much closer and more familiar part of the world: sub-Saharan Africa. Connections across the Sahara had been historically strong but had become weaker over time as the Maghreb had placed more emphasis on its richer and more powerful neighbours to the north and east. In the immediate aftermath of independence, both Algeria and Morocco had developed ties with the other newly independent states of Africa out of post-colonial solidarity, although Morocco shifted under Hassan II to align itself with the Western powers and their allies in the continent after his accession to the throne in 1961. The Western Sahara conflict led to both countries competing for influence in the region, most notably over securing recognition of the SADR by a majority of member states to facilitate its admission to the Organisation of African Unity (OAU). Beyond this, though, relations were of relatively marginal importance to the Maghreb states when compared to those with the Middle East, Europe and the United States. This began to change with the arrival of significant numbers of sub-Saharan migrants into the states of the Maghreb, partly as a consequence of Muammar's Qadhafi's encouragement of African migration into Libya as part of his quixotic vision to make Libya the leading state in the continent, having been disappointed by the lack of enthusiasm shown for his initiatives in the Arab world. Although these migrants primarily affected the Maghreb states' relations with governments in Europe rather than in Africa, through the attempts made by many of them to travel illegally to Europe, their increasingly permanent presence in the region changed the cultural and frequently religious social complexion of the region in ways that were still not fully apparent by the beginning of the second decade of the twenty-first century. Indeed, together with the growth of a small but influential East Asian community and, much more importantly, the rise of the Berber cultural movement (see Chapter 6), a more varied and cosmopolitan Maghrebi society seemed to be emerging that could have potential consequences for states that still primarily thought of themselves as Arab and Islamic in terms of identity and outlook.

The Tunisian Revolution: Putting the Maghreb Back on the International Map?

The pattern of the Maghreb states' relations with the outside world was shaken up once more by the events of the opening months of 2011. The outside world was taken aback by both the speed and nature of the popular uprisings across North Africa and the Middle East and struggled to articulate an appropriate response. The revolts subverted and overturned not only several of the regimes in the region but also nearly all the accepted wisdom about the Arab world at official levels in Europe and the United States. The conventional view, that the region contained passive, fatalistic populations who had no real appetite for either significant political change or democratic government and who were culturally predisposed towards authoritarian rule, rapidly disintegrated with the clear evidence to the contrary coming from the crowds on Avenue Bourguiba in Tunis and Tahrir Square in Cairo; as did the view that any mass opposition movement emerging in the region would inevitably be of radical Islamist colouring. Perhaps most disconcerting of all to European and American foreign policy-makers was the fact that these appeared to be entirely indigenous popular movements, destroying the widely-held assumption that any meaningful political change in the region could only come through outside assistance and intervention.

Western governments' backing of authoritarian regimes in the region automatically aligned them, by default, against the popular movements that emerged in the opening weeks of 2011. Most governments moved to qualify and frequently eventually drop their support for what were clearly deeply unpopular leaders in the region, in the face of calls from the streets for the installation of democratic government—something Western governments had always professed they also wanted. It was perhaps inevitable that the staunchest Western backer of the first state in the Arab world to see a mass protest movement develop would be badly wrong-footed by events. The declaration by the French foreign minister, Michèle Alliot-Marie, that France could offer its 'know-how' (*savoir-faire*) in maintaining public order to the Tunisian authorities as the popular unrest spread to the Tunisian capital in the second week of January, demonstrated how unaware the Quai d'Orsay was about the magnitude of the popular revolt against the despised Ben Ali regime.[117] It also revealed, more seriously, the closeness of the French establishment to the Ben Ali regime and its commitment to its survival. The depth of these connections was gradually revealed in the weeks that followed the departure of Ben Ali with the emergence of evidence of prominent French politicians, most notably Alliot-Marie herself, having benefited from free travel and holidays from members of Ben Ali's now disgraced family; the scandal cost the foreign minister her job.[118] These developments, on top of long-standing French support for the Ben Ali regime, ensured that Paris's standing in Tunisia was badly damaged, especially as public opinion and hostile opposition politicians, who had castigated France's backing of the deposed dictator, began to have a much greater say in the running of the country.[119] Hostility to outside powers that had been insufficiently critical of Ben Ali's regime during its long tenure also extended to the European Union. A Tunisian minister described as 'ridiculous' the Union's initial offer of 17 million Euros extra aid in the tumultuous wake of the revolution.[120] Even when this was increased nearly tenfold to 140 million Euros, the editorial of one leading Tunisian daily newspaper was critical of the apparent linking of aid to efforts to control Tunisian emigration to Europe, which increased substantially following the disappearance of police controls with the collapse of the Ben Ali regime. Significantly, it contrasted Italy's willingness to accept Tunisian migrants with France's criticism of the move which had the 'whiff of xenophobia' and did not come as any surprise to a Tunisian people 'bitterly disappointed' by the behaviour of the French with regard to Ben Ali.[121]

The spread of the popular uprisings to other larger and more high-profile Arab states, most notably Egypt and then Libya, in the weeks that followed the fall of Ben Ali meant that the international attention that had briefly but intensely focused on Tunisia rapidly fell away. Yet the events of January 2011 in Tunisia were destined to have a lasting international impact and importance for some time to come. Firstly, as the country in which the 'Arab Spring' had indisputably begun, Tunisia accrued a level of attention and kudos that it had never previously experienced and which was openly and gratefully acknowledged by the other popular movements that took to the streets across the Arab world in 2011. Secondly, the fact that Tunisia's revolution looked set to be the most comprehensive and far-reaching of all the revolts in the region not only set the standard for uprisings elsewhere but put it on track to be potentially the Arab world's newest and most genuine democracy. To what extent this new-found attention and status extended to Tunisia's western neighbours in Algeria and Morocco was unclear, given the emergence of initially much less powerful protest movements in the two countries. It did, nonetheless, draw international interest and awareness to the Maghreb in new ways, not least in the way it had reversed the traditional relationship with the Mashreq, with the latter taking its lead from events in the former rather than the other way around.

CONCLUSION

As the first decade of the twenty-first century drew to a close, the politics of the states of the central Maghreb seemed to have settled into a stable pattern. Having weathered the political and economic storms of the 1980s and 1990s, Algeria, Morocco and Tunisia appeared to have succeeded in establishing a form of political equilibrium. It was an equilibrium that was remarkably similar to that which had been put in place in the years that followed the achievement of independence from European colonial rule nearly half a century earlier. Most striking was the continuity in the forms of political leadership and structures of power in the three countries: in Morocco, a hereditary monarchy claiming near absolutist authority based on religion ruled; in Tunisia an all-powerful individual president backed by a hegemonic political party held sway; and between them, in Algeria, nearly all the key decisions of state were taken by the senior hierarchy of the country's military. Whilst some of the visible forms of politics had changed over the intervening years, these central realities of political power established in the 1960s in the three states remained remarkably unmoved after nearly five decades. Key political debates and decisions continued to occur behind closed doors carried out by a very small number of people: the king and his advisers in the royal palace in Rabat; the president, his senior advisers and increasingly his family in Tunis; and the conclave of senior military leaders and their civilian allies in Algiers. Significantly, there was little or no meaningful input from the wider populations of the countries into decision-making. Electoral processes had become part of the formal political calendar in all three states by the 1990s, but the elections they produced were wholly incapable of removing or replacing existing political leaders, let alone of fundamentally altering political power structures. In Tunisia, elections were skewed and rigged to ensure the sitting president always won with a crushing majority, whilst in Morocco and Algeria the real wielders of power, the monarchy and the senior military leadership, were by definition unelected and thus outside the scope of any, even theoretical, electoral control.

In the decades following independence, all three political regimes had passed through periods where it had looked as if they might experience some fundamental mutation. In the early 1970s the Moroccan monarchy had narrowly survived extinction through two attempted military coups; and in the late 1980s and early 1990s Tunisia and Algeria opened up their political systems to what appeared to be more genuine competition for power before successfully closing down these openings in the years that followed. In the late 1990s Morocco appeared to be making at least a step in the same direction through the appointment of the *alternance* government led by the long-time opposition USFP party; but this, too, proved to mark no real shift in political power as the monarchy slowly reasserted itself in the 2000s. More profound openings had occurred in Algeria and Morocco, and as political power became centralised once more in the two states there were suggestions that the model they might be seeking to emulate was that of Tunisia. The Ben Ali regime appeared to have succeeded in creating a highly stable political environment accompanied by modernisation and economic prosperity. Any domestic criticism and opposition had been suppressed and marginalised, largely through co-option and state largesse and, in a minority of cases, by force. International approval had been bought through the holding of political processes that mimicked, at least in form, those of liberal democracy and, more crucially, through the argument that the alternative to the existing regime was liable to be a radical and fundamentalist religious one.

The startlingly swift collapse of the Ben Ali regime in the opening weeks of 2011 thus overturned many of the assumptions and much of the received wisdom about the existing and future paths of the regimes and their political systems in the Maghreb. The continuity and resilience of the political structures in the region had come to be seen as perhaps their fundamental characteristic. Indeed, an exploration of the reasons for this had been the original intention of this book. That the forces and dynamics behind Ben Ali's fall were not particular to Tunisia was amply demonstrated by the swiftness with which similar movements of popular protest spread throughout the rest of the Arab world, barely sparing a single country.

Algeria and Morocco felt the impact of these changes, but notably much less so than many countries in the Arab Mashreq. There were clear potential reasons as to why Algeria and Morocco had not experienced the same levels of upheaval witnessed by Egypt, Libya, Yemen, Bahrain and Syria in the months that followed the collapse of the regime in Tunis. Painful memories of the violent turmoil of the 1990s provided the main disincentive for ordinary citizens to come onto the streets of Algeria, together with an ongoing experience of extensive locally based socio-economic unrest that relieved tensions at these levels, and the absence of more personalised and individual political leadership against which popular anger could be focused. In Morocco, similarly recent popular memories of political reform in the 1990s, a generally more liberal political atmosphere and a relatively new head of state, King Mohamed VI, served to dilute popular rage against the regime. As one of the leaders of the 20 February protest movement that emerged in Morocco ruefully remarked, 'If Morocco had been a little less liberal and we had had a Ben Ali in power, we would be achieving much more.'[1] Yet despite the persuasive quality of these explanations as to why the regimes in Algiers and Rabat had not come under serious threat in the early months of what became known as the 'Arab Spring,' they contained strong echoes of the reasons given by observers of the regimes in Cairo, Tripoli, Manama and Damascus in the days following Ben Ali's fall for why Tunisia's revolutionary spirit was highly unlikely to spread to Egypt, Libya, Bahrain or Syria. It therefore remains highly possible that Algeria and Morocco might eventually suffer the sort of upheaval that their smaller Maghrebi neighbour spearheaded. Political stasis, corruption, a lack of democracy, high graduate unemployment and growing gaps between regions and the rich and poor were the major components of the undoing of the Ben Ali regime, and all are also present in Algeria and Morocco. Whilst less abusive rule, recent experiences of political change and modest attempts at constitutional reform may have bought both regimes time, failure to address these problems fully in the longer term is likely to put significant popular and perhaps international pressure on them to change in more fundamental ways.

If fundamental political change remains only a distinct possibility in Algeria and Morocco, it remains a strong probability in Tunisia as of the end of 2011. Developments since the departure of Ben Ali on 14 January most closely resemble a genuine and successful revolution, as the country held a successful election of a constituent assembly in October 2011 to write a new constitution and put in place a new political system and order. It is possible that the structures of political power established by Habib Bourguiba and maintained by Zine al-Abdine Ben Ali may in time reassert themselves in Tunisia, and that the dramatic events of January 2011 will come to be seen, like the *changement* that Ben Ali heralded when he replaced Bourguiba in November 1987, as a temporary and aberrant interruption to a broader and more profound political pattern of control and centralisation of power. Tunisia is not alone in having already seen an apparently fresh reforming president metamorphose with time into a dictatorial and autocratic figure. Sub-Saharan Africa, in particular, is replete with such experiences. One can readily see a new, even democratically elected, president drift into authoritarian excess through the excuse of threats to national unity or prosperity or, like Bourguiba, through a sincere if mistaken belief that only he or she truly understand the real interests of the country. The balance of probability, however, is that substantial political change will come about as an enduring product of the January revolution. Whilst this change is unlikely to meet all the demands of those mainly younger Tunisians who were at the forefront of the protests against Ben Ali and is likely to fall short, certainly in the short term, of many of the proclaimed characteristics of Western liberal democracy, a full return to the political configurations of the country's two post-independence presidents is highly improbable. The truly popular—in both senses—nature of the revolution has given a sense of ownership and involvement to the ordinary population that will push it to avoid being fully marginalised again from political life as it was during the previous fifty years. It is this popular mobilisation, particularly of the youth, that could be the most important legacy of the Tunisian revolution, and its continued engagement will be the test of the long-term success of the revolution and indeed the longevity of the post-revolutionary political system that is put in place. If Tunisia's revolution does succeed in this way, it is likely to have an enduring impact on both the Maghreb and the wider Arab region. Its achievements are likely to become a benchmark, example and possible model for all the surrounding states and societies. A democratic Tunisia is liable to become a deeply subversive presence amongst those authoritarian regimes that manage to survive the popular upheavals of the Arab Spring.

CONCLUSION

As the Maghreb enters the second decade of the twenty-first century it therefore confronts more challenges to the remarkable continuity of its politics than at any other time since the end of European colonial rule in the 1950s and 1960s. It is hoped that this book has provided a useful and accurate portrayal and analysis of these first fifty years of the political life of post-colonial Algeria, Tunisia and Morocco. It is more fervently hoped that any future account of the next fifty years of political life in the region will show a more economically prosperous and politically pluralistic one than this study has been able to show.

NOTES

NOTE ON TRANSLITERATION

1. C. R. Pennell, *Morocco since 1830: A History* (London: Hurst & Co., 2000), xxxiii.

INTRODUCTION

1. See Andrea Liverani, *Civil Society in Algeria: The Political Functions of Associational Life* (London: Routledge, 2008); James Sater, *Civil Society and Political Change in Morocco* (London: Routledge, 2007).

1. THE IMPRINT OF HISTORY

1. Abdallah Laroui, *L'Histoire du Maghreb: Un Essai de Synthèse* (Casablanca: Centre Culturel Arabe, 1995), 15.
2. John Ruedy, 'Historical Influences on Intra-Regional Relations in the Maghrib,' in Halim Barakat (ed.), *Contemporary North Africa: Issues of Development and Integration* (London: Croom Helm, 1985), 89.
3. Ruedy, 'Historical Influences,' 89–92.
4. Wilfrid J. Rollman, 'Introduction,' in Michel Le Gall and Kenneth Perkins (eds), *The Maghrib in Question: Essays in History and Historiography* (Austin: University of Texas Press, 1997), xviii.
5. Ruedy, 'Historical Influences,' 89.
6. John Waterbury, *The Commander of the Faithful: The Moroccan Elite: A Study in Segmented Politics* (London: Weidenfeld and Nicolson, 1970); Mahmoud Benoune, 'Socio-Historical Foundations of the Contemporary Algerian State,' in Ali El-Kenz (ed.), *Algeria: The Challenge of Modernity* (London: CODESRIA, 1991), 50. Mohamed Hachmaoui has noted that tribal affiliation has also retained a degree of political significance in the post-independence period in parts of Algeria; and Hugh Roberts has argued

that traditional forms of organisation from rural Kabylia can be seen in the structures of the revolutionary FLN in the struggle for Algerian independence. Mohamed Hachemaoui, 'Tribalism without Tribes,' Paper presented at the Middle East Studies Association (MESA) Conference, Boston, November 2009; Hugh Roberts, 'The Confiscated Historiography of the Algerian War,' Paper presented at the MESA Conference, Washington DC, November 2008.

7. Jamil Abun-Nasr, *A History of the Maghrib in the Islamic Period* (Cambridge: Cambridge University Press, 1987), 15; Michael Brett, 'Regionalism in the History of North Africa,' Paper presented at 'The Various Interpretations of Integration: Devolution, Decentralisation, Self-determination, Autonomy, Regionalisation, Union, Autonomous Regions, Landers Federation and others' Conference, Rabat, 1–2 April 2011, 1.
8. Laroui, *L'Histoire du Maghreb*, 15
9. For a discussion of Libya's Maghrebi identity see L. Carl Brown, 'Maghrib Historiography: The Unit of Analysis Problem,' in Le Gall and Perkins, *The Maghrib in Question*, 8.
10. The emergence of the Almohads in the mountains of the High Atlas was due to their belief that the Almoravids had themselves fallen into corrupt and un-Islamic ways.
11. Michel Le Gall, 'The Historical Context,' in I. William Zartman and William Mark Habeeb (eds), *Polity and Society in Contemporary North Africa* (Boulder: Westview, 1993), 6.
12. Abun-Nasr, *History of the Maghrib*, 21.
13. Susan E. Waltz, *Human Rights and Reform: Changing the Face of North African Politics* (London: University of California Press, 1995), 52.
14. Ruedy, 'Historical Influences,' 93–4.
15. Le Gall, 'Historical Context,' 9.
16. John Ruedy, *Modern Algeria: The Origins and Development of a Nation* (Bloomington: Indiana University Press, 1992), 1.
17. Le Gall, 'Historical Context,' 7–8.
18. Abun-Nasr, *History of the Maghrib*, 208.
19. Waterbury, *Commander of the Faithful*, 15.
20. Waltz, *Human Rights*, 76.
21. Le Gall, 'Historical Context,' 7. Le Gall also notes that this intermediary role was also shared by the urban religious scholars (*ulema*), thus emphasising the political role of religion in both the urban and rural worlds. Moreover, the influence of sufism was certainly not confined to the rural milieu: *sheikhs* and *tariqa* being active and important in most towns and cities across the Maghreb.
22. Le Gall, 'Historical Context,' 3.
23. These two exceptions were the cities of Sebta/Ceuta and Melilla/Millilia on the coast of Morocco, of which the Portuguese and Spaniards respectively took control during the fifteenth century and which have remained under Spanish control until the modern day.

24. In 1881 Britain allowed France to assert their dominance in Tunisia in return for French recognition of similar rights for Britain vis-à-vis Cyprus. Similarly, German objections to the recognition of the primacy of French interests in Morocco were removed by allowing Germany a free hand in Cameroon.
25. In April 1827 the Dey of Algiers had allegedly struck the French consul to the regency in the face with a fly whisk. The fact that it was not until 1830 that France sent troops into Algeria itself is indicative of the rather fabricated nature of the response that in reality had more to do with French domestic politics (notably the need for a distracting colonial adventure at a time of domestic crisis) than with any genuine feeling of diplomatic injury.
26. Ruedy, *Modern Algeria*, 69.
27. Le Gall, 'Historical Context,' 8.
28. Ruedy, *Modern Algeria*, 92–3.
29. Lisa Anderson, *The State and Social Transformation in Tunisia and Libya, 1830–1980* (Princeton, 1986), 69, cited in Robert J. King, 'The Political Logic of Economic Reform in Tunisia,' in Azzedine Layachi (ed.), *Economic Crisis and Political Change in North Africa* (Westport: Praeger, 1998), 118.
30. Quoted in Anderson, *The State and Social Transformation in Tunisia and Libya*, 87.
31. Clement Henry Moore, *Tunisia Since Independence: The Dynamics of One-Party Government* (Westport: Greenwood Press, 1965), 15.
32. Henry Moore, *Tunisia*, 22–3.
33. Ruedy, *Historical Influences*, 98.
34. Mohamed Kenbib, 'Structural Transformations of the Moroccan State Apparatus Under Pressure from Foreign Penetration,' in Abdelali Doumou, *The Moroccan State in Historical Perspective (1850–1985)* (Dakar: CODESRIA, 1990).
35. Richard Pennell, *Morocco Since 1830: A History* (London: Hurst & Co., 2000), 160.
36. Waterbury, *Commander of the Faithful*, 34.
37. Benjamin Stora and Akram Ellyas, *Les 100 Portes du Maghreb: L'Algérie, Le Maroc, La Tunisie, Trois voies singulières pour allier Islam et modernité* (Paris: Les Editions de l'Atelier, 1999), 121.
38. Henry Moore, *Tunisia*, 27.
39. Waterbury, *Commander of the Faithful*, 34–5.
40. The *salafiyya* movement should not be confused with the movement of the same name (usually referred to as 'salafist') that came to the fore in the latter part of the twentieth century and which endorsed a far more literalist, puritanical, and at times violent, religious agenda.
41. Le Gall, 'Historical Context,' 13.
42. Ruedy, 'Historical Influences,' 99; Ruedy, *Modern Algeria*, 155.

43. Ruedy, 'Historical Influences,' 99.
44. Abun-Nasr, *History of the Maghrib*, 324–5.
45. Kenneth J. Perkins, *Tunisia: Crossroads of the Islamic and European Worlds* (Boulder: Westview, London: Croom Helm, 1986), 95
46. Stora and Ellyas, *Les 100 Portes du Maghreb*, 239.
47. Abdelali Doumou, 'The State and Legitimation in Post-Colonial Morocco,' in Boumou (ed.), *The Moroccan State in Historical Perspective*, 65.
48. Waterbury, *Commander of the Faithful*, 58.
49. Le Gall, 'Historical Context,' 3.

2. POST-INDEPENDENCE STATE-BUILDING

1. Ben Youssef fled first to Tripoli in Libya and then to Cairo, where he continued to try to organise resistance to Bourguiba. Following the failure of an attempt by the regime at reconciliation, in Switzerland in March 1961, Ben Youssef was found murdered in a hotel room in Frankfurt the following August—almost certainly on the orders of Bourguiba. Derek Hopwood, *Habib Bourguiba of Tunisia: The Tragedy of Longevity* (Basingstoke: Macmillan, 1992), 87.
2. Sophie Bessis and Souhayr Belhassen, *Bourguiba. Tome I: A la conquête d'un destin 1901–1957* (Paris: Jeune Afrique Livres, 1988), 170–71.
3. According to Clement Henry Moore, Bourguiba succeeded in getting the *bey* to sign the decree regarding the creation of the Constituent Assembly by threatening to reveal how the *bey* had sought to dissuade the French from assisting Bourguiba against Ben Youssef. Henry Moore, *Tunisia Since Independence*, 72.
4. Bessis and Belhassen, *Bourguiba I*, 174.
5. Perkins, *Tunisia*, 149.
6. Bessis and Belhassen, *Bourguiba I*, 174.
7. I. William Zartman, 'King Hassan's New Morocco,' in Zartman (ed.), *The Political Economy of Morocco* (New York: Praeger, 1987), 3.
8. Waterbury, *Commander of the Faithful*, 147.
9. Waterbury, *Commander of the Faithful*, 175.
10. Only 10 of the 76 members of the National Consultative Assembly appointed in August 1956 were members of the Istiqlal party.
11. Rkia El-Mossadeq, 'Political Parties and Power Sharing,' in I. William Zartman (ed.), *The Political Economy of Morocco* (New York: Praeger, 1987), 62–4.
12. Waterbury, *Commander of the Faithful*, 235.
13. El-Mossadeq, 'Political Parties,' 62.
14. Waterbury, *Commander of the Faithful*, 195.
15. Hugh Roberts, 'The FLN: French Conceptions, Algerian Realities,' in George Joffé (ed.), *North Africa: Nation, State and Region* (London: Routledge, 1993), 130–31.

16. Hugh Roberts has observed that the factionalism of the leadership of the FLN had been exacerbated by the nature of the eight-year liberation struggle with the operational division of the military campaign into *wilayas*, zones, regions and sectors reinforcing 'the long-standing cultural and also political differences resulting from the low level of national integration and the regionally differentiated impact of French colonialism on Algerian society.' Hugh Roberts, 'The Politics of Algerian Socialism,' in R. I. Lawless and A. M. Findlay (eds), *North Africa* (London: Croom Helm, 1984), 7.
17. William B. Quandt, *Revolution and Political Leadership: Algeria, 1954–1968*(Cambridge and London: MIT Press, 1969), 167.
18. David and Marina Ottaway, *Algeria: The Politics of a Socialist Revolution* (Berkeley and Los Angeles: University of California Press, 1970), 179.
19. Hopwood, *Bourguiba*, 80.
20. Henry Moore, *Tunisia Since Independence*, 62.
21. Bessis and Belhassen, *Bourguiba I*, 158,
22. Anderson, *The State and Social Transformation in Tunisia and Libya*, 233; Henry Moore, *Tunisia Since Independence*, 68n.
23. Quandt, *Revolution and Political Leadership*, 172.
24. Ruedy, *Modern Algeria*, 197.
25. Ruedy, *Modern Algeria*, 197.
26. Ottaway and Ottaway, *Politics of a Socialist Revolution*, 8.
27. Sophie Bessis and Souhayr Belhassen, *Bourguiba. Tome 2: Un si long règne 1957–1989* (Paris: Jeune Afrique Livres, 1989), 17.
28. Henry Moore, *Tunisia Since Independence*, 81–2.
29. Henry Moore, *Tunisia Since Independence*, 103.
30. Mohsen Toumi, *La Tunisie de Bourguiba à Ben Ali* (Paris: Presses Universitaires de France, 1989), 32.
31. Ibid., 32.
32. Mustapha Kraiem, *Etat et société dans la Tunisie Bourguibienne* (Tunis: MIP, 2011), 80.
33. For a description of this see Hopwood, *Bourguiba*, 89–92.
34. Waterbury, *Commander of the Faithful*, 149. Interestingly, one of those UNFP leaders arrested in 1963 was Abderrahmane Youssoufi, whom 35 years later in 1998 Hassan would appoint as his prime minister.
35. Pennell, *Morocco Since 1830*, 321.
36. Waterbury, *Commander of the Faithful*, 155; Emad Eldin Shahin, *Political Ascent: Contemporary Islamic Movements in North Africa* (Boulder: Westview, 1997), 48–9.
37. Ahmed Rouadjia, *Grandeur et Decadence de L'État Algérien* (Paris: Karthala, 1994), 131.
38. This aspect of Ben Bella's brief rule was heavily and specifically criticised in the formal communiqué issued by the Council of the Revolution in the wake of the coup. It stated that no one man could 'claim to incarnate alone Algeria': *Le Peuple*, 20 June 1965, quoted in Ottaway and Ottaway, *Politics of a Socialist Revolution*, 187.

39. Ottaway and Ottaway, *Politics of a Socialist Revolution*, 177.
40. Ibid., 192.
41. For a fuller account of the marginalisation of the Oujda Clan see Hugh Roberts, 'Politics of Algerian Socialism,' 17–23.
42. Entelis, *Revolution Institutionalized*, 60.
43. John P. Entelis, *Comparative Politics of North Africa: Algeria, Morocco, and Tunisia* (New York: Syracuse University Press, 1980), 168.
44. Henry Moore, *Tunisia Since Independence*, 95–6.
45. Perkins, *Tunisia*, 150.
46. For the numerous instances of this policy of removal and reintegration see Henry Moore, *Tunisia Since Independence*, 89–93.
47. Waltz, *Human Rights*, 60 and 63.
48. Henry Moore, *Tunisia Since Independence*, 94.
49. Kraiem, *Etat et société dans la Tunisie Bourguibienne*, 67.
50. Waterbury, *Commander of the Faithful*, 269–70 and 146.
51. Ibid., 146 and 148.
52. For example, King Hassan's sister was married to Ahmed Osman, who was prime minister 1972–81. His daughter was married to the son of Abdellatif Filali, who was prime minister 1993–7.
53. Rémy Leveau, *Le Fellah Marocain: Défenseur du Trône* (Paris: Presses de la Fondation des Sciences Politiques, 2ndedn 1985), 235.
54. Ottaway and Ottaway, *Politics of a Socialist Revolution*, 282 and 196.
55. Hugh Roberts has argued that the use of the term 'clan' in this context is misleading because of its associations with kinship, and that 'faction' is a much more useful and accurate way to describe intra-elite divisions. Hugh Roberts, *Demilitarizing Algeria*, *Carnegie Papers*, Middle East Program, no. 86, May 2007 (http://www.carnegieendowment.org/publications/index.cfm?fa=view&id=19153), 7 n.4.
56. Entelis, *Revolution Institutionalized*, 179.
57. Rouadjia, *Grandeur et Decadence*, 154.
58. Perkins, *Tunisia*, 147.
59. Henry Moore, *Tunisia Since Independence*, 99–100. Henry Moore believes that this was particularly the case when Bourguiba faced criticism of his perceived mishandling of the unsuccessful attempt to force the French to withdraw from the town of Bizerte in July 1961.
60. Lars Rudebeck, *Party and People: A Study of Political Change in Tunisia* (Stockholm: Almqvist & Miksell, 1967), quoted in Michel Camau and Vincent Geisser, *Le syndrome autoritaire: Politique en Tunisie de Bourguiba à Ben Ali* (Paris: Presses de Sciences Po, 2003), 160.
61. Kraiem, *Etat et société dans la Tunisie Bourguibienne*, 92.
62. Henry Moore, *Tunisia Since Independence*, 81 and 71.
63. Kraiem, *Etat et société dans la Tunisie Bourguibienne*, 63.
64. Benjamin Stora, *Histoire de l'Algérie depuis l'indépendance* (Paris: La Découverte, 1994), 30.

NOTES pp [66–78]

65. Ruedy, *Modern Algeria*, 200.
66. Ottaway and Ottaway, *Politics of a Socialist Revolution*, 4.
67. Stora, *Histoire de l'Algérie*, 33.
68. Charles-Robert Ageron, *Modern Algeria: A History from 1830 to the Present* (London: Hurst & Co., 1991), 132.
69. Entelis, *Revolution Institutionalized*, 160.
70. Waterbury, *Commander of the Faithful*, 157.
71. El-Mossadeq, 'Political Parties,' 67.
72. Abun-Nasr, *History of the Maghrib*, 410.
73. Ibid., 410.
74. Henry Moore, *Tunisia Since Independence*, 69.
75. Perkins, *Tunisia*, 149–50.
76. Quoted in Noura Borsali, *Bourguiba à l'épreuve de la démocratie 1956–1963* (Sfax: SAMED Editions, 2008), 132.
77. Ottaway and Ottaway, *Politics of a Socialist Revolution*, 27. The one exception to this was the intervention of some ordinary Algerians when fighting broke out between the two rival camps in September 1962, supposedly shouting '*Sabaa Snin Baraka*!' (Seven years, enough.) Benjamin Stora, *Algeria 1830–2000: A Short History* (Ithaca: Cornell University Press, 2001), 127.
78. Roberts, 'Politics of Algerian Socialism,' 11.
79. Ruedy, *Modern Algeria*, 209.
80. Jean Leca and Jean-Claude Vatin, *L'Algérie: Politique, Institutions et Régime* (Paris: Presses de la Fondation Nationale des Sciences Politiques, 1975), 464.
81. Entelis, *Revolution Institutionalized*, 61.
82. For an analysis of the rural revolts see David M. Hart, *Tribe and Society in Rural Morocco* (London: Frank Cass, 2001), Chapter 7.
83. Waterbury, *Commander of the Faithful*, 148.
84. For more details see Laurie A. Brand, *Women, the State and Political Liberalization: Middle Eastern and North African Experiences* (New York: Columbia University Press, 1998), 207–11.
85. *Agence France-Presse* despatch, 1 April 1962, quoted in Raymond Vallin, 'Muslim Socialism in Algeria,' in I. William Zartman (ed.), *Man, State and Society in the Contemporary Maghrib* (London: Pall Mall Press, 1973), 50.
86. Self-management was essentially the idea that workers should manage factories and farms themselves without reference to managers or owners.
87. Ageron, *Modern Algeria*, 140.
88. Abun-Nasr, *History of the Maghrib*, 427.
89. Ruedy, *Modern Algeria*, 208.
90. Leveau, *Fellah Marocain*, 236–8.
91. Waterbury, *Commander of the Faithful*, 155.

3. THE MILITARY

1. Mohamed Harbi, *Le FLN Mirage et Réalité: des origines à la prise de pouvoir (1945–1962)* (Paris: Jeune Afrique, 1980), 372.
2. Rémy Leveau, *Le Sabre et le Turban: L'Avenir du Maghreb* (Paris: François Bourrin, 1993), 207.
3. J. J. Regnier and J. C. Santucci, 'Armée, Pouvoir et Légitimité' in M. Teitler, A. Nousch et al. (eds), *Elites, Pouvoir et Légitimité au Maghreb* (Paris: CNRS, 1973), 168.
4. Pennell, *Morocco Since 1830*, 300–301.
5. Regnier and Santucci, 'Armée, Pouvoir et Légitimité,' 171–2.
6. Leveau, *Le Sabre et le Turban*, 208.
7. John Waterbury, 'The Coup Manqué,' in Ernest Gellner and Charles Micaud (eds), *Arabs and Berbers: From Tribe to Nation in North Africa* (London: Duckworth, 1973), 398.
8. John P. Entelis, *Culture and Counter-Culture in Moroccan Politics* (Maryland: University Press of America, 1996), 94.
9. The crown prince played a leading role in the crushing of the rebellions that occurred in the Rif in 1957–8 (see Chapter 2), as he also did in 1958 in the liberation of Tarfaya in the south of the country which the Spanish had not relinquished in 1956.
10. Waterbury, 'The Coup Manqué,' 398.
11. Abdellah Hammoudi, *Master and Disciple: The Cultural Foundations of Moroccan Authoritarianism* (Chicago: University of Chicago Press, 1997), 27.
12. Leveau, *Le Sabre et le Turban*, 214.
13. Quoted in Abdelhak El Merini, *L'Armée Marocaine à Travers l'Histoire* (Rabat: Editions-Diffusion, 2000), 381.
14. Omar Bendourou, *Le Régime Politique Marocain* (Rabat: Dar Al Qalam, 2000), 130–33.
15. Abun-Nasr, *History of the Maghrib*, 418.
16. Borsali, *Bourguiba*, 87–8.
17. Russell A. Stone, 'Tunisia: A Single Party System Holds Change in Abeyance,' in I. W. Zartman (ed.), *Political Elites in Arab North Africa* (New York: Longman, 1982), 150.
18. Quoted in *Jeune Afrique* (Paris), 13 July 1999.
19. Leveau also believes that the association of Tunisia's military tradition with the former *bey* and the Ottomans also influenced Bourguiba's desire not to emphasise it. Leveau, *Le Sabre et le Turban*, 208.
20. For a full account and discussion of the 1962 plot see Borsali, *Bourguiba*, 145–215. Borsali argues that the plotters were variously motivated by Arab nationalism, Youssefism, unhappiness with Bourguiba's handling of the Bizerte crisis and the general economic situation in Tunisia.
21. Seven military personnel were amongst the thirteen individuals condemned to death in January 1963 for involvement in the December 1962 plot.

22. Rachid Sfar, director of the Tunisian Ministry of Defence 1980–82, to author, Tunis, 17 April 2009.
23. Nicole Grimaud, *La Tunisie: A la Recherche de sa Sécurité* (Paris: PUF, 1995), 94–6.
24. Ottaway and Ottaway, *Politics of a Socialist Revolution*, 198.
25. Quandt, *Revolution and Political Leadership*, 111.
26. I. William Zartman, 'The Algerian Army in Politics,' in Zartman (ed.), *Man, State and Society in the Contemporary Maghrib* (London: Pall Mall Press, 1973), 215–16.
27. Ruedy, *Modern Algeria*, 207; Quandt, *Revolution and Political Leadership*, 241.
28. Hugh Roberts, 'The Struggle for Constitutional Rule in Algeria,' in *Journal of Algerian Studies*, vol. 3 (1998), 24.
29. Leca and Vatin, *L'Algérie politique*, 386; Stora, *Histoire de l'Algérie*, 56–8.
30. National Charter (1976), 100, quoted in Jean-Jacques Lavenue, *Algérie: La Démocratie Interdite* (Paris: L'Harmattan, 1993), 135.
31. UNFP leader Mehdi Ben Barka to *Al-Ahram* newspaper, quoted in Regnier and Santucci, 'Armée, Pouvoir et Légitimité,' 174.
32. For the most comprehensive accounts of the Skhirat coup see Stephen O. Hughes, *Morocco Under King Hassan* (Reading: Ithaca Press, 2001), 159–66; and Waterbury, 'The Coup Manqué.'
33. Waterbury, 'The Coup Manqué,' 402–9. It was also suggested that Medbouh and the other senior FAR officers behind the coup attempt had perhaps acted to forestall a potential coup from more junior and more radical elements within the military, which might seek to eliminate the senior army commanders.
34. Hughes, *Morocco Under King Hassan*, 161.
35. The mystery as to why several F5 jet fighters were unable to shoot down an unarmed airliner is apparently explained by one of the coup plotters, Ahmed Rami, living in exile. In an interview with a Moroccan newspaper he claimed that the jets had been equipped with training rockets by ground staff unaware of the plot. *La Gazette du Maroc* (Casablanca), 19 January 2000.
36. Others connected with the plot, both captured after the coup and also in exile, confirm this. King Hassan himself subsequently asserted that only the defence minister would have the authority to allow the F5 jets to take off. Hassan II, *La Mémoire d'un Roi: Entretiens avec Eric Laurent* (Paris: Librairie Plon, 1993), 168.
37. Stephen Smith, *Oufkir: Un Destin Marocain* (Paris: Calmann-Lévy, 1999), 301–3, 327.
38. Hughes, *Morocco Under King Hassan*, 182.
39. See Hughes, *Morocco Under King Hassan*, 177–8; Interview with Ahmed Rami, *La Gazette du Maroc*, 19 January 2000; *Le Journal* (Casablanca), 25 November 2000.

40. Zartman, 'King Hassan's New Morocco,' 23–4.
41. Quoted in *Tel Quel*, 31 October 2009. Mahjoub Tobji, *Les Officiers de sa Majesté: Les Dérives des Généraux Marocains 1956–2006* (Paris: Fayard, 2006), 9.
42. Fernanda Faria, *Politiques de Sécurité au Maghreb: Les Impératifs de la Stabilité Intérieure* (Lisbon: Cahiers du Lumiar 1, Instituto de Estudos Estuatégicos Internacionais, 1994), 27.
43. Zartman, 'King Hassan's New Morocco,' 23.
44. Alain Claisse, 'Makhzen Traditions and Administrative Channels,' in I. William Zartman (ed.), *The Political Economy of Morocco* (New York: Praeger, 1987), 49.
45. Entelis, *Culture and Counter-Culture*, 95.
46. Two opposite and contending theories have Dlimi plotting a *coup d'état* either to prevent Hassan from making possible concessions in negotiations with Polisario's chief backer, Algeria, or alternatively to allow for concessions through the removal of Hassan, whose overly hard-line stance was prolonging the conflict. Hughes, *Morocco Under King Hassan*, 320–21; Belkassem Belouchi, *Portraits d'Hommes Politiques du Maroc* (Casablanca: Afrique Orient, 2002), 176–7.
47. Claisse, 'Makhzen Traditions,' 50.
48. Leveau, *Le Sabre et le Turban*, 237.
49. L. B. Ware, 'Ben Ali's Constitutional Coup in Tunisia,' in *Middle East Journal*, vol. 42, no. 4 (1988), 594.
50. Stone, 'Tunisia,' 150–51.
51. Leveau, *Le Sabre et le Turban*, 229–30.
52. L. B. Ware, 'The Role of the Tunisian Military in the Post-Bourguiba Era,' *Middle East Journal*, vol. 39, no. 1 (1985), 41n.
53. Camau and Geisser, *Le Syndrome Autoritaire*, 164.
54. Despite promoting Ben Ali, Bourguiba appears to have remained aware of the former's background and its limitations. It is reported that, when frustrated by Ben Ali, Bourguiba would declare, 'You understand nothing, you are only a man of the barracks.' Nicolas Beau and Jean-Pierre Tuquoi, *Notre Ami Ben Ali: L'Envers du 'Miracle Tunisien'* (Paris: La Découverte, 1999), 96.
55. Leveau, *Le Sabre et le Turban*, 229.
56. Toumi, *Tunisie de Bourguiba à Ben Ali*, 214.
57. Only one senior military figure apparently opposed the removal of Bourguiba: the chief of staff of the air force and a nephew of the ousted president. He was subsequently arrested. Beau and Tuquoi, *Notre Ami Ben Ali*, 44.
58. Leveau, *Le Sabre et le Turban*, 221.
59. Entelis, *Revolution Institutionalized*, 208–9.
60. Hugh Roberts, 'The Zeroual Memorandum: The Algerian State and the Problem of Liberal Reform,' in *Journal of Algerian Studies*, vol. 1 (1996), 7.

61. Ruedy, *Modern Algeria*, 197.
62. George Joffé, 'The Army in Algerian Politics and Government,' in Reza Shah-Kazemi (ed.), *Algeria: Revolution Revisited* (London: Islamic World Report, 1997), 105.
63. Peter R. Knauss, 'Algeria Under Boumedienne: The Mythical Revolution 1965 to 1978,' in Issac James Mowoe (ed.), *The Performance of Soldiers as Governors: African Politics and the African Military* (Columbus: University Press of America, 1980), 52; Abdelkader Yefsah, 'Armée et Politique depuis les Evénements d'Octobre 88: l'Armée Sans Hidjab,' in *Les Temps Modernes* (Janvier-Fevrier 1995, no. 580), 159n.
64. Hugh Roberts, 'Demilitarizing Algeria,' 9. Rémy Leveau, however, interprets the reinstatement of the General Staff as an attempt to weaken the regional commanders by removing them from their regional fiefdoms and placing them in the General Staff in Algiers. Leveau, *Le Sabre et le Turban*, 232.
65. Jean-François Daguzan, *Le Dernier Rempart? Forces Armées et Politiques de Défense au Maghreb* (Paris: Publisud, 1998), 29.
66. Roberts, 'Zeroual Memorandum,' 8.
67. General Khaled Nezzar, minister of defence, in *L'Horizon* (Algiers), 13 September 1990, quoted in Yahia H. Zoubir, 'The Painful Transition from Authoritarianism in Algeria,' in *Arab Studies Quarterly*, vol. 15, no. 3 (Summer 1993), 98.
68. See Michael Willis, *The Islamist Challenge in Algeria: A Political History* (Reading, Ithaca University Press, 1996), 183–5.
69. Joffé, 'Army in Algerian Politics,' 106.
70. Willis, *Islamist Challenge in Algeria*, 186.
71. Pierre Dévoluy and Mireille Duteil, *La Poudrière Algérienne: Histoire Secrète d'une République sous Influence* (Paris: Calmann-Lévy, 1994), 41–50.
72. Toumi, *Tunisie de Bourguiba à Ben Ali*, 245.
73. Camau and Geisser, *Le Système Autoritaire*, 212.
74. Foreign journalists who referred to 'General Ben Ali' reportedly received telephoned complaints from local Tunisian diplomats. Beau and Tuquoi, *Notre Ami Ben Ali*, 31n.
75. Beau and Tuquoi, *Notre Ami Ben Ali*, 96.
76. Daguzan, *Le Dernier Rempart*, 74.
77. Camau and Geisser, *Le Syndrome Autoritaire*, 211. It is alleged that Islamist figures within the military had been plotting their coup against Bourguiba on 8 November 1987 and were purposely forestalled by Ben Ali's move the day before (see Chapter 5).
78. *Réalités* (Tunis), 14 March 2011.
79. Yefsah, 'Armée et Politique,' 154–5.
80. Roberts, 'Struggle for Constitutional Rule,' 24–5.
81. Abed Charef, *Algérie: Le Grand Dérapage* (Paris: L'Aube, 1994), 415.

82. There was also the theory that Boudiaf had provoked further suspicion amongst the generals because of his close association with neighbouring Morocco, where he had spent most of his long exile. Some in the Algerian military apparently feared that Boudiaf was planning to make concessions to Morocco, with whom Algeria had been in long-standing conflict over the issue of the Western Sahara (see Chapter 8). For a fuller discussion of the assassination of Mohamed Boudiaf see Lyes Laribi, *L'Algérie des Généraux* (Paris: Max Milo, 2007), 116–33; Hichem Aboud, *La Mafia des Généraux* (Paris: J. C. Lattès, 2002), 149–70.
83. Roberts, 'Struggle for Constitutional Rule,' 25.
84. See Habib Souadia, *La Sale Guerre: Le Témoignage d'un Ancien Officier des Forces Speciales de l'Armée Algérienne* (Paris: La Découverte, 2001), which is the testimony of a former special forces officer. Also Nesroulah Yous, *Qui a Tué à Bentalha?: Algérie: Chronique d'un Massacre Annoncé* (Paris: La Découverte, 2000), which is the testimony of one survivor of a massacre in September 1997.
85. Luis Martinez, *The Algerian Civil War 1992–1998* (London: Hurst & Co., 2000), 162–3.
86. As early as the late 1970s observers were able to conclude that the ANP had 'a virtual monopoly on the external market of the Algerian government' through a bureaucratic body called the *Direction Nationale Co-operative* (DNC), which oversaw the import trade and was able to procure products for individual senior officers. Knauss, 'Algeria Under Boumedienne,' 57–8.
87. Martinez, *The Algerian Civil War*, 164.
88. Aboud, *La Mafia des Généraux*, 36.
89. Leveau, *Le Sabre et le Turban*, 211.
90. It was even argued that the chaos and violence in Algeria during the 1990s was deliberately created and maintained according to the wishes of certain elements in the current French political and military establishment: notably individuals in parliament and the security services who were former *pieds noirs* settlers in Algeria forced to flee in 1962, for whom the destruction in Algeria was some vengeful recompense for their loss.
91. These include a former army officer, who has written a book on the subject (see Aboud, *La Mafia des Généraux*), and a former prime minister during Chadli Benjedid's presidency, Abdelhamid Brahimi, who witnessed the rise of figures such as Larbi Belkheir during this period. Author's interviews with Abdelhamid Brahimi, Algerian prime minister 1984–8, London, 19 December 1994 and 6 September 1995. In March 2000 Ali Kafi, the former interim president following the assassination of Boudiaf, spoke out publicly against the influence of the former French officers in the army. Hugh Roberts, 'Algeria's Army: Changing the Guard,' *Middle East International*, 24 March 2000.
92. Martinez, *The Algerian Civil War*, 67–8; 165.

93. Aboud, *La Mafia des Généraux*, 246.
94. Roberts, 'Demilitarizing Algeria,' 14–16.
95. Leveau, *Le Sabre et le Turban*, 229.
96. Pierre Vermeren, *Le Maroc de Mohamed VI; La Transition Inachevée* (Paris: La Découverte, 2009), 91–2.
97. *Tel Quel*(Casablanca), 2 May 2009.
98. This is the central argument of Tobji, *Les Officiers de sa Majesté*; see also *Le Monde Diplomatique*, August 2000, quoted in Ignace Dalle, *Les Trois Rois: La Monarchie Marocaine de l'Indépendance à Nos Jours* (Paris: Fayard, 2004), 716–21, 682; Vermeren, *Le Maroc de Mohamed VI*, 94.
99. Dalle, *Les Trois Rois*, 688–9.
100. *Le Monde* (Paris), 21 December 2000.
101. Interview with Driss Lachgar, *Le Journal*, 13 May 2006.
102. Faria suggests that large-scale demobilisation of the military would probably be significantly mitigated by troops being maintained in the Sahara to guard the border, with others being involved in civil infrastructure projects. Faria, *Politiques de Sécurité au Maghreb*, 27–8.
103. Tobji, *Les Officiers de sa Majesté*, 11; Dalle, *Les Trois Rois*, 682.
104. Zartman, 'King Hassan's New Morocco,' 24–5.
105. Jean-Pierre Tuquoi, *Le Dernier Roi: Crépuscule d'une Dynastie* (Paris: Bernard Grasset, 2001), 310–11; Dalle, *Les Trois Rois*, 684. According to one former military officer, the head of the gendarmerie, General Hosni Benslimane, had actually been the power behind Basri. Tobji, *Les Officiers de sa Majesté*, 272–3.
106. *Maroc Hebdo International* (Casablanca), 27 January 2006; *Tel Quel*, 13 December 2008.
107. Author's interviews with senior Islamist figures in Morocco.
108. Dalle, *Les Trois Rois*, 682. Mohamed VI is said to keep channels open to the lower ranks in the FAR to keep himself informed about the concerns and morale of the troops. Dalle, *Les Trois Rois*, 691.
109. *Le Journal*, 31 May 2008.
110. Ware, 'Ben Ali's Constitutional Coup,' 594.
111. *Le Monde*, 25 January 2011.
112. For more on *Sécurité Militaire* see Waltz, Human Rights, 92–3 and Leveau, *Le Sabre et le Turban*, 230–31.
113. Roberts, 'Demilitarizing Algeria,' 12.
114. Hocine Malti, *Histoire Secrète du Pétrole Algérien* (Paris: La Découverte, 2010), 11.
115. Zemri Benheddi, 'L'Armée, l'état et le pouvoir,' in Camille and Yves Lacoste (eds), *L'état du Maghreb* (Casablanca: Le Fennec, 1991), 341.
116. Robert Mortimer, 'State and Army in Algeria: The "Bouteflika Effect,"' *Journal of North African Studies*, 11, no. 2 (June 2006), 166.
117 *Le Figaro*(Paris), 24 January 2011.

4. POLITICAL PARTIES

1. Célina Braun, 'A quoi servent les partis Tunisiens? Sens et contre-sens d'une "liberalisation" politique,' *Revue des Mondes Musulmans et de la Méditerranée. Les partis politiques dans les pays Arabes. Tome 2: Le Maghreb*, 111–12 (Paris: Edisud, 2006), 21–3.
2. Emma Murphy, *Economic and Political Change in Tunisia: From Bourguiba to Ben Ali* (London: Macmillan, 1999), 51–2; Perkins, *Tunisia*, 148.
3. Camau and Geisser, *Le syndrome autoritaire*, 160.
4. Perkins, *Tunisia*, 147.
5. Roberts, 'The FLN: French Conceptions, Algerian Realities,' 130–31. Roberts also states that the *tamen* feature of the Kabyle *jama'a* is important to understanding the dynamics of the FLN, and indeed Algerian politics more generally, through the link it forged between constituent clans and the central *jama'a* as a means of ensuring consensus in decision-making.
6. Arun Kapil, 'Algeria,' in Frank Tachau (ed.), *Political Parties of the Middle East and North Africa* (London: Mansell, 1994), 16–17.
7. Roberts, 'Demilitarizing Algeria,' 5–6.
8. Kapil, 'Algeria,' 18.
9. Dalle, *Les Trois Rois*, 360–62.
10. Hughes, *Morocco Under King Hassan*, 130.
11. Tony Hodges, *Western Sahara: The Roots of a Desert War* (Westport: Lawrence Hill & Co., 1983), 180–81.
12. Clement Henry Moore, 'Political Parties,' in I. William Zartman and William Mark Habeeb (eds), *Polity and Society in Contemporary North Africa* (Boulder: Westview, 1993), 50.
13. These three parties were the *Mouvement des Démocrates Socialistes* (MDS), formed by liberal dissidents within the PSD; the Tunisian Communist Party (PCT), which had been allowed briefly to function legally in the aftermath of independence; and the Popular Unity Party (PUP), which was an offshoot of Ben Salah's Movement for Popular Unity (MUP) and which the regime allegedly hoped to use to undermine Ben Salah's movement. For details see Mary-Jane Deeb, 'Tunisia,' in Frank Tachau (ed.), *Political Parties of the Middle East and North Africa* (London: Mansell, 1994), 530–48.
14. Abdelhamid Brahimi, Chadli's prime minister 1984–8, argued that 'I know Chadli very well and he has nothing to do with democracy.' Author's interview, London, 6 September 1995.
15. Author's interview with Mustapha Ben Jaafar, member of the MDS 1978–92, Tunis, 26 May 2004.
16. Braun, 'A quoi servent les partis Tunisiens?,' 43 and 47.
17. For example Stephen J. King, 'Economic Reform and Tunisia's Hegemonic Party: The End of the Administrative Elite,' *Arab Studies Quarterly*, Vol. 20, 1998.

18. Camau and Geisser, *Le syndrome autoritaire*, 214–18; Murphy, *Economic and Political Change*, 212, 231–2.
19. Prospective candidates were legally required to have the formal endorsement of a minimum number of elected representatives. Given the miniscule representation of the opposition parties in parliament and local government, no candidate other than Ben Ali succeeded in meeting this requirement.
20. Henry Moore, *Tunisia Since Independence*, 71.
21. See *The Economist*, 23 October 1999; and Braun, 'A quoi servent les partis Tunisiens?,' 49.
22. Author's interview with Mohamed Mokhtar Jalali, UDU (Union for Democratic Unity) member of parliament 1999–2004, Tunis, 31 May 2004.
23. Author's interview with Nejib Chebbi, leader of the RSP 1980–2001, Tunis, 26 May 2004.
24. These included failing to approve lists of candidates on minor technical grounds and constantly changing rules on eligibility, especially for presidential elections, deliberately to exclude particular candidates.
25. Specifically, the party leader, Mohamed Moadda, had attacked the 'official' results of the local elections of 1995 which credited his party with less than 1per cent of the votes cast. *Financial Times*, 11 October 1995.
26. Willis, *Islamist Challenge in Algeria*, 129.
27. Willis, *Islamist Challenge in Algeria*, 128–30.
28. Interview with Abassi Madani, *Algérie Actualité* (Algiers), 23 February 1989. Abassi Madani had himself been one of the original FLN's earliest militants following its creation in 1954.
29. Lahouari Addi, 'Les partis politiques en Algérie,' *Revue des Mondes Musulmans et de la Méditerranée. Les partis politiques dans les pays Arabes. Tome 2: Le Maghreb*, 111–12 (Paris: Edisud, Paris, 2006), 143. Addi has also pointed out what he sees as clear similarities between the FIS's programme and the FLN's original National Charter. Addi, 'De la permanence du populisme Algérien,' *Peuples Méditerranéens*, nos.2–3 (juillet-septembre 1990), 42–3.
30. *Middle East International*, 24 January 1992.
31. Roberts, 'The FLN: French Conceptions, Algerian Realities,' 112; Roberts, 'Demilitarizing Algeria,' 3.
32. Hugh Roberts, 'Musical Chairs in Algeria,' *Middle East Report (MERIP)* Press Information Note 97, 4 June 2002.
33. Louisa Dris-Ait-Hamadouche and Yahia H. Zoubir, 'Pouvoir et opposition en Algérie: vers une transition prolongée,' *L'Année du Maghreb 2009* (Paris: CNRS Editions, 2009), 117–19.
34. Roberts, 'Musical Chairs in Algeria.'
35. Addi, 'Les partis politiques en Algérie,' 157–8.
36. Dris-Ait-Hamadouche and Zoubir, 'Pouvoir et opposition en Algérie,' 116.
37. The Platform was signed by representatives of the FLN, the FIS, the FFS,

the Islamist An-Nahda party, the leftist Workers' Party (*Parti des Travailleurs*, or PT) and the Movement for Democracy in Algeria (MDA) led by Ahmed Ben Bella. For the full text of the Platform see http://www.santegidio.org/archivio/pace/algeria_19950113_FR.htm
38. The MDA refused to drop references to Arab nationalism in its founding statutes.
39. Roberts, 'Demilitarizing Algeria,' 13.
40. The Kutla parties had made Basri's dismissal a condition of their entry into government following the 1993 parliamentary elections, and Hassan's refusal to agree to this had been the primary reason for their rejection of the palace's offer.
41. *Tel Quel*, 29 September 2007.
42. Mohamed Darif, *al-Islamiyyûn al-maghariba: hisâbât as-siyyâsa fi al-'amal al-islâmî* 1969–1999 (Casablanca, Al-Majalla al-maghribiyya li 'ilm al-ijtima' as-siyyâsî, 1999), 276.
43. Jean-Claude Santucci, 'Le Multipartisme Marocain entre les constraints d'un "pluralisme controlé" et les dilemmes d'un "pluripartisme autortaire,"' *Revue des Mondes Musulmans et de la Mediterranée. Les partis politiques dans les pays Arabes. Tome 2: Le Maghreb*, 111–112 (Paris: Edisud, 2006), 63.
44. Michael J. Willis, 'Political Parties in the Maghrib: The Illusion of Significance?' *Journal of North African Studies*, 7, no. 2 (Summer 2002), 3.
45. Willis, 'Political Parties in the Maghrib: The Illusion of Significance?,' 3–4.
46. Murphy, *Economic and Political Change*, 223–4 and 230.
47. Roberts, 'Demilitarizing Algeria,' 6.
48. See Willis, 'Political Parties in the Maghrib: The Illusion of Significance?' for full details and examples on each of these points.
49. Addi, 'Les partis politiques en Algérie,' 159; Andrea Liverani, *Civil Society in Algeria: The Political Functions of Associational Life* (London: Routledge, 2008), 97–8.
50. Mohamed Abdelhaq and Jean-Bernard Heumann, 'Opposition et elections en Tunisie,' *Maghreb-Machrek*, no. 168 (2000), 35, quoted in Braun, 'A quoi servent les partis Tunisiens?,' 51.
51. Willis, 'Political Parties in the Maghrib: The Illusion of Significance?,' 14–15.
52. Mohamed Hachemaoui, 'Algeria's May 17, 2007 parliamentary elections or the political representation crisis,' *Arab Reform Initiative*, Arab Reform Briefs, 17 July 2007 (http://arab-reform.net/spip.php?article924). Some opposition parties justified their participation in manifestly rigged elections by the government subsidy supplied to parties 'winning' seats in the parliament, which financed the operation of the party. Such was the case with the Ettajdid party in Tunisia. Author's interview with Abdeljaoued Jounaidi, deputy secretary general of the Ettajdid party, Tunis, 20 April 2011.

53. For a full exploration of this argument see Michael J. Willis, 'Political Parties in the Maghrib: Ideology and Identification. A Suggested Typology,' *Journal of North African Studies*, 7, no. 3 (Autumn 2002).
54. Hugh Roberts, 'Algeria: The Subterranean Logics of a Non-Election,' *Real Instituto Elcano*, ARI 68/2009, 22 April 2009 (http://www.realinstitutoelcano.org/wps/portal/rielcano_eng/Content?WCM_GLOBAL_CONTEXT=/elcano/elcano_in/zonas_in/ari68–2009), 7.
55. Author's interview with Nejib Chebbi, leader of the PDP 2001–6, Tunis, 16 April 2009.
56. Michael J. Willis, 'Islamism, Democratization and Disillusionment: Morocco's Legislative Elections of 2007,' Research Paper no. 1, Mohamed VI Fellowship in Moroccan and Mediterranean Studies, St Antony's College, Oxford (http://www.sant.ox.ac.uk/mec/morocco/Islamism-Democratisation-Disillusionment.pdf), 20.
57. Camau and Geisser, *Le syndrome autoritaire*, 249. According to one European diplomat, senior figures in the Tunisian opposition became 'untouchable' by the regime because of their profile abroad (Interview, Tunis, April 2009). Mustapha Ben Jaafar, leader of the FTDL, who tried unsuccessfully to run against Ben Ali in the 2009 presidential election, believes that he has avoided imprisonment largely by virtue of his external connections. Author's interview with Mustapha Ben Jaafar, leader of the FTDL, Tunis, 26 May 2004.
58. National Democratic Institute (NDI), *Final Report on the Moroccan Legislative Elections, September 7, 2007* (Washington: National Democratic Institute, 2007) (http://www.ndi.org/files/2316_ma_report_electionsfinal_en_051508_1.pdf).
59. Hachemaoui, 'Algeria's May 17, 2007 parliamentary elections'; Dris-Ait-Hamadouche and Zoubir, 'Pouvoir et opposition en Algérie,' 116.
60. Amel Boubekeur, 'Tunisia: Beyond illusions of change,' *open Democracy*, 23 October 2009 (http://www.opendemocracy.net/amel-boubekeur/tunisia-beyond-illusions-of-change)
61. *Aujourd'hui Le Maroc* (Casablanca), 21 August 2007; 'Ben Ali: We will sue those who sabotage elections,' *Middle East Online*, 25 October 2009 (http://www.middle-east-online.com/english/?id=35220).
62. Roberts, 'Algeria, The Subterranean Logics,' 5.
63. Ibid., 4–6.
64. Willis, 'Islamism, Democratization and Disillusionment,' 12–14.
65. Author's interview with Mustapha Ramid, head of the PJD group in the Chamber of Deputies, Casablanca, 2 April 2008.
66. Ferdinand Eibl, *The Moroccan Political Party System: the Case of the Party of Authenticity and Modernity (PAM)*, MPhil thesis, University of Oxford, 2010.
67. Liverani, *Civil Society in Algeria*, 129.
68. Camau and Geisser, *Le syndrome autoritaire*, 263–4.

69. Fouad Abdelmoumni, former vice-president of AMDH, to author; Rabat, 15 October 2009.
70. Willis, 'Islamism, Democratization and Disillusionment,' 11–14.
71. Dris-Ait-Hamadouche and Zoubir, 'Pouvoir et opposition en Algérie,' 115.
72. Addi, 'Les partis politiques en Algérie,' 141.
73. Dris-Ait-Hamadouche and Zoubir, 'Pouvoir et opposition en Algérie,' 122.
74 *La Vie Economique* (Casablanca), 28 March 2011.
75 *Réalités*, 5 April 2011.

5. ISLAMIST MOVEMENTS

1. Mohamed Tozy, 'Islam and the State,' in I. William Zartman and William Mark Habeeb (eds), *Polity and Society in Contemporary North Africa* (Boulder: Westview, 1993), 105.
2. Shahin, *Political Ascent*, 56.
3. Ibid., 67, 69.
4. Rachid Ghannouchi, quoted in *Arabia*, April 1985, quoted in Mohamed ElHachmi Hamdi, *The Politicization of Islam: A Case Study of Tunisia* (Boulder: Westview, 1998), 17.
5. Shahin, *Political Ascent*, 70–71, 64–7.
6. Elbaki Hermassi, 'The Islamicist Movement and November 7,' in I. William Zartman (ed.), *Tunisia: The Political Economy of Reform* (London: Lynne Rienner, 1991), 194. Into the early 1980s members of the movement were still swearing allegiance to the 'Tunisian branch of the Muslim Brotherhood.' Former member of the MTI to author, London, June 2009. Camau and Geisser argue, however, that the structures and organisation of the movement owed much more to those of the leftist movements they had encountered on the university campuses than the Muslim Brotherhood. Camau and Geisser, *Le syndrome autoritaire*, 284–5.
7. Shahin, *Political Ascent*, 74–80.
8. Willis, *Islamist Challenge in Algeria*, 38–48.
9. For a study of these independent mosques see Ahmed Rouadjia, *Les frères et la mosquée: Enquête sur le mouvement islamiste en Algérie* (Paris: Karthala, 1990).
10. Willis, *Islamist Challenge in Algeria*, 51–3, 56–61.
11. Shahin, *Political Ascent*, 181–4; Henry Munson, *Religion and Power in Morocco* (New Haven and London: Yale University Press, 1993), 160.
12. Shahin, *Political Ascent*, 186–7.
13. Mohamed Darif, *al-Islamiyyûn al-maghariba: hisâbât as-siyyâsa fi al-'amal al-islâmî 1969–1999* (Casablanca: Al-Majalla al-maghribiyya li 'ilm al-ijtima' as-siyyâsî, 1999), 281.
14. For a full discussion of the letter see Munson, *Religion and Power*, 163–71.
15. Azzam S. Tamimi, *Rachid Ghannouchi: A Democrat Within Islamism* (Oxford: Oxford University Press, 2001), 58–9,

16. François Burgat and William Dowell, *The Islamic Movement in North Africa* (Center for Middle Eastern Studies, University of Texas at Austin, 1993), 188.
17. Shahin, *Political Ascent*, 87–8.
18. Sadri Khiari, *Tunisie: Le Délitement de la Cité. Coercition, Consentement, Résistance* (Paris: Karthala, 2003), 38.
19. Murphy, *Economic and Political Change*, 73; Shahin, *Political Ascent*, 95. The MTI had called on its supporters to vote for candidates from the opposition MDS in the legislative elections of November 1981, an offer the MDS accepted. Khiari, *Tunisie: Le Délitement de la Cité*, 39.
20. Michael Collins Dunn, 'The An-Nahda Movement in Tunisia: From Renaissance to Revolution,' in John Ruedy (ed.), *Islamism and Secularism in North Africa* (London: Macmillan, 1994), 155.
21. Shahin, *Political Ascent*, 99.
22. Hermassi, 'The Islamicist Movement and November 7,' 196.
23. Dunn, 'An-Nahda Movement,' 155–6.
24. These changes included the broadcasting of the call to prayer on national radio, the reopening of the Zaytuna mosque university and the establishment of a Higher Islamic Council.
25. Abdelkader Zghal, 'The New Strategy of the Movement of the Islamic Way: Manipulation or Expression of Political Culture?,' in I. William Zartman (ed.), *Tunisia: The Political Economy of Reform* (London: Lynne Rienner, 1991), 208–10.
26. Hamdi, *Politicisation of Islam*, 67–8. Significantly, Ghannouchi subsequently expressed public doubt about the wisdom of his decision to challenge the regime so directly by contesting so many electoral districts, believing that he had allowed himself to be overly influenced by popular sentiment. Tamimi, *Rachid Ghannouchi*, 70–71.
27. Tamimi, *Rachid Ghannouchi*, 70.
28. Author's interview with Rachid Ghannouchi, London, 18 April 1995.
29. Burgat and Dowell, *Islamic Movement in North Africa*, 234.
30. Hamdi, *Politicisation of Islam*, 69; Burgat and Dowell, *Islamic Movement in North Africa*, 237. It was rumoured that Ben Ali had been minded to legalise An-Nahda in order to bring them into the legal arena, but had been persuaded by others in the regime that this would jeopardise Bourguiba's whole modernising project. Murphy, *Economic and Political Change*, 179.
31. *Le Maghreb*, 10 November 1989, quoted in Hamdi, *Politicisation of Islam*, 69.
32. Hamdi, *Politicisation of Islam*, 67.
33. Murphy, *Economic and Political Change*, 193–5.
34. Amnesty International figures quoted by Shahin, *Political Ascent*, 101.
35. Willis, *Islamist Challenge in Algeria*, 115–18.
36. *Algérie Actualité* (Algiers), 26 April 1990.

37. 'Taking Up Space in Tlemcen: The Islamist Occupation of Urban Algeria,' Interview with Rabia Bekkar in *Middle East Report*, November-December 1992.
38. Willis, *Islamist Challenge in Algeria*, 118–21, 124–30. Hugh Roberts, 'Doctrinaire Economics and Political Opportunism in the Strategy of Algerian Islamism,' in John Ruedy (ed.), *Islamism and Secularism in North Africa* (London: Macmillan 1994), 124–6.
39. For details of the results see Keith Sutton and Ahmed Aghrout, 'Multiparty Elections in Algeria: Problems and Prospects,' in *Bulletin of Francophone Africa*, 2, Autumn 1992, 76–7.
40. Official statement quoted in *L'Humanité* (Paris), 5 March 1992.
41. *The Guardian* (London), 18 January 1992.
42. *Algérie Actualité*, 9 January 1992.
43. Author's interview with Kameredine Kherbane, London, 28 June 1997.
44. Martinez, *The Algerian Civil War*, 106–11. R. Labévière, 'Les Réseaux Européens des Islamistes Algériens: Entre Déshérence et Reconversion,' *Les Cahiers de l'Orient: Algérie: Les Nouveaux Islamistes*, Deuxième Trimestre 2001, no. 62, 146.
45. Abdelbaki Hermassi, 'The Rise and Fall of the Islamist Movement in Tunisia,' in Laura Guazzone (ed.), *The Islamist Dilemma: The Political Role of Islamist Movements in the Contemporary Arab World* (Reading: Ithaca University Press, 1995), 105.
46. Some members of Islamic Jihad were minor former members of the MTI. Burgat and Dowell, *Islamic Movement in North Africa*, 205.
47. Shahin, *Political Ascent*, 98.
48. Hamdi, *Politicisation of Islam*, 57–63.
49. *Al-Sabah*, 19 March 1988, quoted in Hermassi, 'The Islamicist Movement and November 7,' 199. Hamdi, *Politicisation of Islam*, 65.
50. Dunn, 'An-Nahda Movement,' 156–61.
51. Ibid., 162. Amnesty International: 'Tunisia: Amnesty International Concerned About Convictions After Unfair Trial,' MDE 30/WU 04/92 External, 28 August 1992 (http://78.136.0.19/en/library/asset/NWS11/034/1992/en/3f9ff51f-ed8a-11dd-95f6-0b268ecef84f/nws110341992en.html).
52. Hermassi argues that An-Nahda adopted a much harder line following the departure of Ghannouchi abroad and his effective replacement as leader inside the country by Sadok Chorou: Hermassi, 'Rise and Fall,' 120.
53. Dunn, 'An-Nahda Movement,' 159.
54. Tamimi, *Rachid Ghannouchi*, 213.
55. 'Entretien avec Rachid Ghannouchi,' in Olfa Lamloum and Bernard Ravenel (eds), *La Tunisie de Ben Ali: La société contre le régime: Les Cahiers de Confluences* (Paris: L'Harmattan, 2002), 261–2; Hermassi, 'Rise and Fall,' 125.
56. Murphy, *Economic and Political Change*, 200–201.
57. This section draws substantially on Michael J. Willis, 'Justice and Devel-

opment or Justice and Spirituality?: The Challenge of Morocco's Non-Violent Islamist Movements,' in Bruce Maddy-Weitzman and Daniel Zisenwine (eds): *The Maghrib in the New Century: Identity, Religion and Politics* (Gainesville: University of Florida Press, 2007)

58. Shahin, *Political Ascent* p. 172. According to *Al-Adl wal Ihsan*, Abdelkrim Mouti, who had had regular contacts with Yassine in the 1950s and 1960s, had approached Yassine early on to form a political party, but the latter had replied that he did not feel spiritually ready. Author's interview with Nadia Yassine, daughter and spokesperson for Abdeslam Yassine, Salé, 5 July 2001.
59. Munson, *Religion and Power*, 115–48.
60. Munson, *Religion and Power*, 172–3.
61. Author's discussion with Salim Hmimnat, author of *The Religious Policy of the Ministry of Habous and Islamic Affairs 1984–2002*, PhD thesis, Mohamed V University, Rabat 2009, Rabat, 15 October 2009.
62. Author's interview with Abdelwahed El Moutawakil, member of *Al-Adl wal Ihsan*'s *Majlis Irshad* (Guidance Council), Rabat, 28 June 2002. Salim Hmimnat argues that interior minister Driss Basri insisted on a very explicit recognition of the religious authority of the king to prevent *Al-Adl wal Ihsan*'s legalisation as a political party, which he opposed. Author's discussion with Salim Hmimnat.
63. Mohamed Tozy, *Monarchie et Islam Politique au Maroc* (Paris: Presses de Sciences Po, Paris, 1999), 243–4.
64. Author's interview with Abdelkrim Khatib, secretary general of the MPDC 1967–98, Rabat, 6 July 2001.
65. For full details of this see Michael J. Willis, 'Between *Alternance* and the *Makhzen*: At-Tawhid wa Al-Islah's Entry into Moroccan Politics,' *Journal of North African Studies*, 4, no. 3 (Autumn 1999), 46–9.
66. *Al-Islah wa At-Tajdid/At-Tawhid wa al-Islah* was kept organisationally distinct from the PJD to allow the movement to retain a legal organisation if the authorities ever decided to ban the PJD as a political party.
67. Willis, 'Between *Alternance* and the Makhzen,' 50–59.
68. Author's interview with Saad-Eddine Othmani, deputy secretary general of the PJD, Rabat, 7 June 2000.
69. Interview with Abdelilah Benkirane in *Le Figaro*, 30 September 2002.
70. *7 à Dire* (Casablanca), 20 September 2002.
71. For a full account of the PJD's participation in the 2002 legislative elections see Michael J. Willis, 'Morocco's Islamists and the Legislative Elections of 2002: The Strange Case of the Party that Did Not Want to Win,' in *Mediterranean Politics*, vol. 9, no. 1 (Spring 2004).
72. See PJD newspaper *Justice et Développement* (Casablanca), 10 September 2007.
73. Willis, 'Islamism, Democratization and Disillusionment,' 1–10. The elections were monitored by a team from the US democracy promotion NGO,

the National Democratic Institute (NDI). For a copy of the report on the election see NDI, *Final Report on the Moroccan Legislative Elections, September 7, 2007* (Washington: National Democratic Institute, 2007).
74. Willis, 'Islamism, Democratization and Disillusionment,' 12–14.
75. Emilie François, forthcoming DPhil thesis, University of Oxford.
76. *Le Journal*, 22 September 2007.
77. Tozy, *Monarchie et Islam Politique*, 198–9.
78. Author's interviews with Nadia Yassine, Salé, 9 June 2000 and 27 June 2002.
79. Author's interview with Nadia Yassine, Salé, 1 April 2006.
80. Author's interview with Abdeslam Yassine, Salé, 22 June 2000. *Al-Adl wal Ihsan*'s position on the monarchy is that, although the Prophet Mohamed asked people to love his descendants, this should not equate to giving them exclusive political power. Author's interview with Nadia Yassine, Salé, 24 July 2003.
81. For an excellent account of this tradition and these individuals see Munson, *Religion and Power in Morocco*
82. Avi Spiegel, *Islamist Pluralism: Youth Activism and the State in Morocco*, DPhil thesis, University of Oxford, 2009.
83. Emilie François, forthcoming DPhil thesis, University of Oxford.
84. Mohamed Yatimm quoted in Shahin, *Political Ascent*, 190–91.
85. International Crisis Group (ICG), *Islamism, Violence and Reform in Algeria: Turning the Page*, Middle East Report no. 29, 30 July 2004, 13–14.
86. For a full discussion of the massacres and the international reaction to them see Jacob M. Mundy, 'Expert intervention: knowledge, violence and identity during the Algerian crisis, 1997–1998,' *Cambridge Review of International Affairs*, 23, 1 (March 2010) 25–47.
87. International Crisis Group (ICG), *Islamism, Violence and Reform in Algeria*, 12.
88. Gilles Kepel, *Jihad: The Trail of Political Islam* (London and New York: I. B. Tauris, 2003), 254.
89. Louisa Ait-Hamadouche and Yahia H. Zoubir, 'The Fate of Political Islam in Algeria,' in Bruce Maddy-Weitzman and Daniel Zisenwine (eds), *The Maghrib in the New Century: Identity, Religion and Politics* (Gainesville: University of Florida Press, 2007), 116.
90. Author's interview with Djafar Houari, member of the FIS Executive Bureau Abroad, London, 14 January 2000.
91. *El Watan*(Algiers), 9 November 2000.
92. Author's interview with Djafar Houari, member of the FIS Executive Bureau Abroad, London, 11 August 2000.
93. The MSP was launched in 1991 and originally known by the acronym HAMAS (*Harakat al Mujtama al-Islami*—Movement for an Islamic Society) before it bowed to the authorities' demand to drop the reference to Islam in 1997.

94. Author's interview with Sid Ahmed Boulil, MSP minister of transport 1997–9, Algiers, 26 March 2007.
95. Martinez, *The Algerian Civil War*, 181–2; Kepel, *Jihad*, 254.
96. Julien Lariège, 'Ministres Islamistes et Système Politique Algérien: Logique et mode de fonctionnement d'une ouverture politique,' *Les Cahiers de l'Orient. Algérie: La Guerre N'est Pas Fini*, 84 (December 2006), 40–42.
97. Nahnah was officially excluded from being a candidate because of his supposed inability to prove that he had played an active role in the liberation struggle.
98. Michael Willis, 'Algeria's Other Islamists: Abdallah Djaballah and the Ennahda Movement,' *Journal of North African Studies*, 3, no. 3 (1998).
99. International Crisis Group (ICG), *Islamism, Violence and Reform in Algeria*, 19. As one MSP minister distinguished his party from Islah: 'We don't believe in opposition for opposition's sake.' Author's interview with Sid Ahmed Boulil, MSP minister of transport 1997–9, Algiers, 26 March 2007.
100. Willis, 'Algeria's Other Islamists,' 51.
101. Khiari, *Tunisie: Le Délitement de la Cité*, 139.
102. Camau and Geisser, *Le syndrome autoritaire*, 309–11.
103. Algerian Islamist to author, London, August 1997.
104. *Maroc Hebdo International*, 5 October 2001.
105. For a comprehensive examination of the May 2003 attacks in Casablanca see Jack Kalpakian, 'Building the Human Bomb: The Case of the 16 May 2003 Attacks in Casablanca,' *Studies in Conflict and Terrorism*, 28, 2 (March/April 2005).
106. *La Gazette du Maroc*, 9 June 2003.
107. One senior figure in the PJD believed that the break-up of the parties was a deliberate move by the authorities to limit the options for Islamist voters; it also provided an excuse to resist further political reform on the grounds of the supposed continued threat of terrorism. Author's interview with Lahcen Daoudi, Rabat, 13 April 2010.
108. Michael J. Willis, 'Algerian Terrorism: Domestic Origins and International Links,' *South African Journal of International Affairs*, 10, 2 (Winter/Spring 2003), 72–4.
109. International Crisis Group (ICG), *Islamism, Violence and Reform in Algeria*, 13–16; Hamadouche and Zoubir, 'The Fate of Political Islam in Algeria,' 113–14; Camille Tawil, *Brothers in Arms. The Story of Al-Qa'ida and the Arab Jihadists* (London: Saqi Books, 2010), 194–5.
110. See Jeremy Keenan, *The Dark Sahara* (London: Pluto, 2008).
111. International Crisis Group (ICG), *Islamism, Violence and Reform in Algeria*, 17.
112. Tawil, *Brothers in Arms*, 195.
113. Camau and Geisser, *Le syndrome autoritaire*, 304–11.

114. Author's interview with Rachid Ghannouchi, London, 18 April 1995.
115. Interview with Rachid Ghannouchi, *Asharq Alawsat* (London), 8 February 2011.
116. *Tel Quel*, 19 March 2011.
117. *El Watan*, 13 February 2011.
118. International Crisis Group (ICG), *Islamism, Violence and Reform in Algeria*, 5. The ICG argues that the FIS had even more in common with the PPA of the period 1937–54 than with the later FLN.
119. Mohamed Darif, *Al-Islam As-Siyyasa fi Al-Maghrib* (Casablanca, 2002), 317.
120. Rachid Ghannouchi, 'Comment expliquer la supériorité de l'expérience marocaine sur celle de la Tunisie,' www.ezzeitouna.com, October 2002, quoted in Camau and Geisser, *Le syndrome autoritaire*, 312–13.
121. Author's interview with Rachid Ghannouchi, London, 18 April 1995.
122. Leila Nadir-Jones, *Perceptions and Expressions of Religion in the Aftermath of the FIS and the Insurgency in Algeria: Political Islam or Piety?* MPhil thesis, University of Oxford, 2006.
123. Many Maghrebi Islamists were inspired by the events in Iran immediately surrounding the revolution, but their interest and enthusiasm rapidly declined due to the emergence of both the Shi'ite particularities of the new Islamic Republic and its perceived authoritarian excesses.
124. *La Gazette du Maroc*, 7 October 2002.

6. THE BERBER QUESTION

1. The Ibadite communities date back to the eighth century in the Maghreb and emerged from the Kharijite schism in early Islamic history, which placed greater emphasis on personal piety and rejected hereditary rule in the Islamic community.
2. For examples of these different narratives see Salem Chaker, *Berbères Aujourd'hui* (Paris: L'Harmattan, 1998, 2nd edn), esp. 1; and James McDougall, 'Myth and Counter-Myth: "The Berber" as National Signifier in Algerian Historiographies,' *Radical History Review*, 86 (Spring 2003).
3. Stephanie Saad, 'Interpreting Ethnic Quiescence: A Brief History of the Berbers in Morocco,' in R. Kevin Lacey and Ralph M. Coury (eds), *The Arab-African and Islamic Worlds: Interdisciplinary Studies* (New York: Peter Lang, 2000), 169.
4. For an excellent exploration of the origins and nature of the Kabyle Myth in Algeria see Patricia M. E. Lorcin, *Imperial Identities: Stereotyping, Prejudice and Race in Colonial Algeria* (London: I. B. Tauris, 1995).
5. For fuller discussion of the Berber Dahir see Lorcin, *Imperial Identities*, 228–31 and David M. Hart, 'The Berber Dahir of 1930 in Colonial Morocco: Then and Now (1930–1996),' *Journal of North African Studies*, 2, no. 2 (Autumn 1997).

6. Louis-Jean Duclos, 'The Berbers and the Rise of Moroccan Nationalism,' in Ernest Gellner and Charles Micaud (eds), *Arabs and Berbers: From Tribe to Nation in North Africa* (London: Duckworth, 1973); Michael Brett and Elizabeth Fentress, *The Berbers* (Oxford: Blackwell, 1996), 227.
7. Hugh Roberts, 'The Unforeseen Development of the Kabyle Question in Contemporary Algeria,' *Government and Opposition*, 17, no. 3 (Summer 1982), 325–7.
8. Ernest Gellner and Charles Micaud (eds), *Arabs and Berbers: From Tribe to Nation in North Africa*,(London: Duckworth, 1973); Michael Brett and Elizabeth Fentress, *The Berbers* (Oxford: Blackwell, 1996), 271.
9. Jane Goodman, 'Reinterpreting the Berber Spring: From Rite of Reversal to Site of Convergence,' *Journal of North African Studies*, 9, no. 3 (Autumn 2004).
10. Roberts, 'Unforeseen Development,' 328–9.
11. The impact of Arab nationalism on the Algerian nationalist movement had already created tensions within the movement before the creation of the FLN. In 1948 a number of Kabyle members of the nationalist MTLD had protested against the increasingly exclusive Arabo-Islamic definition being given to the Algerian 'nation' by the organisation's leaders. In what became known as the 'Berber Crisis,' this led to a purge of these figures for promoting 'sectarian deviation.' See Gilbert Meynier, *Histoire Intérieure du FLN 1954–1962* (Paris: Fayard, 2002), 94–6.
12. Quoted in Hugh Roberts, 'Historical and Unhistorical Approaches to the Problem of Identity in Algeria,' *Bulletin of Francophone Africa*, 4 (Autumn 1993), 80.
13. Brett and Fentress, *The Berbers*, 273–4.
14. Goodman, 'Reinterpreting the Berber Spring,' 77.
15. Brett and Fentress, *The Berbers*, 274.
16. Chaker, *Berbères Aujourd'hui*, 22–3; Bruce Maddy-Weitzman, 'Ethno-Politics and Globalisation in North Africa: The Berber Cultural Movement,' *Journal of North African Studies*, 11, no. 1 (March 2006), 78.
17. Michael J. Willis, 'The Politics of Berber (Amazigh) Identity: Algeria and Morocco Compared,' in Yahia H. Zoubir and Haizam Amirah-Fernandez (eds), *North Africa: Politics, Region and the Limits of Transformation* (London: Routledge, 2007), 230.
18. Goodman, 'Reinterpreting the Berber Spring,' 72.
19. Roberts, 'Unforeseen Development,' 312.
20. Goodman, 'Reinterpreting the Berber Spring,' 77–8. Goodman plays down the impact of the cancellation by the authorities of the lecture on Berber poetry by Miloud Mammeri at Tizi Ouzou University, which is traditionally cited as the 'spark' that ignited the unrest. Instead she emphasises the longer-term roles played by the Berberist associations at the university and, moreover, of Arabisation, without which, she argues, 'the Berber Spring would likely never have happened.' Goodman, 'Reinterpreting the Berber Spring,' 64–5.

21. Goodman, 'Reinterpreting the Berber Spring,' 62.
22. Roberts, 'Unforeseen Development,' 322–3.
23. Berber-speakers had joined the Istiqlal, but in the view of John Waterbury had done so 'more out of antipathy to the French than out of loyalty to the party,' with many abandoning it after independence. Waterbury, *Commander of the Faithful*, 57.
24. Lahcen Brousky, *Les Berbères face à leur destin* (Rabat: Editions Bouregreg, 2006), 232–3.
25. See Abdaslam Ben Kaddour, 'The Neo-Makhzan and the Berbers,' in Gellner and Micaud, *Arabs and Berbers*.
26. Leveau, *La Fellah Marocain*, 83–7; Brousky, *Les Berbères*, 243.
27. Waterbury, *Commander of the Faithful*, 244.
28. Chaker, *Berbères Aujourd'hui*, 23–4.
29. Bruce Maddy-Weitzman, 'Contested Identities: Berbers, Berberism and the State in North Africa,' *Journal of North African Studies*, 6, no. 3 (Autumn 2001), 30.
30. David Crawford and Katherine E. Hoffman, 'Essentially Amazigh: Urban Berbers and the Global Village,' in R. Kevin Lacey and Ralph M. Coury (eds), *The Arab-African and Islamic Worlds: Interdisciplinary Studies* (New York: Peter Lang, 2000), 123.
31. *La Gazette du Maroc*, 15 April 2002. Early activists in these associations were also motivated by a desire to combat the high levels of illiteracy in the kingdom's rural areas, which they saw as exacerbated by the marginalisation experienced by Berber children in the exclusively Arabic language schools which many of them had experienced first-hand themselves. Fadma Ait Mous, 'Le Réseau Associatif Amazigh: Emergence et Diffusion,' in Hassan Rachik (ed.), *Usages de l'identité Amazighe au Maroc* (Casablanca: 2006), 137–8.
32. Brett and Fentress, *The Berbers*, 276. Brett and Fentress argue that Morocco's Berberophone regions share much more in common with the Aurès region in Algeria.
33. Rémy Leveau argues that colonial rule, particularly Spanish control of the Rif, actually accentuated differences between the various Berber-speaking regions. Leveau, *La Fellah Marocain*, 84.
34. Laura Feliu, 'Le Mouvement culturel amazigh (MCA) au Maroc,' *L'Année du Maghreb 2004* (Paris: CNRS Editions, 2006), 277.
35. Omar Ouakrim, 'La revendication culturelle amazighe,' in Maria-Angels Roque (ed.), *La Société Civile au Maroc* (Clamency: Publisud, 2004), 132; Aziz Chahir, 'Leadership Politique Amazigh,' in Rachik, *Usages de l'identité Amazighe*, 217–18.
36. Salem Mehzoud, 'Glasnost the Algerian Way: The Role of Berber Nationalists in Political Reform,' in George Joffé (ed.), *North Africa: Nation, State and Region* (London: Routledge, 1993).
37. For the text of the Agadir Charter see http://www.tlfq.ulaval.ca/axl/afrique/charte_berbere.htm.

38. Ouakrim, 'La revendication culturelle amazighe,' 141.
39. Maddy-Weitzman, 'Contested Identities,' 31–2; Joël Donnet, 'Renaissance berbère au Maroc,' *Le Monde Diplomatique*, January 1995.
40. Feliu, 'Le Mouvement culturel amazigh,' 279; Brett and Fentress, *The Berbers*, 276.
41. Maxime Ait Kaki, *De la Question Berbère au Dilemme Kabyle à l'Aube du XXIème Siecle* (Paris: L'Harmattan, 2004), 110–12; Maddy-Weitzman, 'Contested Identities,' 39; International Crisis Group (ICG), *Algeria: Unrest and Impasse in Kabylia*, Middle East/North Africa Report no. 15, 10 June 2003, 7.
42. See Abdeslam Yassine, 'Hiwar ma'a sadiqin amazighi' (Casablanca: Imprimerie al-Ufuq, 1997). For a discussion of this book and its contents see Maddy-Weitzman, 'Contested Identities,' 33–4.
43. International Crisis Group, *Algeria: Unrest and Impasse*, 8.
44. Azzedine Layachi, 'The Berbers in Algeria: Politicized Ethnicity and Ethnicized Politics,' in Maya Shatzmiller (ed.), *Nationalism and Minority Identities in Islamic Societies* (Montreal and Kingston: McGill-Queen's University Press, 2005), 207.
45. International Crisis Group, *Algeria: Unrest and Impasse*, 38.
46. The parties received some support in Algiers, due to the significant presence of Kabyles who had moved to the capital.
47. International Crisis Group, *Algeria: Unrest and Impasse*, 6, 12 and 33.
48. International Crisis Group, *Algeria: Unrest and Impasse*, 13, 19 and 31.
49. Layachi, 'The Berbers in Algeria,' 208–11. There were also suggestions that regime manipulation had not been limited to its reaction to the unrest, but had even played a part in provoking it in the first place. One investigation into the outbreak of the protests of April 2001 concluded that outside interference in the police's chain of command had led to the security services being particularly provocative. International Crisis Group, *Algeria: Unrest and Impasse*, 9.
50. Ait Mous, 'Le Réseau Associatif Amazigh,' 156–7.
51. Author's interview with Ahmed Adghrini, Rabat, 2 July 2001.
52. For the text of the Manifesto see http://www.amazighworld.org/human_rights/morocco/manifesto2000.php.
53. Dalle, *Les Trois Rois*, 716–21; *7 à Dire*, 5 July 2002.
54. *La Vie Economique*, 15 April 2002.
55. *Le Reporter* (Casablanca), 14 June 2001.
56. Feliu, 'Le Mouvement culturel amazigh,' 281; Dalle, Les Trois Rois, 722.
57. Feliu, 'Le Mouvement culturel amazigh,' 280.
58. Author's interview with member of IRCAM, Rabat, 8 April 2005. The appointment of a former director of the Royal College, Mohamed Chafik, as the first director of IRCAM demonstrated the palace's wish to prevent any radicalisation within IRCAM, despite Chafik's standing as a respected Berberist.

59. David Crawford, 'Royal Interest in Local Culture: Amazigh Culture and the Moroccan State,' in Maya Shatzmiller (ed.), *Nationalism and Minority Identities in Islamic Societies* (Montreal and Kingston: McGill-Queen's University Press, 2005), 188; Ouakrim, 'La revendication culturelle amazighe,' 136.
60. Author's interview with member of IRCAM, Rabat, 31 March 2008.
61. *La Gazette du Maroc*, 7 March 2005. Author's interview with member of IRCAM, Rabat, 8 April 2005.
62. Dalle, *Les Trois Rois*, 723.
63. Feliu, 'Le Mouvement culturel amazigh,' 285.
64. Interview with Rachid Raha, president of the World Amazigh Congress, *Maroc Hebdo International*, 29 September 2000.
65. Author's interviews with Ahmed Adghrini, secretary general of the PDAM, Rabat, 2 July 2001 and 7 September 2007.
66. *Aujourd'hui Le Maroc*, 21 April 2008.
67. Author's interview with member of IRCAM, Rabat, 8 April 2005.
68. *7 à Dire*, 5 July 2002.
69. Gabi Kratochwil and Abderrahim Lakhbassi, 'Associations Culturelles Amazighes,' in Maria-Angels Roque (ed.), *La Société Civile au Maroc* (Clamency: Publisud, 2004), 141.
70. Author's interview with Ahmed Adghrini, secretary general of the PDAM, Rabat, 7 September 2007.
71. *Tel Quel*, 9 July 2005.
72. Feliu, 'Le Mouvement culturel amazigh,' 273.
73. International Crisis Group, *Algeria: Unrest and Impasse*, 6.
74. Ibid., 6.
75. Roberts, 'Unforeseen Development,' 321.
76. Ferhat Mehenni, *L'Algérie: La Question Kabyle* (Paris: Editions Michalon, 2004), 95. Both the FFS and the RCD were able to attract support outside Kabylia, but this was almost exclusively in parts of Algiers with large Kabyle populations.
77. Salem Chaker, 'Preface,' in Mehenni, *L'Algérie: La Question Kabyle*, 13.
78. Layachi, 'The Berbers in Algeria,' 212.
79. International Crisis Group, *Algeria: Unrest and Impasse*, 25.
80. Mehenni, *L'Algérie: La Question Kabyle*, 95.
81. International Crisis Group, *Algeria: Unrest and Impasse*, 25; Layachi, 'The Berbers in Algeria,' 211–18.
82. *El Watan*, 24 September 2005.
83. At the same time, the Algerian government continued to make concessions in the cultural sphere. In 2007 President Bouteflika announced the establishment of an Algerian Academy for the Amazigh Language and also a High Council for the Amazigh Language. Both were regarded as fruit of the long drawn out negotiations between the regime and the Coordinations Movement since the unrest of 2001. *El Watan*, 20 June 2007 and 21 June 2007.

84. Author's interview with Ahmed Adghrini, secretary general of the PDAM, Rabat, 2 July 2001.
85. *Aujourd'hui Le Maroc*, 10 June 2005.
86. Crawford and Hoffman, 'Essentially Amazigh,' 126; David Crawford, 'Royal Interest in Local Culture: Amazigh Culture and the Moroccan State,' in Maya Shatzmiller (ed.), *Nationalism and Minority Identities in Islamic Societies* (Montreal and Kingston: McGill-Queen's University Press, 2005), 184–7. Stephanie Saad has similarly pointed out that apparent prejudice against Berbers in Morocco is usually related more to specific regions and the urban-rural divide than any Arab-Berber one. Saad, 'Interpreting Ethnic Quiescence,' 173.
87. Crawford, 'Royal Interest in Local Culture,' 173.
88. Crawford and Hoffman, 'Essentially Amazigh,' 119–22.
89. Willis, 'The Politics of Berber (Amazigh) Identity,' 238.
90. Ahmed Adghrini (leader of the PDAM) has, for example, argued that 'what threatens Morocco is the transfer of the Middle East conflict to North Africa. (…) The true threat to our identity is the Arab-Islamic movement who import into here conflicts from outside.' *La Gazette du Maroc*, 15 April 2002.
91. One Berber newspaper in Morocco, for example, argued that official efforts to encourage solidarity with the Palestinians were aimed at undermining Berbers and Berber identity. *Agraw Amazigh*, 4 January 2001.
92. *Tel Quel*, 9 July 2005.
93. Crawford and Hoffman, 'Essentially Amazigh,' 126.
94. *Magharabia*, 6 July 2011 (http://www.magharebia.com/cocoon/awi/xhtml1/en_GB/features/awi/features/2011/07/06/feature-01).

7. POLITICS AND ECONOMICS

1. Robert J. King, 'The Political Logic of Economic Reform in Tunisia,' in Azzedine Layachi (ed.), *Economic Crisis and Political Change in North Africa* (Westport: Praeger, 1998), 111–12.
2. The agricultural reforms were particularly resented by small private landowners—an important constituency for the PSD. This undoubtedly also contributed to the decision to dismiss Ben Salah. Gregory White, *A Comparative Political Economy of Tunisia and Morocco: On the Outside of Europe Looking In* (Albany: State University of New York Press, 2001), 37.
3. King, 'Political Logic,' 113–14.
4. Murphy, *Economic and Political Change*, 78.
5. Stephen King, *Liberalization Against Democracy: The Local Politics of Economic Reform in Tunisia* (Bloomington: Indiana University Press, 2003), 28–9.
6. Rhys Payne, 'Economic Crisis and Policy reform in the 1980s,' in I. William Zartman and William Mark Habeeb (eds), *Polity and Society in Contemporary North Africa* (Boulder: Westview, 1993), 149.

7. Clement M. Henry and Robert Springborg, *Globalization and the Politics of Development in the Middle East* (Cambridge: Cambridge University Press, 2001), 24.
8. Will D. Swearingen, *Moroccan Mirages: Agrarian Dreams and Deceptions, 1912–1986* (Princeton: Princeton University Press, 1987), 188–9.
9. Leveau, *Sabre et Turban*, 69–74.
10. White, *Comparative Political Economy of Tunisia and Morocco*, 129–36.
11. Henry and Springborg, *Globalization*, 108.
12. Philip J. Akre, 'Algeria and the Politics of Energy-Based Industrailization,' in John P. Entelis and Phillip C. Naylor (eds), *State and Society in Algeria* (Boulder: Westview, 1992), 78.
13. Tunisia's population grew from 3.9 to 7.9 million between 1960 and 1989; Algeria's from 9.7 to 24.4 million in the same period; and Morocco's from 11.6 to 24.6 in the years between 1956 and 1989. *United Nations Yearbook 1990*, cited in Mark Tessler, 'Alienation of Urban Youth,' in I. William Zartman and William Mark Habeeb (eds), *Polity and Society in Contemporary North Africa* (Boulder: Westview, 1993), 75.
14. Payne, 'Economic Crisis,' 140.
15. King, 'Political Logic,' 113–14.
16. Kenneth J. Perkins, *A History of Modern Tunisia* (Cambridge: Cambridge University Press, 2004), 169–70.
17. Marguerite Rollinde, 'Les émeutes en Tunisie: un défi à l'état?,' in Didier Le Saout and Marguerite Rollinde (eds), *Emeutes et Mouvements Sociaux au Maghreb* (Paris: Karthala, 1999), 126.
18. White, *Comparative Political Economy*, 133–5.
19. Payne, 'Economic Crisis,' 158.
20. Michael Willis, 'Algeria's Troubled Road Toward Political and Economic Liberalization: 1988–1995,' in G. Nonneman (ed.), *Political and Economic Liberalization: Dynamics and Linkages in Comparative Perspective* (London: Lynne Rienner, 1996), 200–201.
21. Azzedine Layachi, 'Reform and the Politics of Inclusion in the Maghrib,' *Journal of North African Studies*, 5, no. 3 (2000), 18; Payne, 'Economic Crisis,' 139.
22. For an exposition of this viewpoint see Stephen King, *Liberalization Against Democracy*, 7–24.
23. Jean-Pierre Cassarino, 'Participatory Development and Liberal reforms in Tunisia: The Gradual Incorporation of *Some* Networks,' in Steven Heydemann (ed.), *Networks of Privilege in the Middle East: the Politics of Economic Reform Revisited* (New York and Basingstoke: Palgrave Macmillan, 2004), 225–6.
24. Murphy, *Economic and Political Change*, 161, 224.
25. Ibid., 225.
26. Clement M. Henry, 'Crises of Money and Power: Transitions to Democracy?' in John P. Entelis (ed.), *Islam, Democracy and the State in North*

Africa (Bloomington and Indianapolis: Indiana University Press, 1997), 190–91.
27. Béatrice Hibou, 'Fiscal trajectories in Morocco and Tunisia,' in Steven Heydemann (ed.), *Networks of Privilege in the Middle East: the Politics of Economic Reform Revisited* (New York and Basingstoke: Palgrave Macmillan, 2004), 213–15; Béatrice Hibou, 'Domination and Control in Tunisia: Economic Levers for the Exercise of Authoritarian Power,' *Review of African Political Economy*, 33, no. 108 (2006), 199–200.
28. Stephen King, *Liberalization Against Democracy*, 3, 6, 138–9.
29. Ibid., 138–9.
30. Béatrice Hibou, 'Il n'y a pas de miracle Tunisien,' in Olfa Lamloum and Bernard Ravenel, *La Tunisie de Ben Ali: La Societé Contre le Régime* (Paris: L'Harmattan, 2002), 37–9, 42.
31. Béatrice Hibou, 'Il n'y a pas de miracle Tunisien,' 40–41.
32. Camau and Geisser, *Le syndrome autoritaire*, 213; *Libération* (Paris), 23 October 2004.
33. Camau and Geisser, *Le syndrome autoritaire*, 220–24; Christopher Alexander, 'State, Labor and the New Global Economy in Tunisia,' in Dirk Vandewalle (ed.), *North Africa: Development and Reform in a Changing Global Economy* (New York: St Martin's Press, 1996), 178–9, 186; Stephen King, *Liberalization Against Democracy*, 5.
34. Leveau, *Sabre et Turban*, 72.
35. Henry and Springborg, *Globalization*, 172–3.
36. Henry, 'Crises of Money and Power,' 198–200.
37. Melani Cammett, 'Challenges to Networks of Privilege in Morocco: Implications for Network Analysis,' in Steven Heydemann (ed.), *Networks of Privilege in the Middle East: the Politics of Economic Reform Revisited* (New York and Basingstoke: Palgrave Macmillan, 2004), 250.
38. Guilain Denoeux, 'Understanding Morocco's "Sanitisation" Campaign (December 1995–May 1996),' *Journal of North African Studies*, 3, no. 1 (1998), 111–12.
39. Denoeux, 'Understanding Morocco's "Sanitisation" Campaign'; Hibou, 'Fiscal Trajectories in Morocco and Tunisia,' 202–11.
40. Hibou, 'Fiscal Trajectories in Morocco and Tunisia,' 208–10.
41. Denoeux, 'Understanding Morocco's "Sanitisation" Campaign,' 106.
42. Myriam Catusse, 'Acteurs Privés, Action Publique. Patronat et Politique au Maroc,' in Maria-Angels Roque (ed.), *La Société Civile au Maroc: L'Emergence de Nouveaux Acteurs de Développement* (Paris: Publisud, 2004), 173–6.
43. Cammett, 'Challenges to Networks of Privilege,' 266–7.
44. *Le Journal* (Casablanca), 17 June 2006.
45. *La Vérité* (Casablanca), 13 July 2005.
46. *Le Journal*, 29 April 2006 and 17 June 2006. Guilain Denoeux, 'Corruption in Morocco: Old Forces, New Dynamics and a Way Forward,' *Middle East Policy*, 14, no. 4 (2007), 147.

47. Guilain P. Denoeux and Abdeslam Maghraoui, 'The Political Economy of Structural Adjustment in Morocco,' in Azzedine Layachi (ed.), *Economic Crisis and Political Change in North Africa* (Westport: Praeger, 1998), 76.
48. Azzedine Layachi, 'State-Society Relations and Change in Morocco,' in Azzedine Layachi (ed.), *Economic Crisis and Political Change in North Africa* (Westport: Praeger, 1998), 95–6. Thierry Desrues argues, nonetheless, that the ongoing lack of reform in rural Morocco is evidence of the continued importance of the palace's alliance with the rural elites. Thierry Desrues, 'Governability and Agricultural Policy in Morocco: Functionality and Limitations of the Reform Discourse,' *Mediterranean Politics*, 10, no. 1 (2005), 60.
49. Denoeux and Maghraoui, 'The Political Economy of Structural Adjustment in Morocco,' 79.
50. Abdellatif Moutadayene, 'Economic Crises and Democratisation in Morocco,' *Journal of North African Studies*, 6, no. 3 (2001), 78.
51. Denoeux and Maghraoui, 'The Political Economy of Structural Adjustment in Morocco,' 78.
52. Cammett, 'Challenges to Networks of Privilege,' 267.
53. Catusse, 'Acteurs Privés, Action Publique,' 167, 177.
54. Myriam Catusse, *Le temps des entrepreneurs? Politique et transformations du capitalisme au Maroc* (Paris: Maisonneuve & Larose, 2008), 288–95 and 302–11.
55. Vermeren, *Le Maroc de Mohamed VI*, 282–91; Denoeux, 'Corruption in Morocco,' 137–8; Dalle, *Les Trois Rois*, 748–9; *Tel Quel*, 18 July 2009.
56. Rachid Tlemcani, 'Chadli's Perestroika,' *Middle East Report* (March-April 1990); Interview with Belaid Abdeslam, 'By Force of Islam,' *Assignment* BBC TV, June 1991.
57. Lynette Rummel, 'Privatization and Democratization in Algeria,' in John P. Entelis and Phillip C. Naylor (eds), *State and Society in Algeria* (Boulder: Westview, 1992), 59.
58. Rummel, 'Privatization and Democratization,' 57; Roberts, 'Doctrinaire Economics and Political Opportunism,' 131–2.
59. Rafael Bustos, 'Economic Liberalization and Political Change in Algeria: Theory and Practice (1988–92 and 1994–1999),' *Mediterranean Politics*, 8, no. 1 (2003), 9; Roberts, 'Doctrinaire Economics and Political Opportunism,' 126–7.
60. *Projet de Programme du Front Islamique du Salut*, 9 March 1989. Extracts reproduced in M. Al-Ahnaf, Bernard Botiveau and Franck Frégosi, *L'Algérie par ses Islamistes* (Paris: Karthala, 1991), 179–87.
61. Interview with Abassi Madani, *Algérie Actualité*, 4 January 1990.
62. Roberts, 'Doctrinaire Economics and Political Opportunism,' 124–7.
63. For the FIS's economic platform (or lack thereof), see Willis, *Islamist Challenge in Algeria*, 138–40;
64. See Willis, *Islamist Challenge in Algeria*, 49–50.

65. Martinez, *The Algerian Civil War*, 35.
66. George Joffé, 'The Role of Violence Within the Algerian Economy,' *Journal of North African Studies*, 7, no. 1 (2002), 43–4.
67. *Horizons* (Algiers), 5 May 1991.
68. Willis, *Islamist Challenge in Algeria*, 200–201.
69. Willis, 'Algeria's Troubled Road,' 210–12.
70. Martinez, *The Algerian Civil War*, 179.
71. Martinez, *The Algerian Civil War*, 139–46, 122, 171. The absence of attacks on oil pipelines and installations may also be explained by their remoteness from population centres and the relatively high levels of security and surveillance they enjoyed.
72. Martinez, *The Algerian Civil War*, 188–9, 183, 126.
73. Martinez, *The Algerian Civil War*, 121–2.
74. Isabelle Werenfels, 'Obstacles to Privatisation of State-Owned Industries in Algeria: The Political Economy of a Distributive Conflict,' *Journal of North African Studies*, 7, no. 1 (2002), 1.
75. Werenfels, 'Obstacles to Privatisation,' 2.
76. Ibid., 12.
77. Werenfels, 'Obstacles to Privatisation,' 2, 18–19; Ivan Martin, 'Algeria's Political Economy (1999–2002): An Economic Solution to the Crisis?,' *Journal of North African Studies*, 8, no. 2 (2003), 49.
78. Werenfels, 'Obstacles to Privatisation,' 17–20.
79. Ibid., 20.
80. Bradford Dillman. 'The Political Economy of Structural Adjustment in Tunisia and Algeria,' *Journal of North African Studies*, 3, no. 3 (1998), 17.
81. Werenfels, 'Obstacles to Privatisation,' 13.
82. Bustos, 'Economic Liberalization and Political Change in Algeria,' 16.
83. Joffé, 'Violence Within the Algerian Economy,' 41.
84. Martin, 'Algeria's Political Economy,' 65.
85. Ibid., 40
86. Martin, 'Algeria's Political Economy,' 43–4.
87. Joffé, 'Violence Within the Algerian Economy,' 35.
88. Hocine Malti, *Histoire Secrète du Pétrole Algérien*, 345.
89. *El Watan*, 7 February 2011.
90. Denoeux and Maghraoui, 'The Political Economy of Structural Adjustment in Morocco,' 78.
91. Denoeux, 'Understanding Morocco's "Sanitisation" Campaign,' 107–10.
92. Interview with Abderrahmane El Youssoufi, *Libération* (Paris), 24 June 1998. Significantly, El Youssoufi had been much more positive about the Islamist movement in interviews given to the Moroccan press.
93. Martinez, *The Algerian Civil War*, 180.
94. Payne, 'Economic Crisis,' 139.
95. Ibid., 158.
96. Joffé, 'Violence Within the Algerian Economy,' 39.

97. Cammett, 'Challenges to Networks of Privilege,' 246, 262.
98. Murphy, *Economic and Political Change*, 229.
99. Layachi, 'Reform and the Politics of Inclusion,' 16.
100. Iván Martín, 'Recherche Modèle de Développement Désespérément,' *Afkar/Idées*, Printemps/Eté 2006, 73.
101. The World Bank country brief for 2010 had declared that 'Tunisia is far ahead in terms of government effectiveness, rule of law, control of corruption and regulatory quality.' Quoted in *Financial Times*(London), 18 January 2011.

8. REGIONAL RELATIONS

1. John Damis, 'The Western Sahara Dispute as a Source of Regional Conflict in North Africa,' in Halim Barakat (ed.), *Contemporary North Africa: Issues of Development and Integration* (London: Croom Helm, 1985), 140.
2. Damis, 'Western Sahara Dispute,' 140.
3. Nicole Grimaud, *La Politique Extérieure de l'Algérie* (Paris: Karthala, 1984), 199.
4. International Crisis Group (ICG), *Western Sahara: Out of the Impasse*, Middle East/North Africa Report no. 66, 11 June 2007, 12.
5. Grimaud, *Politique Extérieure de l'Algérie*, 197–9.
6. Mohamed Abed Jabri, 'Evolution of the Maghrib Concept: Facts and Perspectives,' in Halim Barakat (ed.), *Contemporary North Africa: Issues of Development and Integration* (London: Croom Helm, 1985), 81–2.
7. Grimaud, *Politique Extérieure de l'Algérie*, 206, 208.
8. Hodges, *Western Sahara*, 85–6.
9. David Seddon, 'Morocco at War,' in Richard Lawless and Laila Monahan (eds), *War and Refugees: The Western Sahara Conflict* (London and New York: Pinter, 1987), 118.
10. Hammad Zouitni, 'Les Intérêts Nationaux: Entre la Pratique de la Politique Extérieure du Maroc et les Besoins d'une Redéfinition par Rapport au Nouveau Système International,' in Mohamed Jari (ed.), *Rapport Annuel sur l'Evolution du Système International (RAESI) 1997* (Rabat: GERSI, 1997), 324.
11. John Damis, *Conflict In Northwest Africa: The Western Sahara Dispute* (Stanford: Hoover Press, 1983), 47–8; Philip C. Naylor, 'Spain, France, and the Western Sahara: A Historical Narrative and Study of National Transformation,' in Yahia H. Zoubir and Daniel Volman (eds), *International Dimensions of the Western Sahara Conflict* (Westport: Praeger, 1993), 23.
12. John Damis, 'The Impact of the Saharan Dispute on Moroccan Foreign and Domestic Policy,' in I. William Zartman, *The Political Economy of Morocco* (New York: Praeger, 1987), 191.

13. John Damis, *Conflict in Northwest Africa*, 50–51.
14. For a full discussion of the ICJ and the Western Sahara see George Joffé, 'The International Court of Justice and the Western Sahara Dispute,' in Richard Lawless and Laila Monahan (eds), *War and Refugees: The Western Sahara Conflict* (London and New York: Pinter, 1987).
15. John Damis, 'King Hassan and the Western Sahara,' *The Maghreb Review* 25, nos.1–2 (2000), 17. For an example of the Moroccan reading of the judgement see Mohamed Ghomari, 'La Défense de l'Intégrité Territorial: la Réponse du Maroc dans une Perspective Historique,' in Mohamed Jari (ed.), *Rapport Annuel sur l'Evolution du Système International (RAESI) 1997* (Rabat: GERSI, 1997).
16. Damis, 'King Hassan and the Western Sahara,' 18.
17. In the run-up to the Green March, negotiations were already underway between Spain and Morocco which helped to ensure that the march did not end in confrontation between the two sides. Damis, *Conflict in Northwest Africa*, 65–6.
18. Boumedienne declared, 'I confirm that Algeria does not have any claim over the Sahara, that its only concern remains the understanding between Morocco and Mauritania. They have reached agreement on the part of the Sahara that should return to each of them. I was present when this agreement was reached; I approve it wholeheartedly and without reservation.' Quoted in Damis, *Conflict in Northwest Africa*, 53. The Moroccans Subsequently released a tape recording of the statement.
19. Quoted in Damis, *Conflict in Northwest Africa*, 56.
20. More credible explanations for Morocco's failure to ratify the treaty relate to Moroccan concerns over suspected Algerian support for leftist guerrillas in Morocco and a desire to have a guarantee that Algeria would not renege on its commitment not to contest Morocco's claim on the Sahara. Paul Balta, *Le Grand Maghreb: Des Indépendances à l'an 2000* (Paris: La Découverte, 1990), 187 and 211.
21. Hodges, *Western Sahara*, 191.
22. Damis, *Conflict in Northwest Africa*, 59. Balta, *Le Grand Maghreb*, 187.
23. Grimaud, *Politique Extérieure de l'Algérie*, 213, 96–7.
24. Hassan II, *La Mémoire d'un Roi*, 90–91.
25. Khadija Mohsen-Finan, *Sahara occidental: Les enjeux d'un conflit régional* (Paris: CNRS Editions, 1997), 33.
26. Balta, *Le Grand Maghreb*, 217.
27. Hodges, *Western Sahara*, 194.
28. See Hugh Roberts, 'The Saharan Cul-de-Sac and the Responsibility of Polisario's Intellectual Sympathisers,' *Journal for the Society of Moroccan Studies* Occasional Papers 1 (1994), 91–3.
29. Toby Shelley, *Endgame in the Western Sahara: What Future for Africa's Last Colony?* (London: Zed Books, 2004), 168.
30. Tony Hodges, 'The Origins of Sahrawi Nationalism,' in Richard Lawless

and Laila Monahan (eds), *War and Refugees: The Western Sahara Conflict* (London and New York: Pinter, 1987).
31. Damis, *Conflict in Northwest Africa*, 72–3.
32. Hodges, *Western Sahara*, 190–91, 193. Balta, *Le Grand Maghreb*, 223. The French journalist Paul Balta claims that Boumedienne asked him as late as December 1975 about the strength of the Sahrawi and whether Algeria should continue to back them. Balta, *Le Grand Maghreb*, 220.
33. Seddon, 'Morocco at War,' 100.
34. Mary-Jane Deeb, *Libya's Foreign Policy in North Africa* (Boulder: Westview, 1991), 85–6.
35. Mauritania had planned to hand its third of the territory over to Polisario, but Morocco moved in to annex the territory. Shelley, *Endgame in the Western Sahara*, 44.
36. Damis, 'The Impact of the Saharan Dispute,' 191–2.
37. Béji Caïd Essebsi, *Habib Bourguiba: Le Bon Grain et l'Ivraie* (Tunis: Sud Editions, 2009), 304, 335–6. Balta, *Le Grand Maghreb*, 201; Abdelaziz Chneguir, *La Politique Extérieure de la Tunisie 1956–1987* (Paris: L'Harmattan, 2004), 127–8.
38. Bourguiba's minister of defence at the time of the agreement believed that Ben Bella's willingness to compromise on the border issue with Tunisia had contributed to his overthrow in June 1965. Essebsi, *Habib Bourguiba*, 330.
39. Balta, *Le Grand Maghreb*, 205; Mary-Jane Deeb and Ellen Laipson, 'Tunisian Foreign Policy: Continuity and Change Under Bourguiba and Ben Ali,' in I. William Zartman (ed.), *Tunisia: The Political Economy of Reform* (London: Lynne Rienner, 1991), 228.
40. Nicole Grimaud, *La Tunisie: A la Recherche de sa Sécurité* (Paris: PUF, 1995), 111–26.
41. *Le Monde*, 1 November 1975, quoted in Grimaud, *La Tunisie: A la Recherche de sa Sécurité*, 126–7.
42. Grimaud, *La Tunisie: A la Recherche de sa Sécurité*, 129; Essebsi, *Habib Bourguiba*, 337–8.
43. Essebsi, *Habib Bourguiba*, 342 and 338.
44. Robert A. Mortimer, 'The Greater Maghreb and the Western Sahara,' in Yahia H. Zoubir and Daniel Volman (eds), *International Dimensions of the Western Sahara Conflict* (Westport: Praeger, 1993), 171–2.
45. Essebsi, *Habib Bourguiba*, 340.
46. Ibid., 308.
47. Balta, *Le Grand Maghreb*, 229 and 232.
48. Morocco officially claimed that its abrogation of the treaty was a result of a communiqué put out jointly by Libya and Syria criticising the visit of the Israeli prime minister, Shimon Peres, to Morocco in July 1986. Deeb, however, is of the view that Libya's growing isolation and pressure from the United States were more likely factors behind Morocco's move. Deeb, *Libya's Foreign Policy in North Africa*, 176–7.

49. Balta claims that initial contacts between Algeria and Morocco began as early as 1977, after Boumedienne realised that King Hassan had not been fatally destabilised by the conflict, he having hoped that the king would be overthrown by the Moroccan military. Balta, *Le Grand Maghreb*, 223–4.
50. Robert Mortimer, 'Algerian Foreign Policy in Transition,' in John P. Entelis and Phillip C. Naylor (eds), *State and Society in Algeria* (Boulder: Westview, 1992), 244–50. Mortimer has noted that the new National Charter introduced by Chadli in 1985 had used much more functionalist language in discussing regional relations when compared to the revolutionary rhetoric of Boumedienne's 1976 constitution.
51. Hassan II, *La Mémoire d'un Roi*, 201.
52. Mary-Jane Deeb, 'The Arab-Maghribi Union and the Prospects for North African Unity,' in I. William Zartman and William Mark Habeeb (eds), *Polity and Society in Contemporary North Africa* (Boulder: Westview, 1993), 192–3.
53. Deeb, 'Arab-Maghribi Union,' 193.
54. Mortimer, 'Algerian Foreign Policy,' 251–3.
55. Mortimer, 'The Greater Maghreb and the Western Sahara,' 182.
56. Deeb and Laipson, 'Tunisian Foreign Policy,' 229.
57. *Traité Instituant l'Union du Maghreb Arabe*, 17 February 1989(http://www.maghrebarabe.org/images/traite_de_marrakech.pdf).
58. Robert Mortimer, 'The Arab Maghreb Union: Myth and Reality,' in Yahia H. Zoubir (ed.), *North Africa in Transition: State, Society, and Economic Transformation in the 1990s* (Gainesville: University Press of Florida, 1999).
59. Yahia H. Zoubir, 'The Dialectics of Algeria's Foreign Relations, 1992 to the Present,' in Ahmed Aghrout and Redha M. Bougherra (eds), *Algeria in Transition: Reforms and Development Prospects* (London: Routledge Curzon, 2004), 159; Charef, *Algérie: Le Grand Dérapage*, 340. In an interview in February 1992, Boudiaf had stated the importance of Algeria and Morocco resolving the conflict in the Western Sahara, thus breaking with the official Algerian position that the parties to the conflict were Morocco and Polisario. Mohsen-Finan, *Sahara occidental*, 143.
60. *El Watan*, 15 February 1994; Zoubir, 'Dialectics of Algeria's Foreign Relations,' 159; Yahia H. Zoubir, 'The Geopolitics of the Western Sahara Conflict,' in Zoubir (ed.), *North Africa in Transition: State, Society, and Economic Transformation in the 1990s* (Gainesville: University Press of Florida, 1999), 201.
61. Morocco revoked the visa requirement for Algerians visiting Morocco in 2004, but this did not lead to Algeria reopening the border.
62. Deeb, 'Arab-Maghribi Union,' 200–201.
63. Mortimer, 'Arab Maghreb Union: Myth and Reality,' 178; Miguel Hernando de Larramendi, 'Intra Maghreb Relations: Unitary Myth and

National Interests,' in Zoubir and Amirah-Fernández (eds), *North Africa*, 180.
64. For full details on this, see Charles Dunbar, 'Saharan Stasis: Status and Future Prospects of the Western Sahara Conflict,' *Middle East Journal*, 4 (2000).
65. This view is supported by Hodges, *Western Sahara*, 193–4, and Balta, *Le Grand Maghreb*, 218–19; but disputed by Damis, *Conflict in Northwest Africa*, 57–8, who claims that Boumedienne and Bouteflika were in constant phone contact during the Rabat meeting and that the release of the final communiqué was delayed until the Algerian foreign minister's return to Algiers.
66. Yahia H. Zoubir, 'Algerian-Moroccan Relations and their Impact on Maghribi Integration,' *Journal of North African Studies*, 5, no. 3 (2000), 60–62.
67. For the two proposals, see United Nations, 'Report of the Secretary-General on the situation regarding the Western Sahara,' S/2001/613 20 June 2001 (http://daccess-dds-ny.un.org/doc/UNDOC/GEN/N01/414/44/IMG/N0141444.pdf?OpenElement) and S/2003/565 23 May 2003 (http://daccess-dds-ny.un.org/doc/UNDOC/GEN/N03/356/98/IMG/N0335698.pdf?OpenElement).
68. *Tel Quel*, 26 June 2004.
69. Rachid El Houdaigui, *La politique étrangère sous le règne de Hassan II* (Paris: L'Harmattan, 2003), 206.
70. For a full discussion of the development of Sahrawi identity and nationalism in the refugee camps, see Pablo San Martin, 'Nationalism, Identity and Citizenship in the Western Sahara,' *Journal of North African Studies*, 10, nos. 3–4 (September-December 2005).
71. International Crisis Group (ICG), *Western Sahara: Out of the Impasse*, 10–15.

9. INTERNATIONAL RELATIONS

1. By one calculation there were 4–5 million Maghrebi nationals living in France together with an estimated 1.5 million Jews, former *pieds noirs* settlers and harkis. Jean-François Daguzan, 'France and the Maghreb: The End of the Special Relationship?,' in Yahia H. Zoubir and Haizam Amirah-Fernández (eds), *North Africa: Politics, Region, and the Limits of Transformation* (Abingdon: Routledge, 2008), 332.
2. Ministère des Affaires Etrangères et Européennes, France Diplomatie: France and Maghreb (http://www.diplomatie.gouv.fr/en/country-files_156/north-africa_5493/france-and-maghreb_5495/france-maghreb-relations_8837.html).
3. Phillip C. Naylor, 'French-Algerian Relations, 1980–1990,' in John P. Entelis and Phillip C. Naylor (eds), *State and Society in Algeria* (Boulder: Westview, 1992), 217.

4. Benjamin Stora, *Algeria 1830–2000: A Short History* (Ithaca and London: Cornell University Press, 2001), 29.
5. *Le Monde*, 8 November 1964, quoted in Naylor, 'French-Algerian Relations,' 217.
6. Deeb and Laipson, 'Tunisian Foreign Policy,' 222, 230.
7. Abdelkhaleq Berramdane, *Le Maroc et l'Occident* (Paris: Karthala, 1987), 334–88; Richard B. Parker, *North Africa: Regional Tensions and Strategic Concerns* (New York: Praeger, 1987), 159.
8. Grimaud, *Politique Extérieure de l'Algérie*, 144, 126–8, 151–2, 160.
9. John Damis, 'The United States and North Africa,' in I. William Zartman and William Mark Habeeb (eds), *Polity and Society in Contemporary North Africa* (Boulder: Westview, 1993), 229.
10. Grimaud, *Politique Extérieure de l'Algérie*, 223–31, 234.
11. Hassan II, *La Mémoire d'un Roi*, 245–7.
12. Michael M. Laskier, *Israel and the Maghreb: From Statehood to Oslo* (Gainesville: University Press of Florida, 2004), 192–3.
13. Paul Balta, 'Maghreb-Machrek: Des relations politiques, mais rarement économiques,' in Camille and Yves Lacoste (eds), *L'état du Maghreb* (Casablanca: Le Fennec, 1991), 512.
14. Bruce Maddy-Weitzman, 'Israel and Morocco: A Special Relationship,' *The Maghreb Review*, 21, nos.1–2 (1996), 37.
15. There is even the claim that Morocco allowed Mossad to establish a covert bureau in the kingdom and supplied the Israelis with intelligence on intra-Arab discussions and summits. Laskier, *Israel and the Maghreb*, 139–42.
16. Algerian hostility towards Israel was also shaped by the support Israel had given to the French during Algeria's liberation struggle. Laskier, *Israel and the Maghreb*, 282–3.
17. Hassan II, *La Mémoire d'un Roi*, 257–60.
18. Daguzan, 'France and the Maghreb,' 337. French military and rhetorical, if not diplomatic, support was reined in by the end of the 1970s. Naylor, 'French-Algerian Relations,' 218–19.
19. See Jacob Mundy, 'Neutrality or complicity? The United States and the 1975 Moroccan takeover of the Spanish Sahara,' *Journal of North African Studies*, 11, no. 3 (2006); Parker, *North Africa*, 161.
20. Grimaud, *Politique Extérieure de l'Algérie*, 147.
21. Damis, 'The United States and North Africa,' 225; Parker, *North Africa*, 159.
22. Damis, 'Impact of the Western Sahara Dispute,' 196.
23. Damis, 'Impact of the Western Sahara Dispute,' 198.
24. Damis, 'The United States and North Africa,' 225–7.
25. Hassan II, *La Mémoire d'un Roi*, 267–74.
26. Grimaud, *La Tunisie: A la Recherche de sa Sécurité*, 182.
27. Pierre Sateh Agate, 'Les pays du Maghreb dans le Système regional Arabe,'

in Hubert Michel and Jean-Claude Santucci (eds), *Le Maghreb dans le Monde Arabe* (Paris: Editions du CNRS, 1987).
28. It is claimed that Algeria established discreet contacts with Israelis in Paris from 1986, but these were discontinued when Israel rejected Algeria's proposal that it recognise the PLO. Laskier, *Israel and the Maghreb*, 276.
29. Hassan II, *La Mémoire d'un Roi*, 263.
30. Yahia H. Zoubir and Stephen Zunes, 'United States Policy in the Maghreb,' in Yahia H. Zoubir (ed.), *North Africa in Transition: State, Society, and Economic Transformation in the 1990s* (Gainesville: University Press of Florida, 1999), 234–45.
31. Olfa Lamloum, 'L'indéfectible soutien français à l'exclusion de l'islamisme Tunisien,' in Bernard Ravenel (ed.), *La Tunisie de Ben Ali: La société contre le régime: Les Cahiers de Confluences* (Paris: L'Harmattan, 2002), 104.
32. The Algerian prime minister at the time of the 1988 riots has claimed that the French president, François Mitterrand, was very influential in persuading Chadli Benjedid to adopt a multi-party political system in the aftermath of the unrest. Author's interview with Abdelhamid Brahimi, prime minister of Algeria 1984–8, London, 19 December 1994.
33. Willis, *Islamist Challenge in Algeria*, 162–4.
34. In justification of these views, many ordinary Maghrebis cite their own personal experiences of Gulf Arabs visiting and especially holidaying in the Maghreb states.
35. Yahia H. Zoubir, 'Reactions in the Maghreb to the Gulf War,' *Arab Studies Quarterly*, 15, no. 1 (1993).
36. Zoubir, 'Reactions in the Maghreb,' 92.
37. Mortimer, 'Algerian Foreign Policy,' 262.
38. Damis, 'Impact of the Western Sahara Dispute,' 198–9; Damis, 'King Hassan and the Western Sahara,' 25–6.
39. Houdaigui, *La politique étrangère sous le règne de Hassan II*, 229–38.
40. Camille Bonora-Waisman, *France and the Algerian Conflict: Issues in Democracy and Political Stability, 1988–1995* (Aldershot: Ashgate, 2003) 196–202.
41. Lamloum, 'L'indéfectible soutien,' 104.
42. For numerous examples of criticism of France and French influence in the literature produced by the FIS in Algeria see M. Al-Ahnaf et al., *L'Algérie par ses islamistes*, 270–88.
43. The fact that the announcement of the 'discovery' of the plot came a matter of hours before the visit of the French foreign minister Roland Dumas has led to suggestions that the announcement was timed to influence French opinion, particularly on the activity of Tunisian exiles in France. Lamloum, 'L'indéfectible soutien,' 109; Phillip C. Naylor, *France and Algeria: A History of Decolonization and Transformation* (Gainesville: University Press of Florida, 2000), 179–80.
44. Bonora-Waisman, *France and the Algerian Conflict*, 22, 29–31.

45. Bonora-Waisman, *France and the Algerian Conflict*, 111–12, 136–8; Jean-François Daguzan, 'France, Democratization and North Africa,' in Richard Gillespie and Richard Youngs (eds), 'Special Issue: The European Union and Democracy Promotion: The Case of North Africa,' *Democratization*, 9 (2002), 141–4.
46. Naylor, *France and Algeria*, 198, 208–13.
47. See Laribi, *L'Algérie des Généraux*, 164–8.
48. Zoubir and Zunes, 'United States Policy in the Maghreb,' 229–31.
49. Nicole Grimaud, *La Tunisie à la recherche de sa sécurité*, 181, 187.
50. Yahia H. Zoubir, 'The United States, Islamism, and Democracy in the Maghreb: The Predominance of Security?' in Zoubir and Amirah-Fernández (eds), *North Africa*, 286.
51. Zoubir and Zunes, 'United States Policy in the Maghreb,' 234–5.
52. Waltz, *Human Rights and Reform*, 205–9.
53. Yousra Bencherif, *The Impact of Foreign Media on Moroccan Foreign Relations: The case of 'The Gilles Perrault Affair,'* Al Akhawyn University Research Paper Series, no. 13 (Social Sciences, 2003), 29–53; Waltz, *Human Rights and Reform*, 209–13.
54. Jean-Pierre Tuquoi, *Majesté, je dois beaucoup à votre père...: France-Maroc, une affaire de famille* (Paris: Albin Michel, 2006), 19–23 and 63–75; Daguzan, 'France and the Maghreb,' 338.
55. Daguzan, 'France, Democratization and North Africa,' 142–6.
56. William Mark Habeeb, 'The Maghribi States and the European Community,' in I. William Zartman and William Mark Habeeb (eds), *Polity and Society in Contemporary North Africa* (Boulder: Westview, 1993), 208–9; George Joffé, 'The European Union and the Maghreb in the 1990s,' in Yahia H. Zoubir (ed.), *North Africa in Transition: State, Society, and Economic Transformation in the 1990s* (Gainesville: University Press of Florida, 1999), 246–7.
57. Mohamed Ben Ali El Hassan Alaoui, *La Coopération entre l'Union Européenne et les Pays du Maghreb* (Paris: Editions Nathan, 1994), 79.
58. Lionel Fontagné and Nicolas Péridy, *The EU and the Maghreb* (Development Centre Studies, OECD, 1997), 71.
59. Barcelona declaration adopted at the Euro-Mediterranean Conference, 27–8 November 1995. Full text available at http://ec.europa.eu/external_relations/euromed/docs/bd_en.pdf.
60. Barcelona declaration adopted at the Euro-Mediterranean Conference, 27–8 November 1995.
61. Fouad M. Ammor, 'Morocco's Perspectives towards the EMP,' in Haizam Amirah Fernández and Richard Youngs (eds), *The Euro-Mediterranean Partnership: Assessing the First Decade* (Madrid: FRIDE, 2005), 151.
62. George Joffé, 'European Policy and the Southern Mediterranean,' in Yahia H. Zoubir and Haizam Amirah-Fernandes (eds), *North Africa: Politics, Region and the Limits of Transformation* (Abingdon and New York: Routledge, 2008), 315.

63. Fontagné and Péridy, *The EU and the Maghreb*, 27.
64. Barcelona declaration adopted at the Euro-Mediterranean Conference, 27–8 November 1995.
65. Richard Gillespie and Laurence Whitehead, 'European Democracy Promotion in North Africa: Limits and Prospects,' in Richard Gillespie and Richard Youngs (eds), 'Special Issue: The European Union and Democracy Promotion: The case of North Africa,' *Democratization*, 9 (2002), 192.
66. Joffé, 'European Policy and the Southern Mediterranean,' 314.
67. Joffé, 'European Policy and the Southern Mediterranean,' 323.
68. Hakim Darbouche, 'Decoding Algeria's ENP Policy: Differentiation by Other Means?' *Mediterranean Politics* 13, no. 3 (2008), 377.
69. Kristina Kausch, 'The European Union and Political Reform in Morocco,' in Driss Maghraoui and Michael J. Willis (eds), 'Special Issue: Reform in the Arab World: The Experience of Morocco,' *Mediterranean Politics*, 14, no. 2 (2009), 170–71; Bechir Chourou, 'The Euro-Mediterranean Partnership and the European Neighbourhood Policy: Results and Prospects,' paper presented at Information and Training seminar for Euro-Med Diplomats, Malta, 11–14 April 2008. http://www.euromed-seminars.org.mt/seminar24/papers/Chourou-MaltaSeminars-April_08-w.pdf.
70. Laskier, *Israel and the Maghreb*, 266–7.
71. It is claimed that President Zeroual established secret contacts with the Israelis in 1994 to secure medical and pharmaceutical suppliers that were needed in Algeria. See Laskier, *Israel and the Maghreb*, 276–7.
72. King Hassan actually called on Israelis of Moroccan origin to make 'the choice of peace' in the 1999 Israeli election and vote for Barak and the Labour party. Laskier, *Israel and the Maghreb*, 271–2.
73. Ahron Bergman, *The Elusive Peace: How the Holy Land Defeated America* (London: Penguin, 2005), 41–2, 107.
74. Laskier, *Israel and the Maghreb*, 276. There were reports that a high-ranking Israeli delegation visited Algeria in the autumn of 1999 to explore the possibility of establishing liaison bureaux there. Laskier, *Israel and the Maghreb*, 277.
75. *Le Journal*, 24 May 2007; *Le Temps* (Casablanca), 17 October 2009.
76. AllAfrica.com, 'Algerian president says terrorism must be fought equally worldwide,' 5 November 2001. Available at http://www.allAfrica.com.
77. *New York Times*, 13 February 2006. On another occasion the US defence secretary also commented: 'I was with President Bouteflika in Algeria not too long ago. What did they go through, 12 years? People were being beheaded in the streets. It was a horrible, bloody insurgency. It was a ghastly period for that country. Today they're fine. How did they get there? Was it easy? No. Was it bloody? You bet. Did it cost lives and money? Yes. And time? Yes. Think of other countries that have gone through an insurgency. In the last analysis, it was Algerians. And in the last analysis it's going to be Iraqis.' Quoted in *Financial Times* (London), 20 October 2006.

78. Donna Miles, 'New Counterterrorism Initiative to Focus on Saharan Africa,' *American Forces Press Service*, Department of Defense, 16 May 2005 (http://www.defense.gov/news/newsarticle.aspx?id=31643).
79. See Jeremy Keenan, *The Dark Sahara* (London: Pluto, 2008).
80. Zoubir and Zunes, 'United States Policy in the Maghreb,' 238.
81. Brieg Tomas Powel, 'The Stability Syndrome: US and EU democracy promotion in Tunisia,' in Francesco Cavatorta (ed.), 'Special Issue: The Foreign Policies of the European Union and the United Sates in North Africa—Diverging or Converging Dynamics?,' *Journal of North African Studies*, 14, no. 1 (2009), 69.
82. 'Bush Says Tunisia Needs Press Freedom, Open Political Process. Bush Hosts Tunisian President Ben Ali in Washington February 18,' 18 February 2004, America.gov. http://www.america.gov/st/washfile-english/2004/February/20040218165932CPataruK0.5092279.html.
83. Author's interview with Nejib Chebbi, leader of the Progressive Democratic Party (PDP) 2001–06, Tunis, 16 April 2009.
84. Zoubir and Zunes, 'United States Policy in the Maghreb,' 227; Zoubir, 'The United States, Islamism, and Democracy,' 267–9.
85. Patrick Holden, 'Security, Diplomacy or Profit? The economic diplomacy of the US and the EU in North Africa,' in Francesco Cavatorta (ed.), 'Special Issue: The Foreign Policies of the European Union and the United Sates in North Africa—Diverging or Converging Dynamics?,' *Journal of North African Studies*, 14, no. 1 (2009), 16–17.
86. Hakim Darbouche, *EU-Algerian Interaction in the Context of the Barcelona Process: Interests, Processes and the Limits of Convergence*, PhD thesis, Liverpool University 2009, 115–19, 129.
87. Lamloum, 'L'indéfectible soutien,' 111–18.
88. *Agence France Presse*, 9 February 2001, quoted in Pia Christina Wood, 'French Foreign policy and Tunisia: Do Human Rights Matter?,' *Middle East Policy*, 9, no. 2 (2002), 104.
89. *Le Monde*, 4 December 2003. Jean-François Daguzan argues that French timidity in raising the issue of human rights was a result of sensitivities about its own record on human rights during the colonial period, and was something that the Maghreb states did not fail to exploit when necessary. Daguzan, 'France and the Maghreb,' 332. Although this was most obviously the case for Algeria, the Tunisians made similar reference to French abuses in the colonial period when French officials expressed unhappiness with the state of human rights in the country in the wake of the 2009 presidential election in Tunisia. *Le Monde*, 17 November 2009.
90. Darbouche, 'Decoding Algeria's ENP Policy,' 375, 379–80. Although the agreement was not finally ratified by Algeria until 2005, Darbouche states that this was due to a packed political and legislative agenda within the country.
91. Reports produced by the European Commission that were critical of Tuni-

sia's human rights record were criticised and even suppressed by southern member states.
92. Brieg Tomos Powel, 'A clash of norms: normative power and EU democracy promotion in Tunisia,' *Democratization*, 16, no. 1 (2009), 200–208; Powel, 'The Stability Syndrome,' 65.
93. Kausch, 'The European Union and Political Reform in Morocco,' 173.
94. Iván Martín, 'Profile: EU-Morocco Relations: How Advanced is the "Advanced Status"?,' *Mediterranean Politics*, 14, no. 2 (2009), 239–42.
95. Kausch, 'The European Union and Political Reform in Morocco,' 174.
96. Ibid., 176; Powel, 'A clash of norms,' 208; Darbouche, 'Decoding Algeria's ENP Policy,' 380.
97. Darbouche, 'Decoding Algeria's ENP Policy,' 380–85.
98. Haizam Amirah-Fernandez, 'Spain's Policy Towards Morocco and Algeria: Balancing Relations with the Southern Neighbours,' in Zoubir and Amirah-Fernández (eds), *North Africa*, 354.
99. Richard Gillespie, *Spain and the Mediterranean: Developing a European Policy Towards the South* (Basingstoke: Macmillan, 2000), 63, 53, 55.
100. Gillespie, *Spain and the Mediterranean*, 42.
101. Ibid., 43 and 68; Haizam Amirah-Fernandez, 'Spain's Policy,' 350. It has been argued that Morocco used the issue of Sebta and Mellila in securing the Tripartite Agreement of 1976. Hodges, *Western Sahara*, 216.
102. Gillespie, *Spain and the Mediterranean*, 50.
103. Richard Gillespie, '"This Stupid Little Island": A Neighbourhood Confrontation in the Western Mediterranean,' *International Politics*, 43 (2006), 114–15.
104. Interestingly, trade between Morocco and Spain actually *increased* during the period of the crisis. Amirah-Fernandez, 'Spain's Policy,' 353.
105. *Maroc Hebdo International*, 30 November 2001.
106. Miguel Hernando de Larramendi, 'La politique étrangère de l'Espagne envers le Maghreb. De l'adhésion à l'Union européenne à la guerre contre l'Iraq,' in *L'Année du Maghreb 2004* (Paris: CNRS Editions, 2006), 33–6 and 41. Spain signed a Treaty of Friendship and Cooperation with Tunisia in 1995, but the ties between the two countries remained very limited when compared to those with Morocco and Algeria.
107. *La Vie éco* (Casablanca), 19 March 2004.
108. Amirah-Fernandez, 'Spain's Policy,' 357–9.
109. Darbouche, 'Decoding Algeria's ENP Policy,' 380–81.
110. Amirah-Fernandez, 'Spain's Policy,' 353.
111. Hernando de Larramendi, 'La politique étrangère de l'Espagne,' 40–42.
112. George Joffé, 'European Policy and the Southern Mediterranean,' 318.
113. Daguzan, 'France and the Maghreb,' 335–6.
114. Richard Gillespie, 'Profile: A "Union for the Mediterranean"…or for the EU?,' *Mediterranean Politics*, 13, no. 2 (July 2008).

115. *L'Expression* (Algiers), 19 June 2008.
116. See *Libération* (Paris), 10 February 2010; *L'Express* (Paris), 27 November 2009; *Aujourd'hui Le Maroc*, 1 December 2010.
117. *Le Monde*, 11 January 2011,
118. *Le Monde*, 1 February 2011.
119. The leading opposition politician, Nejib Chebbi, who became a cabinet minister in the interim government put together in the immediate aftermath of the departure of Ben Ali, had long argued that 'France is against change in Tunisia. It has a dominant position in the country and does not want that to change.' Author's interview with Nejib Chebbi, leader of the Progressive Democratic Party (PDP) 2001–06, Tunis, 16 April 2009.
120. *Le Temps* (Tunis), 19 February 2011.
121. *Le Temps* (Tunis), 13 April 2011.

CONCLUSION

1. A leader and founder of the 20 February Movement to author, Rabat, 1 April 2011.

SELECT BIBLIOGRAPHY

Aboud, Hichem, *La Mafia des Généraux* (Paris: J.C. Lattès, 2002)
Abun-Nasr, Jamil, *A History of the Maghrib in the Islamic Period* (Cambridge: Cambridge University Press, 1987)
Addi, Lahouari, 'Les partis politiques en Algérie,' *Revue des Mondes Musulmans et de la Mediterranée. Les partis politiques dans les pays Arabes. Tome 2: Le Maghreb*, 111–12 (Paris: Edisud, 2006)
Ageron, Charles-Robert, *Modern Algeria: A History from 1830 to the Present* (London: Hurst & Co., 1991)
Amirah-Fernández, Haizam, 'Spain's Policy Towards Morocco and Algeria: Balancing Relations with the Southern Neighbours,' in Yahia H. Zoubir and Haizam Amirah-Fernández (eds), *North Africa: Politics, Region, and the Limits of Transformation* (Abingdon: Routledge, 2008)
Balta, Paul, *Le Grand Maghreb: Des Indépendances à l'an 2000* (Paris: La Découverte, 1990)
Beau, Nicolas and Jean-Pierre Tuquoi, *Notre Ami Ben Ali: L'Envers du 'Miracle Tunisien'* (Paris: La Découverte, 1999)
Bessis, Sophie and Souhayr Belhassen, *Bourguiba. Tome 1: A la conquête d'un destin 1901–1957* (Paris: Jeune Afrique Livres, 1988); *Tome 2: Un si long règne 1957–1989* (Paris: Jeune Afrique Livres, 1989)
Bonora-Waisman, Camille, *France and the Algerian Conflict: Issues in Democracy and Political Stability, 1988–1995* (Aldershot: Ashgate, 2003)
Braun, Célina, 'A quoi servent les partis Tunisiens? Sens et contre-sens d'une "liberalisation" politique,' *Revue des Mondes Musulmans et de la Méditerranée. Les partis politiques dans les pays Arabes. Tome 2: Le Maghreb*, 111–12 (Paris: Edisud, 2006).
Brett, Michael and Elizabeth Fentress, *The Berbers* (Oxford: Blackwell, 1996)
Camau, Michel and Vincent Geisser, *Le syndrome autoritaire: Politique en Tunisie de Bourguiba à Ben Ali* (Paris: Presses de Sciences Po, 2003)
Charef, Abed, *Algérie: Le Grand Dérapage* (Paris: L'Aube, 1994)
Crawford, David and Katherine E. Hoffman, 'Essentially Amazigh: Urban Berbers and the Global Village,' in R. Kevin Lacey and Ralph M. Coury (eds),

SELECT BIBLIOGRAPHY

The Arab-African and Islamic Worlds: Interdisciplinary Studies (New York: Peter Lang, 2000)

Daguzan, Jean-François, *Le Dernier Rempart? Forces Armées et Politiques de Défense au Maghreb* (Paris: Publisud, 1998)

────── 'France and the Maghreb: The End of the Special Relationship?,' in Yahia H. Zoubir and Haizam Amirah-Fernández (eds), *North Africa: Politics, Region, and the Limits of Transformation* (Abingdon: Routledge, 2008)

Dalle, Ignace, *Les Trois Rois: La Monarchie Marocaine de l'Indépendance à Nos Jours* (Paris: Fayard, 2004)

Damis, John, *Conflict in Northwest Africa: The Western Sahara Dispute* (Stanford: Hoover Press, 1983)

────── 'The Western Sahara Dispute as a Source of Regional Conflict in North Africa,' in Halim Barakat (ed.), *Contemporary North Africa: Issues of Development and Integration* (London: Croom Helm, 1985)

────── 'The Impact of the Saharan Dispute on Moroccan Foreign and Domestic Policy,' in I. W. Zartman (ed.): *The Political Economy of Morocco* (New York: Praeger 1987)

────── 'The United States and North Africa,' in I. William Zartman and William Mark Habeeb (eds), *Polity and Society in Contemporary North Africa* (Boulder: Westview, 1993)

Darbouche, Hakim, 'Decoding Algeria's ENP Policy: Differentiation by Other Means?,' *Mediterranean Politics*, 13, no. 3 (2008)

Darif, Mohamed, *al-Islamiyyûn al-maghariba: hisâbât as-siyyâsa fi al-'amal al-islâmî 1969–1999* (Casablanca: Al-Majalla al-maghribiyya li 'ilm al-ijtima' as-siyyâsî, 1999)

Denoeux, Guilain, 'Understanding Morocco's 'Sanitisation' Campaign (December 1995–May 1996),' *Journal of North African Studies*, 3, no. 1 (1998)

────── and Abdeslam Maghraoui, 'The Political Economy of Structural Adjustment in Morocco,' in Azzedine Layachi (ed.), *Economic Crisis and Political Change in North Africa* (Westport: Praeger, 1998)

Dris-Ait-Hamadouche, Louisa and Yahia H. Zoubir, 'Pouvoir et opposition en Algérie: vers une transition prolongée,' *L'Année du Maghreb 2009* (Paris: CNRS Editions, 2009)

Dunn, Michael Collins, 'The An-Nahda Movement in Tunisia: From Renaissance to Revolution,' in John Ruedy (ed.), *Islamism and Secularism in North Africa* (London: Macmillan, 1994)

Entelis, John P., *Algeria: The Revolution Institutionalized* (Boulder: Westview, 1986)

────── *Culture and Counter-Culture in Moroccan Politics* (Maryland: University Press of America, 1996)

────── and Phillip C. Naylor (eds), *State and Society in Algeria* (Boulder: Westview, 1992)

Essebsi, Béji Caïd, *Habib Bourguiba: Le Bon Grain et l'Ivraie* (Tunis: Sud Editions, 2009)

SELECT BIBLIOGRAPHY

Feliu, Laura, 'Le Mouvement culturel amazigh (MCA) au Maroc,' *L'Année du Maghreb 2004* (Paris: CNRS Editions, 2006)

Gellner, Ernest and Charles Micaud (eds), *Arabs and Berbers: From Tribe to Nation in North Africa* (London: Duckworth, 1973)

Gillespie, Richard, *Spain and the Mediterranean: Developing a European Policy Towards the South* (Basingstoke: Macmillan, 2000)

Goodman, Jane, 'Reinterpreting the Berber Spring: From Rite of Reversal to Site of Convergence,' *Journal of North African Studies*, 9, no. 3 (Autumn 2004)

Grimaud, Nicole, *La Politique Extérieure de l'Algérie* (Paris: Karthala, 1984)

——— *La Tunisie: A la Recherche de sa Sécurité* (Paris: PUF, 1995)

Hamdi, Mohamed ElHachmi, *The Politicization of Islam: A Case Study of Tunisia* (Boulder: Westview, 1998)

Hassan II, *La Memoire d'un Roi: Entretiens avec Eric Laurent* (Paris: Plon, 1993),

Henry Moore, Clement, *Tunisia Since Independence: The Dynamics of One-Party Government* (Westport: Greenwood Press, 1965)

——— 'Crises of Money and Power: Transitions to Democracy?,' in John P. Entelis (ed.), *Islam, Democracy and the State in North Africa* (Bloomington and Indianapolis: Indiana University Press, 1997)

——— and Robert Springborg, *Globalization and the Politics of Development in the Middle East* (Cambridge: Cambridge University Press, 2001)

Hermassi, Elbaki, 'The Islamicist Movement and November 7,' in I. William Zartman (ed.), *Tunisia: The Political Economy of Reform* (London: Lynne Rienner, 1991)

Hibou, Béatrice, 'Il n'y a pas de miracle Tunisien,' in Olfa Lamloum and Bernard Ravenel, *La Tunisie de Ben Ali: La Société Contre le Régime* (Paris: L'Harmattan, 2002)

——— 'Fiscal trajectories in Morocco and Tunisia,' in Steven Heydemann (ed.), *Networks of Privilege in the Middle East: the Politics of Economic Reform Revisited* (New York and Basingstoke: Palgrave Macmillan, 2004)

Hodges, Tony, *Western Sahara: The Roots of a Desert War* (Westport: Lawrence Hill, 1983)

Hopwood, Derek, *Habib Bourguiba of Tunisia: The Tragedy of Longevity* (Basingstoke: Macmillan, 1992)

Houdaigui, Rachid El, *La politique étrangère sous le règne de Hassan II* (Paris: L'Harmattan, 2003)

Hughes, Stephen O., *Morocco Under King Hassan* (Reading: Ithaca Press, 2001)

International Crisis Group (ICG), *Algeria: Unrest and Impasse in Kabylia*, Middle East/North Africa Report no. 15, 10 June 2003

——— *Islamism, Violence and Reform in Algeria: Turning the Page*, Middle East Report no. 29, 30 July 2004

——— *Western Sahara: Out of the Impasse*, Middle East/North Africa Report no. 66, 11 June 2007

SELECT BIBLIOGRAPHY

Joffé, George, 'The Army in Algerian Politics and Government,' in Reza Shah-Kazemi (ed.), *Algeria: Revolution Revisited* (London: Islamic World Report, 1997)
—— 'The European Union and the Maghreb in the 1990s,' in Yahia H. Zoubir (ed.), *North Africa in Transition: State, Society, and Economic Transformation in the 1990s* (Gainesville: University Press of Florida, 1999)
—— 'The Role of Violence Within the Algerian Economy,' *Journal of North African Studies*, 7, no. 1 (2002)
—— 'European Policy and the Southern Mediterranean,' in Yahia H. Zoubir and Haizam Amirah-Fernández (eds), *North Africa: Politics, Region and the Limits of Transformation* (Abingdon and New York: Routledge, 2008)
Kapil, Arun, 'Algeria,' in Frank Tachau (ed.), *Political Parties of the Middle East and North Africa* (London: Mansell, 1994)
Kausch, Kristina, 'The European Union and Political Reform in Morocco,' in Driss Maghraoui and Michael J. Willis (eds), 'Special Issue: Reform in the Arab World: The Experience of Morocco,' *Mediterranean Politics*, 14, no. 2 (2009)
King, Stephen, *Liberalization Against Democracy: The Local Politics of Economic Reform in Tunisia* (Bloomington: Indiana University Press, 2003)
Kraiem, Mustapha, *Etat et société dans la Tunisie Bourguibienne* (Tunis: MIP, 2011)
Lacey, R. Kevin and Ralph M. Coury (eds), *The Arab-African and Islamic Worlds: Interdisciplinary Studies* (New York: Peter Lang, 2000)
Lamloum, Olfa and Bernard Ravenel (eds), *La Tunisie de Ben Ali: La Société Contre le Régime* (Paris: L'Harmattan, 2002)
Laroui, Abdallah, *L'Histoire du Maghreb: Un Essai de Synthèse* (Casablanca: Centre Culturel Arabe, 1995)
Laskier, Michael M., *Israel and the Maghreb: From Statehood to Oslo* (Gainesville: University Press of Florida, 2004)
Layachi, Azzedine(ed.), *Economic Crisis and Political Change in North Africa* (Westport: Praeger, 1998)
—— 'Reform and the Politics of Inclusion in the Maghrib,' *Journal of North African Studies*, 5, no. 3 (2000)
—— 'The Berbers in Algeria: Politicized Ethnicity and Ethnicized Politics,' in Maya Shatzmiller (ed.), *Nationalism and Minority Identities in Islamic Societies* (Montreal and Kingston: McGill-Queen's University Press, 2005)
Le Gall, Michel, 'The Historical Context,' in I. William Zartman and William Mark Habeeb (eds), *Polity and Society in Contemporary North Africa* (Boulder: Westview, 1993)
Leveau, Rémy, *Le Fellah Marocain: Défenseur du Trône* (Paris: Presses de la Fondation des Sciences Politiques, 2ndedn, 1985)
—— *Le Sabre et le Turban: L'Avenir du Maghreb* (Paris: François Bourrin, 1993)
Maddy-Weitzman, Bruce, 'Contested Identities: Berbers, Berberism and the State in North Africa,' *Journal of North African Studies*, 6, no. 3 (Autumn 2001)

SELECT BIBLIOGRAPHY

Martín, Iván, 'Algeria's Political Economy (1999–2002): An Economic Solution to the Crisis?,' *Journal of North African Studies*, 8, no. 2 (2003)

Martinez, Luis, *The Algerian Civil War 1992–1998* (London: Hurst & Co., 2000)

Mortimer, Robert, 'Algerian Foreign Policy in Transition,' in John P. Entelis and Phillip C. Naylor (eds), *State and Society in Algeria* (Boulder: Westview, 1992)

—— 'The Arab Maghreb Union: Myth and Reality,' in Yahia H. Zoubir (ed.), *North Africa in Transition: State, Society, and Economic Transformation in the 1990s* (Gainesville: University Press of Florida, 1999)

Munson, Henry, *Religion and Power in Morocco* (New Haven and London: Yale University Press, 1993)

Murphy, Emma, *Economic and Political Change in Tunisia: From Bourguiba to Ben Ali* (London: Macmillan, 1999)

Naylor, Phillip C., 'French-Algerian Relations, 1980–1990,' in John P. Entelis and Phillip C. Naylor (eds), *State and Society in Algeria* (Boulder: Westview, 1992)

—— *France and Algeria: A History of Decolonization and Transformation* (Gainesville: University Press of Florida, 2000)

Ottaway, David and Marina, *Algeria: The Politics of a Socialist Revolution* (Berkeley and Los Angeles: University of California Press, 1970)

Parker, Richard B., *North Africa: Regional Tensions and Strategic Concerns* (New York: Praeger, 1987)

Payne, Rhys, 'Economic Crisis and Policy Reform in the 1980s,' in I. William Zartman and William Mark Habeeb (eds), *Polity and Society in Contemporary North Africa* (Boulder: Westview, 1993)

Pennell, Richard, *Morocco Since 1830: A History* (London: Hurst & Co., 2000)

Perkins, Kenneth J., *Tunisia: Crossroads of the Islamic and European Worlds* (Boulder: Westview, London: Croom Helm, 1986)

Quandt, William B., *Revolution and Political Leadership: Algeria 1954–1968* (Cambridge and London: MIT Press, 1969)

Roberts, Hugh, 'The Unforeseen Development of the Kabyle Question in Contemporary Algeria,' in *Government and Opposition*, vol. 17, no. 3 (Summer 1982)

—— 'The Politics of Algerian Socialism,' in R. I. Lawless and A. M. Findlay (eds), *North Africa* (London: Croom Helm, 1984)

—— 'The FLN: French Conceptions, Algerian Realities,' in George Joffé (ed.), *North Africa: Nation, State and Region* (London: Routledge, 1993)

—— 'Doctrinaire Economics and Political Opportunism in the Strategy of Algerian Islamism,' in John Ruedy (ed.), *Islamism and Secularism in North Africa* (London: Macmillan 1994)

—— 'Algeria's Ruinous Impasse and the Honourable Way Out,' in *International Affairs*, 71, 2 (1995)

―――― 'The Zeroual Memorandum: The Algerian State and the Problem of Liberal Reform,' in *Journal of Algerian Studies*, vol. 1(1996)

―――― 'The Struggle for Constitutional Rule in Algeria,' in *Journal of Algerian Studies*, vol. 3(1998)

―――― 'Demilitarizing Algeria,' *Carnegie Papers*, Middle East Program, no. 86, May 2007 (http://www.carnegieendowment.org/publications/index.cfm?fa=view&id=19153)

Ruedy, John, 'Historical Influences on Intra-Regional Relations in the Maghrib,' in Halim Barakat (ed.), *Contemporary North Africa: Issues of Development and Integration* (London: Croom Helm, 1985)

―――― *Modern Algeria: The Origins and Development of a Nation* (Bloomington: Indiana University Press, 1992)

―――― (ed.), *Islamism and Secularism in North Africa* (London: Macmillan, 1994)

Shahin, Emad Eldin, *Political Ascent: Contemporary Islamic Movements in North Africa* (Boulder: Westview, 1997)

Shelley, Toby, *Endgame in the Western Sahara: What Future for Africa's Last Colony?* (London: Zed Books, 2004)

Stora, Benjamin, *Histoire de l'Algérie depuis l'Indépendance* (Paris: La Découverte, 1994)

Tachau, Frank (ed.), *Political Parties in the Middle East and North Africa* (London: Greenwood Press, 1994)

Tamimi, Azzam S., *Rachid Ghannouchi: A Democrat within Islamism* (Oxford: Oxford University Press, 2001)

Toumi, Mohsen, *La Tunisie de Bourguiba à Ben Ali* (Paris: Presses Universitaires de France, 1989)

Tozy, Mohamed, *Monarchie et Islam Politique au Maroc* (Paris: Presses de Sciences Po, 1999)

Vermeren, Pierre, *Le Maroc de Mohamed VI: La Transition Inachevée* (Paris: La Découverte, 2009)

Waltz, Susan E., *Human Rights and Reform: Changing the Face of North African Politics* (London: University of California Press, 1995)

Ware, L. B., 'The Role of the Tunisian Military in the Post-Bourguiba Era,' *Middle East Journal*, vol. 39, no. 1 (1985)

―――― 'Ben Ali's Constitutional Coup in Tunisia,' in *Middle East Journal*, vol. 42, no. 4 (1988)

Waterbury, John, *The Commander of the Faithful: The Moroccan Elite: A Study in Segmented Politics* (London: Weidenfeld and Nicolson, 1970)

―――― 'The Coup Manqué,' in Ernest Gellner and Charles Micaud (eds), *Arabs and Berbers: From Tribe to Nation in North Africa* (London: Duckworth, 1973)

Werenfels, Isabelle, 'Obstacles to Privatisation of State-Owned Industries in Algeria: The Political Economy of a Distributive Conflict,' *Journal of North African Studies*, 7, no. 1 (2002)

White, Gregory, *A Comparative Political Economy of Tunisia and Morocco:*

SELECT BIBLIOGRAPHY

On the Outside of Europe Looking In (Albany: State University of New York Press, 2001)

Willis, Michael J., *The Islamist Challenge in Algeria: A Political History* (Reading: Ithaca Press, 1996)

―― 'Between *Alternance* and the *Makhzen*: At-Tawhid wa Al-Islah's Entry into Moroccan Politics,' *Journal of North African Studies*, 4, no. 3 (Autumn 1999)

―― 'Political Parties in the Maghrib: The Illusion of Significance?,' *Journal of North African Studies*, 7, no. 2 (Summer 2002)

―― 'Justice and Development or Justice and Spirituality? The Challenge of Morocco's Non-Violent Islamist Movements,' in Bruce Maddy-Weitzman and Daniel Zisenwine (eds), *The Maghrib in the New Century: Identity, Religion and Politics* (Gainesville: University of Florida Press, 2007)

―― 'The Politics of Berber (Amazigh) Identity: Algeria and Morocco Compared,' in Yahia H. Zoubir and Haizam Amirah-Fernandez (eds), *North Africa: Politics, Region and the Limits of Transformation* (London: Routledge, 2007)

―― 'Islamism, Democratization and Disillusionment: Morocco's Legislative Elections of 2007,' Research Paper no. 1, Mohamed VI Fellowship in Moroccan and Mediterranean Studies, St Antony's College, Oxford, 2008 (http://www.sant.ox.ac.uk/mec/morocco/Islamism-Democratisation-Disillusionment.pdf)

Zartman, I. William, 'King Hassan's New Morocco,' in I. William Zartman (ed.), *The Political Economy of Morocco* (New York: Praeger, 1987)

―― (ed.), *The Political Economy of Morocco* (New York: Praeger 1987)

―― (ed.), *Tunisia: The Political Economy of Reform* (London: Lynne Rienner, 1991)

―― and William Mark Habeeb (eds), *Polity and Society in Contemporary North Africa* (Boulder: Westview, 1993)

Zoubir, Yahia H., 'Reactions in the Maghreb to the Gulf War,' *Arab Studies Quarterly*, 15, no. 1 (1993)

―― (ed.), *North Africa in Transition: State, Society, and Economic Transformation in the 1990s* (Gainesville: University Press of Florida, 1999)

―― 'The United States, Islamism, and Democracy in the Maghreb: The Predominance of Security?,' in Yahia H. Zoubir and Haizam Amirah-Fernández (eds), *North Africa: Politics, Region, and the Limits of Transformation* (Abingdon: Routledge, 2008)

―― and Stephen Zunes, 'United States Policy in the Maghreb,' in Yahia H. Zoubir (ed.), *North Africa in Transition: State, Society, and Economic Transformation in the 1990s* (Gainesville: University Press of Florida, 1999)

―― and Haizam Amirah-Fernández (eds), *North Africa: Politics, Region, and the Limits of Transformation* (Abingdon: Routledge, 2008)

INDEX

Abbas, Ferhat: 26, 29, 32, 157; support for ALN, 50
Abdeslam, Belaid: 253
Abdu, Mohamed: 26; influence of, 156
Adghrini, Ahmed: Berber identity theories of, 225–6
Adib, Mustapha: 113, 115
Afghanistan: 320; mujahidin, 173, 194; Soviet Invasion of (1979–89), 173
Agadir Charter (1991), 215, 222
Al-Adl wal Ihsan: 192, 197–8; boycotting of elections, 152; growth of, 184; Guidance Council, 180; members of, 186; opponents of, 185; origins of, 180
Ait Ahmed, Hocine: leader of FFS, 130, 214
Al Haraka Shaabia: see Mouvement Populaire
Al-Islah wa At-Tajdid: 180
Al Qaeda: 192, 320; influence of, 194
Al Qaeda in the Islamic Maghreb (AQIM): 195; formerly GSPC, 193
Al Qiyam: association, 161
Alliot-Marie, Michèle: French Foreign Minister, 333
Africa: 9; provinces of Roman Empire in, 11; Saharan Desert, 12; sub-Saharan, 5, 293, 331-2

Alawite dynasty: 16; origins in Tafilalet region of Morocco, 93
Algeria: 3, 11, 14, 17, 19, 33–5, 49, 62–3, 66, 70–1, 77–8, 81, 87–8, 93–4, 103, 128–9, 131, 139–41, 144, 146–7, 150, 152, 155, 157–8, 164, 167, 177, 198–200, 223, 231–2, 262, 265, 277, 279–80, 282–3, 300, 305–6, 315, 339; *Assemblée Populaire Nationale* (APN), 67; borders of, 270, 274, 277; Charter of Peace and National Reconciliation (2005), 112, 225; Civil War (1991–2002), 105; Constantine, 26, 33; Constitution of (1963), 48, 67–8; Constitution of (1976), 90; Constitution of (1989), 100–1, 168; Council of Ministers, 67; Council of the Revolution, 48–9, 57–8, 67, 77, 89; *Départment du Renseignement et de la Sécurité* (DRS), 118, 195, 320; economy of, 76, 130, 236, 238, 240, 253, 255–8, 261; founding member of Arab Maghreb Union, 5; French colonial influence in, 19–20, 23, 26–7, 30–2, 110, 208, 213, 331; Government of, 164, 173, 238, 303; *Haut Commissariat à l'Amazighité* (HCA), 217; High Council of State, 105–

INDEX

6, 172; Independence of (1962), 30, 37, 45, 78, 82, 121, 123, 233, 293–4; Islamism in, 108–10, 115, 139, 151, 156, 160–2, 168, 171–2, 174, 178, 186, 190, 193, 195, 198, 214, 216–17, 307, 309, 319, 321; Kabylia, 151, 209–10, 213, 216, 218, 225, 258, 268; Kabyle tribes of, 204–5, 210, 223, 227; member of Rejection Front, 301; military of, 82, 88-90, 97-103, 105-12, 116, 136, 161, 286; Ministry of Defence, 97; National Assembly, 67, 103, 137–9, 170–1; nationalism in, 27–9, 139, 285; Ottoman influence in, 18, 22; parliamentary elections in (2007), 149; recognition of SADR (1976), 281; rejection of ENP, 324; role in shuttle diplomacy (1974), 297; Rome Platform (1995), 139; Treaty of Friendship and Cooperation (1992), 327; War of Independence, (1954–62) 30–1, 33, 207, 267, 294; Zeralda, 282

Algiers, 15–16, 19, 33, 101, 153, 172, 191, 205–6, 210, 263, 266, 280, 282, 298, 302, 308, 320, 330, 335–6;

Algiers Charter (1964): 76

Almohads (*al-muwahhidun*): significance of, 12–13, 342

Almoravids (*al-murabitum*): significance of, 12–13, 342

Alternance: 113, 142–4, 149–50, 153, 219, 336; impact on credibility of Istiqlal and USFP, 183

Amazigh *see* Berbers

Amazigh (revue): first edition of (1980), 213

Amazigh Cultural Movement (MCA): 215; demands of, 216; supporters of, 222

Ammar, General Rachid: role in removal of Zine Al-Abidine Ben Ali from power (2011), 116–19

Amnesty International: condemnation of trials of An-Nahda members (1991), 176

Amir Al-Muminim: concept of, 55

An-Nahda party (Algeria): 190

An-Nahda party (Tunisia): 132, 153, 168, 170, 172, 175, 198, 310, 322; activists, 168; election victory of 2011, 201; members of, 167, 191, 195; opposition to, 134–5; successor to MTI, 155; support for Iraq during Persian Gulf War, 304; supporters of, 196; trial of members (1991), 176–7, 200

Annahj Addimocrati: boycotting of elections, 152

Arab Cooperation Council: 283

Arab League: expulsion of Egypt (1979), 301; Rabat Summit (1974), 301

Arab Maghreb Union (AMU): 282-7; founding of (1989), 5, 283; members of, 287, 292; Treaty of Marrakech (1989), 283–5

Arab Spring: 4, 151, 258, 334, 338; Algerian protests (2011), 151–3; Tunisian Revolution (2011), 1, 116–19, 151, 197, 243, 264, 332, 334, 337–8

Arabs: 13; arrival in Maghreb, 11–12

Arabs and Berbers: view of contributors, 206–7

Arafat, Yasser: 317; declaration of Palestinian Independence (1987), 302

Arme de Libération Nationale (ALN): 86, 90; activities of, 46; created by FLN (1954), 85; members of, 47, 89; renamed as ANP, 48, 88; supporters of, 50

Armée Nationale Populaire (ANP):

INDEX

90, 99–101, 107–9, 286; ceasefire with AIS (1997), 187; formerly ALN, 48, 88; role in organisation of FLN party congress, 97

Army of Islamic Salvation (AIS): 174; ceasefire with ANP (1997), 187; members of, 188

Association of Algerian Ulema: 32, 156, 161, 211; formation of (1931), 27; support for FLN, 158

Association Marocaine des Droits de l'Homme (AMDH): activists of, 150

At-Tawhid wa al-Islah: 184, 193

Ataturk, Mustafa Kemal: influence of, 158

Aznar, Jose Maria: Spanish Prime Minister, 326

Bahrain: 337; Manama, 337

Baker, James: resignation of, 289; UN special envoy, 288

Balafrej, Ahmed: Prime Minister of Morocco, 45

Bandung Conference (1955): 296

Barak, Ehud: Prime Minister of Israel, 317, 382

Barcelona Conference and Declaration (1995): 312-6, 325, 327

Basri, Driss: dismissal of (1999), 112, 115; Moroccan Minister of Interior, 112, 117, 127, 142, 246, 361

Belgium: Moroccan diaspora in, 226; Brussels, 329

Belhadji, Ali: deputy leader of FIS, 197; released from prison (2003), 188

Belkheir, General Larbi: 107; Algerian Interior Minister, 102, 110

Ben Ali, Zine Al-Abidine: 133, 135, 146, 149, 152, 167, 176, 240, 242, 321, 334, 338; assumption of Defence portfolio (1987–9), 104; background of, 96, 117; corruption under, 242–3; director of national security at Tunisian Ministry of Interior, 95–6, 117; family of, 4, 243; Prime Minister of Tunisia, 96–7; regime of, 104–5, 116, 179, 191, 195–6, 247, 310, 317, 333, 336–7; removed from power (2011), 1, 116, 118–19, 197, 229, 243, 249, 264, 336; role in removal of Habib Bourguiba from power (1987), 54, 95–6, 129, 133, 155, 166, 284, 303; supporters of, 321, 333

Ben Badis, Abdelhamid: 26, 158

Ben Barka, Mehdi: murder of (1965), 296, 310

Ben Bella, Ahmed: 47–9, 58–9, 62–3, 66–7, 75, 161, 207–8, 267–8, 292; appointment of supporters to National Constituent Assembly by, 56; *autogestion* policies of, 234; leader of MDA, 130; named as first president of independent Algeria, 48, 86, 123; relationship with Gamal Abdul Nasser, 297; removed from power (1965), 48, 57, 59, 66, 77, 88–9, 298, 376; secretary general of FLN, 57, 68

Ben Jaafar, Mustapha: attempt to run in Tunisian presidential election (2009), 357

Ben Salah, Ahmed: 122, 160, 164; economic policies of, 128; exile of, 128–9; former head of UGTT, 61, 75; Prime Minister of Tunisia, 232; sacked (1969), 232–3, 235; shortcomings of, 61; supporters of, 244

Ben Youssef, Salah: 73, 279; conflict with Habib Bourguiba, 39–40, 49, 51, 71, 74, 232; exile of (1956), 39; murder of, 344; rejection of Franco-Tunisian Autonomy Conventions (1955), 38–9

397

INDEX

secretary general of Neo-Destour, 38; supporters of, 53, 87, 158

Benjedid, Chadli: 106–7, 125, 130–1, 135, 162, 170, 238, 250, 256, 281, 306; allies of, 251; background of, 97–8; foreign policy of, 282, 284, 303; President of Algeria, 82, 97–8, 100, 124, 280, 282; resignation of (1992), 103, 105, 137, 286; support for FIS, 136

Benkirane, Abdelilah: leader of PJD, 184, 186, 197

Berber Cultural Movement (MCB): 218, 224, 332; origins of, 214; supporters of, 216

Berber Manifesto: announcement of (2000), 220; signatories of, 220

Berber Spring (1980), 124, 210, 214, 217–18, 224

Berbers: 12, 203-29; arrival in Maghreb (*c.* 2000 BC), 11; Chaouia. 211; identity of, 214, 222, 227, 229; languages of, 204–6, 210, 215–20, 228; political presence of, 44; presence within FAR, 83; presence within FLN, 206, 223; territory populated by, 13

Bey, Lamine: 41; role in creation of Tunisian Constituent Assembly (1956), 40

Bey, Moncef: death of (1948), 30; exile of (1943), 40

Bin Laden, Osama: 194

Bouazizi, Mohamed: suicide of (2010), 243

Boudiaf, Mohamed: 107; assassination of (1992), 106, 286; co-founder of FLN, 105–6; head of Algerian High Council of State, 105

Boumedienne, Houari: 58–9, 63, 67, 71, 73, 75, 78, 98, 208, 273, 288, 291–2, 376; announcement of 'Socialist Revolution' (1971), 72, 76, 90, 252; attempted coups against, 87; chief of staff of ALN, 47, 85; coup d'état led by (1965), 76; creation of Council of Ministers, 89; death of (1978), 63, 68, 90, 97, 124, 162, 238; development strategy of, 77; economic policies of, 268; foreign policy of, 282; industrialisation programmes of, 253; leader of Council of the Revolution, 48–9, 57–8; nationalisation of hydrocarbon reserves (1971), 295; President of Algeria, 82; reconstruction of regime of, 58; relationship with military, 124; view of partitioning of Spanish Sahara, 274–5

Bourguiba, Habib: 4, 29, 41–2, 52, 56–7, 63–4, 66–7, 70–1, 74–5, 78, 123, 129, 133, 157–9, 164, 198, 232–3, 299, 301, 306, 338; background of, 25; circulation of senior figures within regime of, 60–1; conflict with Salah Ben Youssef, 39–40, 49, 51, 71, 74, 232; economic policies of, 128; exclusion of Tunisian military from politics, 86, 88, 104; foreign policy of, 295; influence of, 64; *Le Monde* interview (1975), 280; modernisation aims, 74; party president of Neo-Destour, 38, 48; President of Tunisia, 40; proclamation of self as 'President for Life' (1974), 53; removed from power (1987), 54, 95–6, 105, 129, 133, 155, 166, 282, 284, 303; speeches of, 52; use of Neo-Destour, 64–5, 122, 278–9, 294

Bouteflika, Abdelaziz: 48, 273, 291, 368; Algerian Foreign Minister, 98, 107, 267; foreign policy of, 319, 329; President of Algeria, 107, 111–12, 288, 318, 321; opposition to *Tamazight*

398

INDEX

as national an official language, 225; supporters of, 140
Brahimi, Abdelhamid: prime minister of Algeria (1984-8), 352, 354, 380
Britain: 167, 343 *see also* London
Bush, George W.: 319, 321; administration of, 321; foreign policy of, 321

Camp David Accords (1978): 301
Casablanca: 162, 233, 249, 318; bombings (2003), 192, 320, 363; riots in (1965) 69, 73, 85, 91, 126.
Carter, Jimmy: administration of, 300; foreign policy of, 300
Carthage: establishment of, 11
Chad: 281
Chaker, Salem: support for MAK, 224
Chami, Hassan: President of CGEM, 246–7
Chechnya: 194
China: influence of, 331
Chirac, Jacques: background of, 311; foreign policy of, 312, 321; President of France, 311, 322, 329; relationship with King Hassan, 311-2; visit to Tunisia (2003), 322
Chorou, Sadok: 360
Christianity: 18
Clinton, Bill: 318
Cold War: 283, 295, 301; end of, 302
Colonialism: 209; French, 5, 19–20, 23, 26–7, 30, 32, 41, 54, 82–4, 99, 110, 203, 205, 208, 213, 265, 270–1, 294, 331; Italian, 5; legacy of, 76; Spanish, 19–20, 41, 82–3, 203, 270–1, 324
Communism: 27, 65; Algerian, 124
Confédération Générale des Enterprises du Maroc (CGEM): 246, 248, 262; members of, 246–7

Conference of Tangier (1958): participants in, 266
Conseil National pour les Libertés en Tunisie (CNLT): 150
Coordinations Movement: El Kseur Platform, 219

Daddah, Mokhtar Ould: overthrow of (1978), 278; President of Mauritania, 278
de Gaulle, Charles: ending of war in Algeria, 32; retirement of (1970), 296; severance of relations with Morocco, 296
Destour party: 25, 27; formation of (1920), 24
al-Din, Khayr: Prime Minister of Tunisia, 21
Djaballah, Abdallah: 191; former leader of An-Nahda (Algeria), 190; founder of *Islah* (1999), 190
Dlimi, General Ahmed: 112, 117, 350; death of (1975), 94; military forces commanded by, 94

Egypt: 81, 160, 279, 297, 337; Cairo, 49, 283, 297–8, 301, 332, 337; expulsion from Arab League (1979), 301; recognition of Israel, 285; Tahrir Square, 332
d'Estaing, Valéry Giscard: 310; President of France, 299
Ettajdid party (Tunisia): 356
Euro-Mediterranean Partnership Initiative (EMPI) (1995): 313, 316, 325, 329–30; expectations regarding, 260, 313–14; shortcomings of, 260, 314
European Community (EC): change to EU (1993), 287, 312; creation of (1957), 287; enlargement of, 283
European Economic Community (EEC): Association Agreements, 312

INDEX

European Parliament: 315; suspension of financial aid to Morocco (1992), 260, 313

European Union (EU): 145, 259, 312, 315–16, 322, 327, 330, 333; expansion of (2004), 315; formerly EC, 287, 312; Free Trade Agreement (1995), 262, 314; Neighbourhood Policy (ENP), 315–16, 323–4, 329

Al Fassi, Abbas: leader of Istiqlal, 143

Al-Fassi, Allal: leader of Istiqlal, 42, 296; presence at Bandung Conference (1955), 296

February 20th Movement (Morocco), 152, 197, 228–9, 249, 337

Fédération de France du Front de Libération Nationale (FFFLN): formation of, 46

Fez: 12, 25–6, 33, 112, 211, 302, 305

Filali, Abdelatif: Moroccan Prime Minister, 215, 346

First World War (1914–18): Maghrebi soldiers serving in, 24; outbreak of, 18

Forum Démocraqtique pour le Travail et les Libertes (FDTL); 135

France: 49, 96, 199, 206, 260, 275, 287, 294-5, 301, 306-9, 321-2, 330; *Académie Berbère*, 209; colonial military of, 82–4, 99, 110; colonialism, 5, 19–20, 23, 26–7, 30, 32, 41, 54, 82–4, 99, 110, 203, 205, 208, 213, 265, 270–1, 294, 331; Government of, 32, 311; *Le Monde*, 113, 280; military of, 296; Paris, 20, 25, 31, 91, 158, 209, 294, 296, 306, 308, 311, 328; political influence in Maghreb, 3; Saint Cyr Military Academy, 97, 104

Franco, General Francisco: 273; death of (1975), 324; relationship with King Hassan II, 270

Free Officers Movement: 81

Front de Libération Nationale (FLN): 49, 67–8, 72, 100, 105, 122–4, 131, 138, 140, 168, 170, 190, 251, 256; Berber-speakers in, 206, 223; Central Committee, 100; creation of (1954), 68, 105–6, 123; creation of ALN (1954), 85; division of, 46; ideology of, 46; Kabyle presence in, 206; members of, 31, 50, 57, 59, 67–8, 129, 137; party congress of, 97–8; presence in Conference of Tangier (1958), 266; relationship with UNFP, 268–9; role in Algerian War of Independence, 31; supporters of, 158, 207, 297–8

Front des Forces Socialistes (FFS): 129–30, 139, 218, 224. 355, 368; founding of (1963), 214; led by Hocine Ait Ahmed, 130, 214; members of, 215

Front Islamique du Salut (FIS): 101, 106, 151, 155, 174, 177, 186, 224, 251–2, 258, 307, 309; banned (1992), 137, 192, 200, 216, 253, 308; electoral performance (1990), 136, 168, 170, 254; electoral performance (1991), 102–3, 108, 136, 171, 254; formation of (1989), 169, 306; members of, 136, 172–3, 189, 197; support for Iraq during Persian Gulf War, 304; supporters of, 102, 136, 169, 191, 255

Front pour la Défense des Institutions Constitutionelles (FDIC): 125

Gafsa, 95, 280

Gas, 109, 235, 238, 254, 257, 259, 291, 297, 324, 327-8

INDEX

Germany: 287, 330, 343; Moroccan diaspora in, 226

Ghana: 81

Ghannouchi, Rachid: 164, 175, 196, 199–200; arrest and imprisonment of (1987), 165–6, 176; disavowal of violent extremism, 176, 191; elected as Emir of Islamic Group (1979), 161; in London, 191, 195, 196; return to Tunisia (2010), 196, 201; voluntary exile of (1989), 167, 196

GIA *(Groupes Islamiques Armés—Jamat Islamiyya Mousalaha)*: 187–8, 308; ideology of, 173–4, 188, 194

Gorbachev, Mikhail: 283

Gouvernement Provisoire de la République Algérienne (GPRA): 85–6, 267; antipathy toward, 63; formation of (1958), 46; members of, 50, 279; relationship with FLN, 46–7; supporters of, 47–8

Green March (1975): 126, 272–3;

Gulf War (1990–1): 141, 179, 201, 305, 307, 310, 317; impact of, 306; Invasion of Kuwait (1990), 168, 303–4

Hachani, Abdelkader: interim leader of FIS, 172

Hadj, Messali: 27–8, 57; leader of MTLD, 31, 46; rivals of, 32

Hafsids: 14

Hamas (Algeria): 362 *see also* Movement of a Society for Peace (MSP)

Hamas (Palestine): 1; electoral performance of (2006), 321

Hamrouche, Mouloud: economic reform programmes of, 251; Prime Minister of Algeria, 251

Harbi, Mohamed: 82

Hassan II, King: 57, 62, 73, 117, 141, 146, 163, 178, 215, 233–4, 245, 268, 275, 280–1, 294, 296, 299, 301, 305, 310–11, 325–6, 331; acceptance of Treaty of Fraternity, Good Neighbourliness and Cooperation in Ifrane (1970), 269; attempted coup against (1971), 91, 126, 234, 272, 277; attempted coup against (1972), 91–2, 126, 234, 272, 277; attempted expansion of *Amir Al-Muminim*, 55; death of (1999), 112, 288, 317; declaration of 'State of Exception' (1965), 69, 126; dissolving of parliament and suspension of constitution (1965), 85; economic policies of, 249; family of, 54, 94, 127, 298, 318–19; chief of staff of FAR, 83–4; meeting with Polisario Front (1989), 287; political use of Islam by, 55–6; reign of, 54, 226; relationship with General Francisco Franco, 270; relationship with Moroccan military, 84, 90, 92–3, 113–15; support for demands of Amazigh Cultural Movement, 219

El Himma, Fouad Ali: contesting of Moroccan elections (2007), 144

Hizb-Fransa: conspiracy theories regarding, 110–11, 308

Hussaynids: *beys*, 20; origins of, 15

Ibadite Communities: 203, 211, 364

Ibn Khaldun: theory of *asabiyya*, 50

Ibrahim, Abdullah: Prime Minister of Morocco, 45

Ibrahimi, Ahmed Taleb: Algerian Foreign Minister, 189

Ifrane: 269, 274

Ifriquia: 14

Institut Royal de la Culture Amazigh (IRCAM), 220–1, 367

401

INDEX

International Court of Justice (ICJ): 271; rulings of, 271–2

International Crisis Group (ICG): 291; observations of Kabylia, 218, 223–5

International Monetary Fund (IMF): 236–7, 242, 253, 264; part of 'Washington Consensus', 236, 239–40, 259; reform programmes, 239, 254–5, 257–8, 261

Iran: 165; Hostage Crisis (1979–81), 303; Islamic Revolution (1978–9), 200, 300; Maghreb Islamists and, 364

Iraq: 1, 81, 283; Invasion of Kuwait (1990), 168, 303–4; Operation Iraqi Freedom (2003–11), 329, 382

Islah party : founded by Abdallah Djaballah (1999), 190

Islam: 16, 200, 206; introduction to Maghreb, 11–12; political use of, 17–18, 28–9, 55–6, 156–7, 167; puritanical interpretations of, 13; Qur'an, 27, 217; Ramadan, 55, 158; Sharia law, 74; *takfir*, 187, 194

Islamic Jihad (Tunisia): bombing campaigns of, 175, 360.

Islamic Tendency Movement (MTI): 169, 175–7, 186, 198, 306; arrest of leadership (1987), 165, 175; formerly Islamic Group, 164; links with UGTT, 165; members of, 165–6; succeeded by An-Nahda party, 155

Islamism: 109, 111, 117, 128, 136, 155-201, 249, 255, 307; Algerian, 108–10, 115, 139, 151, 156, 160–2, 168, 171–2, 174, 178, 186, 190, 193, 195, 198, 214, 216–17, 307, 309, 319, 321; fear of, 177; growth in Maghreb region, 157, 178, 182; militant, 260; Moroccan, 156, 160, 162, 178, 186, 199, 201, 214, 221; political presence of, 1, 95–6, 130, 132, 152, 156, 168, 188, 304; radical, 101, 148, 322; Tunisian, 104–5, 151, 156, 159, 162, 168–9, 171–2, 174–5, 178, 186, 192, 195, 201, 233, 237, 306–7

Israel: 1, 93, 192, 298–9, 203, 316-318, 376, 379, 380-2; conflict with Palestinians, 1–2, 183; Invasion of Lebanon (1982), 302; Jerusalem, 301, 317; Labour Party, 302; recognition of, 285, 318; Temple Mount/Haram al-Sahrif, 317; Tel Aviv, 317–18; US support for, 296

Israeli-Egyptian Peace Treaty (1979): 301

Istiqlal party: 27, 41–3, 69, 73, 82, 84, 127, 141, 151, 159, 211–12, 270, 296; boycott of Moroccan constitutional referendum and elections (1965), 69; conflict within (1958–9), 45, 62; extraordinary party congress (1955), 43; formerly *Kutla al-Amal al-Watani*, 26; impact of connection to *alternance*, 183; influence of, 55; led by Abbas Al Fassi, 143, 296; members of, 42, 83, 127; presence in Conference of Tangier (1958), 266; relationship with Moroccan monarchy, 125; relationship with UNFP, 126; supporters of, 30

Italy: 334; colonialism, 5; Rome, 139

Jamaa Islamiyyyah (Islamic Group—Tunisia): origins of, 160; renamed as MTI (1981), 164

Jews: 203, 299, 378; Jewish community in Morocco, 298-99

Jordan: 283; recognition of Israel, 285

INDEX

Judaism: presence in Maghreb region, 203, 298

Kabylia: 151, 205, 207-11, 216, 217-9, 223-5, 258, 268, 342, 368; in French colonial period, 204-5, 210
Kafi, Ali: 352; appointed president of Algeria, 106
Kairouan: 12; consolidation of Maliki school of Islamic law in, 13
Kashmir: 194
Khatib, Abdelkrim: background of, 180; leader of MPDC, 180
al-Khattabi, Abd al-Krim: revolt led by, 24, 26
Kherbane, Kameredine: 173
Khider, Mohamed: evicted by Ahmed Ben Bella (1963), 124; secretary general of FLN, 123
Kissinger, Henry: shuttle diplomacy, 297
Kutla Alliance: members of, 143; revival of, 141
Kuwait: Iraqi Invasion of (1990), 168, 303-4

Lachgar, Driss: 113–14
Laroui, Abdallah: view of process of establishment of Maghrebi identity, 12; view of portrayal of Maghreb, 9–10
Lebanon: 1–2; expulsion of PLO from (1982), 301–2; Israeli Invasion of (1982), 302
Libya: 5, 13–14, 81, 87, 265, 279–80, 282–3, 291, 300, 310, 337, 376; borders of, 277; Civil War, 2, 6, 292; founding member of Arab Maghreb Union, 5; oil reserves of, 279; support for Tunisian dissidents, 95; Tripoli, 15, 46, 75, 279, 337
Ligue Algérienne pour la Défense des Droits de l'Homme (LADDH): influence of, 150
Ligue Tunisienne des Droits de l'Homme (LTDH): activity of, 150
London: Rachid Ghannouchi in, 191, 195, 196
Lyautey, Marshall Louis-Hubert-Gonzales: first French *Résident Général* (1922-5), 22

Madani, Abassi: 252; president of FIS, 136, 251; released from prison (2003), 188
Madrid: bombing (2004), 328
Madrid Peace Conference (1991): representatives present at, 316
Maghreb: 6, 10–11, 13–14, 32–3, 59, 79, 81, 145, 148, 203, 227, 236, 257, 302, 334, 336, 338–9; colonial impact on, 34; Hilalian invasions, 12; growth of Islamism in, 157, 199; introduction of Islam to, 11–12, 156; Jewish populations of, 203, 298; media focus on, 1–3; Ottoman influence in, 16, 18; states of, 9
Malek, Redha 253
Maliki school of Islamic law: 13
Mali: 270
Mansouri, Yassine: first civilian head of DGED, 115
Marrakech, 33, 163, 193, 283, 286
Mashreq: 13, 334, 337; Arab, 5; media focus on, 1–2
Mauritania: 5, 270–1, 273, 282, 291; founding member of Arab Maghreb Union, 5; Nouakchott, 277, 279; recognised by Tunisia, 279; recognition of Israel (1999), 285; recognition of SADR (1984), 281
Mdaghri, Abdelkebir Alaoui: Moroccan Minister of Religious Affairs, 179

403

INDEX

Medbouh, General: role in attempted coup d'état against King Hassan II (1971), 91, 349

Medienne, General Tewfiq: head of DRS, 118

Mehenni, Ferhat: role in creation of MAK (2001), 224

Mekhloufi, Said: 173

Melilla (Mililia) 325-6, 342, 384

Mitterand, Danielle: 311

Mitterand, François: President of France, 310–11, 380

Mohamed, Prophet: descendants of, 16, 55, 158, 178

Mohamed V, Sultan: 40–1, 73, 186, 212; death of (1961), 54; exiled by French authorities, 30; family of, 54, 298; recognition of UNFP and *Mouvement Populaire* (1959), 125; relationship with Gamal Abdul Nasser, 298; relationship with Moroccan military, 82; return from exile (1955), 55

Mohamed VI, King: 117, 149, 249, 313, 337; accession of (1999), 112, 288; advisers to, 328; control over FAR General Staff, 94; economic policies of, 249; family of, 94, 318–19; IRCAM Dahir (2001), 220; proposal for revision of Moroccan Constitution (2011), 153

Morocco: 2–3, 11, 14, 17, 19, 21, 29, 33, 35, 57, 61, 65, 70–1, 77, 81, 88, 94, 96, 114, 118, 138, 140, 142, 147–8, 152, 155, 164, 198–9, 201, 223, 231–2, 236, 250, 258, 260–3, 265, 268, 271, 282–3, 298, 305–6, 320, 331, 335–6, 339ALN external forces in, 85; American, French and Spanish military bases in, 296; Association Agreement with EEC (1969), 312; Berber *dahir* (1930), 28, 205, 211; black economy of, 245–6; borders of, 274; Constitution (1962), 44, 54–5, 125; designated as major non-NATO ally (2004), 320; economy of, 240, 247, 249, 255–7; El Hajeb, 91; external security services (DGED), 115; *Forces Armées Royales* (FAR), 83–5, 90–2, 94, 112–15; founding member of Arab Maghreb Union, 5; French and Spanish influence in, 19–20, 30, 43, 270–1; Goulmima, 215–16; Government of, 164, 227, 237–8, 303, 318; High Atlas tribes, 206; Independence of (1956), 32, 37, 43, 45, 77, 121, 233, 293, 312; Islamism in, 156, 160, 162, 178, 186, 199, 201, 214, 221; Jewish community in, 298; land confiscation in, 21; military of, 82, 92–3, 113, 116, 272, 278; Ministry of Defence, 85; Ministry of Interior, 42, 93, 112, 212, 246, 296; national budget (1970), 85; National Defence Administration, 93; nationalism in, 25–8, 45, 125–7, 212; Ottoman influence on, 15–18; Oujda, 281; 'pacification' of rural tribes, 24; parliamentary elections in (2007), 149; population of, 179; presence at Madrid Peace Conference (1991), 316; Rif mountains, 226–7, 245; Royal Palace, 91; Sidi Ifni, 270; Skhirat, 91–2; Souss Valley, 226–7; Tarfaya, 270, 348; Treaty of Friendship and Cooperation (1991), 325

Mouti, Abdelkrim: 180, 361; background of, 162

Mouvement des Démocrates Socialistes: 354, 359; (MDS—Tunisia): arrest of members (1995), 135

Mouvement Démocratique et Social (MDS –Algeria) role in Algerian protests (2011), 153

404

INDEX

Mouvement National Algérien (MNA): 32

Mouvement Populaire (MP): 44, 142, 212, 215, 221–2; recognised by King Mohamed V (1959), 125; use against Istiqlal, 44–5

Mouvement Populaire Démocratique et Constituitionnel (MPDC): 182–3; led by Abdelkrim Khatib, 180

Mouvement pour la Triomphe des Libertés Démocratiques (MTLD): 365; led by Messali Hadj, 31

Movement for the Autonomy of Kabylia (MAK): founding of (2001), 224; ideology of, 225; supporters of, 224

Movement for Democracy in Algeria (MDA): 356; led by Ahmed Ben Bella, 130

Movement of a Society for Peace (MSP): 362; led by Mahfoud Nahnah, 189–90; rejection of Rome Platform, 139; scission within (2009), 191; supporters of, 255

Muslim Brotherhood: model of, 160, 200, 358

Mzali, Mohamed: Tunisian Prime Minister, 280

Nahnah, Mahfoud: excluded from Algerian presidential election (1999), 190, 363; leader of MSP, 189–90

Nasser, Gamal Abdul: 296–7; death of, 299; ideology of, 75, 305; relationship with Ahmed Ben Bella, 297; relationship with King Mohamed V, 298; rise to power (1952), 81; support for FLN, 207, 297–8

National Action Bloc: 28

National Bloc (*al-Kutla al-Wataniyya*): formation of (1970), 126; members of, 126–7

National Council for the Algerian Revolution (CNRA): Berber-speakers in, 206; Tripoli Conference (1962), 46, 50, 75, 234

Nationalism: 23–4, 34, 40, 83, 102, 127, 206, 261; Algerian, 27–9, 139, 285; Arab, 207–8, 212, 285, 298, 305; Moroccan, 25–8, 45, 54, 125–7, 212; radical, 82; Tunisian, 27–8, 38, 64

Neo-Destour, 25–7, 30, 40–2, 68, 70–1, 87, 123, 279; Central Committee, 65, 122; creation of, 64; factions of, 294; members of, 38, 60; renamed as PSD (1964), 71, 122, 232; Party Congress (1955), 39; presence in Conference of Tangier (1958), 266; used by Habib Bourguiba, 64–5, 122, 278–9

Netanyahu, Benjamin: Prime Minister of Israel, 317

Nezzar, General Khaled: 107; Algerian Minister of Defence, 101, 110; role in resignation of Chadli Benjedid (1992), 103, 137

North Atlantic Treaty Organization (NATO): 118

Oil: 109, 11, 169, 233, 235, 237, 238, 253, 254, 257-9, 279, 282, 283, 291, 297, 319, 331, 373

Omnium Nord-Africain (ONA): 244–7, 249

Organisation of African Union (OAU): 268, 331; charter of, 267; Rabat Summit (1972), 269

Organisation of the Islamic Conference: Al-Quds Committee, 301, 317

Oslo Accords: 318; collapse of, 314; supporters of, 317, 320

Osman, Ahmed: 346; role in creation of RNI (1978), 127

Othmani, Saad-Eddine: deputy leader of PJD, 182

405

INDEX

Ottoman Empire: 14, 22, 35, 40; role in political development in Maghreb, 16, 18, 74; territory of, 15, 18

Oufkir, Mohamed: 96, 117; Moroccan Interior Minister, 91; role in attempted coup d'état against King Hasan II (1972), 91–2

Oujda Clan: 346; origins of, 58

Palestine: 1, 201, 228, 298; conflict with Israel, 1–2; Gaza, 302, 318; West Bank, 302, 318

Palestinian Liberation Organisation (PLO): 299; expulsion from Lebanon (1982), 301–2; recognition as representative of Palestinians (1974), 301; Tunis headquarters air strike (1985), 310

Palestinian National Council (PNC): 302

Palestinians: 201, 228, 369, 297, 299, 318, 369; intifada, 302

Parti Communiste Marocain (PCM): rebranded as PPS, 127

Parti Communiste Tunisien (PCT): 354

Parti Démocrate Amazigh Marocain (PDAM): constitution annulled (2008), 222; ideology of, 226; members of, 225

Parti de l'Avant-Garde Socialiste (PAGS): formerly Algerian Communist Party, 124; members of, 130

Parti Démocratique de l'Indépendance (PDI): origins of, 44

Parti Socialiste Destourian (PSD): 87, 96, 123, 128, 135, 237; change to RCD, 103, 132; Congress, 87; formerly Neo-Destour, 71, 122, 232; members of, 233

Parti Socialiste Unifié (PSU): electoral performance of, 152

Party of Authenticity and Modernity (PAM): 150; creation of (2008), 144, 149; growth of, 147

Party of Justice and Development (PJD): 144, 148, 153, 192–3, 199, 201; creation of, 143; electoral performance of (2007), 183, 322; election of 2011, 201 ideology of, 155–6; members of, 149, 182, 186, 197

Party of Progress and Socialism (PPS): formerly PCM, 127

Perrault, Gilles: *Notre Ami le Roi* (1990), 311

Peres, Shimon: 302, 317, 376

Phoenicians: 12; role in establishing Carthage, 11

Polisario Front: 2, 284, 289–90, 303, 320; Nouakchott attacks (1976/1978), 277; meeting with King Hassan II (1989), 287; origins of (1973), 275–6; proclamation of SADR (1976), 277; supporters of, 281

Popular Party (Spain): electoral performance of (2000), 328

Portugal: 16; inclusion in EC, 283

Powell, Colin: US Secretary of State, 321

Progressive Democratic Party (PDP): 148; formerly RSP, 135

Qadhafi, Colonel Muammar: 302, 332; regime of, 300; removed from power (2011), 292; seizure of power (1969), 5–6, 279; support for national liberation movements, 277, 281

Al-Qadir, Amir Abd: banner of, 33; revolt led by, 23

Rabat, 7, 25, 93, 114, 211, 266, 273, 281–2, 285, 288, 296, 301, 317–18, 325–6, 330

Rabin, Yitzhak: signatory of Oslo Accords (1993), 317

INDEX

Rassemblement Constitutionnel Démocratique (RCD—Tunisia): 133–5, 152, 167, 218, 240, 242; electoral performance (1989), 131; electoral performance (1984), 132; formerly PSD, 103, 132
Rassemblement National Démocratique (RND): 138–9, 190; creation of (1997), 137
Rassemblement National des Indépendants (RNI): 142; creation of (1978), 127, 137, 144
Rassemblement pour la Culture et la Démocratie (RCD – Algeria): 218, 224, 368; creation of (1989), 214; ideology of, 217; role in Algerian protests of 2011, 153, 229
Rassemblement Socialiste Progressiste (RSP): change to PDP (2001), 135
Reagan, Ronald: foreign policy of, 300–1
Reda Guedira, Ahmed: Moroccan Defence Minister, 83
Rejection Front: Algerian membership of, 301
Rif mountains and region: 24, 73, 206, 213, 226, 227, 245, 348, 366
Roman Empire: 11–12; African provinces of, 11
Ruedy, John: 30; view of portrayal of Maghreb, 9–10
Rumsfeld, Donald: 319

Saadian dynasty: 16; rise of, 18
Sadat, Anwar: relationship with King Hassan, 299; visit to Israel (1977), 301
Saharan Arab Democratic Republic (SADR): 280, 284, 290; proclaimed by Polisario Front (1976), 277; recognition of, 278, 281, 300, 331

Salafism: 343
Salafist Group for Preaching and Combat (GSPC): appeal of, 194; renamed as AQIM (2007), 193
Salafiyya movement: 156, 159, 343; emergence of 26; and nationalist movements, 29
Sahbani, Ismail: secretary general of UGTT, 244
Sahel: 5
Sarkozy, Nicolas: 329–30
Saudi Arabia: 168, 304–5
Sebta (Ceuta): 325–6, 342, 384
Second World War (1939–45): 23
Senegal: 270
Shabiba Islamiyya al-Maghribiyya (Moroccan Islamic Youth): 179, 193; accusation of role in assassination of USFP member (1975), 162–3; formation of, 162; members of, 162
Sifi, Mokdad: Prime Minister of Algeria, 216–17
Six-Day War (1967): 296–7, 299
Socialism: 24, 133, 292, 297; antipathy to, 251; revolutionary Arab, 75
Society for the Preservation of the Quran: origins of, 160
Soviet Union (USSR): 283, 295, 301; Invasion of Afghanistan (1979–89), 173; military hardware supplied by, 296–7, 303; Moscow, 296–7, 300
Spain: 11, 16, 272, 276, 298, 324-9, 330; Moroccan diaspora in, 226; Atocha bombing (2004), 328; Barcelona, 313, 325; colonial military of, 82–3; colonialism, 19–20, 41, 82–3, 203, 270–1, 324; enclaves of, 325; inclusion in EC, 283; Islamic conquest of, 3; Madrid, 325–6; military of, 24, 296, 328–9; Treaty of Friendship and Cooperation

407

INDEX

with Morocco (1991), 325, 327; Treaty of Friendship and Cooperation with Algeria (2002), 327
Spanish Sahara: 93, 269–70, 276; Moroccan claim on, 270–2; partitioning of, 273–4, 288
Sudan: 279
Sufism: 178, 342; brotherhoods of, 33; *sheikhs*, 17; *zaouia*, 163
Suliman, Sultan Moulay: isolationist policies of, 22
Syria: 81, 337, 376; Damascus, 337; Golan, 93

Tangier: 266, 270
Terrorism: 193, 319, 320, 322, 323, 330, 363
Tindouf: 277, 311
Tlemcen: 12
Trabelsi, Leila: family of, 4, 243; revilement of, 4
Treaty of Fraternity, Good Neighbourliness and Cooperation (1969): 269
Tribal structures: 11, 12, 17, 50, 62, 123; influence on FLN in Algeria, 46, 341-2
Tripartite Agreement (1975): participants in, 273; signing of, 276
Tunis, 7, 14–15, 20, 24, 40, 51, 117, 159, 165, 168, 191, 279–80, 285, 310, 318, 330, 332; Tunis University, 75
Tunisia: 1–3, 5, 15–16, 19, 29, 33, 35, 48–50, 52, 57, 61, 66, 70–1, 74, 77–8, 81–2, 94, 103, 123, 128, 131, 136, 139–41, 144, 146–7, 150, 152, 155, 158, 170, 198–9, 231–2, 245, 250, 261, 265, 282–3, 291, 301, 306, 310, 320, 335–6, 339; ALN external forces in, 85; Association Agreement with EEC (1969), 312; Avenue Bourguiba, 332; *Banque Internationale Arabe de Tunisie* (BIAT), 241; Berber population of, 229; Bizerte, 294; Constituent Assembly, 40–1, 51; Constitution (1959), 66; Constitution (1989), 103; Djerba, 39, 192, 203, 320, 322; economy of, 233, 237, 240, 255–7, 263–4; founding member of Arab Maghreb Union, 5; French influence in, 19–21, 30, 41, 162; Government of, 164, 193, 238, 303, 307; Higher Islamic Council, 166; Independence of (1956), 32, 37, 45, 78, 121, 233, 278, 293, 312; Islamism in, 104–5, 151, 156, 159, 162, 168–9, 171–2, 174–5, 178, 186, 192, 195, 201, 233, 237, 306–7; land confiscation in, 21; legislative elections (1989), 131; military of, 87, 95, 103, 116, 155; Ministry of Defence, 86; Ministry of Interior, 87, 103; Monastir, 175; National Assembly, 66, 166–7, 233; National Pact (1988), 129, 166, 241; National Solidarity Fund (NSF), 241; nationalism in, 27–8, 38, 64; Ottoman influence in, 18, 22, 40; parliamentary elections in (2007), 149; population of, 179, 200, 262; recognition of Mauritania, 279; Revolution (2010–11), 1, 116–19, 151, 197, 243–4, 249, 258, 264, 332, 334, 337–8; Saket Sidi Youssef, 294; Sfax, 39; Sidi Bouzid, 243; Sousse, 175; State Security Court, 165;

Union Constitutionnel (UC): 138; creation of (1983), 127, 137, 144
Union Générale des Travailleurs Tunisiens (UGTT): 39, 95, 164, 232, 279; detachment from RCD (1988), 244; general strike organised by (1978), 130, 237; links

with MTI, 165; members of, 61, 75, 244; role in Tunisian Revolution (2010–11), 243–4
Union Nationale des Forces Populaires (UNFP): 73, 84, 162, 296; boycott of Moroccan constitutional referendum and elections (1965), 69; creation of (1959), 45; influence of, 55; members of, 55, 126; recognised by King Mohamed V (1959), 125; relationship with FLN, 268–9; relationship with Istiqlal, 126
Union Socialiste des Forces Populaires (USFP): 127, 141, 151, 290, 310–11, 336; led by Abderrahamane El Youssoufi, 142; impact of connection to *alternance*, 183; members of, 127, 162; origins of, 126
United Nations (UN): 2, 271, 287, 290; Peace Plan on Western Sahara, 310; peacekeeping forces of, 92–3; plan for partitioning of Palestine (1947), 298
United States of America (USA): 4, 96, 119, 145, 182, 275, 293, 295, 299, 302, 305, 328; 9/11 attacks, 111, 118, 183, 191, 261, 319, 321–3, 329–30; Department of Defense, 320; influence of, 23; Manhasset, 289; military of, 168, 296; State Department, 310, 320; support for Israel, 296; Washington DC, 118, 296–7, 303, 309–10, 317–19, 321
US-North Africa Economic Partnership (USNAEP): launch of (2000), 321

Vedrine, Hubert: French Foreign Minister, 322
Vietnam War (1959–75): 296

Wahhabism: criticisms of, 185

War on Terror: 118, 183, 261, 319, 329
Western Sahara: 2, 114, 126, 127, 141, 146, 163, 216, 226, 236, 237, 269, 271, 272, 274–8, 280–90, 292, 299–301, 303, 305, 310, 318, 324, 326, 327, 328, 331, 352, 377
World Amazigh Congress (1997):227
World Bank: 236, 242, 264; part of 'Washington Consensus', 236, 239–40, 259; reform programmes, 239; Report (2000), 255

Yahiaoui, Salah: director of FLN, 98
Yassine, Abdeslam: 198–9; background of, 163; family of, 185; released from house arrest (2000), 185; supporters of, 179; writings of, 163, 180, 184, 217
Yassine, Nadia: 192; family of, 185
El Yazigh, Mohamed: deputy leader of USFP, 192
Yemen: 283, 337
Yom Kippur War (1973): 297, 301; Moroccan involvement in, 93, 299; Tunisian involvement in, 299
El Youssoufi, Abderrahamane: 113' 345, 373; imprisonment of, 142; leader of USFP, 142; Prime Minister of Morocco, 142–3, 260; shortcomings of government of, 143

Zaim: role of, 62
Zaire: 93
Zapatero, J.L.R.: administration of, 328–9; Spanish Prime Minister, 327
Zaytouna mosque/university (Tunis): 158, 159, 359
Zbiri, Tahar: attempted coup d'état

led by (1967), 58, 88–9, 99; chief of staff of ANP, 58

Zeroual, Lamine: Algerian Minister of Defence, 106; background of, 140; President of Algeria, 82, 106, 140